T0156066

Communications
in Computer and Information Science 1644

Rationale
The CCIS series is devoted to the publication of proceedings of computer science conferences. Its aim is to efficiently disseminate original research results in informatics in printed and electronic form. While the focus is on publication of peer-reviewed full papers presenting mature work, inclusion of reviewed short papers reporting on work in progress is welcome, too. Besides globally relevant meetings with internationally representative program committees guaranteeing a strict peer-reviewing and paper selection process, conferences run by societies or of high regional or national relevance are also considered for publication.

Topics
The topical scope of CCIS spans the entire spectrum of informatics ranging from foundational topics in the theory of computing to information and communications science and technology and a broad variety of interdisciplinary application fields.

Information for Volume Editors and Authors
Publication in CCIS is free of charge. No royalties are paid, however, we offer registered conference participants temporary free access to the online version of the conference proceedings on SpringerLink (http://link.springer.com) by means of an http referrer from the conference website and/or a number of complimentary printed copies, as specified in the official acceptance email of the event.

CCIS proceedings can be published in time for distribution at conferences or as postproceedings, and delivered in the form of printed books and/or electronically as USBs and/or e-content licenses for accessing proceedings at SpringerLink. Furthermore, CCIS proceedings are included in the CCIS electronic book series hosted in the SpringerLink digital library at http://link.springer.com/bookseries/7899. Conferences publishing in CCIS are allowed to use Online Conference Service (OCS) for managing the whole proceedings lifecycle (from submission and reviewing to preparing for publication) free of charge.

Publication process
The language of publication is exclusively English. Authors publishing in CCIS have to sign the Springer CCIS copyright transfer form, however, they are free to use their material published in CCIS for substantially changed, more elaborate subsequent publications elsewhere. For the preparation of the camera-ready papers/files, authors have to strictly adhere to the Springer CCIS Authors' Instructions and are strongly encouraged to use the CCIS LaTeX style files or templates.

Abstracting/Indexing
CCIS is abstracted/indexed in DBLP, Google Scholar, EI-Compendex, Mathematical Reviews, SCImago, Scopus. CCIS volumes are also submitted for the inclusion in ISI Proceedings.

How to start
To start the evaluation of your proposal for inclusion in the CCIS series, please send an e-mail to ccis@springer.com.

Ilsun You · Hwankuk Kim · Pelin Angin
Editors

Mobile Internet Security

6th International Symposium, MobiSec 2022
Jeju, South Korea, December 15–17, 2022
Revised Selected Papers

 Springer

Editors
Ilsun You ⓘ
Kookmin University
Seoul, Korea (Republic of)

Hwankuk Kim ⓘ
Sangmyung University
Cheonan-si, Korea (Republic of)

Pelin Angin ⓘ
Middle East Technical University
Ankara, Türkiye

ISSN 1865-0929   ISSN 1865-0937 (electronic)
Communications in Computer and Information Science
ISBN 978-981-99-4429-3   ISBN 978-981-99-4430-9 (eBook)
https://doi.org/10.1007/978-981-99-4430-9

This Springer imprint is published by the registered company Springer Nature Singapore Pte Ltd.
The registered company address is: 152 Beach Road, #21-01/04 Gateway East, Singapore 189721, Singapore

Preface

During the past two decades, mobile Internet technologies have been dramatically growing, leading to a paradigm shift in our lives. Despite their revolution, mobile Internet technologies open doors to various security threats, which should be addressed to keep mobile Internet environments secure and trusted. Recent technologies including 5G-Advanced/6G networks, large-scale and massive IoT/CPS, and quantum computing among others have also exacerbated the problems in the mobile security arena by introducing a larger attack surface and continue to introduce new security challenges.

This volume contains revised and selected papers presented at the 2022 International Symposium on Mobile Internet Security held on Jeju Island, Republic of Korea, during December 15–17, 2022. The purpose of MobiSec 2022 was to bring together academic and industrial researchers and practitioners working on different aspects, to exchange ideas and explore new research directions to address the challenges in mobility Internet security. MobiSec 2022 focused on publishing high-quality papers which are closely related to various theories and practical applications in mobility management, to highlight state-of-the-art research.

MobiSec 2022 provided an international forum for sharing original research results among specialists in fundamental and applied problems of mobile Internet security. The symposium was organized by the Korea Institute of Information Security and Cryptology (KIISC) Research Group on 5G Security and Kookmin University Cryptography & Information Security Institute, hosted by KIISC, and sponsored by Huawei Korea and the Electronics and Telecommunications Research Institute (ETRI), Korea Information Security Agency (KISA), National Security Research Institute (NSR), and Korea Institute of Science and Technology Information (KISTI).

A total of 60 papers related to significant aspects of theory and applications of mobile Internet security were accepted for presentation at MobiSec 2022. The symposium was further powered by the invited talks of Kim Kwang Raymond Choo (University of San Antonio, USA), Fang-Yie Leu (Tunghai University and Ming Chuan University, Taiwan) and Jungmin Kang (National Security Research Institute, South Korea). All papers were reviewed by at least 3 professionals in the field, and only 24 papers were selected for publication in CCIS. The success of the symposium was assured by the collective efforts of sponsors, organizers, reviewers, and participants. We would like to acknowledge the contribution of the individual Program Committee members and thank the paper reviewers. Our sincere gratitude goes to the participants of the conference and all authors of submitted papers.

We wish to express our gratitude to the Springer team for their help and cooperation.

March 2023

Ilsun You
Hwankuk Kim
Pelin Angin

Organization

Honorary Chair

Okyeon Yi   Kookmin University, South Korea

Advisory Committee Chairs

Souhwan Jung   Soongsil University, South Korea
Kyung-Hyune Rhee   Pukyong National University, South Korea
Jaecheol Ryou   Chungnam National University, South Korea

General Chair

Ilsun You   Kookmin University, South Korea

Organizing Committee Chair

Kiwook Sohn   SSNC, South Korea

Program Chairs

Pelin Angin   Middle East Technical University, Türkiye
Hwankuk Kim   Sangmyung University, South Korea

Poster Chairs

Haehyun Cho   Soongsil University, South Korea
Taek-Young Youn   Dankook University, South Korea

Publication Chairs

Yuh-Shyan Chen   National Taipei University, Taiwan
Igor Kotenko   SPIIRAS and ITMO University, Russia

Local Arrangement Chair

Ji Won Kang   Sejong University, South Korea

Publicity Chairs

Hsing-Chung Chen   Asia University, Taiwan
Siu Ming Yiu   University of Hong Kong, China

Web Chairs

Jiyoon Kim   Gyeongsang National University, South Korea
Jungsoo Park   Soongsil University, South Korea

Advisory Committee

Xiaofeng Chen   Xidian University, China
KwangHee Choi   KISA, Executive Director, South Korea
Ik-Kyun Kim   ETRI, Executive Director, South Korea
Kibom Kim   NSR, Executive Director, South Korea
Francesco Palmier   University of Salerno, Italy
Kouichi Sakurai   Kyushu University, Japan
Antonio Skarmeta   Universidad de Murcia, Spain
Willy Susilo   University of Wollongong, Australia
Jianhua Yang   Columbus State University, USA
Huachun Zhou   Beijing Jiaotong University, China

Organizing Committee

Hyo-Beom Ahn   Kongju National University, South Korea
Dong-Guk Han   Kookmin University, South Korea

Ki Hyo Nam	UMLogics Ltd., South Korea
Hee-Un Park	KISA, South Korea
Jong-Geun Park	ETRI, South Korea
Jung Taek Seo	Gachon University, South Korea
Jungsuk Song	KISTI, South Korea

Program Committee Members

Hiroaki Anada	Aomori University, Japan
Ramón Alcarria	Universidad Politécnica de Madrid, Spain
Philip Virgil Astillo	University of San Carlos, Philippines
Ram Basnet	Colorado Mesa University, USA
Jorge Bernal Bernabe	University of Murcia, Spain
Yuanlong Cao	Jiangxi Normal University, China
Dooho Choi	Korea University, South Korea
Michal Choraś	Bydgoszcz University of Science and Technology, Poland
Gaurav Choudhary	Technical University of Denmark, Denmark
Salvatore D'Antonio	University of Naples "Parthenope", Italy
Jianfeng Guan	BUPT, China
Shoichi Hirose	University of Fukui, Japan
Kihoon Hong	Soongsil University, South Korea
Huisu Jang	Soongsil University, South Korea
Peter Kieseberg	St. Pölten University of Applied Sciences, Austria
Jongkil Kim	University of Wollongong, Australia
Yong-Soo Kim	ETRI, South Korea
Gokhan Kul	University of Massachusetts Dartmouth, USA
Hyun Kwon	Korea Military Academy, South Korea
Manhee Lee	Hannam University, South Korea
Mun-Kyu Lee	Inha University, South Korea
Sokjoon Lee	Gachon University, South Korea
C. Mala	NIT Trichy, India
Alessio Merlo	University of Genoa, Italy
Ki-Woong Park	Sejong University, South Korea
Sandi Rahmadika	State University of Padang, Indonesia
Vishal Sharma	Queen's University Belfast, UK
Kunwar Singh	NIT Trichy, India
Seog Chung Seo	Kookmin University, South Korea
Sang Uk Shin	Pukyong National University, South Korea
SeongHan Shin	AIST, Japan
Simon Tjoa	St. Pölten University of Applied Sciences, Austria

Kunwar Singh   NIT Trichy, India
Kunlin Tsai   Tunghai University, Taiwan
Noriki Uchida   Fukuoka Institute of Technology, Japan
Fulvio Valenza   Polytechnic University of Turin, Italy
Elena Vlahu-Gjorgievska   University of Wollongong, Australia
Akihiro Yamamura   Akita University, Japan
Toshihiro Yamauchi   Okayama University, Japan
Naoto Yanai   Osaka University, Japan
Baokang Zhao   National University of Defense Technology,
                                 China

Contents

5G Advanced and 6G Security

Attacks Against Security Context in 5G Network

Zhiwei Cui[1], Baojiang Cui[1(✉)], Li Su[2], Haitao Du[2], Hongxin Wang[1], and Junsong Fu[1]

[1] Beijing University of Posts and Telecommunications, Beijing, China
`{zwcui,cuibj,wanghongxin,fujs}@bupt.edu.cn`
[2] China Mobile Research Institute, Beijing, China
`{suli,duhaitao}@chinamobile.com`

Abstract. The security context used in 5G authentication is generated during the Authentication and Key Agreement (AKA) procedure and stored in both the user equipment (UE) and the network sides for the subsequent fast registration procedure. Given its importance, it is imperative to formally analyze the security mechanism of the security context. The security context in the UE can be stored in the Universal Subscriber Identity Module (USIM) card or in the baseband chip. In this work, we present a comprehensive and formal verification of the fast registration procedure based on the security context under the two scenarios in ProVerif. Our analysis identifies two vulnerabilities, including one that has not been reported before. An attacker can exploit these vulnerabilities to register to the network with the victim's identity and then launch other attacks. To ensure that these attacks are indeed realizable in practice, we have responsibly confirmed them through experimentation in three operators. Our analysis reveals that these vulnerabilities stem from design flaws of the standard and unsafe practices by operators. We finally propose several potential countermeasures to prevent these attacks. We have reported our findings to the GSMA and received a coordinated vulnerability disclosure (CVD) number CVD-2022-0057.

Keywords: Security context · 5G network · Attack

1 Introduction

The Universal Subscriber Identity Module (USIM) card stores critical authentication credentials for subscribers to access the 5G network. The Authentication and Key Agreement (AKA) procedure utilizes these credentials to complete key derivation and mutual authentication between the user equipment (UE) and the network to ensure communication security. Usually, a security context is created

Supported by the National Natural Science Foundation of China (No. 62001055 and 61872386), and the Beijing University of Posts and Telecommunications-China Mobile Research Institute Joint Innovation Center.

as the result of the AKA procedure and maintained by the UE and the network. Then the UE can use this security context to quickly register to the network in a following period without going through the AKA procedure.

The UE consists of the USIM card and the mobile equipment (ME). The 3rd Generation Partnership Project (3GPP) stipulates that the security context can be stored in the USIM or ME [1,2]. If the security context is not present on the USIM, it is stored in the baseband chip in the ME together with the permanent identity. Moreover, 3GPP has proposed some protection measures to defend against attacks on the security context. The PIN-based access control can prevent malicious access to the security context in the USIM card [3]. The security context stored in the baseband chip can only be used if the permanent identity from the USIM matches the identity stored in the non-volatile memory. And the standard specifies that the security context should be deleted from the baseband chip in some scenarios, such as the USIM is removed from the ME when the ME is in power on state [4,5].

Whether these methods can achieve the intended purpose and whether there will be shortcomings in the implementation stage are still worth discussing. However, existing works have at least one of the following limitations: (A) Some studies did not pay attention to the security of the security context itself [6,7]; (B) Another situation that the security context stored in the baseband chip is not considered [8]; (C) These studies were conducted through ad-hoc manual analyses [6–8].

In this paper, we systematically model the fast registration procedure based on the security context using the formal method. And we use ProVerif, an automatic symbolic protocol verifier [9], to automatically investigate whether the safeguards proposed by 3GPP for the security contexts under multiple storage methods can achieve their intended purpose. Unfortunately, the results yield a negative answer. We have uncovered two vulnerabilities, one of which is novel. An attacker could exploit these vulnerabilities to register to the network as the victim. Additionally, we discuss further attacks (e.g., forging location information and stealing privacy) that an attacker can launch after registering to the network. Our analysis reveals that these vulnerabilities are caused by design weaknesses of the 3GPP standard and unsafe practices by operators. In the end, we discuss potential countermeasures.

2 Background

2.1 USIM

The USIM card is a smart card specified in [3] and contains a microprocessor, three types of memory, which are RAM, ROM and EEPROM, and some security functions. Each USIM card has a unique integrate circuit card identity (ICCID). The USIM card can be viewed as a black box interfacing with ME through the standard application programming interface (API) [10]. A mobile user can access the 5G network through the ME equipped with a valid USIM card to consume services, including the Internet, voice, and SMS.

The USIM card stores various critical information for a subscriber, such as identities, permanent authentication keys, security contexts, phone number, etc. These parameters are stored in the form of files. Each file has a unique identifier and can be set with different access conditions determined by the mobile carrier. The access conditions indicated in the file header can be divided into 4 types [8,10]: (1) Always (ALW): the command is executable on the file with no restrictions; (2) PIN: the command is executable on the file after entering the correct PIN unless the verification is disabled; (3) ADM: the command is executable on the file after entering the correct administrative key owned by the mobile carrier; (4) Never (NEV): the command cannot executable on the file. The applications (e.g., the baseband chip, card reader, and APP) can send application protocol data unit (APDU) to the USIM card to read or update these files.

In our experiments, a total number of three files will be involved: the international mobile subscriber identity (IMSI) in file IMSI (ID: 6F07), the globally unique temporary identifier (GUTI) in file EPSLOCI (ID: 6FE3), and the 4G Non-Access-Stratum (NAS) security context in file EPSNSC (ID: 6FE4). The 3GPP standard stipulates that the read permission of these files should be set to PIN mode [3]. If the PIN verification is enabled, the card holder needs to input the correct PIN to unlock the USIM card after inserting the card to a new device or restarting the phone. The length of the PIN is usually set to 4-8 digits and the number of consecutive incorrect PIN entries is limited. If the limit is exceeded, the USIM card will be automatically locked or destroyed.

2.2 5G Registration Procedure

The 5G protocol stacks are divided into the control plane and the user plane. The registration procedure belongs to the control plane, which is the responsibility of the access and mobility management function (AMF). The base station (BS) provides the wireless network for the UE and the AMF to communicate with each other. Figure 1 shows the registration procedure [1,2,8]. The registration procedure includes the initial registration and the fast registration.

Initial Registration. To protect subscriber privacy, the ME initiates an initial registration request message containing the Subscription Concealed Identifier (SUCI) instead of the Subscription Permanent Identifier (SUPI) [5]. If the AMF confirms that the identity is valid, it initiates the authentication procedure, also known as the AKA procedure. The AMF sends an authentication request message to the ME, containing a random number (RAND) and authentication token (AUTN) generated based on the permanent key and RAND. Then the ME forwards these two parameters to the USIM card in the form of APDU. The USIM card calculates cipher key (CK), integrity key (IK) and authentication response through the permanent key and security algorithms preset in the USIM card, and returns them to the ME. Then the ME and the network derive several keys for data encryption and integrity protection. Next, the ME and the network negotiate encryption and integrity protection algorithms to activate security. Finally, when the ME initiates the deregistration procedure (e.g., turns on the airplane mode or powers off), the UE (including the USIM and the ME) and the network maintain a security context simultaneously. For the UE, the security context is stored in the ME or the USIM card.

Fast Registration. The 3GPP standard specifies a fast registration procedure when a 5G security context is stored in the UE [1,2]. The cached context includes 5G-GUTI and 5G NAS security context. If the UE has a cached context, it shall send a registration request message containing 5G-GUTI as an identity, not SUCI. With the 5G NAS security context, the sent message shall be ciphered in a NAS container which is ciphered and shall also be integrity protected [8]. If the AMF has the same security context, and successfully decrypts the NAS container and verifies the integrity of the registration request message, the AKA procedure may be omitted. Then the UE and the network derive the keys required for subsequent communication based on this security context to activate security. It's worth noting that the 3GPP standard does not mandate skipping the AKA procedure, which depends on the operator. The three operators involved in this paper all provide fast registration services.

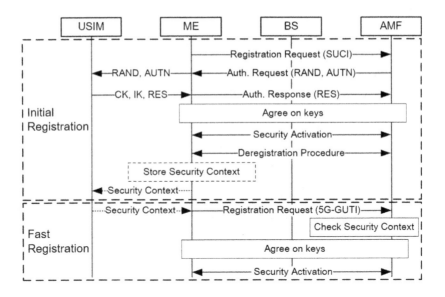

Fig. 1. 5G registration procedure

2.3   5G Security Context

The UE and the network need to establish a security context before activating security. Usually, a security context is generated as the result of an AKA procedure between the UE and the network and maintained by the UE and the network simultaneously. The 5G security context discussed in this paper includes the 5G-GUTI and the 5G NAS security contexts. If the USIM supports storing the 5G security context, then the 5G-GUTI and the 5G NAS security context will be stored in file EF5GS3GPPLOCI (ID: 4F01) and file EF5GS3GPPNSC (ID: 4F03) respectively in the form of files. Otherwise, they will be stored in the baseband chip together with the permanent identity SUPI of the subscriber. The 5G NAS security context contains K_{AMF} with the associated key set identifier (ngKSI), the UE security capabilities, and the uplink and downlink NAS COUNT values. The UE security capabilities identify the selected NAS integrity and encryption algorithms. The UE derives the NAS encryption and integrity keys according to K_{AMF}, and uses these algorithms to complete the protection of the registration request message as mentioned above. In addition, the registration request message contains the 5G-GUTI, the ngKSI and the uplink NAS COUNT in plaintext. The AMF queries the corresponding security context through the 5G-GUTI and the ngKSI. The uplink and downlink NAS COUNT values are used to resist replay attacks.

In order to prevent the security context from being used illegally, the 3GPP proposes some security protections [3–5]: (1) The PIN-based access control prevents malicious reading of the security context stored in the USIM card. (2) In order to use the security context stored in the baseband chip, the permanent identity of the USIM card inserted into the ME shall match the permanent identity corresponding to the security context.

3   Modeling the Fast Registration Procedure in ProVerif

In this section, we present the formal model for the fast registration procedure. First, we introduce the security assumptions and goals. Then we briefly introduce the formal verification tool ProVerif and present the modeling of security goals and the fast registration procedure.

3.1   Security Assumptions

The security assumptions are very strong in the 3GPP specifications [4,5]. However, many deployments of operators do not strictly follow them. To provide a more precise analysis, we take the real-world scenarios into account when defining security assumptions.

Assumptions on Cryptographic Algorithms. We assume that all cryptographic algorithms are public and secure. An attacker without the correct key cannot encrypt or decrypt the message.

Assumptions on Entities and Channels. In the fast registration procedure, the entities related to our research include UE and AMF. We assume that the UE and AMF jointly maintain a valid security context. The communications between UE and AMF use a wireless channel. An attacker can eavesdrop the communications on the channel, but cannot decrypt the encrypted messages. In addition, the attacker can create malicious entities to send plaintext messages to UE or AMF. Only the attacker with the correct key can send the encrypted messages to UE or AMF. The UE consists of USIM and ME as mentioned above.

We assume that the USIM's PIN is set to default value. And the attacker has physically access to the USIM and ME. In real life, there are indeed chances for other people to physically access the UE. For example, when a confidential meeting is held, the relevant personnel are required to put their mobile phones together outside the meeting room.

Assumptions on Data Protections. We assume the following data are public and available to the attacker: the default PIN and SUPI. If the operator strictly follows the 3GPP standard, the attacker cannot obtain SUPI. However, the three operators involved in this paper disable SUPI protection, which will lead to the leakage of SUPI [11].

Assumptions on Authentications. We assume that the UE and the AMF complete the mutual authentication through the security context. If the AMF can correctly process the UE's encrypted and integrity-protected registration request based on the security context, the AMF will skip the AKA procedure.

3.2   Security Goals

We now describe the security goals of the fast registration procedure based on the security context.

Authentication Properties. The 3GPP standard describes the 5G subscriber authentication properties in the document. We have identified the relevant statements and translated them into formal security goals. We use Lowe's taxonomy of authentication properties to precisely formalize the goals [12]. Lowe's taxonomy specifies four levels of authentication between two agents A and B from A's point of view: (i) aliveness: it ensures that B has run the protocol previously, but not necessarily with A; (ii) weak agreement: it ensures that B and A have run the protocol previously, but not necessarily with the same data. This prevents impersonation attacks; (iii) non-injective agreement: it ensures that B and A have run the protocol previously and agree on the data. This prevents message tampering attacks; (iv) injective agreement: on the basis of non-injective agreement, it ensures that for each run of the protocol of A there is a unique matching run of B. This prevents replay attacks. The AMF and the UE should be able to complete mutual authentication. During the fast registration procedure, these authentications are ensured by both parties being able to complete key confirmation. And the uplink and downlink NAS COUNT values prevent replay attacks as described above. Formally, the AMF must obtain injective agreement on the fast registration procedure with the UE. Conversely, so does the UE.

Confidentiality Properties. While it is not clearly specified, obviously the confidentiality of the security context should be ensured. The 3GPP proposes protection measures for the security context stored in the USIM card or the baseband chip [3,5]. Since all the data in the security context except K_{AMF} will be transmitted in plaintext, K_{AMF} should be guaranteed to be confident. Formally, the cryptographic key K_{AMF} protected by these measures should remain secret in the presence of the attacker.

3.3   Overview of ProVerif

To analyze the fast registration procedure based on the security context, we used the ProVerif prover [9]. ProVerif is a protocol verification tool for the symbolic model, which is able to prove the security properties of protocols, including confidentiality properties, authentication properties and privacy properties. Although ProVerif does not support XOR operation, which is important for 5G key derivation, it can still be used to verify the fast registration procedure. Since we assume that the cryptographic algorithm is secure, we can simplify the key derivation procedure.

ProVerif can automatically deduce the logical derivation of the security goals to be proved based on the formal description of the protocol. If a goal is violated, it will give the detailed attack method. In ProVerif, messages are described as terms. A term is constructed by constructors. Taking symmetric encryption as an example, we define the type key, and $senc(m, k)$ represents the message m encrypted using the k, where $senc(bitstring, key)$ is a constructor. And the equation $sdec(senc(m, k), k) = m$ represents that the decryption of the plaintext with the same k.

```
1  type key.
2  fun senc(bitstring, key): bitstring.
3  reduc forall m: bitstring, k: key;
4      sdec(senc(m, k), k) = m.
```

3.4   Formalizing Security Goals

ProVerif can prove correspondence assertions, reachability properties.

Authentication properties can be checked via the correspondence assertions. The correspondence assertions are used to capture relationships between events. It can be expressed that if a specified event with some arguments has been executed, then the other with the same arguments event has been previously executed. For example, If the AMF is able to verify an encrypted and integrity-protected registration request message with information elements (including 5G-GUTI, ngKSI, uplink NAS COUNT), NAS container, and message authentication code (MAC) (event amf_verify), then it means that the UE has initiated a unique registration request with the same parameters (event ue_init). We can use the following query to check the injective agreement on these data.

```
1  query x: ies, y: container, z: mac;
2  inj-event(amf_verify(x, y, z)) ==> inj-event(ue_init(x,
       y, z)).
```

Confidentiality is a reachability property. Verifying reachability properties is the most basic capability of ProVerif. The tool can prove which terms are available to an attacker by checking all possible protocol executions and attacker behaviors. Using the following query statements, ProVerif can test secrecy of the term *Key* in the model.

```
1 query attacker(Key).
```

3.5   ProVerif Model of the Fast Registration Procedure

We now model the fast registration procedure in ProVerif, which takes 240 lines of ProVerif code. Due to a large amount of modeling code, we only describe some key codes in this section.

Channel and Cryptographic Algorithm. We have defined a channel between UE and AMF. The channel is public under the attacks of malicious users. In addition, we also define the auxiliary cryptographic algorithms, including symmetric encryption, integrity protection, and key derivation. Specifically, the symmetric encryption and the integrity protection are used to protect the registration request message; the key derivation is used to obtain encryption and integrity protection keys from K_{AMF}.

UE. There are two storage methods for the security context in the UE. To do this, we pass a parameter to the UE process. If the value of this parameter is ME, the security context is stored in the baseband chip. Otherwise, the security context is stored in the USIM card. In addition, to indicate that the correct PIN code is required to read the security context stored in the USIM card, we solve this problem with symmetric encryption. Specifically, the security context is encrypted with a PIN code in a symmetric encryption manner, and the correct PIN code needs to be used as a key for decryption. Similarly, for the scenario where the security context is stored in the baseband chip, we have done the same trick, but the key has become SUPI.

AMF. We define a table to represent the correspondence between GUTI, ngKSI and security context. The AMF can query the corresponding security context according to the GUTI and ngKSI sent by the UE. Then the AMF judges whether the registration request message is correctly encrypted and integrity protected according to the security context, and verifies whether it is replayed through the uplink NAS COUNT value.

4   Vulnerabilities

In this section, we present the formal verification results of the fast registration procedure using the security context. The existing security mechanism cannot meet the security goals of the fast registration procedure. Specifically, the AMF and the UE cannot satisfy injective agreement on the fast registration procedure. That is to say, the completion of the authentication of the UE by the AMF does not mean that the UE initiates an authentication request. This shows that the attacker can impersonate the UE to complete the mutual authentication with the AMF. Moreover, an attacker can obtain keys, which defeats the confidentiality properties of the fast registration procedure. Combined with the attack paths automatically generated by ProVerif, we analyze the discovered vulnerabilities from the perspective of how the security context is stored. In addition, we tested 3 operators and found that they have vulnerabilities in both cases where the security context is stored in the USIM card or the baseband chip. Exploiting these vulnerabilities, we designed 3 attacks, which are validated on these operators. Table 1 summarizes our findings and the results of testing on 3 operators. We denote the three operators as OP-I, OP-II, and OP-III for the privacy concern. It is worth noting that the discussions below and the vulnerabilities also apply to the 4G network.

Table 1. Summary of our findings on the security context vulnerabilities and attacks

OP	Vulnerability		Attack		
	in USIM	in baseband	Impersonation	Auth. bypass	Location spoofing
OP-I	Yes	Yes	Yes	Yes	Yes
OP-II	No	Yes	Yes	Yes	Yes
OP-III	Yes	Yes	Yes	Yes	Yes

The Security Context Stored in the USIM Card. We analyze the operators' insecure practices regarding the security context stored in the USIM card. The 3GPP standard stipulates that the PIN-based access control can prevent the security context stored in the USIM card from being maliciously read [3]. However, the PIN-based access control cannot achieve the desired effect [8]. First, the USIM card cannot differentiate between various entities accessing the card through the PIN verification. To make matters worse, operators usually set a default PIN and disenable the PIN verification. Therefore, an attacker can access the security context saved in the USIM card, which uses the default PIN, with a card reader, malware, etc. In this paper, we have tested USIM cards from three operators and found that they all use 1234 as the default PIN. In addition, only one of the three operators has enhanced the USIM card to prevent the use of the card reader to obtain the security context.

The Security Context Stored in the Baseband Chip. We analyze the security of the security context stored in the baseband chip from the protocol perspective. The 3GPP standard stipulates that the security context stored in the baseband chip shall correspond to the subscriber's permanent identity. It also specifies that the security context stored in the baseband chip should be deleted from the baseband chip in the following cases [4,5]: (1) The USIM card is removed from the ME when the ME is in power on state; (2) The ME is turned on and finds that there is no USIM card in the ME; (3) The ME is turned on and discovers that the USIM card is different from the one which was used to create the security context. However, we find that if the ME is in airplane mode or turned off, the baseband chip cannot capture the USIM card being removed or replaced. The security context stored in the baseband chip can only be used if the permanent identity from the USIM matches the identity associated with the security context. Therefore, an attacker may construct a USIM card with the same permanent identity, and replace the legitimate USIM card with the fake USIM card when the phone is in airplane mode or turned off to illegally use the stored security context.

5   Attacks

In this section, we describe the proposed attacks that exploit the discovered vulnerabilities. First, we introduce our attack model and experimental setup. Then we show the two impersonation attacks by exploiting the vulnerabilities of the security context. Finally, we present two other attacks (i.e., one-tap authentication bypass and location spoofing) that result from a successful impersonation attack. We have validated them on three operators as shown in Table 1.

5.1   Attack Model

We assume an attacker can perform attacks in the following two scenarios. In the first scenario, we assume the attacker can obtain the valid security context stored in the victim's USIM card. This can be achieved with one-time physical access through hardware (e.g., the card reader) or malware installed on the victim's phone [8]. There are many types of malware, such as worms, backdoors, viruses, Trojans, that easily threaten smartphones which can be employed by attackers to steal the private information in potential. In addition, attackers can leverage the USIM sticker to extract sensitive files from the victim's USIM [8]. In this paper, we take advantage of the card reader to obtain these target parameters. In the second scenario, we assume the attacker can obtain a mobile device, which stores a valid security context of the victim. This does work in real life. For example, on some special occasions, several people will take turns using a mobile phone, and each person will use a different USIM card. An attacker who is one of the members can then attack the previous user. Alternatively, the attacker can trick the victim into inserting their USIM card into the attacker's phone in front of the victim and then return the USIM card. The attacker only needs to ensure that the phone is turned off or in airplane mode when the victim's USIM card is pulled out. It is worth noting that attackers can use their own USIM cards to launch the above attack and forge their location information as described in Sect. 5.5. Moreover, we assume that the attacker needs to know some basic knowledge about 4G/5G, and have the ability to use the card reader to read and write the USIM card.

Ethics Discussion. We perform all the experiments in a responsible way: all USIM cards and mobile devices involved in the experiments are our own to prevent affecting other users. We have notified operators about the unsafe implementations. At the same time, we have submitted the discovered protocol vulnerability to the GSMA for mitigation and obtained a coordinated vulnerability disclosure (CVD) number CVD-2022-0057.

5.2   Experimental Setup

The setup consists of a computer with the Windows operating system. The computer is equipped with the software which sends APDUs to interact with the USIM card, and cooperates with a card reader to read and write the USIM card. In addition, we used a Huawei Mate30 5G as the test phone, which can connect to the 4G and 5G networks of the three operators. There are two kinds of USIM cards used in our experiments. One is a legal 5G USIM card that is assigned by the operator and facilitates the subscriber to access the 4G/5G network (we name it a real card). And the other is a programmable USIM card (we named it a fake card). The files (e.g., IMSI, EPSLOCI and EPSNSC) stored in the fake card can be read and written at will.

We found that when using the real card to access the operator's 5G network, the security context is stored in the baseband chip, and when accessing the 4G network the security context is stored in the USIM card. Therefore, in order to verify the impersonation attack using the security context in USIM, we choose to access the 4G network. And when verifying the impersonation attack using the security context in the baseband chip, we choose to access the 5G network.

5.3   Impersonation Using the Security Context in USIM

The PIN-based access control cannot effectively protect the security context stored in the USIM card. If the operator does not enhance the security of the USIM, an attacker can use hardware or software to obtain these security contexts. Then the attacker can leverage the vulnerability and the fast registration procedure to perform several attacks, such as traffic eavesdropping, MITM attack, and impersonation [8]. The impersonation attack described in [8] is implemented using the open-source software srsLTE [13]. However, since the software utilizes software-defined radio (SDR) to send wireless signals, it is not as stable as mobile devices equipped with a baseband chip. In this paper, our impersonation attack based on this vulnerability is performed with a commercial mobile device.

Attack Procedure. We assume that the victim has connected to the operator's 4G network using a mobile phone equipped with the real card. At this point, a valid 4G security context is already stored in the real card. The attacker can then launch the impersonation attack. First, the attacker uses the card reader to obtain the files (i.e., IMSI, EPSLOCI and EPSNSC) required for the fast registration procedure. Second, the attacker uses the same method to write these files into the fake card. Then the attacker inserts the fake card into the phone and uses the fast registration service to access the operator's 4G network as the victim. Figure 2 shows the NAS signaling messages. The attach request signaling includes the NAS key set identifier (in file EPSNSC) and the GUTI (in file EPSLOCI), and the 4G network does not initiate an AKA procedure. Both sides use the key in file EPSNSC to derive various keys to ensure the security of subsequent communications.

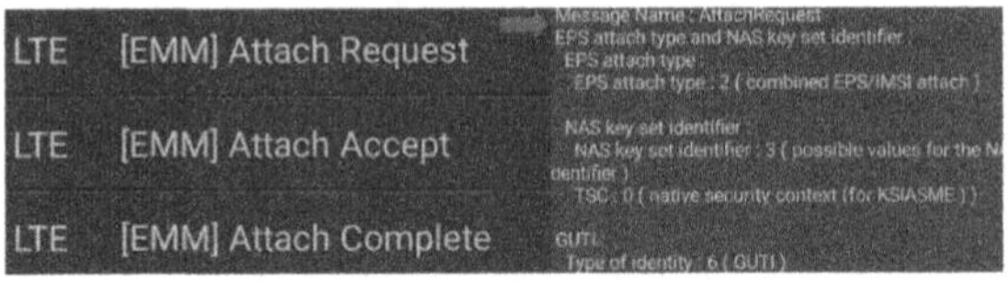

Fig. 2. The NAS signaling messages of the impersonation attack in a 4G network

5.4   Impersonation Using the Security Context in Baseband Chip

The security protection proposed by the 3GPP standard for the security context stored in the baseband chip cannot achieve its intended purpose. First, when the mobile phone is in airplane mode or turned off, the baseband chip cannot determine whether the mobile phone card has been pulled out or replaced. Secondly, the baseband chip decides whether to use the security context for fast registration procedure by judging whether the permanent identity in the USIM card is consistent with the identity corresponding to the saved security context. In this paper, we propose an impersonation attack that exploits the security context stored in the baseband chip.

Attack Procedure. First, the attacker determines the permanent identity SUPI of the victim's USIM card. Since these three operators have not enabled protection against SUPI, SUPI is transmitted over the air interface in the form of IMSI at this time [11]. Then the attacker writes it to the fake card. Second, the attacker would need to obtain a phone with a legitimate security context. Third, the attacker inserts the fake card into the phone, and then turns off airplane mode or turns the phone on. Since the permanent identity in the fake card is consistent with the identity corresponding to the security context, the mobile phone determines that the saved security context is valid, and uses it to initiate a fast registration procedure. Finally, the attacker can use the fake card to access the operator's 5G network as shown in Fig. 3.

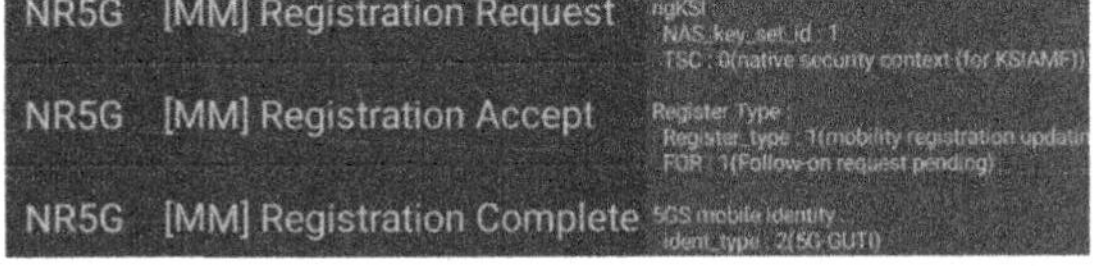

Fig. 3. The NAS signaling messages of the impersonation attack in a 5G network

5.5   Other Attacks

After the attacker has successfully launched the impersonation attack, the attacker can also launch some other attacks, including one-tap authentication bypass and location spoofing.

One-tap Authentication Bypass. The one-tap authentication service allows users to quickly sign up or log in to their application accounts using the tokens provided by the operator [14]. All three operators discussed in this paper support this service. The service is based on cellular network status. The attacker's device needs to have the same cellular network state as the victim to bypass this authentication. Since the attacker can launch impersonation attacks, the attacker can bypass this authentication to log into the victim's application account. This poses a great threat to user privacy.

Location Spoofing. Operators can locate subscribers based on which base station the subscribers are connected to. However, the attacker with the security context can launch impersonation attacks far from the victim, which will challenge operators to locate users. Moreover, this could also be exploited by criminals to forge evidence.

6 Countermeasures

The vulnerabilities stem from the design flaw of the 3GPP protocol and the unsafe practices by operators. We propose the following countermeasures from three perspectives.

The Operator. First, the operator should enhance the security of the USIM card to prevent the security context saved in the USIM card from being illegally read. Second, operators can disable the fast registration services. For each registration request, the network initiates an AKA procedure to ensure security. Moreover, for the UE that has already accessed the network, it is better for the operator to reinitiate an AKA procedure at regular intervals to update the security context. Third, the 5G USIM card should be enhanced to support storing the 5G security context.

The 3GPP Protocol. Checking the validity of the security context stored in the baseband chip should incorporate other parameters (e.g., ICCID), not just the permanent identity. This will greatly increase the difficulty of the attack.

The Equipment Manufacturer. Mobile phone manufacturers and baseband chip manufacturers should coordinate the transmission of USIM card status information. When the mobile phone is in airplane mode or turned off, the baseband chip should be able to know the change of the USIM card status information, and then decide whether to delete the security context.

7 Related Work

We discuss the related work with the following two categories, namely, impersonation attacks in mobile networks, and security research on the USIM card.

Impersonation Attacks in Mobile Networks. Meyer et al. [15] present that an attacker could exploit the inherent authentication flaws of the GSM network to imitate the victim's access to the GSM network. Rupprecht et al. [16] propose the impersonation attack that exploits the lack of integrity protection on the user plane and the reflection mechanism of Internet Control Message Protocol (ICMP). Zheng et al. [17] find one vulnerability in Circuit Switched Fallback (CSFB) where the authentication step is missing, which allows an attacker to impersonate a victim.

Security Research on the USIM Ccard. Liu et al. [18] present how to copy a 3G/4G USIM card via the side-channel attack. An attacker can launch the SIMjacker attack to track user location without the user's awareness [19]. Zhao et al. [8] uncover three vulnerabilities of the PIN-based access control of the USIM card. In this paper, we analyze the security context generated by the USIM card.

8   Conclusion

In this work, we use the formal approach to model a fast registration procedure based on the security context. We find two vulnerabilities, which are caused by the insecure implementations of operators or the 3GPP protocol flaws. We propose two novel impersonation attacks based on these vulnerabilities and confirm them in three operators. Furthermore, we also discuss two other security threats that can arise from impersonation attacks. Finally, we propose several countermeasures from multiple perspectives to defend against the attack.

References

1. 3GPP: Non-access-stratum (nas) protocol for 5g system. Technical Report, 24.501
2. 3GPP: Non-access-stratum (nas) protocol for evolved packet system (eps). Technical Report, 24.301
3. 3GPP: Characteristics of the universal subscriber identity module (usim) application. Technical Report, 31.102
4. 3GPP: 3gpp system architecture evolution (SAE); security architecture. Technical Report, 33.401
5. 3GPP: Security architecture and procedures for 5g system. Technical Report, 33.501
6. Schneider, P., Horn, G.: Towards 5g security. In: 2015 IEEE Trustcom/BigDataSE/ISPA, pp. 1165–1170. IEEE (2015)
7. Shaik, A., Borgaonkar, R., Park, S., Seifert, J.P.: New vulnerabilities in 4g and 5g cellular access network protocols: exposing device capabilities. In: 12th Conference on Security and Privacy in Wireless and Mobile Networks, pp. 221–231. ACM (2019)
8. Zhao, J., Ding, B., Guo, Y., Tan, Z., Lu, S.: Securesim: rethinking authentication and access control for sim/esim. In: 27th Annual International Conference on Mobile Computing and Networking, pp. 451–464. ACM (2021)
9. Blanchet, B., et al.: Modeling and verifying security protocols with the applied pi calculus and proverif. Found. Trends® Privacy Secur. 1(1–2), 1–135 (2016)

10. Savoldi, A., Gubian, P.: Sim and usim filesystem: a forensics perspective. In: the 2007 ACM Symposium on Applied Computing, pp. 181–187. ACM (2007)

11. Nie, S., Zhang, Y., Wan, T., Duan, H., Li, S.: Measuring the deployment of 5g security enhancement. In: 15th ACM Conference on Security and Privacy in Wireless and Mobile Networks, pp. 169–174. ACM (2022)

12. Lowe, G.: A hierarchy of authentication specifications. In: 10th Computer Security Foundations Workshop, pp. 31–43. IEEE (1997)

13. Gomez-Miguelez, I., Garcia-Saavedra, A., Sutton, P.D., Serrano, P., Cano, C., Leith, D.J.: srslte: an open-source platform for LTE evolution and experimentation. In: 10th ACM International Workshop on Wireless Network Testbeds, Experimental Evaluation, and Characterization, pp. 25–32. ACM (2016)

14. Zhou, Z., Han, X., Chen, Z., Nan, Y., Li, J., Gu, D.: Simulation: demystifying (insecure) cellular network based one-tap authentication services. In: 52nd Annual IEEE/IFIP International Conference on Dependable Systems and Networks (DSN), pp. 534–546. IEEE (2022)

15. Meyer, U., Wetzel, S.: On the impact of GSM encryption and man-in-the-middle attacks on the security of interoperating GSM/UMTS networks. In: 15th International Symposium on Personal, Indoor and Mobile Radio Communications, pp. 2876–2883. IEEE (2004)

16. Rupprecht, D., Kohls, K., Holz, T., Pöpper, C.: Imp4gt: impersonation attacks in 4g networks. In: NDSS (2020)

17. Zheng, Y., Huang, L., Shan, H., Li, J., Yang, Q., Xu, W.: Ghost Telephonist impersonates you: Vulnerability in 4g LTE CS fallback. In: 2017 IEEE Conference on Communications and Network Security (CNS), pp. 1–9. IEEE (2017)

18. Liu, J., et al.: Small tweaks do not help: differential power analysis of MILENAGE implementations in 3G/4G USIM cards. In: Pernul, G., Ryan, P.Y.A., Weippl, E. (eds.) ESORICS 2015. LNCS, vol. 9326, pp. 468–480. Springer, Cham (2015). https://doi.org/10.1007/978-3-319-24174-6_24

19. New simjacker vulnerability exploited by surveillance companies for espionage operation. https://simjacker.com/

A Systematic Approach to Security Management in the MonB5G Architecture

Sławomir Kukliński[1,2](✉) and Jacek Wytrębowicz[1]

[1] Warsaw University of Technology, Warsaw, Poland
jacek.wytrebowicz@pw.edu.pl
[2] Orange Polska, Obrzeżna 7, 02-691 Warsaw, Poland
slawomir.kuklinski@orange.com

Abstract. Network slicing management and orchestration typically use centralised OSS/BSS combined with an ETSI MANO orchestrator. In [20], it has been proposed a concept in which network slicing system management is autonomic, distributed, and slice management is a part of the Network Slice (NS). The MonB5G project has enhanced the idea. The approach can be nicely used for security due to separate management planes of NSs and reducing the common part of all slices. Our paper describes how the MonB5G framework features contribute to network slicing security and how the framework mechanisms can be used to detect and mitigate attacks. In particular, it describes the security roles of the MonB5G framework components. Some examples show the advantages of the proposed approach over the classical ETSI MANO approach. The features of the concept fit well with the requirements of the future mobile network.

Keywords: Network slicing · Network security · Network management

1 Introduction

The Network Slices (NSs) enable the creation of virtual networks atop shared infrastructure composed of typically virtualised resources (computing, storage, and connectivity). Despite sharing common infrastructure, NSs form logical networks that are isolated. The isolation is understood in a broad sense – any activity related to one NS should not be visible nor impact other NSs. The NS template has no functional limitation and may include different NS-level security-related functions, e.g. authentication, data ciphering, integrity check, firewall, intrusion detection, and deep packet inspection. Please note that the NS instance, deployed accordingly to its NS template, can be modified during slice runtime – a feature which also can be used for the dynamic deployment of functions dedicated to security. Network slicing is a part of the Standalone version of the 5G network. The 3GPP approach to orchestration and management [1–3] supports NS (at the level of network function, sub-network slice, network slice and communication service management) using ETSI NFV mechanisms [11,12].

I. You et al. (Eds.): MobiSec 2022, CCIS 1644, pp. 18–32, 2023.
https://doi.org/10.1007/978-981-99-4430-9_2

The ETSI NFV lies on centralised orchestration and common OSS/BSS for all NSs that raise isolation and scalability issues. Moreover, the single OSS/BSS not only degrades NS isolation. A new approach to network slicing has already been proposed in [20] and detailed in [19]. Its enhanced multi-domain version, which uses AI, has been described in [18]. In this concept, the functionalities of OSS/BSS have been distributed, and a slice has its private OSS/BSS, which is part of the NS template, and the OSS/BSS of NS may request orchestration events. The approach provides separation of the slice management plane. It provides the capability to orchestrate the slices and management part of the slice, which is of premium importance for security. In the paper, we provide a systematic approach to using the MonB5G framework and its mechanisms for security. We are focused on the slice runtime phase because, in this phase, the MonB5G approach differs significantly from other NS management and orchestration approaches. To that end, we will describe the benefits of the security management approach and how the distributed management plane mechanisms can be used to provide the NSs and the overall NS framework security. Section 2 of the paper describes the threats related to virtualised solutions and network slicing. Section 3 describes the related work concerning security in network slicing solutions. Section 4 outlines the decomposition of the MonB5G management system (orchestration is part of it). Section 5 details the roles of each management component of MonB5G in security. In Sect. 6, some usage examples of the presented concept are outlined, and finally, Sect. 7 concludes the paper.

2 Threats Related to the Network Slicing Ecosystem

The threats related to network slicing concern the NS lifecycle, NS management and orchestration and the virtualised infrastructure. When it comes to NS lifecycle, the NS preparation phase threats, the NS installation phase threats, the NS runtime phase threats, and NS decommissioning phase threats can be identified. Threats related to the management of NSs (OSS/BSS), as well as end-user hosts and devices, have been divided into two categories – classical and nontrivial [7]. Classical threats are common in other network systems and include eavesdropping on NS management interfaces, traffic injection, etc. Non-trivial threats include passive and active side-channel across slices that share resources and end-device vulnerabilities. Threats related to the ETSI NFV MANO orchestrator and NSs have been described in [8]. The report lists the threats related to virtualisation, hardware, and also lists potential areas of concern, including NS topology validation and enforcement, secure boot and crash, performance isolation, user and tenant authorisation and authentication, and business actors' isolation. ENISA [21] has identified threats related to: infrastructure resources isolation and issues associated with Trust Model creation.

3 Related Work on Network Slicing Security

The OSS/BSS functions for network slicing had not been defined by 3GPP nor ETSI, and the common for all slices OSS/BSS centralisation raises, among others, isolation and security issues, as described in [14]. The 3GPP specifications do not define the security mechanisms of NSs. ETSI NFV has provided several specifications concerning NFV security. In [9], the NFV security and trust guidance related to NFV development, architecture and operations have been described, and in [10], the security of MANO components and reference points has been specified. This document describes a high-level Security Management Framework. It defines Virtual Security Functions (as a part of NS), the NFVI Security Manager, Security Element Managers (SEMs) and the NFV Security Manager (NSM). All the components form a slightly distributed management plane of the framework, as NSM can be a part of OSS/BSS. A survey of approaches to NS and related issues can be found in [4,5,13]. In [15], an abstraction layer is introduced to assure end-to-end NS isolation. In [22], possible attack points for intra-slice and inter-slice security have been described as well as security recommendations considering different stages of the lifecycle of an NS. In [25], it has been defined slices with varying levels of security. In [19,20], the management plane of each slice is separated and embedded. The management operations, including security, are driven by multiple control loops. An extension of the idea presented in [16,18] defines the AI-driven distributed management architecture with the programmability of slice management. The security approach using the MonB5G architecture has been outlined in [23]. In [6], a network-slicing security orchestration framework for NS in multiple domains using the MonB5G approach has been described. Our paper uses the MonB5G concept; however, we systematically analysed all the mechanisms of the MonB5G framework that can be exploited for security. Specifically, following the idea described in [17], we assume that OSS/BSS of each slice can trigger the orchestration operations, i.e., adding or removing Network Functions (NFs) to its NSs. We assume the security service is just one of the management plane services, what is justified by the reusability of common components for security, performance, accounting and fault management.

4 Management Decomposition in the MonB5G Architecture

The MonB5G management and orchestration architecture [16,18] use multiple control loops, which generic structure is shown in Fig. 1. Each control loop is composed of Monitoring Subsystem (MS), one or more Analytic Engines (AEs), a Decision Engine (DE) and an Actuator (ACT). These elements are involved in reconfigurations driven by the management plane. In the MonB5G management system, multiple control loops exist, and each of them may have a different goal. For example, some DEs may optimise system security, while others focus on system performance or fault management.

The overall decomposition of the MonB5G management and orchestration architecture is shown in Fig. 2. The main difference between the approach and the classical ETSI NFV MANO is the decomposition of the management plane. In the MonB5G concept, each NS has a management plane (it also concerns

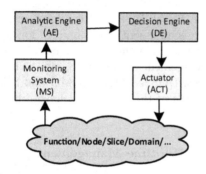

Fig. 1. MonB5G generic control loop.

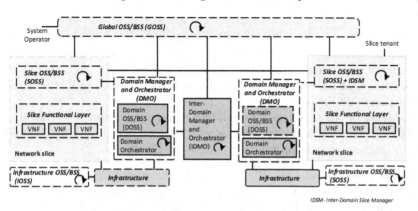

Fig. 2. MonB5G simplified architecture.

the multi-domain NSs) called in the paper Slice OSS (SOSS). Each Orchestration Domain has OSS/BSS, called Domain OSS (DOSS). The Infrastructure has Infrastructure OSS (IOSS), and the Inter-Domain operations are handled by the Inter-Domain Manager & Orchestrator (IDMO). Finally, there is the Global OSS/BSS (GOSS), which is responsible for the overall management of the framework. The approach provides a good separation of concerns and isolation between NSs – the NS management operations are isolated, and orchestration domain operations are focused on resources and agnostic to NSs. Finally, in the NS runtime phase, the GOSS is only involved in administrative and cross-OSS management. That way, clear objectives for each management subsystem can be defined. Please note that slice-level management, i.e. SOSS, is a part of the NS template; therefore, it can be customised for each NS. In the paper, we will follow the concept presented in [17], in which the management plane offers management services. In the mentioned paper, the author has followed the well-known FCAPS approach (Fault Management, Configuration Management, Accounting, Performance Management and Security Management) in the context of SOSS, which is called in the paper In-Slice Management. In the approach, each service is control-loop based (can be AI-driven) except for accounting. The Configuration Management Service is an essential mechanism for achieving performance, fault and security management. In this paper, we go beyond SOSS and discuss the overall MonB5G management architecture, which, in a multi-domain case, is a combination of GOSS, DOSSs, IOSSs, IDMO and SOSSs. During NS runtime management, the OSSs of the framework have different roles and scopes, described below.

4.1   SOSS Role in NS Runtime Management

The SOSS is the NS management plane, a part of the NS template, and is typically based on multiple control loops. Following [17], the control loops can change NS configuration by:

- NS parameters modifications, which is a typical management operation;
- resource scaling in proactive (data-driven) and reactive (resource consumption-driven) ways. The resource scaling is an orchestrator-based operation that lies on change in the allocation of resources to Virtual Network Functions (VNFs) of an NS;
- modifying of NS topology. The modification may concern NS Control, User Planes, and SOSS and can be done by adding or removing VNFs or making their migrations (redeployment in a different cloud).

Please note that in the MonB5G approach, the above operations are driven by multiple and independent AI pipelines used to implement fault, performance, and security management. In the paper, we follow [17] and use the decomposition (see Fig. 3) of SOSS into:

- Autonomic Monitoring Sublayer (AMS). It collects information from all sources (VNFs, Infrastructure) and processes the monitoring data, including data aggregation and filtering. The AMS has a database that keeps all the monitoring information (Monitoring Database) and NS topology (Topology Database). The AEs are also part of AMS, which, as already mentioned, is programmable. The programmability concerns monitoring operations and the ability to add new AEs if needed. The AEs not only analyse the monitoring data by looking for anomalies but can also make predictions of their future values;
- Intelligent Reconfiguration Sublayer (IRS). The NS reconfigurations, enforced by IRS, can be triggered by SOSS services, slice tenant, DOSS or GOSS. Each reconfiguration request may have assigned priority. Whereas a SOSS service (typically the performance management service) can trigger proactive scaling of NS-allocated resources (based on the change of NS users, traffic growth, etc.), the IRS may trigger reactive resource scaling based on the level of the consumed resources. The IRS subscribe to AMS to take decisions about reactive resource scaling. The reconfigurations' history is kept in the Reconfiguration Database. Please note that resource scaling procedures are susceptible to security attacks;

- Management Services. Independent management services deal with performance, fault and security; however, in this paper, we have focused on the Security Management Service (SMS) only;
- Auxiliary Management Functions (AMF). The functions are essential for SOSS's overall operations. They enable the system operator or NS tenant to perform NS configuration, inter-domain NS operations, and Policy-Based Management (PBM). The reconfigurations are described in detail in [18]; therefore, the details of the functions will be omitted in the paper.

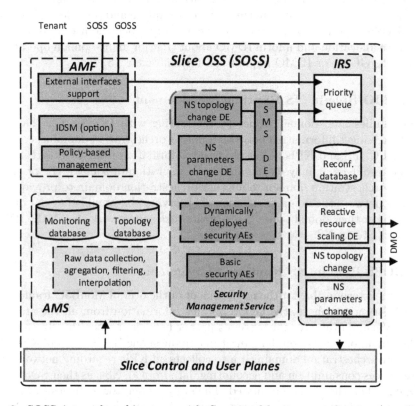

Fig. 3. SOSS internal architecture with Security Management Service (simplified, generic example).

The AMS and IRS sublayers are common for all management services. The AMS provides generic and dedicated, programmable monitoring, and the IRS is responsible for synchronising, coordinating and executing operations related to NS reconfigurations that come from different management services. In the case of NSs deployed in multiple domains, the SOSSs of domain-level NSs are integrated using the Inter-Domain Slice Manager (IDSM). The IDSM is a part of one of the integrated SOSSs (see Fig. 3). The IDSM's role is to exchange information between the SOSSs regarding management operations and provide the tenant interface.

4.2   DOSS Role in NS Runtime Management

According to the MonB5G assumption, the DOSS is agnostic to managed NSs, i.e. it is not directly involved in NS management. In the NS runtime phase, it is focused on its orchestration domain. DOSS operations are concentrated in the FCAPS of the underlying orchestrator, allocation of resources to NSs, and inter-slice issues by analysing NSs' Key Performance Indicators (KPIs) degradation. The DOSS provides orchestrator abstraction as it is used to interact with it. The orchestrator can be seen as a simplified version of ETSI NFV MANO. Internally, similarly to SOSS, the DOSS may use multiple control loops. It interacts with SOSS for resource scaling and runtime NS orchestration and provides an interface to the DOSS operator. DOSS may observe abnormal behaviour of NSs in terms of resource allocation and inform IDMO about that for multi-domain operations. The DOSS, GOSS, or IDMO request can terminate an NS.

4.3   IDMO Role in NS Runtime Management

IDMO handles inter-domain issues by interacting with DOSSs. For that purpose, it exchanges information between different orchestration domains, comparing their FCAPS and KPIs. After obtaining information from DOSSs regarding available resources, it may decide about the migration of some VNFs of an NS from one orchestration domain to another orchestration domain to provide load balancing between the domains. Moreover, observing abnormal behaviour of end-to-end NSs or their domain-level components (aka subnetwork slices), the IDMO may terminate an NS.

4.4   GOSS Role in NS Runtime Management

The GOSS is responsible for the management of the overall MonB5G framework. In the NS runtime phase, the GOSS obtains information from all the architecture's OSSs and evaluates the system's proper behaviour ('health'). In case of a problem in an orchestration domain, it may request the IDMO to deploy the NS in another orchestration domain. It also collects all KPIs regarding network NSs and resources consumption and accounting data from all NSs, as their SOSSs will disappear when the NS is terminated. The system operator manages GOSS and may request execution of any management or orchestration operation. GOSS is also used by NS tenants when requesting NS deployment or termination.

4.5   IOSS Role in NS Runtime Management

IOSS is focused on Infrastructure management and is involved in all operations related to hardware, hypervisor and virtualised resources. It can be seen as a cloud management system or a federation of clouds. Similarly to other OSSs of the framework, it performs FCAPS of its domain. The IOSS may exchange with DOSS and GOSS essential information concerning FCAPS. Similarly to other OSSs, The IOSS should be based on multiple control loops to implement FCAPS.

5   Network Slicing Security Mechanisms in the MonB5G Architecture

A simplified security management architecture of MonB5G, showing only the management part during the runtime phase of a single NS, is presented in Fig. 4. Each of the presented OSSs has a specific role in security, which is seen as a management service. All the OSSs cooperate to identify the threats and mitigate them. Please note that the trust issue should also be addressed in a multi-stakeholder environment.

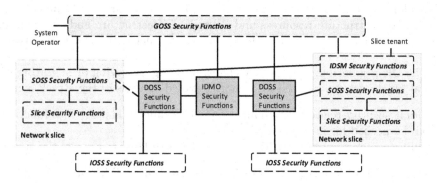

Fig. 4. MonB5G security architecture.

5.1   Usage of SOSS Mechanisms for Security

The SOSS is defined in an NS template as the NS management plane and is specific to the NS functional part (i.e. user and control planes); therefore, it may have incorporated all the mechanisms needed for the security management of the NS. It is up to the NS template provider how to implement these mechanisms; thus, each NS may have different levels of security. The NS security mechanisms concern the definition of the NS functional part and security management functions (called in the paper Security Management Service, SMS). The NS functional part may deal with data ciphering, data integrity checks and authentication of users and devices. This part may also have some security-dedicated nodes, such as firewalls and honeypots. The [9] can be used as a guideline for creating the NS template. Due to virtualisation and MonB5G architecture, it is possible to deploy such virtual security functions dynamically (in the form of VNFs). This includes the possibility of dynamic change of NS topology to complicate the attack reconnaissance phase. The modification of the NS functional part is typically SOSS driven. The AMS (see Fig. 3) of SOSS collects information from all virtual functions of the NS functional part and processes them. The processing includes monitoring data aggregation, correlation, interpolation, and filtering. Finally, the preprocessed data are recorded in Monitoring

Database. Security AEs consume the information stored in the database. Each of such AEs has been designed to detect an anomaly or direct security threat. Until these units see a threat, the other components of the SMS are idle. The AEs are also involved in the analysis of the attack. The DoS/DDoS attacks can be easily observed by monitoring the anomalies of NS user plane traffic by respective user plane AE. A DoS/DDoS attack on the control plane that lies on intensive NS attachments can be detected by monitoring control plane traffic. The AMS also collects information regarding resource scaling (mechanism incorporated in SOSS). A respective AE can analyse this information to detect an on/off attack (aka Yo-Yo attack) on the resource scaler that forces the scaler for continuous resource scaling. Such behaviour causes unnecessary usage of Infrastructure resources and degrades Infrastructure and orchestrator performance (DDoS attack on scaler) that may further lessen isolation between NSs.

The DE responsible for topology change (adding, removing or migrating NS virtual functions) can be used for a more detailed analysis of the attack by:

– adding security-related virtual functions to NS functional part. Such functions can be needed for in-depth analysis of attack;
– adding attack-respective entities to SOSS (AEs or DEs) to analyse the attack.

AEs provide the details of an attack to security DEs (SMS part), which are responsible for the mitigation of the attack. Different actions can be taken in the attack mitigation phase:

– the DE that is responsible for NS configuration parameters can block traffic flows, make traffic redirection and isolate malicious nodes. The information about the detected attack is sent to DOSS and IDMO in the case of multi-domain NSs;
– the DE dedicated to resource scaling attacks may block resource scaling mechanisms or impose some limits on resource scaling. Such operation may impact the performance of NS; therefore, the part of the management system that is involved in NS performance management, as well as DOSS, should be informed about the attack and its mitigation method;
– the DE responsible for topology change (adding, removing or migrating of NS virtual functions) can be used to modify the topology of the functional part of NS; for example, for Moving Target Defence (MTD) or for blocking the attack in a specific part of the NS.

5.2   Usage of DOSS Mechanisms for Security

The security role of DOSS is to keep the orchestrator secure and to analyse and correlate attacks on multiple NSs. Moreover, the DOSS can analyse the behaviour of the SOSS as it also can be a subject of an attack. DOSS collects information about security incidents from all the NSs of its domain via interaction with SOSSs; however, it is agnostic to the deployed NSs. It also observes the consumption of the domain resources allocated to NSs and interacts with SOSSs regarding resource scaling and NS instance updates (adding/removing or migrating NS virtual functions). Consequently, DOSS can discover the malicious behaviour of a SOSS, and it informs GOSS and can stop increasing or even decide to decrease the resources allocated to the attacked NS. Please note that the increased resource consumption of one NS may degrade the KPIs of other NSs, and DOSS monitors such impact. In relatively rare situations where the attack cannot be mitigated, the DOSS interacting with GOSS can terminate the attacked NS. Multiple DOSSs are involved in the NS termination if NS is multi-domain NS.

5.3 Usage of IDMO Mechanisms for Security

The IDMO collects information about security incidents from all DOSSs and correlates the results. The data can be collected from AEs of SOSSs and DOSSs, and as a result, situation awareness can be achieved using correlation. Such an approach enables the detection of DDoS very early, giving more time for attack mitigation. It is assumed that the IDMO is trusted and is not susceptible to attacks.

5.4 Usage of IOSS Mechanisms for Security

In the MonB5G concept, each orchestrator is attached to an isolated (dedicated) Infrastructure that IOSS manages. IOSS interfaces should use ciphering and authentication. The IOSS can observe the overall resource consumption patterns, detect anomalies and cooperate with the DOSS to contribute to situation awareness. The IOSS is also responsible for detecting and mitigating attacks within its domain (e.g. on hardware or hypervisor). The IOSS may not trust to DOSSs and vice versa; therefore, appropriate mechanisms related to trust-building have to be built-in in IOSS. The Infrastructure provider manages the IOSS.

5.5 Usage of GOSS Mechanisms for Security

GOSS interacts with the system operator, with NS tenants (for NS lifecycle management) and with all other OSSs and business actors of the framework. It is involved in all operations related to NS deployment and termination. During the NS lifetime, it collects all information regarding the suspicious behaviour of NSs and mitigations taken. It may decide to terminate an NS (it also concerns the multi-domain NSs). It is assumed that GOSS obtains synthetic information from other OSSs and is not directly involved in identifying threats and their mitigation, which is the role of other OSSs. The SOSS, DOSS, IDMO, GOSS and Infrastructure interactions must be authenticated and ciphered.

6 Examples of the Usage of the Approach

This section will outline some security use cases that use the described framework. Three of them will be related to the attacks on the user, control, and orchestration planes, and the fourth one concerns utilising the framework for situation awareness.

6.1   DDoS Attack on the NS User Plane

The DoS or DDoS attack on the user plane is among the most popular attacks. It generates intensive user plane traffic that leads to user plane congestion and, therefore, degradation of the user data exchange. In virtualised networks, the resource allocation mechanism can provide more resources, shifting away from the congestion problem; however, malicious traffic can consume these resources. In case of such an attack, the dedicated AE of SOSS should analyse the traffic patterns from all NS sources and destinations. It should analyse the traffic history (such as dependence on the time of day), the number of users and sessions, process some analytical data, and on that basis, identify the DDoS attack. The AI algorithms can be used as AE. The role of the architecture components in such an attack is the following:

- SOSS: an AE detects the attack. The DE of SMS responsible for resource allocation imposes limits on resource allocation or reduces resources allocated to the NS. The DE is responsible for NS parameter change to block malicious traffic, and after the attack, it releases the constraints concerning resource scaling.
- DOSS: it may observe the change in resource scaling of the attacked NS and cooperate with the SOSS of the affected NS in the attack detection phase. It checks if such an attack also concerns other slices in its domain (informs other SOSSs about the attack).
- IDMO: it collects information about the DDoS attack from the DOSS and informs other DOSSs about the attack. The DOSSs may, in turn, inform AEs of their SOSSs that an attack is taking place.
- GOSS: it is informed about all attacks, and this information is stored in the GOSS repository. If the attack mitigation is ineffective or takes too much time, the GOSS may request NS termination.

6.2   Attack on the NS Control Plane

The attack on the NS control plane typically lies in the degradation of the control plane efficiency (e.g. by the increasing number of false transactions). Such an attack is usually invoked by sending incomplete requests or making a DoS/DDoS attack on the control plane. The attack handling is similar to the previous case; however, more than one AE of SOSS should be involved (one for detecting incomplete control plane transactions and another for control plane DoS/DDoS detection). The role of other components of the management architecture is almost identical to the one described in Sect. 6.1.

6.3   DDoS Attack on the Management Plane

An attack on the management (and orchestration) plane can force the resource allocation mechanism to scale resources continuously, or it may give the attacker complete control over SOSS (or SOSSes). The scaler attack can be achieved by increasing the attacker's load of an NS function, which triggers the scaler to allocate more resources. The attacker may know that the scaler has assigned the resources to NS as its perceived quality of service has improved. After that, the attacker reduces traffic, and in response to that, the resource scaler requests a reduction of resources allocated to NS. As a result of such periodic activity, the scaler is continuously busy, which may cause degradation of its performance and inefficient allocation of resources to NSs or degradation of isolation between them. The roles of the system entities in such an attack are the following:

- SOSS: An AE monitors the allocation of resources to NS. In the case of the detection of malicious behaviour, the variation of resource allocation changes is limited by the DE of SMS responsible for resource allocation to the attacked NS. The DE, responsible for NS parameter change, after root cause analysis, blocks the malicious traffic, and the constraints concerning resource scaling are released.
- DOSS: The DOSS may observe the change in resource scaling of the attacked NS and cooperate with its SOSS in the attack detection phase. It checks if such an attack also concerns other slices in its domain. However, even if not, it informs other SOSSs about the attack.
- IDMO: The IDMO collects information about the attack from DOSSs and provides details of the attack to other DOSSs, which may inform AEs of their SOSSs that this type of attack is ongoing or already took place.
- GOSS: The GOSS is informed about all attacks stored in the GOSS repository. If the attack mitigation is ineffective or takes too much time, the GOSS may request NS termination. Especially in cases when there is a high probability that the SOSS of the malicious NS is under attacker control.

DOSS can do the detection of the SOSS that the attacker controls. To that end, DOSS observes resource allocation to an NS combined with NS KPIs. In detecting appropriate behaviour, the GOSS and slice tenants are informed about the fact.

6.4 Situation Awareness

Many attacks conduct a reconnaissance in their early phase. A reconnaissance detection lies in the correlation of information coming from multiple sources. In the case of the described framework, the analysed information may come from the infrastructure (IOSS), NSs (SOSSs) of all domains, IDMO and DOSSs. In each orchestration domain, there are AEs responsible for detecting even minor anomalies, and IDMO analyses all these 'low-level' anomalies. In such a case, the detection of suspicious behaviour is not based on the 'value' of the anomaly, but on the number of relatively minor anomalies collected. In case anomalies are significant, malicious behaviour is detected, and some actions must be taken. The approach is widely referred to as situation awareness, and its application goes beyond security. In this use case, the role of the components of the discussed framework is the following:

- SOSS: a dedicated, highly sensitive AE detects anomalies and sends information about them to DOSS;
- DOSS: it collects information obtained from SOSSs of its domain and sends them to IDMO;
- IDMO: it collects information from DOSSs and IOSSs, and its AE analyses them. A respective DE of IDMO estimates the probability of the early phase of the attack. In case of a high likelihood of an episode, it informs DOSSs, which in turn informs the SOSSs about an early attack phase;
- SOSS: in response to information about the early attack phase, it takes some measures to make the reconnaissance phase harder, for example, by triggering the Moving Target Defence mechanism [24];
- GOSS: it is informed about the enforced actions.

7 Conclusions

In the paper, we analysed the value of the MonB5G concept in the context of security. We have focused on the NS runtime phase, as other phases are similar to a classical ETSI MANO approach. We have found that the most complex operations related to security are embedded in SOSS, which is a part of NS, customised to NS type (e.g. IoT or streaming). Besides, the security benefits from the programmability of the functional layer of NS and SOSS. Moreover, some self-tuning of security countermeasures can be applied immediately due to the use of control loops based operations. The other OSSs of the framework are agnostic to NSs, and their security mechanisms do not have to be changed when a new NS is deployed. The roles of the systems in security have been in the paper clearly defined. Due to a strong separation of concerns, the proposed distributed management approach contributes to the overall security architecture as each OSS-subsystem has a different scope, and no more single OSS/BSS is used for the overall system management. The possible impact of all threats mentioned in Sect. 2 is weaker due to the MonB5G architecture, which provides better separation of NSs. An attacker that infects a device or process in one NS has more barriers to access elements in data, control, and management planes of other NSs. In addition, more specialised security functions can process network events, which are well classified, filtered, and aggregated.

The paper has shown a very high complexity of NS system management that also concerns the high complexity of NSs security management. The same complexity also exists in the ETSI MANO framework – in which case, all the mentioned functions must be implemented in a single OSS/BSS, which has to interact with multiple tenants. Moreover, unlike MonB5G, the approach does not provide any programmability of the NS management plane. The problem with the MonB5G is the large footprint of NS templates, as each has a dedicated SOSS. The solution to the problem has already been proposed [18], and if the footprint of NS is critical, a SOSS can manage several NSs. Especially, NSs of the same type can share a common SOSS. However, the approach raises new issues we plan to address in the following paper, together with implementation details and some experiments of the described security concept. Another foreseen activity concerns MonB5G framework security in the NS preparation, deployment and termination phases.

Acknowledgements. The work has been supported by the EU H2020 project MonB5G (grant no. 871780) and by the National Science Centre of Poland (grant no. 2018/30/E/ST7/00413).

References

1. 3GPP: 5G; Management and orchestration; Generic management services, 16.4.0, 3GPP TS 28.532. Technical Report, ETSI, Sophia Antipolis, August 2020
2. 3GPP: 5G; Management and orchestration; Provisioning, version 16.6.0, 3GPP TS 28.531. Technical Report, ETSI, Sophia Antipolis, August 2020
3. 3GPP: Management of network slicing in mobile networks; Concepts, use cases and requirements, 3GPP TS 28.530, v17.1.0. Technical Report, 3GPP, April 2021
4. Afolabi, I., Taleb, T., Samdanis, K., Ksentini, A., Flinck, H.: Network slicing and softwarization: a survey on principles, enabling technologies, and solutions. IEEE Commun. Surv. Tutorials **20**(3), 2429–2453 (2018). https://doi.org/10.1109/COMST.2018.2815638
5. Barakabitze, A.A., Ahmad, A., Mijumbi, R., Hines, A.: 5G network slicing using SDN and NFV: a survey of taxonomy, architectures and future challenges. Comput. Netw. **167**, 106984 (2020). https://doi.org/10.1016/j.comnet.2019.106984
6. Chafika, B., Taleb, T., Phan, C.T., Tselios, C., Tsolis, G.: Distributed AI-based security for massive numbers of network slices in 5G & beyond mobile systems. In: 2021 Joint European Conference on Networks and Communications & 6G Summit (EuCNC/6G Summit), pp. 401–406. IEEE, June 2021. https://doi.org/10.1109/EuCNC/6GSummit51104.2021.9482418
7. Cunha, V.A., et al.: Network slicing security: challenges and directions. Internet Technol. Lett. **2**(5), e125 (2019). https://doi.org/10.1002/itl2.125
8. ETSI GR NFV-SEC 001: Network Functions Virtualisation (NFV); NFV Security; Problem Statement, V1.1.1. Technical Report, ETSI, October 2016
9. ETSI GR NFV-SEC 003: network functions virtualisation (NFV); NFV security; security and trust guidance, v1.2.1. Technical Report, ETSI, August 2016
10. ETSI GR NFV-SEC 014: network functions virtualisation (NFV); NFV security; security specification for mano components and reference points, v3.1.1. Technical Report, ETSI, April 2018
11. ETSI GS NFV-EVE 012: network functions virtualization (NFV); evolution and ecosystem; report on network slicing support with ETSI NFV architecture framework, V3.1.1. Technical Report, ETSI, December 2017
12. ETSI GS NFV-MAN 001: network functions virtualisation (NFV); management and orchestration, V1.1.1. Technical Report, ETSI, December 2014
13. Foukas, X., Patounas, G., Elmokashfi, A., Marina, M.K.: Network slicing in 5G: survey and challenges. IEEE Commun. Mag. **55**(5), 94–100 (2017). https://doi.org/10.1109/MCOM.2017.1600951
14. Gonzalez, A.J., et al.: The isolation concept in the 5G network slicing. In: 2020 European Conference on Networks and Communications (EuCNC), pp. 12–16. IEEE, June 2020. https://doi.org/10.1109/EuCNC48522.2020.9200939
15. Kotulski, Z., et al.: Towards constructive approach to end-to-end slice isolation in 5G networks. EURASIP J. Inf. Secur. **2018**(1), 1–23 (2018). https://doi.org/10.1186/s13635-018-0072-0

16. Kuklinski, S.: Deliverable D2.4 final release of the MonB5G architecture (including security) (2021). https://www.monb5g.eu/wp-content/uploads/2021/11/D2.4_MonB5G-Architecture.pdf
17. Kuklinski, S.: In-slice management decomposition and implementation issues. In: IEEE 5th Future Networks World Forum (FNWF 2022), Montreal. IEEE (2022). https://ieeexplore.ieee.org/xpl/conhome/1826784/all-proceedings
18. Kuklinski, S., et al.: MonB5G: AI/ML-capable distributed orchestration and management framework for network slices. In: IEEE (ed.) 2021 IEEE International Mediterranean Conference on Communications and Networking (MeditCom), pp. 29–34. IEEE, Athens, September 2021. https://doi.org/10.1109/MeditCom49071.2021.9647681
19. Kuklinski, S., Tomaszewski, L.: DASMO: a scalable approach to network slices management and orchestration. In: NOMS 2018–2018 IEEE/IFIP Network Operations and Management Symposium, pp. 1–6. IEEE, April 2018. https://doi.org/10.1109/NOMS.2018.8406279
20. Kuklinski, S., et al.: A reference architecture for network slicing. In: 2018 4th IEEE Conference on Network Softwarization and Workshops (NetSoft), pp. 217–221. IEEE, June 2018. https://doi.org/10.1109/NETSOFT.2018.8460057
21. Marinos, L., Patseas, L., Barros Lourenço, M. (eds.): ENISA: threat landscape for 5G networks. In: European Agency for Cybersecurity (2020). https://doi.org/10.2824/802229
22. Olimid, R.F., Nencioni, G.: 5G network slicing: a security overview. IEEE Access 8, 99999–100009 (2020). https://doi.org/10.1109/ACCESS.2020.2997702
23. Phan, C.T., Rahali, M., Morin, C.: Threat detection and mitigation with MonB5G components in the aLTEr scenario. In: 2021 IEEE International Mediterranean Conference on Communications and Networking (MeditCom), pp. 1–2. IEEE, September 2021. https://doi.org/10.1109/MeditCom49071.2021.9647575
24. Sengupta, S., Chowdhary, A., Sabur, A., Alshamrani, A., Huang, D., Kambhampati, S.: A survey of moving target defenses for network security. IEEE Commun. Surv. Tutorials 22(3), 1909–1941 (2020). https://doi.org/10.1109/COMST.2020.2982955
25. Wichary, T., Mongay Batalla, J., Mavromoustakis, C.X., Żurek, J., Mastorakis, G.: Network slicing security controls and assurance for verticals. Electronics 11(2), 222 (2022). https://doi.org/10.3390/electronics11020222

A Study on 5G Security Activities in Japan

SeongHan Shin[✉]

National Institute of Advanced Industrial Science and Technology (AIST), 2-3-26,
Aomi, Koto-ku, Tokyo 135-0064, Japan
seonghan.shin@aist.go.jp

Abstract. With enhanced mobile broadband, massive machine-type communications, and ultra-reliable and low-latency communications, 5G is expected to create new services that have never been imagined before in a variety of sectors. In this paper, we survey recent activities related to 5G security in Japan. Specifically, we introduce "5G Security Guideline Version 1" [13], published by the Ministry of Internal Affairs and Communications (MIC) of Japan. Then, we explain several activities toward local 5G deployment in Japan and "Local 5G Security Guideline 1st Edition" [12], published by the ICT Information Sharing and Analysis Center (ICT-ISAC) Japan.

Keywords: 5G Security · Local 5G Deployment/Security · Guideline

1 Introduction

Mobile communication speeds have improved dramatically with each generation, and the current 5G (5th Generation) [1] has a peak data rate of 20 Gbps, which is 20 times faster than 4G (4th Generation). In [16], ITU-R has defined the following main usage scenarios of 5G: 1) Enhanced Mobile Broadband (eMBB) to deal with hugely increased data rates, high user density, and very high traffic capacity for hotspot scenarios, as well as seamless coverage and high mobility scenarios with still-improved used data rates; 2) Massive Machine-type Communications (mMTC) for the IoT, requiring low power consumption and low data rates for very large numbers of connected devices; and 3) Ultra-reliable and Low Latency Communications (URLLC) to cater to safety-critical and mission-critical applications. With these superior characteristics (eMBB, mMTC, and URLLC), 5G would make it possible to create new services (e.g., advanced telemedicine and remote monitoring) that have never been imagined before in a variety of sectors [17]. On the other hand, the further utilization of virtualization technology and the introduction of new mechanisms such as edge computing and network slicing are increasing security considerations in their constructions and operations.

I. You et al. (Eds.): MobiSec 2022, CCIS 1644, pp. 33–47, 2023.
https://doi.org/10.1007/978-981-99-4430-9_3

Currently, many efforts to ensure the security and reliability of 5G systems are being progressed worldwide. In [4], NSA and CISA developed four-part series of security guidance for 5G cloud infrastructures which specifically focuses on threats, vulnerabilities, and mitigations that apply to the deployment of 5G cloud infrastructures. Also, NCCoE [2] is conducting a 5G security project in order to provide information that organizations can use to design, acquire, integrate, implement and operate 5G networks taking into consideration the security of hardware and software stack. In EU, ENISA published a report [3] that outlines the contribution of standardization to the mitigation of technical risks in the 5G ecosystem, and a document [5] that contains a 5G technology profile supplementing the technology-neutral guideline on security measures under the EECC (European Electronic Communications Code). This document gives additional guidance to competent national authorities about how to ensure the implementation and strengthening of security measures by mobile network operators for the mitigation of risks to 5G networks.

In this paper, we survey recent activities related to 5G security in Japan. Specifically, we introduce "5G Security Guideline Version 1" [13] published by the Ministry of Internal Affairs and Communications (MIC) of Japan on April 22nd, 2022. Next, we explain several activities toward local 5G deployment in Japan and then introduce "Local 5G Security Guideline 1st Edition" [12] published by the ICT Information Sharing and Analysis Center (ICT-ISAC) Japan on March 31st, 2022.

2   5G Security Guideline

The Ministry of Internal Affairs and Communications (MIC) of Japan released a document, "5G Security Guideline Version 1" [13], on April 22nd, 2022. The objective of this document is to provide a comprehensive guide to ensuring the security of 5G systems in practice.[1] Fig. 1 illustrates various network domains in a 5G system and their associated criticality levels where 5G core network, and NFV (Network Function Virtualization) management and supporting system are the most important components to be protected. Of course, criticality levels can be interpreted as a priority of relevant security measures.

2.1   Security Threat Analysis

First, we describe common security threats generally applicable across all domains of 5G systems and then describe specific security threats in individual domains of 5G systems. Here, threats are classified according to the STRIDE-LM threat model [13], and each "Threat ID" starts with the symbol "#."

Common Security Threats.

Spoofing[#TC_S_01] Network spoofing, [#TC_S_02] Software package spoofing, [#TC_S_03] Phishing

---

[1] Open RAN security considerations can be found in Appendix A of [13].

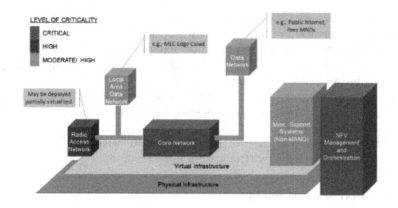

Fig. 1. Criticality levels of different network domains in 5G system [13]

Manipulation[#TC_T_01] Tampering data in transit, [#TC_T_02] Tampering physical platform, [#TC_T_03] Tampering software package, [#TC_T_04] Tampering stored dat, [#TC_T_05] Data poisoning

Repudiation[#TC_R_01] Tampering log data, [#TC_R_02] Account hijacking

Information leakage[#TC_I_01] Cryptanalysis attack, [#TC_I_02] Side-Channel attack, [#TC_I_03] System fingerprinting, [#TC_I_04] Malicious software, [#TC_I_05] Social engineering, [#TC_I_06] Intentional data breach

Denial of service[#TC_D_01] Volumetric attack, [#TC_D_02] Protocol DoS attack, [#TC_D_03] Attack on the application layer, [#TC_D_04] Physical sabotage, [#TC_D_05] Ransomware, [#TC_D_06] Violation of the law

Elevation of privilege[#TC_E_01] Vertical elevation of privilege, [#TC_E_02] Horizontal elevation of privilege

Lateral movement[#TC_L_01] Network lateral movement

Threats to NFV Infrastructure and MANO.

Spoofing[#TM_S_01] NFV workload spoofing (If software certificate validation fails during NFVI deployment, an attacker can take control of the associated MANO (MANagement and Orchestration) components to provision harmful NFV workloads)

Manipulation[#TM_T_01] Tampering VNF image (Software tampering can lead to the insertion of malicious code into the VNF (Virtualized Network Function) image or to vulnerabilities in the VNF image), [#TM_T_02] Tampering data in transit between MANO components (The lack of integrity protection between MANO components can lead to a security incident affecting a large part of the network)

Information leakage[#TM_I_01] Unreliable NFV workload (e.g., single root I/O virtualization, shared folders between host and guest operating systems, direct access to host sockets such as Docker daemon sockets), [#TM_I_02] VNF Sprawl (creation of unlimited new workloads)

Denial of service[#TM_D_01] Resource exhaustion due to NFV workloads (resource allocation failure), [#TM_D_02] Unavailable service provider (The provided infrastructure is no longer available)

Elevation of privilege[#TM_E_01] Guest-host escape (hypervisor infringement due to hardware emulation defects, hypervisor management tools, or graphics driver defects)

Lateral movement[#TM_L_01] Lateral movement within NFVI/MANO (by compromising the central virtualization infrastructure)

Threats to NFV Workloads.

Spoofing[#TW_S_01] Spoofed host platform, [#TW_S_02] Spoofed MANO communication

Manipulation[#TW_T_01] Active VNF introspection

Information leakage[#TW_I_01] Passive VNF introspection, [#TW_I_02] Communication between NFV workloads

Threats to Radio Access Network (RAN).

Spoofing[#TR_S_01] Rogue base station

Manipulation[#TR_T_01] Downgrade of user equipment or network functionality, [#TR_T_02] Traffic tampering in the user plane, [#TR_T_03] Traffic tampering in the control plane

Information leakage[#TR_I_01] Eavesdropping on subscription identifier, [#TR_I_03] Eavesdropping on user plane traffic, [#TR_I_02] Eavesdropping on the control plane traffic

Denial of service[#TR_D_01] Jamming and interference of wireless communications, [#TR_D_02] Attack on mid-haul and backhaul networks

Threats to Core Network.

Spoofing[#TN_S_01] Spoofing user plane traffic (e.g., impersonation between gNB and UPF (User Plane Function) instances (N3 interface), impersonation between different UPF instances (N9 interface), impersonation between UPF and other data networks (N6 interface)), [#TN_S_02] Spoofing control plane traffic (Potential targets of attack are an interface between internal NFs (Network Functions), interface exposed to peer mobile networks (e.g., N32 between SEPP (Security Edge Protection Proxy)), interface exposed to other data networks (e.g., N33 between NEF (Network Exposure Function) and AF (Application Function)), interface for legacy interworking (e.g., N26 between 5G AMF (Access and Mobility Management Function) and 4G MME (Mobility Management Entity))), [#TN_S_03] Spoofed registration request (High volume of unauthorized registration requests can lead to a high load on core network function and unexpected malfunction when processing malformed SUPI/SUCI values)

Manipulation[#TN_T_01] Tampering user plane traffic (Countermeasures should be implemented in N9 interface between different UPF instances, and in N6 interface between UPF and other data networks (e.g., the public Internet, LADN (Local Area Data Network))), [#TN_T_02] Tampering control plane traffic (Integrity protection of control plane should be implemented in the interface between internal NFs, N32 interface between SEPP, N33 interface between NEF and AF, N26 interface between 5G AMF and 4G MME, communication between NF and SCP (Service Communication Proxy), communication between SCP internal components, and communication between different SCP instances)

Information leakage[#TN_I_01] Eavesdropping on user plane traffic (e.g., in N9 interface and N6 interface due to lack of implementation of network security protocols such as IPsec), [#TN_I_02] Eavesdropping on control plane traffic (e.g., in the interface between internal API-driven NFs, N26 interface between 5G AMF and 4G/LTE MME, N32 interface between SEPP, N33 interface between NEF and AF, communication between NF and SCP, communication between SCP internal components, and communication between different SCP instances)

Denial of service[#TN_D_01] Signal spike (This is especially relevant to M2M communications when a large number of IoT devices with the same communication pattern initiate a large number of signal transmissions at the same time (e.g., primary authentication)

Elevation of privilege[#TN_E_01] Attack against OAuth 2.0 authentication framework (An attacker may attempt to elevate granted authority at the following times (e.g., during service discovery by NRF (Network Repository Function), during access token request, during access to a service)

Lateral movement[#TN_L_01] Lateral movement in service mesh instances (It is desirable to split SCP into multiple instances)

Threats to Network Slicing.

Spoofing[#TNS_S_01] Spoofing slice identifier, [#TNS_S_02] Spoofing slice management communication

Information leakage[#TNS_I_01] Leakage of slice-specific information

Denial of service[#TNS_D_01] DoS attack against network slice, [#TNS_D_02] Security policy for network slice-to-slice communication

Elevation of privilege[#TNS_E_01] Network slices with different security policies

Threats to MEC.

Spoofing[#TE_S_01] Spoofing MEC management communication

Manipulation[#TE_T_01] Tampering MEC control plane data

Information leakage[#TE_I_01] Processing and storage of sensitive assets in LADN, [#TE_I_02] Unexpected MEC workload

Denial of service[#TE_D_01] Abuse of AF-assisted routing, [#TE_D_02] Resource sharing between MEC workload and network function, [#TE_D_03] MEC UserApps exploit

Elevation of privilege[#TE_E_01] Violation of lawful communication interception function in LADN

Lateral movement[#TE_L_01] Moving workload in LADN

2.2 Security Measure Requirements

This section describes recommended security measures related to the development and integration of 5G technology, and the operation of 5G systems. Each security measure addresses the threats outlined in Sect. 2.1, where the first "[]" indicates degrees of relative priority and the second "[]" shows corresponding threats.

Organizational Measures[Critical] [Multiple] Security organization, [Critical] [#TC_D_06] Security policy framework, [Critical] [#TM_D_02, #TC_I_06] Security in contracts, [Critical] [Multiple] Organizational risk management, [Critical] [#TM_D_02] Business Continuity Plan (BCP), [Critical] [#TM_I_01, #TW_I_02, #TC_I_04, #TC_I_06] Vendor due diligence

Human Measures[Critical] [#TC_I_05, #TC_S_03] Security education and awareness, [High] [#TC_I_05, #TC_S_03] Positive security culture

Measures in Operation[Critical] [#TC_T_03, #TC_S_02, #TC_T_05] Secure software development process, [Critical] [Multiple] Product security maintenance, [Critical] [#TC_I_01, #TC_I_03, #TC_I_04, #TC_D_03, #TC_E_01, #TC_E_02] Security assurance, [Critical] [#TM_I_02] Asset management, [Critical] [#TM_I_02] Change management, [Critical] [#TC_I_04] Patch management, [Critical] [#TC_R_01, #TC_L_01] Security monitoring, [High] [#TC_I_04, #TC_D_05] Backup and recovery procedures, [Critical] [#TC_L_01, #TC_I_04, #TC_D_05] Security incident reporting and response, [Moderate/High] [#TC_I_04, #TC_D_05] Threat intelligence, [High] [#TC_I_06] Restriction of information flow

Physical Measures[Critical] [#TC_T_02] Secure facility design, [Critical] [#TC_T_02, #TC_D_04] Restriction on physical access, [Critical] [#TC_D_04] Monitoring physical access

Technical Measures. Here, we describe technical measures, both general and specific to a particular 5G system domain.

General measures[Critical] [#TC_I_03, #TC_D_02, #TC_D_03, #TC_E_01] Secure system engineering, [Critical] [#TC_D_01, #TC_L_01, #TM_L_01] Secure network engineering, [Critical] [#TC_I_01] Secure crypto algorithms [8], [Critical] [#TC_R_02, #TC_E_01, #TC_E_02, #TW_T_01, #TW_I_01] Identity and access management (It is strongly recommended that a logical identity be associated with a digital certificate or actual cryptographic key (a private/public key pair).), [Critical] [#TC_R_02] Key management [11] (It should be ensured that a secure cryptographic module is present in system components that handle sensitive keys. It should be ensured the integrity and confidentiality of keys by storing and using the keys only within a secure environment. Whenever key information is available outside of the cryptographic module, an alternative method (encryption, non-encryption, or physical mechanisms) should be used to ensure the same level of protection. Sensitive key-related information after its lifetime should be securely disposed.), [Critical] [#TC_T_04] Secure boot procedure (This requires a Root of Trust (RoT) in the system, such as Trusted Platform Module (TPM). The methods to guarantee system integrity include measured boot (recording low-level system measurements that can be verified by a 3rd party) and trusted/secure boot (cryptographically verifying each step of the boot procedure against expected values).), [High] [#TC_T_04] Monitoring system integrity (It continuously monitors system changes and compares detection results to known "good conditions."), [Critical] [#TC_S_01, #TW_S_02, #TN_S_01, #TC_T_01] Secure management communication (It should be ensured that management protocols utilize secure crypto algorithms in accordance with the organization's cryptography policy. It should enforce strict mutual authentication, ideally tied to the organization's PKI. It should prohibit the use of insecure legacy protocols.), [Critical] [#TC_R_01] Secure log file collection and storage

Measures for virtualization[Critical] [#TC_T_02, #TW_S_01] Hardware-based Root of Trust (Sensitive information and critical cryptographic functions should be stored or supported by Hardware-based Root of Trust (HBRT) such as security elements and hardware security modules.), [Critical] [#TM_I_01] Robustness of NFVI hosts (NVFI (Network Functions Virtualization Infrastructure) hosts are exposed to additional risks due to the workloads.), [Critical] [#TM_I_01, #TM_D_01, #TM_E_01, #TM_L_01, #TW_I_02] Robustness of virtualization layer (The hypervisor (a primary component responsible for resource allocation and isolation of virtual workloads) should be configured to strictly limit resource usage of each guest system.), [Critical] [#TM_S_01, #TM_T_02, #TC_T_03, #TM_T_01, #TW_S_02] MANO security (The MANO component forms the backbone of NFV deployment, transmitting and storing some of the most sensitive information.)

Measures for RAN[High] [#TC_T_01, #TR_T_02] Protection of user plane (5G operators need to ensure that the integrity of user plane traffic transmitted over radio access is protected and that tampering is prevented in data on the air interface and in data processed by RAN system components.), [High] [#TR_T_03] Protection of control plane (5G operators need to ensure that control plane traffic is not transferred in an unprotected manner between radio segments or 5G NR components.), [High] [#TC_T_01, #TR_T_02, #TR_T_03, #TR_I_02, #TR_I_03] Mid-haul and backhaul security [10] (5G technology suppliers and 5G operators should ensure that mutual authentication, confidentiality and integrity protection are provided at all interfaces between 5G NR components.), [High] [#TR_D_02] Redundancy of access network (for improving network resiliency), [Critical] [#TC_S_01, #TC_T_01] Secure non-3GPP access (It is desirable to establish trust and secure subsequent communications between the 5G core and mobile handsets connected via an untrusted non-3GPP access network.)

Measures for core network[Critical] [#TC_T_01, #TN_T_01, #TN_I_ 01] Protection of user plane (e.g., in N3, N9 and N6 interfaces), [Critical] [#TC_T_01, #TN_S_02, #TN_T_02, #TN_I_02] Signal security in PLMN (Control plane signals inside the 5G core should be protected.), [Critical] [#TC_S_01, #TN_E_01] Signal security between PLMNs [9] (Control plane traffic between PLMNs (Public Land Mobile Networks) and network itself should be protected from threats on the interconnection interface between mobile networks.), [Critical] [#TN_E_01, #TC_E_02, #TNS_I_01] Enforcement of API access control (The authentication methods allowed in the 3GPP security specification are transport layer authentication using TLS and implicit authentication using NDS (Network Domain Security)/IP. In particular, NF API should use token-based authentication based on the OAuth 2.0 authentication framework.), [High] [#TR_T_03] Protection of initial NAS messages (The integrity of initial NAS messages transmitted between UE and AMF should be guaranteed.), [Critical] [#TR_ I_01, #TN_S_03] Subscriber privacy [10,11] (It is desirable to ensure the protection of a subscriber's permanent identifier in 5G systems. Regarding SUPI concealment, 1) The 5G security policy under which the calculation of hidden SUPI is performed should be described in USIM or ME (Mobile Equipment); 2) A subscription profile to specify where SUCI concealment is to be performed and which concealment scheme is to be used should be prepared within USIM; 3) It should be ensured that 5G core network does not accept SUCI generated with a null scheme except when UE is accessing emergency services; and 4) 5G operators should provide all UEs with public keys of home network for SUPI confidentiality. Regarding temporary subscriber IDs, 1) 5G operators should enforce frequent reassignment of 5G-GUTI; and 2) 5G operators should ensure that 5G-TMSI (Temporary Mobile Subscriber Identity), a random component of 5G-GUTI, is generated in a process that guarantees sufficient entropy and unpredictability.), [Critical] [#TN_L_01] Service mesh security (5G operators need to secure SCP according to best practices for software-defined mesh networks. The SCP is a key element of 5G core network, connecting to all control plane network functions and supporting basic communication tasks such as service discovery, message routing and load balancing.), [Moderate/High] [#TC_S_01] Enhanced home control (It is desirable to prevent unauthorized requests sent to home network on behalf of subscribers.), [Critical] [#TC_D_01, #TC_D_02, #TN_D_01] DDoS countermeasure (Network functions that are at risk of DDoS attacks or unintended traffic spikes should be protected from excessive traffic loads.)

Measures for network slicing[Critical] [#TNS_D_01, #TC_I_02, #TNS _D_02] Separation of network slices [15] (Network slices, including supporting platforms and applications should be effectively separated from each other (soft network slicing and hard network slicing).), [Critical] [#TNS_S_ 02,

#TNS_D_01] Virtual network security (It is desirable to ensure that the migration from physical to virtual networks does not result in a reduction of security measures.), [Critical] [#TNS_S_01, #TNS_I_01, #TC_E_02] Network slice access control (Resources associated with a particular network slice instance should only be accessible by clients of that slice (strict authentication and slice-specific authorization in network communications).), [Critical] [#TNS_E_01] Security policy for network slicing (If UE subscribes to multiple slices with different security requirements, security policy should be implemented in a manner that does not compromise network slices with a higher level of security guarantees.)

Measures for MEC[Moderate/High] [#TE_I_01, #TE_I_02] MEC application audit (5G providers should define security requirements (e.g., secure communication, key management, identity and access management) to be met by 3rd party MEC applications to ensure the security (e.g., protection of subscriber data) of network and communication data being processed.), [Moderate/High] [#TE_S_01] MEC access control (Unauthorized access to MEC applications should be prevented. 5G secondary authentication can be used to authenticate mobile users using MEC applications. This mechanism allows external parties to perform additional EAP-based authentication procedures before granting access to OTT (Over The Top) services.), [Moderate/High] [#TE_S_01, #TE_T_01] Protection of MEC control data (It is desirable to prevent tampering control plane data communicated between internal MEC components and external interfaces.), [Moderate/High] [#TE_I_01] Protection of MEC user data (User plane traffic should be protected during communication and within MEC environment.), [High] [#TE_D_02, #TE_I_02, #TE_E_01, #TE_L_01] Separation of MEC environment (It is desirable to ensure strict separation between MEC environment and surrounding network components.), [Moderate/High] [#TE_D_01] Controlled management of MEC apps by 3rd party (The Interaction between MEC application and supporting 3rd party application functions and/or MEC UserApps should be monitored and controlled as appropriate.)

3   Toward Local 5G Deployment

In Japan, 5G mobile communication systems that can be used by various entities according to local and individual needs are referred to as "local 5G." Local 5G is a new mechanism that allows local businesses, local governments, and other entities to flexibly build and use networks with assigned radio frequencies on a spot basis within their own buildings and premises, in addition to nationwide 5G services provided by cell phone operators. It is expected to be used to solve local issues and meet a variety of other potential needs. In Japan, the launch of 5G services was followed by local 5G services starting in 2020.

Since the fiscal year of 2020, the Ministry of Internal Affairs and Communications (MIC) of Japan has been implementing a project called "Development and Demonstration Project for Realization of Problem-Solving Local 5G" [7], which involves technical studies on radio propagation as well as creating solutions utilizing local 5G under a wide variety of actual usage environments. This project has been conducted in many sectors, including agriculture, fishing, forestry, factory, power plant, airports and ports, railroads and roads, transportation, mobility, construction, smart city, infrastructure, culture and sports, tourism and e-sports, disaster prevention and mitigation, prevention against crime, work style, medical and healthcare.[2] These project results can be found in [6].

In December 2019, MIC of Japan published a document, "Guidelines for Local 5G Deployment," and its final revision [14] was released on March 31st, 2022. The purpose of this document is to clarify systems (e.g., application procedures for local 5G radio station licenses, an applicable relationship of the Radio law and the Telecommunications Business law) related to local 5G and so on from the viewpoint of promoting local 5G deployment. Regarding local 5G security, this document briefly mentioned as follows:

> "Local 5G must be secure, and adequate cyber security measures, including supply chain risk response, must be in place."

4 Local 5G Security Guideline

In local 5G, local wireless networks are deployed where they are installed, so it is important to implement appropriate methods for securing local 5G networks. The ICT Information Sharing and Analysis Center (ICT-ISAC) Japan released a document, "Local 5G Security Guideline 1st Edition" [12], on March 31st, 2022. Currently, there are no other security guidelines for private/local 5G, except [12]. In Table 1, we describe major risks and examples of countermeasures for local 5G, where threats and vulnerabilities are classified basically based on the STRIDE threat model.

Spoofed Unauthorized Logins to Vulnerable IoT Devices

Risk Malware is planted in vulnerable IoT devices (connected to local 5G network) to exploit access IDs and passwords to shared resources, and confidential information on shared resources is leaked.

Threat Unauthorized login by spoofing

Countermeasure Local 5G service providers should stipulate and operate password setting rules for IoT devices. Also, it is desirable to periodically inspect IoT devices for vulnerabilities and only use devices that have passed the inspection with vulnerability scanner and penetration testing tools. In addition, it is recommended that security tools capable of detecting and removing malware be operated.

---

[2] In particular, the medical and smart factory sectors need a higher level of security than other sectors.

Table 1. Major risks, and examples of threats and countermeasures against risks

Major risks	Examples of threats and countermeasures against risks
Device spoofing	Spoofed unauthorized logins to vulnerable IoT devices
	Spoofed unauthorized login due to unauthorized use of SIM card
Spoofing of inter-station relay equipment	Data tampering by battery drain attack
DoS attack on equipment	Malicious message attack on 5G core
	Mass signaling message attacks from IoT devices
Communication quality degradation	Radio interference due to obstruction
Misuse of devices by theft or eavesdropping	Theft due to inadequate device access control management
	Unencrypted data eavesdropping
	Inadequate device installation management
Physical vulnerability	Deletion of trail logs by intruder
	Internal infection by stepping on IoT devices
	Bringing in IoT equipment or changing facility configuration by contractor
	Malfunction or security hole due to mishandling or misconfiguration of remote management

Spoofed Unauthorized Login Due to Unauthorized Use of SIM Card

Risk A malicious attacker steals the SIM card of an IoT device, and then uses the SIM card to log in to the system with an unauthorized device (SIM swapping).

Threat Unauthorized login by spoofing

Countermeasure Since local 5G systems are self-managed, it is desirable to have measures for users to centrally manage and monitor all devices and their security status. The countermeasure against SIM swapping attack is required to ensure the authenticity of devices (e.g., by combining a device identification number IMEI (International Mobile Equipment Identifier) and a SIM identification number IMSI (International mobile subscriber identity)).

Data Tampering by Battery Drain Attack

Risk A malicious attacker disables the power-saving mode function of an IoT device by using a relay equipment installed between the IoT device and the base station, draining the battery of the IoT device with frequent reconnections (battery drain attack).

Threat Data tampering

Countermeasure Local 5G service providers need to properly manage whether unmanaged relay equipments are physically installed in the network between IoT devices and base stations.

Malicious Message Attack on 5G Core

Risk When 5G core receives messages with abnormal format or abnormal parameters from outside networks and insufficient processing for validation or discarding is taken, 5G system performance is severely degraded or halted due to software failure.

Threat DoS due to specific vulnerability

Countermeasure Local 5G service providers need to ensure that packet verification and error handling are reasonable so that 5G core only processes packets that are operationally expected. As a specific measure, fuzzing tests to discover product-specific vulnerabilities should be conducted in addition to system security tests to discover known vulnerabilities during 5G core development.

Mass Signaling Message Attacks from IoT Devices

Risk Mass IoT devices maliciously controlled by malware send large amounts of signaling that exceed system's capacity and bring the system to a halt.

Threat DoS due to specific vulnerability

Countermeasure Local 5G service providers need to ensure that measures against unauthorized access to IoT devices are implemented.

Radio Interference Due to Obstruction

Risk Communications are delayed due to communication obstructions/shields placed in the coverage area by non-administrator. One of the local 5G frequencies, 28.2 GHz to 28.3 GHz band, is vulnerable to obstructions.

Threat Communication quality degradation due to external factor

Countermeasure Before building a local 5G network, local 5G service providers need to implement an area design that takes into account obstacles affecting radio propagation. Furthermore, it is desirable for local 5G service providers to agree in advance with users on guidelines for equipment expansion, layout changes and so on.

Theft Due to Inadequate Device Access Control Management

Risk Due to inadequate control of access privileges, firmware, configuration information and logs of local 5G components can be stolen from the equipment by a malicious attacker.

Threat Theft

Countermeasure Local 5G service providers should determine access privilege settings based on the service specification. If access privileges are changed during maintenance and operation, the change history should be securely recorded and shared within the maintenance and operation team.

Unencrypted Data Eavesdropping

Risk Data transmitted through C-Plane/U-Plane are intercepted due to inappropriate configuration that allows use of weak cryptographic algorithms or omission of cryptographic operations.

Threat Theft

Countermeasure Local 5G service providers should establish a policy regarding cryptographic algorithms and key lengths to be used in local 5G system, and guarantee that secure cryptographic algorithms in accordance with the policy are used in each 5G component. During security negotiation with user equipment, it should be verified that, even if a user equipment presents an invalid configuration parameter, it will not be accepted.

Inadequate Device Installation Management

Risk Local 5G components in a location where anyone can access them are stolen by a malicious attacker. Also, there is a risk of unauthorized modifications or malware being embedded in the device, once it has been stolen. Then, the device can be used as a foothold for fraudulent activities after it is reconnected to the network.

Threat Theft

Countermeasure When devices are installed outdoors, it is necessary to take physical measures such as restricting access to the device installation location and firmly securing the device so that a 3rd party cannot inadvertently contact or remove it. These measures should also be considered indoors to prevent internal fraud.

Deletion of Trail Logs by Intruder

Risk Logs are deleted and there is a risk to be unaware of unauthorized intrusion.

Threat Other (deletion of logs)

Countermeasure Recording logs in multiple locations or obtaining backups should be considered. If a trace is deleted due to an unauthorized intrusion, the logs can be traced by cross-referencing the time period of the deleted logs and related logs in the vicinity.

Internal Infection by Stepping on IoT Devices

Risk IoT devices infected with Mirai and other malware are connected to local 5G network, and internal devices are infected as well. In addition, infected devices are used as stepping stones for DDoS attacks by remote control from a C&C (Command and Control) server.

Threat Other (malware infection, stepping stone)

Countermeasure Regarding the risk of internal infection, it should prevent unauthorized devices from being connected by means of device authentication. It is desirable to consider installing systems (IPS/IDS) capable of detecting unauthorized communications within local 5G network. Each device should stop unnecessary applications, close ports and apply latest security patches to prevent infection. Also, it should prevent access to the C&C server by placing communication devices with reputation function.

Bringing in IoT Equipment or Changing Facility Configuration by Contractor

Risk Unexpected communication behaviors or failures happen due to IoT equipment brought in or facility configuration change by contractors (e.g., manufacturers, installers, operators, inspectors, maintenance providers).

Threat Other

Countermeasure Rules for bringing equipment into areas where local 5G services are provided and for using wireless communications should be agreed upon in advance among local 5G service providers, operators, and users, and it is necessary to check whether these rules are being followed.

Malfunction or Security Hole Due to Mishandling or Misconfiguration of Remote Management

Risk Malfunction or security hole (e.g., unauthorized external access, malware infection) can occur due to security vulnerability, mishandling or misconfiguration of equipment that remotely manages local 5G base station and GW. That is, safety and stable operation of local 5G base station and GW may be threatened.

Threat Other

Countermeasure When base station, gateway and terminal equipment connected by local 5G need to be monitored and maintained remotely, it is necessary to conduct proper risk assessment and introduce appropriate security control measure for communication equipments, networks and business operation processes. Specifically, these measures could include the use of multi-factor authentication, connection over closed networks instead of the Internet, and introduction of tools that can detect security incidents at an early stage.

5 Conclusion

In this paper, we surveyed recent activities related to 5G security in Japan. Specifically, we introduced "5G Security Guideline Version 1" [13], where security threats in all domains of 5G systems, and recommended security measures related to the development and integration of 5G technology and the operation of 5G systems are described. Next, we explained several activities, including the

Japanese government's project and guidelines toward local 5G deployment, and then introduced "Local 5G Security Guideline 1st Edition" [12], where major risks and examples of countermeasures for local 5G are described. We hope that this paper could be helpful to stakeholders who are concerned with 5G security.

Acknowledgements. We sincerely appreciate the anonymous reviewers' constructive and valuable comments on this paper.

References

1. 5G. https://www.etsi.org/technologies/mobile/5g
2. 5G cybersecurity. https://www.nccoe.nist.gov/5g-cybersecurity
3. 5G cybersecurity standards. https://www.enisa.europa.eu/publications/5g-cybersecurity-standards
4. 5G security and resilience. https://www.cisa.gov/5ghttps://www.cisa.gov/5g
5. 5G supplement - to the guideline on security measures under the EECC. https://www.enisa.europa.eu/publications/5g-supplement-security-measures-under-eecc
6. GO! 5G. https://go5g.go.jp/
7. Ministry of internal affairs and communications. https://www.soumu.go.jp/menu_news/s-news/01ryutsu06_02000325.html
8. 3GPP TS 33.210: network domain security (NDS); IP network layer security (Release 17), September 2022. https://portal.3gpp.org/desktopmodules/Specifications/SpecificationDetails.aspx?specificationId=2279
9. 3GPP TS 33.310: network domain security (NDS); Authentication framework (AF) (Release 17), September 2022. https://portal.3gpp.org/desktopmodules/Specifications/SpecificationDetails.aspx?specificationId=2293
10. 3GPP TS 33.501: security architecture and procedures for 5G system (Release 17), September 2022. https://portal.3gpp.org/desktopmodules/Specifications/SpecificationDetails.aspx?specificationId=3169
11. ENISA: security in 5G specifications - controls in 3GPP, February 2021. https://www.enisa.europa.eu/publications/security-in-5g-specifications
12. ICT information sharing and analysis center (ICT-ISAC) Japan: Local 5G security guideline 1st edition (Japanese), 31 Mar 2022. https://www.ict-isac.jp/news/2_Local_5G_Security_Guideline.pdf
13. Ministry of internal affairs and communications: 5G security guideline version 1 (Japanese), 22nd April 2022. https://www.soumu.go.jp/main_content/000812253.pdf
14. Ministry of internal affairs and communications: guidelines for local 5G deployment (Final Revision) (Japanese), March 2022. https://www.soumu.go.jp/main_content/000804382.pdf
15. NGMN alliance: 5G security recommendations package #2: Network Slicing, April 2016. https://ngmn.org/wp-content/uploads/Publications/2016/160429_NGMN_5G_Security_Network_Slicing_v1_0.pdf
16. Recommendation ITU-R M. 2083-0: IMT vision - framework and overall objectives of the future development of IMT for 2020 and beyond, September 2015. https://www.itu.int/dms_pubrec/itu-r/rec/m/R-REC-M.2083-0-201509-I!!PDF-E.pdf
17. Stallings, W.: 5G Wireless: A Comprehensive Introduction. Pearson, London (2021)

Spatial Multiplexing Techniques and Multifrequency Cells for Massive Machine-type Communications in Future 6G Networks

Borja Bordel[1,3]([✉]) [iD], Ramón Alcarria[1,3] [iD], Joaquin Chung[1] [iD], and Ivan Armuelles Voinov[2] [iD]

[1] Argonne National Laboratory, Lemont, IL, USA
{ralcarriagarrido,chungmiranda}@anl.gov
[2] Universidad de Panamá, Panama City, Panama
ivan.armuelles@up.ac.pa
[3] On leave from: Universidad Politécnica de Madrid, Madrid, Spain
bbordelsanchez@anl.gov

Abstract. Future 6G networks are envisioned to provide communication services to very dense infrastructures, where up to ten million devices per square kilometer could be deployed. With such a large number of devices, human intervention is not feasible and the entire communication process and management must be automated. Besides, while some applications will require enhanced broadband communications, other scenarios will be supported by channels with a limited bitrate. In this context, 6G verticals are designed to pack the required network resources for specific applications and isolate one scenario from the others, with each one providing the needed Quality-of-Service. Nevertheless, even in verticals fully prepared for massive communications, direct management of such an incredible number of devices is challenging (if not impossible) for base stations. There are, nevertheless, two scenarios where the management burden could be mitigated: when devices are slept for long periods and when devices transmit an extremely reduced bitrate. In this paper, we propose a solution for massive machine type communications for devices with an extremely reduced throughput. The proposed solution defines two levels of cells, the first level operating at native 6G frequencies, while the second one operating at high frequency (shortwave). Symbols and bit stream in the first-level cells are spatially multiplexed to cover second-level cells. In that way, hardware devices do not employ a full OFDM (Orthogonal frequency-division multiplexing) symbol, but only use one orthogonal subcarrier each. Coding and modulation at the interface between the two levels of cells are configured to make possible the access of all hardware devices to communication services. In order to validate the proposed technology, we describe our experimental evaluation based on a simulation scenario. The results show how the management workload is reduced more than ten times in 6G base stations thanks to our proposed solution.

I. You et al. (Eds.): MobiSec 2022, CCIS 1644, pp. 48–62, 2023.
https://doi.org/10.1007/978-981-99-4430-9_4

Keywords: 6G networks · massive machine-type communications · spatial multiplexing · cellular networks · multifrequency cells

1   Introduction

Future 6G networks [22] are envisioned to improve the Quality-of-Service (QoS) already achieved by 5G mobile technologies [12]. Specifically, 6G communication services will be characterized by four technical requirements and two business requirements [15]. Namely:

- **Extremely high data rate** [6]: typically known as enhanced Mobile Broadband communications (eMBBC) in the context of 5G networks. 6G networks must be designed to support peak data rates above 100 Gbps, while the core network capacity should increase 100 times the existing capacity in 5G networks.
- **Extreme Low Latency** [34]: Named as Low Latency Communications (LLC) in 5G scenarios, in 6G networks end-to-end delays cannot exceed one millisecond under any circumstances.
- **Extreme High Reliability** [35]: typically referred to as Ultra-Reliable Communications (URC) in the context of 5G mobile technologies. In 6G scenarios this requirement is enhanced and network reliability should reach 99.99999%
- **Extreme Massive Connectivity** [11]: this last technical requirement for future 6G networks is very related to the most popular massive machine-type communications (mMTC) that are a relevant research challenge in 5G networks. This QoS requirement refers to communication services supporting very dense deployments including up to ten million devices per square kilometer. Besides, massive connectivity must enable other associated enriched services such as high precision positioning services (with a precision higher than one centimeter).
- **Extreme low energy and cost** [28]: this new business requirement is a novelty of 6G solutions compared to previous 5G scenarios. Millimetric waves (mmWave) or even frequencies in higher bands are currently managed through very expensive and energy-consuming transmission chains. Future 6G networks must address this challenge, future 6G devices must not need to be charged for extended periods of time and they must be "affordable".
- **Extreme coverage** [2]: finally, the 6G business model must include gigabit connectivity and coverage anywhere on Earth. Additionally, new "locations" are added to traditional 4G and 5G scenarios. Specifically, 6G services must be provided to flying locations up to 10,000 m above the sea level; and also must be provided to cruising locations in the sea up to 200 nautical miles from the closer port.

While in traditional 5G applications, eMBBC, URLLC, and mMTC are considered independent scenarios, and all three QoS parameters are not implemented together (at least not with very demanding KPI -Key Performance

Indicators-); in 6G scenarios, new combinations of extreme requirements will arise for specific use cases [21]. These new use cases may be very challenging, as some KPI and QoS requirements are opposed. To address this challenge, the future 6G network will be organized in verticals [8]. A network vertical is a pack of network resources (e.g., physical, logical, and computational resources) that are exclusively dedicated to support a certain application or scenario. Verticals are independent of each other, thus congestion or malfunctions of one vertical should not affect the remaining sectors of the network [13]. Moreover, by using verticals, it is possible to ensure that new critical applications can meet the expected extreme QoS or business requirements.

With the 6G verticals approach, for example, massive machine-type communications (mMTC) will be feasible, even if they are combined with strict latency requirements. However, although 6G verticals may ensure the availability of enough network resources to provide one millisecond delay communication links to millions of devices, managing such a large number of devices is still very challenging (if not impossible) for base stations [25]. Actually, control processes (e.g., error control, timers, or keep-alive protocols) may consume a significant amount of resources in those situations. On the other hand, human intervention is not efficient or even feasible when millions of devices are communicating, therefore all operations must be fully automated. In this context, completely new and innovative network or base station designs are needed. Nevertheless, this fact is opposite to the integration of 5G New Radio (NR) technologies into future 6G networks [19]. However, there are two special scenarios where it is possible to address the challenge of 6G mMTC, even employing 5G NR technologies. In the first one, although millions of devices are deployed, not all of them communicate at the same time, as most of the time the hardware devices sleep [33]. This scenario is quite common in non-realtime Internet of Things applications. For instance, in systems for environmental monitoring, sensor nodes only transmit new information for a couple of seconds every few minutes (up to one hour). The second scenario in which mMTC may be feasible is where hardware devices have an extremely low throughput [9]. Devices may also have hard latency requirements, but very low bitrates open the door to complex data mixing or multiplexing solutions, enabling the operation of the entire dense deployment. In any case, although mMTC are envisioned to be feasible in those scenarios and circumstances, new technologies to enable the actual operation of 6G networks in those contexts are still needed. This paper fills this gap and aims to describe a new 6G radio technology capable of supporting mMTC when hardware devices have a very limited output bitrate.

In this paper, a new 6G solution for mMTC is proposed. The described technology includes multi-frequency cells organized in two levels. The first level is supported by native 6G radio technologies in the millimetric wave band. The second level multiplexes the original 6G radio links in several different bit streams transmitted over high-frequency (HF) radio channels. Each HF channel codifies information using Huffman optimal coding and analog amplitude modulation. All multiplexed bit streams are later combined in a standard OFDM (Orthogonal frequency-division multiplexing) modulation, so every hardware device does not consume the entire bandwidth of the OFDM channel, but only one subcarrier. The throughput is then reduced, but enough for one-bit sensors (such as movement detectors, photon detectors, passive infrared sensors, etc.).

The remainder of the paper is organized as follows. Section 2 describes the state of the art on 6G and 5G solutions for massive machine-type communications. Section 3 describes the proposed multifrequency technology, including modulation and coding schemes at both levels of cells. Section 4 presents the experimental methodology and simulation scenario that validate the performance of our proposed solution, as well as the results and discussion. Finally, Sects. 5 and 6 present some security challenges and conclude the paper.

2   State of the Art

Among all the challenges introduced by 5G and 6G networks, massive connectivity is probably the least studied. Most of the work on 5G and 6G is focused on Ultra-Reliable Low Latency Communications (URLLC) [3] or enhanced Mobile Broadband Communications (eMBBC) [6]. In fact, most future 6G communication services such as holographic communications [16], present difficult QoS requirements in terms of bitrate and latency. However, massive connectivity requirements are much less common and typically restricted to massive Internet of Things [23], resource-constrained environments [7], or massive Smart Cities [36].

Massive connectivity may be achieved through two basic approaches: radio signals or protocols. The most common approach for radio signals to support massive extreme connectivity is Multiple-Input and Multiple-Output (MIMO) antennas [20]. Different approaches have been reported for high energy efficiency [32], MIMO for millimetric waves [5], MIMO for precise device location [39], analog-to-digital converters for MIMO systems [42] or array antennas for MIMO schemes [40], and beamforming techniques for managing MIMO antennas [41]. Furthermore, several studies on challenges [17], open questions [31], and research opportunities [29] on MIMO technologies have been published. However, this approach cannot be controlled by network operators or application owners as MIMO technologies must be specifically designed for the same frequency bands, base station equipment, and user devices.

Another approach based on radio signals for massive connectivity is efficient resource allocation. Some authors have proposed multiple-access hybrid solutions, where time slots and radio channels are shared according to the dynamic needs of devices [1]. Additionally, schemes for media access management adapted to massive connectivity scenarios have also been reported [4]. Instruments such as artificial intelligence algorithms are integrated to improve precision and reaction time in resource allocation [30]. However, no solution is fully successful, and several authors consider that the allocation of radio resources for massive communications remains an open question in future 6G networks [25].

On the other hand, efficient protocols for managing massive 6G communications have been described [18]. This approach is not as common as the one previously described, but still different proposals may be found. Schemes for random access [37], truly grant-free protocols and technologies [27] have been reported to enable light-weight management of massive communications.

Finally, several works attempt to address massive machine-type communications not from a general perspective but from the point of view of an specific applications. Industry 4.0 scenarios supported by Artificial Intelligence [10], Artificial Intelligence interfaces [24], massive Internet of Things with Big Data collection [26] or green communications [38] are the most studied scenarios.

Contrary to the approaches described in this section, in this paper we focus on a general technology and approach, provided that hardware devices present an extremely reduced throughput.

3 Multifrequency Cells and Spatial Multiplexing for 6G mMTC

A device with an extremely reduced throughput is a sensor with a one-bit state that evolves slowly or changes only sporadically. Therefore, the $i-th$ sensor in our scenario is represented by a one-bit digital signal $b_i(t)$, where the corresponding Fourier transform in the frequency space $B_i(\omega)$ has a bandwidth of W_i Hertz (1). As the sensor output changes only sporadically, we can only focus on the period $[0, T_i]$, so the sensor output changes only one time (2). Here T_1 and T_2 are the starting and ending time instants of the change in the sensor output. In this context, it is possible to find the analytical expression for the Fourier transform $B_i(\omega)$ and the bandwidth W_i (3). Here A is a constant depending on the value of W_i.

$$B_i(\omega) = \begin{cases} 0 & -W_i/2 \geq \omega \geq W_i/2 \\ F\{b_i(t)\} & otherwise \end{cases} \tag{1}$$

$$b_i(t) = \begin{cases} 1 \ T_1 \leq t \leq T_2 \\ 0 \ otherwise \end{cases} \quad t, T_1, T_2 \in [0, T_i] \tag{2}$$

$$B_i(\omega) = A\frac{sin\left(\frac{\pi\omega}{W_i}\right)}{\pi\omega} W_i = \frac{1}{T_2 - T_1} \tag{3}$$

All devices in the scenario are aggregated into clusters. Each of these clusters is provided with a 6G gateway. In general, every gateway is managing a cluster with N devices. Also, the 6G gateways are connected to the 6G base stations. Eventually, only one base station may be enough to manage several radio channels and cells. Figure 1 shows the described scenario.

The 6G base stations and the 6G gateways define a first level of cells. In these cells, usual 6G mobile communications are employed. Specifically, Frequency Range 2 (FR2) is used. In order to maximize the bitrate to be multiplexed in the second-level cells, the 60 GHz band (V-band) is employed. In addition, as in 5G standards, in native 6G radio channel OFDM modulation may be used. Numerology (OFDM subcarrier spacing) is variable and will be adjusted according to the number of devices in every cluster (see Sect. 3.2).

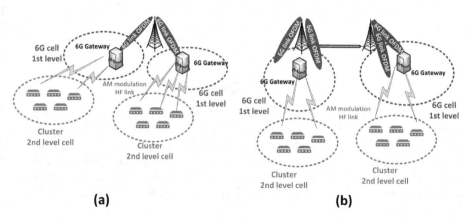

Fig. 1. Proposed scenario with the multifrequency cell scheme: (a) Only one multi-channel base station (b) Several single-channel base stations.

However, device clusters, together with 6G gateways, define a second level of cells. In these cells, traditional analog modulation and frequency bands are employed (see Sect. 3.1). In particular, amplitude modulation in High Frequency (HF) bands is employed. Radio channels in the HF range will be assigned to devices in the cluster. Transmission power will be very reduced in order to avoid inter-cluster interference. Gateways will collect several bits from each device to apply a Huffman coding procedure and obtain complex symbols to be injected into the OFDM modulation.

The following subsections describe in detail each level of cells.

3.1   Device Clusters and Analog One-bit Modulation

Devices in every cluster are provided with a radio channel in the High Frequency (HF) range. Each of these channels have a central frequency f_c^i and a small bandwidth σ_i (4). Traditionally, the HF band includes all frequencies between 3 and 30 MHz, so there is a limit to the number of devices N_{max} that can be included in every cluster (5). All devices in the cluster must be provided with a different HF radio channel, as the media access in these second-level cells is based on FDMA (frequency division multiple access) techniques. However, HF channels are reused in all clusters, so to avoid inter-cluster interference, transmitted power must be limited. Considering d as the geographical distance between two devices belonging to different clusters, the maximum power to be transmitted P_{max} can be calculated using the Friis formula, being I_{max} the maximum interference tolerated by the devices and c the light speed in vacuum (6).

$$\sigma_i = 2 \cdot W_i \tag{4}$$

$$\sum_{i=1}^{N_{max}} \sigma_i \leq 27 \cdot 10^6 \tag{5}$$

$$P_{max} = \frac{c^2}{4\pi d^2 f_c^i} I_{max} \tag{6}$$

The data signals $b_i(t)$ are then transmitted to the 6G gateways using an analog amplitude modulation scheme (see Fig. 2). The radio signal to be transmitted $y_i(t)$ can be easily calculated both in the time domain (7) and in the frequency domain (8). Furthermore, the amplitude C for the carrier frequency and the dynamic range for the data signal $b_i(t)$ should be selected to ensure that the transmitted power is below the maximum (9), but also to guarantee there is no overmodulation (10).

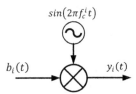

Fig. 2. Amplitude modulation scheme for the second level cells.

$$y_i(t) = \left[1 + \frac{b_i(t)}{C}\right] \cdot \sin\left(2\pi f_c^i t\right) \tag{7}$$

$$B_i(\omega) = \frac{1}{2} C \cdot A \frac{\sin\left(\frac{\pi\left[\omega - 2\pi f_c^i\right]}{W_i}\right)}{\pi\left[\omega - 2\pi f_c^i\right]} \tag{8}$$

$$max\{\|B_i(\omega)\|^2\} = \frac{C^2 A^2}{4} = P_{max} \tag{9}$$

$$1 + \frac{b_i(t)}{C} > 0 \tag{10}$$

Modulated signals are continuously transmitted to the 6G gateway, where they can be easily demodulated using a simple rectification circuit and a lowpass filter (see Fig. 3). In this proposal, both elements are implemented using electronic devices (basically a diode, a capacitor, and a resistor).

Once the 6G gateway obtains the demodulated signal, it samples the data flow (11) with period τ_s. In order to guarantee signals are correctly acquired, the sampling period must meet the Nyquist criterion (12). Furthermore, the gateway generates binary words $\alpha_i[n]$ with M_i bits by considering together the consecutive M_i bits received from each device (13). This M_i-bit symbols α_i^r are then codified using a Huffman coding (14) with R different symbols. Where λ_i^r

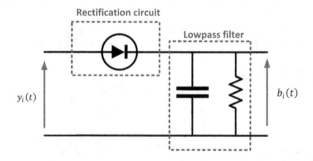

Fig. 3. Amplitude demodulation scheme.

is the probability of occurrence (or weight) of symbol γ_i^r; Γ_{opt} is the Huffman coding and Γ_k is any other possible coding.

$$\beta_i[n] = b_i(n \cdot \tau_s) \tag{11}$$

$$\frac{1}{\tau_s} \geq 2W_i \tag{12}$$

$$\alpha_i[n] = \beta_i[n]\,\beta_i[n-1]\,\beta_i[n-2]\ldots\beta_i[n-M_i] \tag{13}$$

$$\mathcal{L}(\Gamma_{opt}) = \sum_{r=1}^{R} \lambda_i^r \cdot length\,(\gamma_i^r) \leq \mathcal{L}(\Gamma_k) \quad \forall\, \Gamma_k \tag{14}$$

The Huffman symbols $\gamma_i[n]$ are finally injected into the first-level cells through the 6G gateway.

3.2   Native 6G Cells

When streams of Huffman symbols $\gamma_i[n]$ are received in the first-level cell, they are spatially multiplexed to create an OFDM symbol. Figure 4 shows the proposed scheme for this spatial multiplexing.

To multiplex all streams from the devices, the next Huffman symbol $\gamma_i[n]$ is taken from every stream belonging to each device in the massive deployment. Then, N Huffman symbols are collected and used to create the global OFDM symbol. To do that, first, the Huffman symbols are modulated using a QAM (Quadrature Amplitude Modulation) baseband modulation (15). After that, all QAM symbols $z_i[n]$ are injected in parallel into a module to obtain the Inverse Fourier Transform. In this way, the final OFDM symbol $s(t)$ is calculated (16). It is enough to use a Digital-to-Analog converter (DAC) and a frequency mixer to transmit the OFDM symbol to the 6G base station using the $f_0 = 60\,\text{GHz}$ band.

$$x_i(t) = I_i[n] \cdot \sin(2\pi f_0 t) + Q_i[n] \cdot \cos(2\pi f_0 t) =$$
$$= (I_i[n] + jQ_i[n]) \cdot e^{-j2\pi f_0 t} = z_i[n] \cdot e^{-j2\pi f_0 t} \tag{15}$$
$$z_i[n] = I_i[n] + jQ_i[n]$$

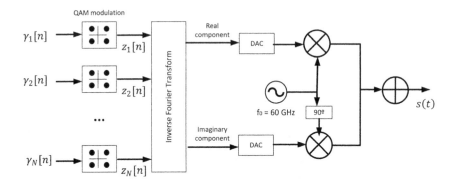

Fig. 4. OFDM modulation and multiplexing in 6G cells

$$s\left(t\right) = \sum_{i=1}^{N} z_i[n] \cdot e^{j2\pi f_i t}$$

$$f_i = f_0 + (i \cdot \varDelta f) \tag{16}$$

The subcarrier spacing $\varDelta f$ in OFDM modulation must be selected according to the 5G NR standard (17). Up to 3300 subcarriers can be considered in one 6G radio channel. With the proposed approach, each device transmits information over one subcarrier in the OFDM spectrum, so the effective bitrate V is limited according to the second Shannon law (18), where SNR is the Signal-to-Noise Ratio in the radio channel. However, from a base station perspective, it is capable of communicating with up to 3300 devices through a single radio link. This reduces management cost and enables the provision of extremely massive connectivity.

$$\varDelta f = 2^{\mu} \cdot 15KHz$$

$$\mu \in [1, 4] \tag{17}$$

$$V = \varDelta f \cdot log_2(1 + SNR) \tag{18}$$

4   Experimental Validation: Simulation Results

To evaluate the performance of the proposed solution and validate it enables massive machine-type communications, an experimental phase was planned and conducted. The experimental evaluation was based on simulation scenarios and tools. Specifically, MATLAB 2022a software was used to describe and execute the scenario.

The simulation scenario consisted of a variable number of devices in a very dense deployment (up to 10^{10}). Twenty 6G gateways were also described. In addition, only one multichannel 6G base station operating in the 60 GHz frequency band was deployed. The devices represented photon detectors in a large scientific facility. These photon detectors are one-bit sensors: the output is zero, but it turns one during a period when a photon is detected. HF channels in the second-level cells had a bandwidth of 3 KHz. In clusters, radio channels are assigned to devices in order: from the lowest frequencies to the highest. Geographically, the simulation scenario was 1400 square meters (a similar size of existing scientific facilities [14]). The clusters are separated by 2.5 m, one from each other. Symbols for the Huffman coding where 128-bit symbols ($M_i = 128 \; \forall \; i$). Only thermal noise was considered in the scenario and power transmission was modeled as in free space. Experiments were repeated for different values of numerology (sub-carrier spacing in OFDM modulation).

To analyze whether the proposed approach generates any improvement compared to the state of the art, a simulation based on direct 6G links between the base station and the devices was also conducted.

All experiments simulated an operating time of 24 h. All simulations were repeated 12 times and the results were obtained as the average of all partial simulations. All simulations were performed using a Linux-based system (Ubuntu 22.04 LTS) with the following hardware characteristics: Dell R540 Rack 2U, 96 GB RAM, two processors Intel Xeon Silver 4114 2.2 G, HD 2TB SATA 7,2K rpm.

With this scenario and infrastructure, two different variables were monitored. On the one hand, end-to-end communication delay between devices and the base station was monitored. On the other hand, the management cost (delay) required by the 6G base station to operate the entire massive deployment was also studied. As specific values for delays are not relevant (they depend on the selected frequencies, hardware simulation, software configuration, etc.), we are normalizing results to study the evolution and scalability.

Figure 5 shows the results for communication delay and management delay at 6G base stations.

As can be seen, both delays increase as the number of devices in the scenario increases. On the one hand, as 6G radio channels are getting sparse, they must be shared using TDMA (Time-Division Multiple Access) techniques, which increases the communication delay. This is a normal situation in all communication systems. However, as shown in Fig. 5, the increase in speed is very different. Actually, for scenarios with a number of devices below one hundred million, the proposed solution with higher numerology improves the communication delay by up to ten times. When all 6G radio channels are already shared, the delay does not increase any more. But while this situation is achieved in traditional approaches when two hundred devices are deployed in the scenario, thanks to our technology, we can increase this number to one billion devices. On the other hand, the management delay has a similar behavior. As can be seen, evolution is also exponential (Fig. 5 are logarithms on the horizontal axis), but with very different increasing speeds. In this case, the improvement is more relevant since the increase in speed for the proposed approach is so slow that, even for massive scenarios including one billion devices, the management delay in 6G base stations with the proposed solution is only 40% of the corresponding delay in

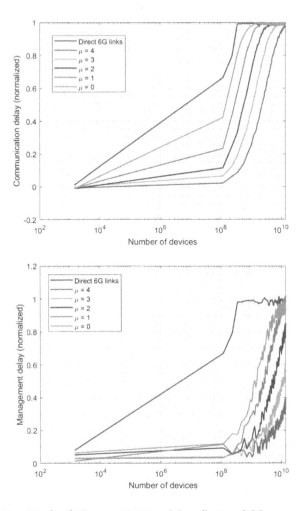

Fig. 5. Results: (top) Communication delay, (bottom) Management delay

traditional schemes. This guarantees scalability for future massive scenarios with densities greater than ten million devices per square kilometer.

Finally, in Fig. 5 (bottom), it can also be seen how results get more noise as the number of devices increase. Actually, as more devices are considered, the measurements' dispersion tend to be higher (because of second round effects such as congestion, interference, etc.) so average values can fluctuate more than in scenarios where a small of devices is considered. But it is also important to highlight that this noise effect gets amplified by the logarithmic graphic. Points that are linearly spaced are much more compressed in upper segments of the horizontal axis than in lower segments, and lines are not equally smooth.

5   Security Challenges and Considerations

From a technological point of view, there is no limit or restrictions to the geographical distribution of devices within the application scenario. Although the proposed scheme is designed to work and improve the efficiency in massive machine-type communications, it could be successfully employed in scenarios with a standard device density. However, security aspects may advise against its implementation is wide area applications.

As explained in Sect. 3, no encryption (or, in general, security) mechanism is considered in the proposed solution. Ciphers introduce delays and consume computational power, and even if lightweight technologies are employed, the consumption may be relevant in massive deployments. Additionally, the proposed model for sensing devices consists of extremely sparse computational and communication resources, so the most efficient way to interact with those elements is through hardware-based analog technologies. But analog encryption solutions are extremely weak against modern cyberattacks, so they are not actually useful but when integrated into complex security mechanisms which are very difficult to provide to every single device in a massive scenario.

Thus, the proposed technology is only secure under some restrictions, which can be found in the described application scenario. When the device density is very high, but the area under study is small, data signals' power can be reduced. In that scenario, the 6G gateway can still communicate with sensing devices, but information signal are undetectable from the outsides of the area under study. That area, moreover, in real scenarios where massive sensing services are deployed (such scientific infrastructures) is under surveillance and physical access to the hardware elements is not feasible. Once data are collected by the 6G gateway, standard cryptography and security solutions could be applied.

It is a pending challenge to find a hardware solution to provide high-integrity and high-security encryption to nodes with ultra-reduced capabilities.

6   Conclusions and Future Works

In this paper, we propose a solution for massive machine-type communications for devices with an extremely reduced throughput. The proposed solution defines two levels of cells, the first is operating at native 6G frequencies, while the second one is operating at high frequency (shortwave). Symbols and bit stream in the first-level cells are spatially multiplexed to cover second-level cells. In that way, hardware devices do not employ a full OFDM (Orthogonal Frequency-Division Multiplexing) symbol, but only use one orthogonal subcarrier each. Coding and modulation at the interface between the two levels of cells are configured to make possible the access of all hardware devices to communication services.

The results show that the proposed solution improves the communication delay and the management delay at the 6G base station, reducing up to ten times the computational cost compared to traditional approaches based on the direct link between the 6G base stations and all devices. Additionally, scalability is also improved, so future massive scenarios (with more than ten million devices per square kilometer) will also be supported.

In future work, the proposed solution will be implemented in mobile network simulators considering additional effects, and, eventually, the solution will be tested in real 6G/5G deployments.

Acknowledgments. This publication was produced within the framework of Ramón Alcarria and Borja Bordel's research projects on the occasion of their stay at Argonne National Laboratory (José Castillejo's 2021 grant). This work is supported by Comunidad de Madrid within the framework of the Multiannual Agreement with Universidad Politécnica de Madrid to encourage research by young doctors (PRINCE project).

References

1. Al-Eryani, Y., Hossain, E.: The D-OMA method for massive multiple access in 6G: performance, security, and challenges. IEEE Veh. Technol. Mag. **14**(3), 92–99 (2019)
2. Voinov, I.A., Chung, J., Kettimuthu, R., Bordel, B., Alcarria, R., Robles, T.: A review of the solutions ecosystem for 5G systems on rural and remote environments. In: 2022 17th Iberian Conference on Information Systems and Technologies (CISTI), pp. 1–6, June 2022
3. Bairagi, A.K., et al.: Coexistence mechanism between eMBB and uRLLC in 5G wireless networks. IEEE Trans. Commun. **69**(3), 1736–1749 (2021)
4. Bockelmann, C., et al.: Massive machine-type communications in 5g: physical and MAC-layer solutions. IEEE Commun. Mag. **54**(9), 59–65 (2016)
5. Bogale, T.E., Le, L.B.: Massive MIMO and mmWave for 5G wireless HetNet: potential benefits and challenges. IEEE Veh. Technol. Mag. **11**(1), 64–75 (2016)
6. Bordel, B., Alcarria, R., Chung, J., Kettimuthu, R., Robles, T.: Evaluation and modeling of microprocessors' numerical precision impact on 5G enhanced mobile broadband communications. In: Rocha, Á., Ferrás, C., López-López, P.C., Guarda, T. (eds.) ICITS 2021. AISC, vol. 1330, pp. 267–279. Springer, Cham (2021). https://doi.org/10.1007/978-3-030-68285-9_26
7. Bordel, B., Alcarria, R., Martín, D., Sánchez-De-Rivera, D.: An agent-based method for trust graph calculation in resource constrained environments. Integr. Comput.-Aided Eng. **27**(1), 37–56 (2020)
8. Bordel, B., Alcarria, R., Robles, T.: An optimization algorithm for the efficient distribution of resources in 6G verticals. In: Rocha, A., Adeli, H., Dzemyda, G., Moreira, F. (eds.) Information Systems and Technologies. WorldCIST 2022. Lecture Notes in Networks and Systems, vol. 468, pp 103–114. Springer, Cham (2022). https://doi.org/10.1007/978-3-031-04826-5_11
9. Bordel, B., Alcarria, R., Robles, T.: Lightweight encryption for short-range wireless biometric authentication systems in Industry 4.0. Integr. Comput.-Aided Eng. **29**(2), 153–173 (2022)
10. Bordel, B., Alcarria, R., Robles, T.: Recognizing human activities in Industry 4.0 scenarios through an analysis-modeling- recognition algorithm and context labels. Integr. Comput.-Aided Eng. **29**(1), 83–103 (2022)
11. Bordel, B., Alcarria, R., Robles, T., Iglesias, M.S.: Data authentication and anonymization in IoT scenarios and future 5G networks using chaotic digital watermarking. IEEE Access **9**, 22378–22398 (2021)

12. Bordel, B., Alcarria, R., Robles, T., Sánchez-De-Rivera, D.: Service management in virtualization-based architectures for 5G systems with network slicing. Integr. Comput.-Aided Eng. **27**(1), 77–99 (2020)

13. Bordel, B., Alcarria, R., Sánchez-de-Rivera, D., Sánchez, Á.: An inter-slice management solution for future virtualization-based 5G systems. In: Barolli, L., Takizawa, M., Xhafa, F., Enokido, T. (eds.) AINA 2019. AISC, vol. 926, pp. 1059–1070. Springer, Cham (2020). https://doi.org/10.1007/978-3-030-15032-7_89

14. Bordel, B., Alcarria, R., Sánchez-Picot, Á., Sánchez-de-Rivera, D.: Cyber-physical systems for environment and people monitoring in large facilities: a study case in public health. In: Rocha, Á., Ferrás, C., Paredes, M. (eds.) ICITS 2019. AISC, vol. 918, pp. 406–416. Springer, Cham (2019). https://doi.org/10.1007/978-3-030-11890-7_40

15. Bordel, B., de Rivera, D.S., Alcarria, R.: Virtualization-based techniques for the design, management and implementation of future 5G systems with network slicing. In: Rocha, Á., Adeli, H., Reis, L.P., Costanzo, S. (eds.) WorldCIST'18 2018. AISC, vol. 746, pp. 133–143. Springer, Cham (2018). https://doi.org/10.1007/978-3-319-77712-2_13

16. Strinati, E.C., et al.: 6G: the next frontier: from holographic messaging to artificial intelligence using subterahertz and visible light communication. IEEE Veh. Technol. Mag. **14**(3), 42–58 (2019)

17. Chataut, R., Akl, R.: Massive MIMO systems for 5G and beyond networks-overview, recent trends, challenges, and future research direction. Sensors **20**(10), 2753 (2020)

18. Chen, X., Ng, D.W.K., Wei, Yu., Larsson, E.G., Al-Dhahir, N., Schober, R.: Massive access for 5G and beyond. IEEE J. Sel. Areas Commun. **39**(3), 615–637 (2021)

19. Dogra, A., Jha, R.K., Jain, S.: A survey on beyond 5G network with the advent of 6G: architecture and emerging technologies. IEEE Access **9**, 67512–67547 (2021)

20. Elijah, O., Leow, C.Y., Rahman, T.A., Nunoo, S., Iliya, S.Z.: A comprehensive survey of pilot contamination in massive MIMO-5G system. IEEE Commun. Surv. Tutorials **18**(2), 905–923 (2016)

21. Giordani, M., Polese, M., Mezzavilla, M., Rangan, S., Zorzi, M.: Toward 6G networks: use cases and technologies. IEEE Commun. Mag. **58**(3), 55–61 (2020)

22. Gui, G., Liu, M., Tang, F., Kato, N., Adachi, F.: 6G: opening new horizons for integration of comfort, security, and intelligence. IEEE Wirel. Commun. **27**(5), 126–132 (2020)

23. Guo, F., Yu, F.R., Zhang, H., Li, X., Ji, H., Leung, V.C.: Enabling massive IoT toward 6G: a comprehensive survey. IEEE Internet Things J. **8**(15), 11891–11915 (2021)

24. Hoydis, J., Aoudia, F.A., Valcarce, A., Viswanathan, H.: Toward a 6G AI-native air interface. IEEE Commun. Mag. **59**(5), 76–81 (2021)

25. Lee, Y.L., Qin, D., Wang, L.C., Sim, G.H.: 6G massive radio access networks: key applications, requirements and challenges. IEEE Open J. Veh. Technol. **2**, 54–66 (2021)

26. Lv, Z., Lou, R., Li, J., Singh, A.K., Song, H.: Big data analytics for 6g-enabled massive internet of things. IEEE Internet Things J. **8**(7), 5350–5359 (2021)

27. Ma, Y., Yuan, Z., LI, W., LI, Z.: Truly grant-free technologies and protocols for 6G (2021)

28. Mareca, P., Bordel, B.: Robust hardware-supported chaotic cryptosystems for streaming commutations among reduced computing power nodes. Analog Integr. Circ. Sig. Process. **98**(1), 11–26 (2019)

29. Kammoun, A., Debbah, M., Alouini, M.S.: Design of 5G full dimension massive MIMO systems. IEEE Trans. Commun. **66**(2), 726–740 (2018)
30. Nawaz, S.J., Sharma, S.K., Mansoor, B., Patwary, M.N., Khan, N.M.: Non-coherent and backscatter communications: enabling ultra-massive connectivity in 6G wireless networks. IEEE Access **9**, 38144–38186 (2021)
31. Papadopoulos, H., Wang, C., Bursalioglu, O., Hou, X., Kishiyama, Y.: Massive MIMO technologies and challenges towards 5G. IEICE Trans. Commun. **E99.B**(3), 602–621 (2016)
32. Surya Vara Prasad, K.N.R., Hossain, E., Bhargava, V.K.: Energy efficiency in massive MIMO-based 5G networks: opportunities and challenges. IEEE Wirel. Commun. **24**(3), 86–94 (2017)
33. Robles, T., Bordel, B., Alcarria, R., de Andrés, D.M.: Mobile wireless sensor networks: modeling and analysis of three-dimensional scenarios and neighbor discovery in mobile data collection. Ad-Hoc Sens. Wirel. Netw. **35**(1–2), 67–104 (2017)
34. Bordel Sánchez, B., Alcarria, R., Robles, T.: Managing wireless communications for emergency situations in urban environments through cyber-physical systems and 5G technologies. Electron **9**(9), 1524 (2020)
35. Siddiqi, M.A., Yu, H., Joung, J.: 5G ultra-reliable low-latency communication implementation challenges and operational issues with IoT devices. Electronics **8**(9), 981 (2019)
36. Taneja, A., Saluja, N., Rani, S.: An energy efficient dynamic framework for resource control in massive IoT network for smart cities. Wirel. Netw. **2022**, 1–12 (2022)
37. Valentini, L., Faedi, A., Chiani, M., Paolini, E.: Coded random access for 6G: intra-frame spatial coupling with ACKs. In: Proceedings of 2021 IEEE Globecom Workshops, GC Wkshps 2021 (2021)
38. Verma, S., Kaur, S., Khan, M.A., Sehdev, P.S.: Toward green communication in 6g-enabled massive internet of things. IEEE Internet Things J. **8**(7), 5408–5415 (2021)
39. Wen, F., Wymeersch, H., Peng, B., Tay, W.P., So, H.C., Yang, D.: A survey on 5G massive MIMO localization. Digital Sig. Process. **94**, 21–28 (2019)
40. Yang, B., Zhiqiang, Yu., Dong, Y., Zhou, J., Hong, W.: Compact tapered slot antenna array for 5G millimeter-wave massive MIMO systems. IEEE Trans. Antennas Propag. **65**(12), 6721–6727 (2017)
41. Yang, B., Zhiqiang, Yu., Lan, J., Zhang, R., Zhou, J., Hong, W.: Digital Beamforming-Based Massive MIMO Transceiver for 5G Millimeter-Wave Communications. IEEE Trans. Microwave Theor. Tech. **66**(7), 3403–3418 (2018)
42. Zhang, J., Linglong Dai, X., Li, Y.L., Hanzo, L.: On low-resolution ADCs in practical 5G millimeter-wave massive MIMO systems. IEEE Commun. Mag. **56**(7), 205–211 (2018)

Building and Utilizing Small-Scale Testbed for Research on 5G SA Network-Related Security Vulnerabilities

Dowon Kim[1,2], Ilsun You[2], Seongmin Park[1,2], and Sungmoon Kwon[1(✉)]

[1] Korea Internet & Security Agency, Naju-si, Jeollanam-do 58324, South Korea
{kimdw,smpark,skwon}@kisa.or.kr
[2] Department of Financial Information Security, Kookmin University, Seoul 80523, South Korea
isyou@kookmin.ac.kr
https://www.kookmin.ac.kr , https://www.kisa.or.kr

Abstract. When it comes to the fourth-generation mobile networks (4G, Long Term Evolution (LTE)) and, to go one step further, 5G Non-Standalone (NSA) relying on 4G core, it was possible to easily set up testbeds using open source projects and Software Defined Radio (SDR) hardware. In particular, the sheer power of open source solutions like, srsLTE [35] and OpenLTE [42], with the use of low-cost SDR devices like Universal Software Radio Peripheral (USRP) [33] and LimeSDR [26], unbridled the race toward 4G/5G NSA testbeds capable of providing radio network coverage, They have been actively utilized by the research community, thereby successfully finding a number of security threats and troubling vulnerabilities. Despite the foregoing, those open source implementations are not completed, as far as 5G Standalone (SA) mobile networks are concerned, so those are considered as incapable of creating testbeds and inapplicable for security threat assessment in the real ecosystem. In such contexts, this article in an attempt to establish a foothold for research of 5G Core network security will introduce considerations and approaches to set up a small-scale lab testbed for 5G SA mobile networking.

Keywords: 5G Standalone (SA) · Testbed · 5G SA security · Vulnerability research

1 Introduction

5G mobile networks provide speeds up to 20 times faster, 10 times more connected and 10 times lower latency, than 4G [19], employing far more advanced technology that not only delivers voice and data services with the use of 4G smartphones but also allows a variety of IoT devices to communicate with each other. The technological advancement of kind is also accelerating from the perspective of 5G SA. Among them the most noteworthy is softwarized architecture

© The Author(s), under exclusive license to Springer Nature Singapore Pte Ltd. 2023
I. You et al. (Eds.): MobiSec 2022, CCIS 1644, pp. 63–81, 2023.
https://doi.org/10.1007/978-981-99-4430-9_5

through Software-Defined Networking(SDN) and Network Function Virtualiza-
tion(NFV) to foster openness, scalability and flexibility in the cellular arena,
while 5G SA Core is more segmented by more detailed functions. Such segmentation as Fig. 2 in the function framework leads to increase complexity in
developing 5G open-source testbeds, compromising perfection in terms of creating features and functions.

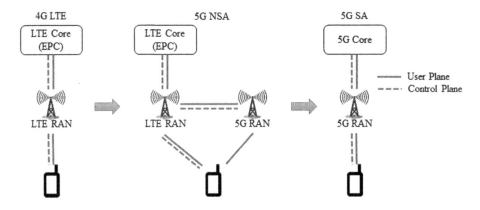

Fig. 1. 4G/5G NSA/5G SA Network Modes

Despite the fact that 3GPP (3rd Generation Partnership Project) Release
15 [13], forming fundamental radio specifications for 5G SA, was released in
2019 and first launched by the U.S.A. [2] in August, 2020, it is not yet broadly
enforced since, as of December, 2021, only 20 telecom companies across 12 countries adopt this set of standards [34]. Korea is also in an initial stage as ushered
only by KT that rolled out 5G SA service in July, 2021. Under the situation
like that, setting up testbeds is currently not active although related technology
for open source networking hardware and software is expected to evolve along
with more popularized 5G SA services. Given that 5G SA service is already
commercialized, making its way for more deployment, there is no other option,
from a standpoint of testbed builders, but to wait until open source networking
hardware and software truly dedicated to 5G SA are unveiled. It is rationally
anticipated that 5G SA-based private 5G network deployments will surge over
the coming years, leading to a deluge of private 5G RAN and Core in enterprise
security level. Now more than that, the imperativeness of research and analysis focused on 5G SA network-associated security risks and vulnerabilities is
manifest as a proactive approach. Such activities require collective intelligence,
meaning that more valuable deliverables can come true from the collaborative
and concerted efforts by more researchers. In this sense, it is important to be
able to build testbeds in an easier and cost-effective manner in order for a great
number of individuals to more easily get started with research of security threats
and vulnerabilities. A small-scale lab-based testbed for 5G SA would be much

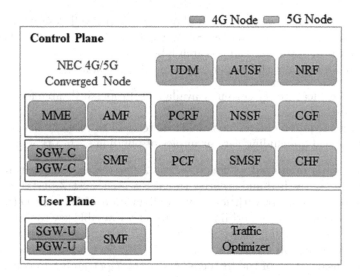

Fig. 2. 4G vs. 5G Nodes

better to facilitate participation of more students and researchers, In this study, it is aimed to build a testbed as an enabler for research on potential vulnerabilities associated with the 5G SA network, such as connection between UEs (User Equipment) and base stations, user authentication process and user data transmission. The detailed scope of research in this paper is as follows:

Table 1. The detailed scope of research

Div.	Index	Description
Research Scope 1	RS.1	Problems that many occur due to request processing by a base station or core with respect to request non-compliant with protocol
Research Scope 2	RS.2	Abnormal behavior that possibly occurs in a base station or core despite compliance with protocol
Research Scope 3	RS.3	Research on security vulnerabilities such as message manipulation, denial of service in user terminal, information leakage, authentication bypass and encryption disabling caused by man in the middle attack via False Base Station (FBS)

Based on the objective mentioned above, this paper will describe a comparison between currently available 5G SA testbed platforms as well as their build and utilization in academia and research labs.

The contributions of this paper can be outlined as follows:

- It scrutinizes features of currently available solutions utilizable for building a 5G SA testbed
- It analyzes requirements for a small-scale testbed to research 5G SA related security threats, including case examples of building such a type of testbeds

This paper is organized as follows: Sect. 2 pertaining to literature review with focus on 5G testbed and security threat research; Sect. 3 pertaining to the background of this study with focus on configuration of 5G core network and principal procedure; Sect. 4 pertaining to currently available key tools for 5G SA, with description in a comparative manner; Sect. 5 pertaining to case examples of building small-scale lab-based testbeds for 5G SA; Sect. 6 pertaining to assessment and consideration of the testbeds; and, Sect. 7 pertaining to conclusion of this thesis.

2   Related Work

2.1   5G Testbed

When focused only on 5G NSA mobile networks, a number of researches are easily searchable from prior literature, which introduce ways for building testbeds based on open source and SDR [3,16]. Most of them describe how to configure physical channels and core as well as UEs. Figure 3 below shows a simplest form of testbed for 5G NSA by only using servers necessary for the network operation, hardware to construct physical channel, such as USRP, and open source software.

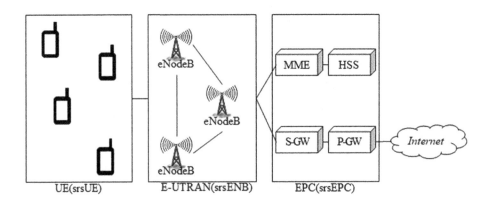

Fig. 3. Building testbed for 5G NSA

It is possible to simulate MITM (Man In The Middle Attack) through combination and configuration as shown in Fig. 4 and verify the behavioral anomaly that has occurred in malicious packet via changing communication packet reception/transmission. By way of versatile and flexible experiments using such a testbed, an array of more precise test sets can be formulated and put in practice to analyze security vulnerabilities targeted on real commercial networks of 5G NSA.

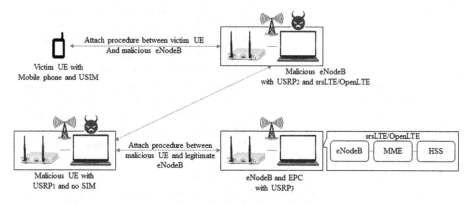

Fig. 4. MITM attack by utilizing srsLTE/OpenLTE

Meanwhile, topics that appeared most frequently in 5G SA testbed-related literature are Software-Defined Networking focused on network slicing, and decentralization and virtualization of the core network, and how to build an environment capable of realizing network function virtualization and testing security of new network functions [27]. There is also a technique to create an environment enabling testing whether a 5G mobile network works normally, without denial of service, over massive IoT devices connected [32]. These testbeds are appropriate for testing security of new 5G features and use cases in the 5G mobile network, but fairly impracticable for addressing manipulation of 5G communication packets that pose vulnerability to protocols and cause malfunction in core systems. In particular, security vulnerabilities associated with 5G mobile network protocols closely involve network operations of 5G core, typically targeted on manipulation and processing of packets in Control Plane (CP) and User Plane (UP) of the core network. Therefore, an ideal testbed should focus on processing mechanism of 5G core, rather than the efficiency e.g. in processing an unprecedented amount of data traffic in wireless communication.

2.2 Security Threats in 5G NSA Networks

In [30] a testbed is built, as shown in Fig. 3 and Fig. 4, to identify potential threat vectors involving 5G NSA networks. Moreover, a set of test cases specific to RAN/Core were constructed and run to probe into security vulnerabilities. Table 2 lists out security vulnerabilities found.

Table 2. Test Result & Vulnerability Disclosure

No	Test case	Type	Vulnerability Description
1	RRC Connection DoS	RAN	According to the standard, it is defined not to verify subscriber ID in base-stations, so access is allowed when sending RRC connection request with a victim's ID
2	RRC Security mode command		There is threat of avoiding authentication when a base station ignores authentication value (MAC) from the terminal for received RRC Security mode command and sends RRC Security mode complete, thus it is processed normally in the base-station
3	RRC Connection reconfiguration		There is a threat of avoiding authentication when a base station ignores authentication value (MAC) from the terminal for received RRC Connection reconfiguration and sends RRC Connection reconfiguration complete, thus it is processed normally in the base-station.
4	NAS Integrity Spoofing [4]	Core Network	There is a threat of avoiding authentication when a base station ignores authentication value (MAC) from the terminal for received RRC Connection reconfiguration and sends RRC Connection reconfiguration complete, thus it is processed normally in the base-station
5	NAS Ciphering Spoofing [4]		There is a threat of eavesdropping when ciphering is not used by changing the EEA field in UE Network Capability of victim's attach request to 0
6	NAS Security mode command [20]		There is threat of avoiding authentication when MME ignores authentication value (MAC) from the terminal for received Security mode command and sends Security mode complete, thus it is processed normally in the MME
7	NAS Attach accept [20]		There is threat of avoiding authentication, when MME ignores authentication value (MAC) from the terminal for received Attach Accept and sends attach mode complete, thus it is processed normally in the MME
8	EPC Scanning [31]		EPC equipment IP can be identified through the response message received after injecting GTP-C echo request into the user data and sending it to CN

3   Background

This Section describes 5G SA system architecture, connection between UE and base station and the procedure for packet processing in 5G Core, as part of an effort to build a testbed platform for researching security vulnerabilities in 5G SA networks, and defines 5G core network functions necessary for the research.

3.1   5G SA System Architecture

The 5G SA core network architecture comprises split NFs (network functions) and entities [15]. The main network functions of the 5G core are enumerated in Fig. 5, below which brief description of each component is provided.

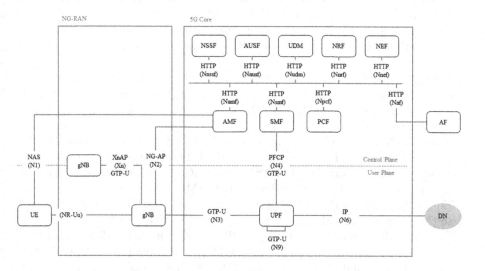

Fig. 5. 5G SA System Architecture

- User Equipment (UE): A user terminal connected to the mobile core network including Mobile Equipment (ME) and Subscriber Identity Module (SIM), to use network services
- Next generation Node B (gNB) : A base station that supports 5G New Radio (NR)
- Access and mobility Management Function (AMF): A 5G core network function that performs registration, connection, reachability, mobility management, etc.
- Session Management Function (SMF): A 5G core network function that manages subscriber session
- User Plane Function(UPF): A 5G core network function that supports packet routing/forwarding, interconnect to Data Network (DN), etc. with respect to UE's UP data

- Authentication Server Function (AUSF): A 5G core network function that supports authentication and security features with respect to UE being connected to 5G core network
- Policy Control Function (PCF): A 5G core network function that controls integrated policy on the behavior of the 5G network in its entirety and delivers policy to other control plane network functions (NFs)
- Unified Data Management (UDM): A 5G core network function for the storage and management of user subscription data and authentication data
- Unified Data Repository (UDR): A 5G core network Function that provides data storage and inquiry functions to 5G NF
- Network Exposure Function (NEF): A 5G core network function responsible for securely using or controlling system information when allowing external applications (service provider or subscriber) to interwork with 5G core NFs
- Network Repository Function (NRF): A 5G core network function that performs managing functions for monitoring service status and interworking information (e.g. IP address, FQDN, etc.) of 5G core NFs which change dynamically
- Network Slice Selection Function (NSSF): A 5G core network function that supports selection of the optimal network slice available for the service requested by the user in the 5G network environment where various services are provided
- Non-3GPP Inter-Working Function (N3IWF): A function responsible for interworking between untrusted non-3GPP networks and the 5G core
- Short Message Service Function (SMSF): A 5G core network function necessary for providing SMS over NAS through AMF
- Equipment Identity Register (EIR): A 5G core network function which is used to check the status of Permanent Equipment Identifier (PEI)
- Security Edge Protection Proxy (SEPP): A 5G core network function that provides message filtering and policy and topology hiding at the inter-PLMN (Public Land Mobile Network) Control Plan Interface among 5G core network functions
- DN: Refers to the service part of the system outside 5G core network, including Internet and service provider

3.2   5G SA Registration Procedure and PDU Session Establishment

As schematically depicted in Fig. 6, the 5G SA Registration procedure can largely be divided into three processes: the first relates to establishing radio connection between the UE and network, covering from RRC Setup Request to RRC Setup (corresponding to procedure (0) in Fig. 6); the second relates to registration of the UE to the network, covering from Registration Request to Registration Accept (corresponding to procedures (1) through (5) in Fig. 6); and, third relates to IP allocation and session creation, covering from PDU Session Establishment Request to PDU Session Resource Response (corresponding to procedures 6 and 7 in Fig. 6 [14]. This paper aims to build a testbed allowing for research of security vulnerabilities that may occur in processes as demonstrated in Fig. 6. For this,

UE, NR (gNB), and 5G SA Core are required. Functions to constitute a 5G core network require UDM additionally, based on such main network functions as AMF, SMF, AUSF, and UPF.

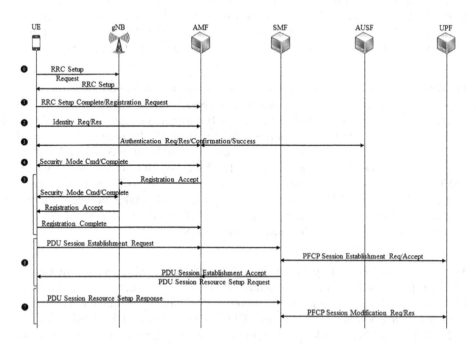

Fig. 6. 5G SA System Architecture

4   5G SA Network Testbed Toolkits

This Section discusses a comparative analysis between software products implementable for 5G core and those utilizable for 5G RAN/UE, in building a 5G SA testbed.

4.1   5G SA Core

For further supplement to introduction in Sect. 3, this Section gets into more detail about open source software and commercial software that can realize 5G SA system architecture, with 5G SA procedure, defined in 3GPP Release 15 and beyond. The former includes Open5GS and free5GC, while the latter includes M5, NetTest 5G, and Open5GCore. As far as 5G SA is concerned, open-source labeled software is distributed by different entities, with Core and RAN separated, but commercial software is provided with Core and RAN packaged together.

Open5GS. Open5GS is a C-language open source implementation for 5G core network as defined by 3GPP Release 16, which is distributed under the GNU AGPLv3.0 license. Commercial license is owned by NextEPC, Inc [21]. The project offers basic components for 5G SA core, such as AUSF, NRF, UDM, UDR, PCF, NSSF and BSF, in addition to AMF, SMF, and UPF [22]. Implementing a 5G RAN is recommended to use UERANSIM that is open source software [23]. The entire code of Open5GS can be found at Github [24].

Free5GC. Free5GC is an open source implementation of 5G core, which is written in the Go programming language under development by National Yang Ming Chiao Tung University, Taiwan, and distributed under the Apache License v2.0, offering a 5G core network environment defined in 3GPP Release 15 and beyond [5]. This implementation whose development was completed in April, 2020, offers various core functions such as AMF, SMF, UPF, AUSF, NSSF, NRF, UDM, UDR, and PCF [6]. It also offers N3IWF (Non-mobile access Network Function) that supports non-3GPP access as well as ULCL (Up Uplink Classifier). Implementing a 5G RAN is recommended, like Open5GS, to use UERANSIM [7]. The entire code of Free5GC can be found at Github [8].

M5. M5, manufactured by Valid8.com, Inc. [40], is a testing equipment for 5G SA that provides functions to emulate both of 5G SA core network and 5G RAN. It provides 3GPP release 15-compliant 5G core environments. The tester provides such CN functions as AUSF, UDM, UDR, NRF, PCF, NSSF, N3IWF and SMSF, in addition to key 5GC functions like AMF, SMF and UPF. The 5G RAN is a hardware solution that offers a set of capabilities, such as frequency band of not greater than 6 GHz, frequency division duplex (FDD) and time division duplex (TDD), and wireless coverage of approx. 10 m [41]. It offers a tool for writing and editting test scenarios, as shown in Fig. 7, for the study of security vulnerabilities. It further offers functions capable of performing 5G SA call flow simulation in a web-based GUI environment and operating/managing gNodeB and emulation nodes. As software of the emulator that mimics 5GC and RAN is complied in the binary form, however, the user cannot make a change as he wishes to the source code itself.

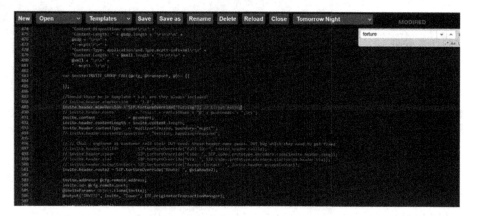

Fig. 7. Code editor for 5G SA test

NetTest 5G. NetTest 5G, manufactured by Polaris Networks [28], is an emulator for testing 5G SA. It incorporates software that simulates elements of 5G SA core network and 5G RAN. The solution based on 3GPP Release 16 specifications offers 5GC functions such as AMF, SMF, UPF, AUSF, NSSF, UDM, UDR, PCF, and SEPP (Security Edge Protection Proxy) [29]. It provides the ability to test standard functional operations over varied network topologies (normal test) but also simulate abnormal network behavior (negative test). It also provides GUI environment for operation and APIs (Application Programming Interface for test automation) for test automation. The software is compiled in the binary form allowable for virtualization.

Open5GCore. Open5GCore, manufactured by Fraunhofer FOKUS [10], is an emulator for 5G SA testing. It provides emulators allowing the user to demonstrate 5G core network functionality (AMF, SMF, UPF, PCF, NEF, NRF, UDM, NSSF and N3IWF) and simulate RAN and UE. It is also possible to test roaming through interworking between core networks by using SCP (Service Communication Proxy) [11]. Another feature enables the user to add new subscriber profile on the UDM, offering GUI environment for management and monitoring [12]. The toolkit will undergo continuous update with additional features according to an established roadmap as shown in Fig. 8. Unlike other commercial peers (e.g. M5, NetTest 5G), this software is provided with binary code and source code as well, meaning that the developer who constructs a testbed has the freedom to change the source code at his disposal for the testing purpose.

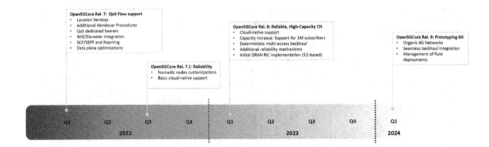

Fig. 8. Roadmap for Open5GCore [10]

Table 3 shows a comparison of 5G SA core products.

4.2 5G SA RAN and UE

For 5G SA RAN, there are open source projects such as UERANSIM and srsRAN, and commercial software suites such as AMARI Callbox. Besides, 5G SA Core software products described in Sect. 4.1 also provide RAN and UE functions.

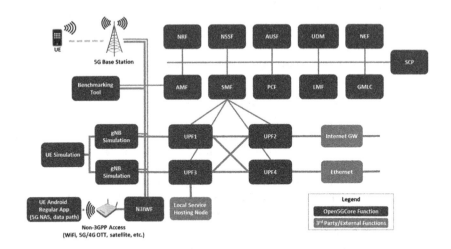

Fig. 9. Open5GCore Architecture [10]

Table 3. Comparison of 5G SA Core products

Div	Open5GS	Free5GC	M5	NetTest 5G	Open5GCore
Make	Sukchan Lee	National Yang Ming Chiao Tung University	Valid8	Polaris Networks	Fraunhofer FOKUS
License	Open Source	Open Source	Commercial Product	Commercial Product	Commercial Product
Core components	AMF, SMF, UPF, AUSF, NRF, UDM, UDR, PCF, NSSF, BSF	AMF, SMF, UPF, AUSF, NSSF, NRF, UDM, UDR, PCF	AMF, SMF, UPF, AUSF, UDM, UDR, NRF, PCF, EIR NSSF, N3IWF, SMSF	AMF, SMF, UPF, AUSF, NSSF, UDM, UDR, PCF, SEPP	AMF, SMF, UPF, PCF, NEF, NRF, UDM, NSSF, N3IWF, SCP
Standard	3GPP Release 16	3GPP Release 15	3GPP Release 15	3GPP Release 16	3GPP Release 16
Programming	Source Code	Source Code	Binary	Binary	Binary & Source Code
RAN	-	-	Hardware	Emulator	Emulator
UE	-	-	Hardware	Emulator	Emulator

UERANSIM. UERANSIM, aligned with 3GPP Release 15, is the project based on C-language open-source software [17], supporting the development of 5G RAN. It follows GPL 3.0 license, and is allowed to combine 5G core open source projects like Open5GS. However, there is no interface that actually receives/transmits wireless signals over SDRs. As of today, its development is complete, while bug fixing has been underway. The entire code thereof can be found at Github [18].

srsRAN. srsRAN developed by Software Radio Systems is the project based on a free and open-source 5G full-stack software suite written in C/C++, It is distributed under the AGPLv3 license and compliant with 3GPP Release 15 [36]. The software suite comprises srsENB compatible with gNB application for 5G SA and srsUE acting as an UE, both codes being downloadable from Github [37]. srsRAN can build an interface that receives/transmits wireless signals using a SDR device. However, capabilities of both srsENB and srsUE when operating in 5G SA mode are limited to 15 kHz SCS (Sub-Carrier Spacing) that only supports the use of FDD bands and a bandwidth of 10 MHz [38], so such pitfalls must be taken into consideration during the build process. srsRAN is interoperable with Open5GS, an open source project, and provides 5G SA features enabling the user to test all of the UE, base station and core setups [39].

AMARI Callbox. AMARI Callbox is a solution provided by Amarisoft, allowing testing of NSA, LTE, LTE-M and NB-IoT devices, as well as 3GPP release 16-compliant 5G SA [1]. It supports all FDD and TDD frequency bands below 6 GHz, with support of encryption in 5G networks using the AES, SNOW3G and ZUC algorithms, The solution provides NG interface that supports NG Application Protocol (NGAP) and GTP-U and provides the function of interworking with 5G core.

5G SA UE. UE that supports 5G SA encompasses Samsung Galaxy S22, Samsung Galaxy S21, Samsung A22, Huwei P40 lite5G, OnePlus 10 Pro 5G, OnePlus Nord 5G, Hisense F50+, etc. These UEs, even though having successfully communicated with a specific base station having the 5G over-the-air test environment, may fail to connect to the real-world commercial 5G network depending on 5G SA sharing deployment of network operators.

5 Testbeds Build

Section 4 described testbed tools necessary for research on security vulnerabilities, in a 5G SA environment, involving connection of UEs with base stations, user authentication procedure and process for user data transmission, Testbeds built by using those solutions are surely utilizable for research on security threats/vulnerabilities but need to extend their usage to formulate test scenarios for security validation of real mobile communication networks or 5G SA networks of private 5G service providers. The latter is particularly prone to be built by inexperienced service providers, unlike telecom operators, thus being far more susceptible at its onset to a variety of security threats. From the perspective of researchers engaged in 5G SA related security vulnerabilities, therefore, it is all the more necessary to build 5G testbeds and create test scenarios exclusively for 5G.

The objective in building testbeds and the scope of research for security threats are as described in Sect. 1. Security vulnerabilities other than them, such as those associated with network slice and MEC interworking, are excluded from the scope hereof, as they can be addressed by test scenarios of mobile network operators currently providing wireless communication services.

The requirements of the testbed to be built are as follow:

Table 4. The requirements of the testbed

No	Requirement
1	It needs to be economical according to a small-scale testbed (e.g. budget: Maxium 140,000 US$)
2	It supports key functions such as AMF, SMF, AUSF, UDM, NRF, and UPF to test basic behavior and security of 5G SA core
3	It provides source code to change to suit study scope and test purpose
4	It is configured as similar to the real 5G communication environment as possible (e.g. UE, base station and 5G SA Core Network are independent hardware)
5	It supplies continuous and rapid product updates and technical support for changes to 3GPP standards and the advent of new 5G services

A testbed built by the authors of this paper incorporated Open5GCore for 5G SA Core and AMARI Callbox for RAN (gNodeB). Open sources of 5G SA core and Open5GCore meet the requirement 1–3. while no hardware RAN testing has yet been performed against free5GC [9], Open5GC has been tested with hardware RAN [25], as far as requirement 4 is concerned. For requirement 5, in light of continuing update in terms of 5G SA core network functionality to respond to 3GP Release 17 and beyond in the future, we deemed that Open5GCore, a commercial software suite, is more preferred than its open-source competitors. Our choice of Open5GCore, out of several commercial software products, is owning to provision of source code, meaning that it allows for editting at our disposal the program to be fit to our testing purpose. In the case of RAN, we selected a hardware product, AMARI Callbox, to create a most realistic wireless communication environment enabling connection to real UEs, rather than testing by using an emulator. Our scheme in building a 5G SA testbed is not the right answer, which means that other types of tools enumerated in Sect. 4 can be flexibly combined depending on the scope of research budget, testing purpose and the extent to which the test is to be carried out.

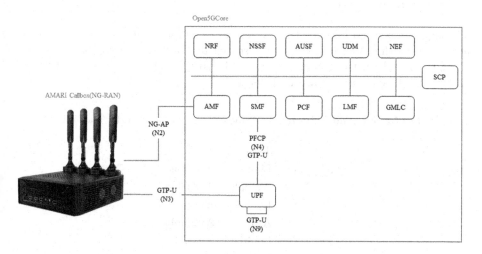

Fig. 10. Example of building a testbed with AMARI Callbox and Open5GcCore

A possible way for testing security threats is to make/install an app on smartphones necessary for testing in the 5G SA network to probe into vulnerabilities associated with the User Plane. Security vulnerabilities associated with the Control Plane may require smartphone routing for in-depth research on e.g. IP spoofing or authentication message manipulation. If such routing is not easy to facilitate, due to diverse security functions provided by most-recent smartphones, it is possible to perform various tests by modifying RAN source code of Open5GCore and interworking it with AMF of the 5G SA core network to be tested, as shown in Fig. 11.

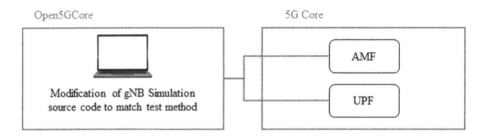

Fig. 11. Test example connecting gNB Simulation source code with AMF and UPF

6   Consideration

Through the testbed built by the authors of this paper, the test was conducted according to the described scope of research in Table 1. The results of testing the CP and UP in the configuration as Fig. 10 (TB 1) and Fig. 11 (TB 2) for each research scope are shown in Table 5.

Table 5. Test availability by the scope of research using TB 1 and TB 2

Div.		TB 1	TB 2
RS. 1	CP	Limited	Available
	UP	Available	Available
RS. 2	CP	Limited	Available
	UP	Available	Available
RS. 3	CP	Limited	Unavailable
	UP	Limited	Unavailable

In the research(RS 1, RS 2) of Control Plane vulnerabilities using TB 1, restriction such as mobile phone routing existed. In the case of RS3, the MITM using FBS could be configured by installing srsUE and srsRAN in the USRP. However, while srsUE and srsRAN only support FDD, the latest 5G SA phones only support TDD, so RS 3 could not be tested using the phones in TB 1. The TB2 configuration could test the CP and UP of RS1 and RS2, while RS3 could not configure the same as the real FBS. It will be a future work to implement MITM in the form of a FSB by connecting the UE emulator with the modified emulator of the gNodeB simulation source code.

7   Conclusion

5G, characterized by ultra-fast wireless speeds, low-latency and hyper connectivity, will be put in reality by virtue of 5G SA networks. Along with massive

IoT devices with different levels of security connected to 5G networks, a variety
of security issues could emerge by exploiting low security-level devices, resulting in user authentication bypass, encryption disabling, denial of service and
user information leakage. Therefore, when private 5G networks are on a wide
scale, maintaining higher level of security is crucial, otherwise inevitably pro-
voking security issues caused by weaknesses in security. The kind of penetration
testing to find the vulnerabilities attackers are looking for and plug them proactively will significantly improve stability in use of 5G. As part of such efforts,
this paper addresses a way for building a testbed to serve as a foothold for 5G
security. We expect that the scheme proposed herein becomes a shared norm
among researchers in building testbeds for finding more vulnerabilities associated with 5G SA networks. We further hope that our scheme is more refined by
the research community toward most advanced 5G testbed capable of not only
embracing network slicing, interworking with MEC systems and new specifications to be released by 3GPP, but also deducing test scenarios enough to deal
with a wide range of security vulnerabilities.

References

1. Amarisoft: AMARI Callbox. https://www.amarisoft.com/app/uploads/2021/10/AMARI-Callbox-Mini.pdf
2. Association, G.: T-Mobile US taunts rivals with SA 5G launch. 04 Aug 2020. https://www.mobileworldlive.com/featured-content/home-banner/t-mobile-us-taunts-rivals-with-sa-5g-launch
3. Brennan, D.M., Marojevic, V.: Uhd-dpdk performance analysis for advanced soft-ware radio communications. In: 2022 18th International Conference on Distributed Computing in Sensor Systems (DCOSS), pp. 420–425. IEEE (2022)
4. Chlosta, M., Rupprecht, D., Holz, T., Pöpper, C.: Lte security disabled: misconfig-uration in commercial networks. In: Proceedings of the 12th Conference on Security and Privacy in Wireless and Mobile Networks, pp. 261–266 (2019)
5. Communication service/Software laboratory, the college of computer science, N.Y.M.C.T.U.: free5GC. https://www.free5gc.org
6. Communication service/Software laboratory, the college of computer science, N.Y.M.C.T.U.: free5GC. https://www.free5gc.org/roadmap
7. Communication service/Software laboratory, the college of computer science, N.Y.M.C.T.U.: free5GC. https://www.free5gc.org/installations/stage-3-sim-install
8. Communication service/Software laboratory, the college of computer science, N.Y.M.C.T.U.: free5GC. https://github.com/free5gc
9. Communication service/Software laboratory, the college of computer science, N.Y.M.C.T.U.: free5GC. https://www.free5gc.org/installations/stage-3-free5gc/
10. Fokus, F.: Fraunhofer FOKUS, Open5GCore. https://www.fokus.fraunhofer.de, https://www.open5gcore.org
11. FOKUS, F.: Open5GCore. https://www.open5gcore.org/open5gcore/fundamental-core-functionality
12. FOKUS, F.: Open5GCore. https://www.open5gcore.org/open5gcore/testbed-management

13. 3rd Generation Partnership Project (3GPP), T.: 3GPP Release 15. https://www.3gpp.org/release-15
14. 3rd Generation partnership project (3GPP), T.: Procedures for the 5G system (5GS). TS.23.502. https://portal.3gpp.org/desktopmodules/Specifications/SpecificationDetails.aspx?specificationId=3145
15. 3rd generation partnership project (3GPP), T.: System architecture for the 5G system (5GS). TS.23.501. https://portal.3gpp.org/desktopmodules/Specifications/SpecificationDetails.aspx?specificationId=3144
16. Gomez-Miguelez, I., Garcia-Saavedra, A., Sutton, P.D., Serrano, P., Cano, C., Leith, D.J.: srslte: an open-source platform for LTE evolution and experimentation. In: Proceedings of the Tenth ACM International Workshop on Wireless Network Testbeds, Experimental Evaluation, and Characterization, pp. 25–32 (2016)
17. GÜNGÖR, A.: UERANSIM. https://github.com/aligungr/UERANSIM
18. GÜNGÖR, A.: UERANSIM. https://github.com/aligungr/UERANSIM/releases
19. ITU: emerging trends in 5G/IMT2020. September 2016. https://www.itu.int/en/membership/documents/missions/gva-mission-briefing-5g-28sept2016.pdf
20. Kim, H., Lee, J., Lee, E., Kim, Y.: Touching the untouchables: dynamic security analysis of the LTE control plane. In: 2019 IEEE Symposium on Security and Privacy (SP), pp. 1153–1168. IEEE (2019)
21. Lee, S.: Open5GS. https://open5gs.org/open5gs/support
22. Lee, S.: Open5GS. https://open5gs.org/open5gs/docs/guide/01-quickstart
23. Lee, S.: Open5GS. https://nickvsnetworking.com/my-first-5g-core-open5gs-and-ueransim
24. Lee, S.: Open5GS. https://github.com/open5gs
25. Lee, S.: Open5GS. https://open5gs.org/open5gs/docs/hardware/01-genodebs
26. Microsystems, L.: LimeSDR. https://limemicro.com
27. Murthy, A.K., Parthasarathi, R., Vetriselvi, V.: Security testbed for next generation mobile networks. In: 2020 Third ISEA Conference on Security and Privacy (ISEA-ISAP), pp. 122–129. IEEE (2020)
28. Networks, P.: NetTest 5G. https://www.polarisnetworks.net
29. Networks, P.: NetTest 5G. https://www.polarisnetworks.net/5g-NetTest-5g-platform.html
30. Park, S., Kim, D., Park, Y., Cho, H., Kim, D., Kwon, S.: 5g security threat assessment in real networks. Sensors **21**(16), 5524 (2021)
31. Park, S., Kim, S., Son, K., Kim, H., Park, J., Yim, K.: Real threats using GTP protocol and countermeasures on a 4g mobile grid computing environment. Int. J. Web Grid Serv. **13**(1), 3–24 (2017)
32. Ravi, N., Selvaraj, M.S.: Tefens: testbed for experimenting next-generation-network security. In: 2018 IEEE 5G World Forum (5GWF), pp. 204–209. IEEE (2018)
33. Research, E.: USRP. https://ettus.com
34. mobile Suppliers Association (GSA), G.: Executive Summary 5G Standalone - January 2022. https://gsacom.com/paper/executive-summary-5g-standalone-january-2022. January 2022
35. Systems, S.R.: srsLTE. https://srslte.com
36. Systems, S.R.: srsRAN. https://www.srsran.com
37. Systems, S.R.: srsRAN. https://github.com/srsran/srsran
38. Systems, S.R.: srsRAN. https://docs.srsran.com/en/latest/app_notes/source/5g_sa_COTS/source/index.html#limitations
39. Systems, S.R.: srsRAN. https://docs.srsran.com/en/latest/app_notes/source/5g_sa_E2E/source/index.html

40. Valid8: M5. https://www.valid8.com/m5
41. Valid8: M5. https://www.valid8.com/datasheets/mobile-ue-tester
42. Wojtowicz, B.: OpenLTE. http://openlte.sourceforge.net

AI for Security

Parameters Transfer Framework for Multi-domain Fake News Detection

Rafał Kozik[✉], Krzysztof Samp, Michał Choraś, and Marek Pawlicki

Bydgoszcz University of Science and Technology, Al. prof. S. Kaliskiego 7,
85-796 Bydgoszcz, Poland
rafal.kozik@pbs.edu.pl

Abstract. Recently, various BERT-based architectures for fake news detection have been proposed. In many cases, these methods work well on various benchmark datasets. However, the performance quickly deteriorates when the models are tested with samples coming from distributions which essentially differ from the ones the model has been trained on. To overcome this obstacle, in this paper, we have proposed a framework for the model's parameter transfer in order to redefine fake news detection as a multi-domain classification problem. The proposed solution is intended to possibly leverage different elements of the classification model's configuration to maximise global performance. The research presented in this paper utilises six publicly available, open benchmark datasets, presents the motivation, the architecture and the technical details of the proposed solution, and reports the achieved results with an array of well-known evaluation metrics. The presented results are promising and open the space for further research.

Keywords: NLP · Fake News · BERT · Machine Learning

1 Introduction

Presently, anyone can become a content creator and spread their views as they please, despite their level of expertise, education or experience. By means of the Internet, content creators can keep their identities a secret if they wish. As with many other contemporary technologies, with all the advantages of the Internet came a novel set of challenges. The fact that anyone can spread their opinion without having to worry about editors, communication commissions and broadcasting licences is a clear aid in free speech and bolsters democratic values. At the same time, malicious users are free to abuse the system for reasons motivated politically, monetarily, or sometimes simply out of spite. This reality set the scene for the emergence of the fake news phenomenon. Although the dissemination of falsified information is most likely as old as human speech, the development of modern media, with a strong emphasis on social media, which can facilitate viral spread of news that are not fact-checked, and are designed to play on the users' emotions and into their prejudices, has significantly changed

I. You et al. (Eds.): MobiSec 2022, CCIS 1644, pp. 85–96, 2023.
https://doi.org/10.1007/978-981-99-4430-9_6

the way deception is spread; as a consequence, it has become a highly powerful weapon.

The machine-learning-based methods have been proved to be effective, accurate and powerful aids in various NLP-related challenges. Natural Language Processing (NLP) is one of the novel research fields, which sits at the crossroads between computer science, artificial intelligence and linguistics. The field attempts to handle the processing and analysis of natural language, allowing for accurate performance in tasks which include text classification, named entity recognition, sentiment analysis and others. Currently, the deep learning (DL) methods are showing especially considerable promise.

However, fake news detection is far more complex than sentiment analysis or named entity recognition tasks. The key observation coming from our experiments [11,23] is that the BERT-based architectures work well when various datasets are considered. Bidirectional Encoder Representations from Transformers (BERT) are one of the premier techniques used very successfully in many tasks in NLP. The method was developed by Google [8,19]. The method leverages pre-training and fine-tuning, a technique which demonstrated effectiveness in Computer Vision in models based on the ImageNET dataset [7,26]. The phenomenon allows to train a deep neural network using a dataset of considerable size, which facilitates the learning of meaningful features in a particular task, and then to formulate a well-performing classifier by using a small dataset to finetune the pre-trained network. However, the performance quickly deteriorates when the models are tested with samples coming from distributions which essentially differ from the ones the model has been fine-tuned to. On top of that, researchers are stumbling with the availability of labelled data [9], as even though the recent explosion of big data made unlabelled data abundant, the preparation of the data for supervised machine learning approaches and the process of dataset labelling is highly time-consuming, problematic and thus costly [27].

This creates a need for addressing the transfer learning challenge. Transfer Learning (TL) is a domain of research which revolves around the utilisation of knowledge accumulated on one task to successfully perform a different task [24].

Therefore, as the major contribution of this paper, we have proposed a framework for the model's parameter transfer in order to redefine fake news detection as a multi-domain classification problem.

The paper is structured as follows. First, we present the related work. Next, we introduce the proposed framework for parameters transfer. The experiments and results are given thereafter. Finally, the paper is concluded with final remarks and perspectives on future work.

2 Related Work

As a result of the tremendous efforts of the community in procuring, curating and labelling textual data, researchers have reported impressive results in many challenging tasks like text translation, text classification, text summarization, and many others. Usually, to solve the most challenging NLP tasks, complex

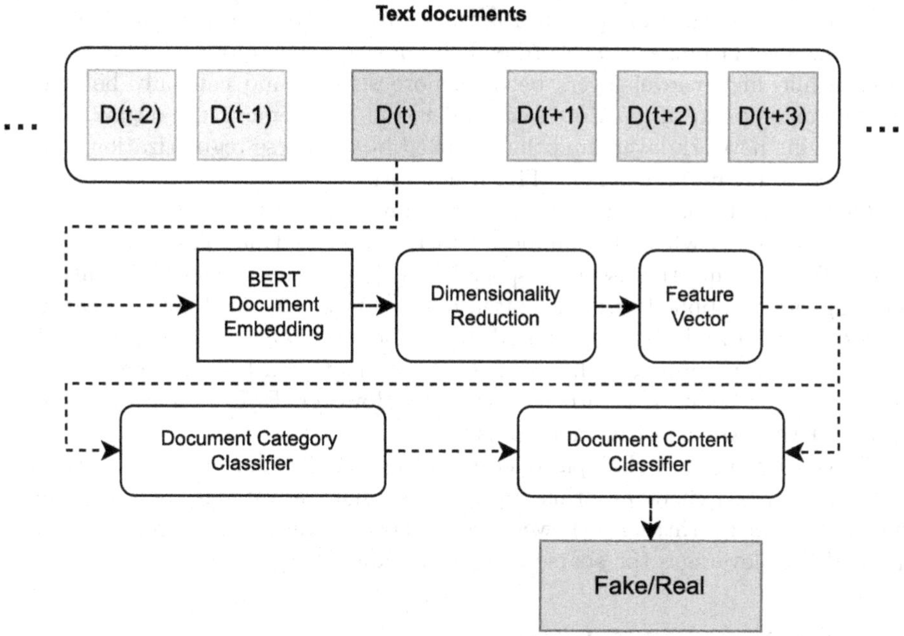

Text documents

Fig. 1. The architecture of the proposed solution.

models with enormous numbers of parameters are trained on vast amounts of labelled data. To circumvent the costly procedure of data labelling in domains that are similar, but different to the domain the enormous, complex models are trained on, transfer learning can be utilised. In the literature [20], there are several approaches to addressing transfer learning, namely: (i) Cross-lingual learning [14], (ii) Domain adaptation [17], and (iii) Multi-task learning [6].

The solution falling into the first category (Cross-lingual learning) MetaXL framework, which is a meta-learning approach that learns to convert representations from auxiliary languages to a target one and obtains their representation spaces nearer to each other, was proposed in [25].

On the other hand, in [12], a solution falling into the "domain adaptation" category is presented. In particular, the authors used the categorical information of both the source and the target domains to guide the pre-training process towards a more domain- and category invariant representation. According to the authors, this approach allows for closing the gap between the domains.

The third category of transfer learning (and the most popular one) is "Multi-task learning" (MTL). In this technique, a good generalization is achieved by learning to jointly solve related or similar problems. An interesting analysis has been performed in [5]. The authors have identified tasks that can always benefit others, as well as tasks that can always be harmed by others. They also noted that their MTL approach reveals the natural clustering of semantic and syntactic tasks. Since the emergence of MTL, researchers investigated various parameter transfer schemes. For example, in [15], the authors noted that for neural network NLP, low-level layers, such as word embeddings, are generally useful for all NLP tasks, while higher-level layers become more specific and can only be shared among more similar tasks. Moreover, Ruder et al. [21] demonstrated that sharing task-specific network layers and the so-called block-sparse regularization can be combined to create an efficient MTL framework.

One of the obvious drawbacks of MTL approaches is the difficulty to scale up. This is a problem when the number of tasks varies and samples arrive dynamically. To overcome this issue, a special case (an online version) of multi-task learning can be applied. It is also often referred to as so-called lifelong learning. In [22], Ruvolo and Eaton proposed an Efficient Lifelong Learning Algorithm (ELLA). In this approach, the parameter vector of each task is then modelled as a linear combination of latent basis tasks. However, ELLA achieves the scalability at the expense of memory consumption.

Driven by the fact that parameter sharing schemes have been successfully used by the researchers, and this approach has many advantages (e.g. it reduces the chances of overfitting [4]), we have proposed a model's parameter sharing method that leverages the sparse coding principles.

3   The Proposed Solution

The proposed framework assumes that in each iteration the training algorithm may receive a batch of labelled data for some task t (a new one or previously trained). Moreover, it is assumed that the number of tasks is not predefined and thus the algorithm must be flexible. This is roughly presented in Fig. 3.

The concept of a task appears in many formal definitions of machine learning models [16]. For example, when considering NLP-related problems, it is often difficult to distinguish when a particular task finishes and the subsequent one starts, i.e. the writer is informing about health-related matters, expressing a political claim, or presenting an opinion/fact. The proposed method defines the parameter transfer as a learning problem combined of supervised learning tasks, where each task $Z^{(t)} = \left(M^{(t)}, X^{(t)}, Y^{(t)} \right)$ is defined by training data $X^{(t)}$, training labels $Y^{(t)}$, and a prediction model $M^{(t)} : X^{(t)} \to Y^{(t)}$.

In the proposed schema, we can distinguish two key stages of operation, namely: (i) Prediction stage (see Fig. 2), where the feature vector is obtained, the model's parameter estimated (using a dictionary of parameters), and finally, the prediction label is returned; and (ii) the Training and Transfer stage (see Fig. 4), where parameters' dictionary is updated accordingly to the incoming training data.

3.1   Prediction Stage

The prediction stage consists of three steps. First, the document category is predicted using a dedicated Document Category Classifier. This is necessary to obtain sparse representation $h^{(t)}$. There is a direct linear mapping between t and

$h^{(t)}$. In the next step, we obtain parameters of Document Content Classifier (the final block of the logic diagram shown in Fig. 3) using sparse representation $h^{(t)}$ and the parameters dictionary D.

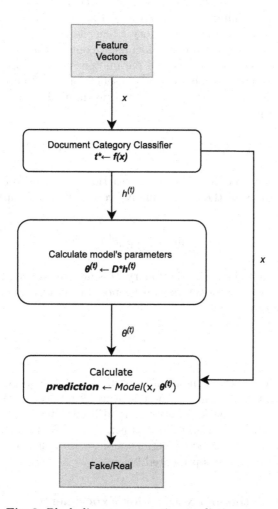

Fig. 2. Block diagram presenting prediction stage.

3.2 Training and Transfer Stage

The training and transfer follow the idea of lifelong learning proposed by Ruvolo and Eaton in [22]. In particular, we hypothesise that the parameters of the classification models can be approximated using a dictionary of task-invariant global parameters. However, in contrast to [22], we incorporated sparse coding together with stochastic gradient descent, instead of closed form solution proposed by Ruvolo and Eaton.

As it is shown in Fig. 4, there are several actions that happen at this stage. In the current implementation, we assume that for each training iteration we obtain a batch of labelled training data (X, Y) (e.g. text followed by real/fake annotation) together with documents category t (e.g. health, sport, politics, news). The labelled data is used to train the document content classification model for category t. Afterwards, we extract the parameters of the model (indicated as $\theta^{(t)}$ in Fig. 4) and calculate their sparse representation $h^{(t)}$. In order to find optimal sparse code vector $h^{(t)}$ (for a given $\theta^{(t)}$), we minimize the energy function $E_D(\theta^{(t)}, h^{(t)})$, which is given by Eq. 1.

$$E_D(\theta^{(t)}, h^{(t)}) = \frac{1}{2}\|\theta^{(t)} - Dh^{(t)}\|_2^2 + \lambda\|h^{(t)}\|_1 \tag{1}$$

The energy function combines the reconstruction error and an L_1 penalty to incentives the sparsity of the code. Finally, we update dictionary D according to the Eq. 2.

$$D^* = \arg\min_D \frac{1}{T}\sum_1^T \frac{1}{2}\|\theta^{(t)} - Dh^{(t)}\|_2^2 \tag{2}$$

It must be noted that the entire dictionary D is affected during the parameters update. This makes the parameters transfer possible and thus lets the classifiers benefit from each other.

4   Results

In this section, an overview of the results obtained with the proposed approach is given. To ensure reproducibility of the performed study the work utilised open, publicly available, benchmark datasets. The utilised datasets were leveraged in the completion of the NLP classification task, which was the aim of the experiments. The details of the used collections along with a succinct description of the premise of the datasets is presented below.

4.1   Data and Methodology Used for Experiments

In all the experiments, six different datasets related to the fake news detection problem were used. These are being referred to as tasks, according to the following numbering:

1. COVID-19 Fake News – The dataset contains the list of COVID Fake News or Claims. It is publicly available on Zenodo repository. The data set contains more than 9700 fake news samples and relatively few (~500) legitimate news items. The dataset was published to answer the popular demand of a compilation of fake news and false claims being popularised in the Internet [2]

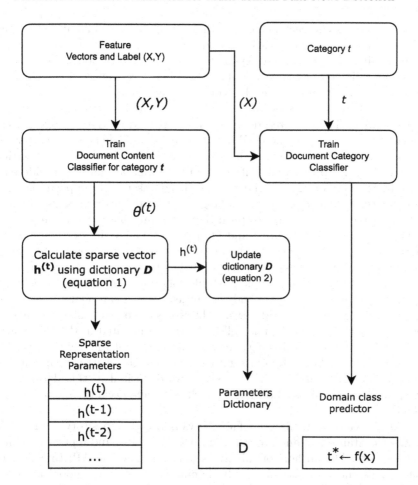

Fig. 3. Block diagram presenting single iteration of model training and parameters transfer procedure.

2. MM-Covid – A Multilingual and Multimodal Data Repository for Combating COVID-19 Disinformation. This dataset provides the multilingual fake news items and the relevant social context. The authors have collected ∼4000 documents representing fake news content and ∼7000 trustworthy pieces of information from English, Spanish, Portuguese, Hindi, French and Italian, and 6 different languages. In the case of the English language, there are more than 1200 fake and ∼4700 legitimate documents. The dataset was collected to oppose and fight hate speech and incorrect information that could affect physical health and mental well-being [13].
3. PubHealth – The dataset contains documents related to public health, including biomedical subjects (e.g. infectious diseases, stem cell research) and government healthcare policy (e.g. abortion, mental health, and women's health). Each instance in the dataset has an associated label (true, false, unproven,

mixture). Moreover, each instance in the dataset has an explanation text field. The explanation is a justification for which the claim has been assigned a particular label. The presented explanations are crafted by journalists and are based on reliable, publicly available and explicitly referenced documentation, which the authors refer to as the 'gold standard' [10].

4. Q-Prop – The corpus contains more than 50000 articles from more than 100 news sources. The collected documents are labelled by the authors as either "legitimate" or "propaganda". When developing and labelling the corpus, the authors have used the distant supervision technique. In that regard, articles are labelled as "propaganda" if the source (outlet/author) is considered as such by the human expert. The focus of this dataset is on propaganda detection, which is defined as the use of language that deliberately aims to impact either individuals or groups to push them in a pre-chosen direction [3].

5. ISOT – Information Security and Object Technology dataset contains two files: one with fake news and the other with real (true) news. The dataset contains a total of 44898 documents, 21417 of which are trustworthy documents and 23481 are fake items. Each file contains four columns: article title, text, article publication date and the subject, which can relate to one of six types of information (world-news, politics-news, government-news, middle-east, US news, left-news). The collection was formulated in the Information Security and Object Technology research laboratory at the University of Victoria in Canada. The datapoints gathered in this set are articles coming from the years of 2016 and 2017. The fake news deposited in this dataset were flagged as unreliable by Politifact, which is a fact-checking service based in the USA [1].

6. GRAFN – Getting Real about Fake News is Kaggle repository dataset. The dataset contains text and metadata from 244 websites and represents almost 13000 posts. The authors of this dataset used webhose.io API to collect the data. This entire dataset is mostly dominated by political information and news from around the world. The collection was formed directly to help data scientists push back against the viral spread of fake news. The fake news in this set were flagged as dubious ('bs') by a well-known tool named 'BS Detector' [18].

In order to compare various classification performance metrics (Accuracy, Balanced Accuracy, Recall, Precision, F1-score, G-mean) achieved by different algorithms, we have used the 5×2 Cross-validation technique. In that approach, standard 2-fold cross-validation is used and the results are averaged. Moreover, the standard deviation from the mean value is calculated to illustrate the volatility and the significance of differences.

4.2 Performance of Base Classifier on Separated Classification Tasks

In this section, we compare the BERT-based classifier on different datasets (tasks). Table 1 demonstrates various performance metrics. For each of the datasets separately, we incorporated 5×2 cross-validation and reported the results. To comply with the research standards in the classification field, the accuracy, precision and recall are reported. The harmonic mean of precision and recall known as the F1-score is also given. To counter the fact that accuracy is not considered a good metric for unbalanced data the balanced accuracy (BACC) and the geometric mean (G-Mean) are also presented. In general, the classifier achieves relatively good results and the balanced accuracy varies from 78% to 99%.

Table 1. Performance of BERT-based classifier evaluated on different datasets (tasks).

Task	Accuracy	BACC	F1	G-mean	Precision	Recall
1	97.0 ± 0.2	77.3 ± 1.3	96.7 ± 0.2	74.1 ± 1.8	96.7 ± 0.2	97.0 ± 0.2
2	92.2 ± 0.3	87.6 ± 0.8	91.9 ± 0.4	87.0 ± 0.9	92.2 ± 0.3	92.2 ± 0.3
3	80.2 ± 0.5	78.8 ± 0.5	80.2 ± 0.5	78.6 ± 0.5	80.2 ± 0.5	80.2 ± 0.5
4	93.1 ± 0.1	76.7 ± 0.4	92.6 ± 0.1	73.8 ± 0.6	92.5 ± 0.1	93.1 ± 0.1
5	99.2 ± 0.0	99.3 ± 0.0	99.2 ± 0.0	99.3 ± 0.0	99.2 ± 0.0	99.2 ± 0.0
6	88.9 ± 0.1	79.9 ± 0.2	88.5 ± 0.1	78.4 ± 0.2	88.4 ± 0.1	88.9 ± 0.1

4.3 Evaluation of Parameter Transfer Method

In this section, we compare methods in the multi-task classification scenario. The quantitative results have been presented in Table 2 and Fig. 4. Single Task Learning (STL) indicated the average performance of the classifier trained only on a single task. In other words, we train the model on one task and check how it generalises to other tasks. From the results shown in Table 2, it can be seen that the performance is significantly worse than the one expected from Table 1. Therefore, we cannot efficiently detect fake news if the texts come from a category other than the given classifier was trained on.

To overcome this limitation one may train the classifier on all the available data. This is indicated as "Multi-Task Learning (MTL)" both in Table 2 and Fig. 4. However, as the results show, this approach will not work for some of the tasks (e.g. tasks 1 and 3).

Finally, the results obtained with the proposed method have been presented in the last column of Table 2. It can be noticed that it allows us to achieve the best performance with respect to other methods. In most cases, the proposed approach significantly surpasses the MTL and STL approaches.

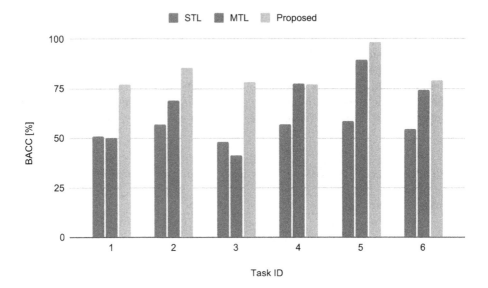

Fig. 4. Comparison of the average BACC for multitask learning scenarios.

Table 2. Multi-task performance (BACC reported).

Task	Single Task Learning	Multi Task Learning	Proposed Method
1	50.8 ± 13.78	50.1 ± 0.4	77.0 ± 1.0
2	56.9 ± 15.20	68.9 ± 0.4	85.5 ± 1.1
3	48.1 ± 14.90	41.3 ± 0.5	78.4 ± 1.1
4	57.0 ± 17.17	77.3 ± 0.2	76.9 ± 0.6
5	58.7 ± 23.76	89.4 ± 0.1	98.5 ± 0.2
6	54.7 ± 14.58	74.1 ± 0.1	78.9 ± 0.2

5   Conclusion

In this paper, we have proposed a framework for the model's parameter transfer in order to tackle the multi-domain fake news detection problem. The key observation coming from our experiments is that the BERT-based text classification methods work well when various datasets are considered (in this research, we have used 6 different datasets). As noted in the introduction and supported by the provided results the performance of BERT-based methods quickly deteriorates when the models are tested on samples coming from distributions, which differ from the ones the model has been trained on. The method presented in this paper works to overcome that predicament, leveraging those elements of classifier configuration that will allow for achieving significantly better global performance. The proposed method is tested on six different, publicly available, benchmark datasets, ensuring the reproducibility of the study. The technical details are provided, along with the architecture of the used approach. The performance of the method is measured with industry-standard metrics and validated using the 5×2 cross-validation approach. The performance metrics are compared across the six datasets and with regard to other approaches, namely single-task learning and multi-task learning. The study shows that the novel, proposed transfer learning method can considerably boost the performance of BERT-based fake news detectors on data coming from outside of the fine-tuning data distribution. The presented results are promising and open the space for further research.

Acknowledgement. This publication is co-financed by the National Center for Research and Development within INFOSTRATEG program, number of application for funding: INFOSTRATEG-I/0019/2021-00.

References

1. Ahmed, H., Traore, I., Saad, S.: Detecting opinion spams and fake news using text classification. Secur. Priv. **1**(1), e9 (2018). https://doi.org/10.1002/spy2.9. https://onlinelibrary.wiley.com/doi/abs/10.1002/spy2.9
2. Banik, S.: Covid fake news dataset [data set]. Zenodo, Online (2020). https://doi.org/10.5281/zenodo.428252
3. Barrón-Cedeño, A., Da San Martino, G., Jaradat, I., Nakov, P.: Proppy: organizing the news based on their propagandistic content. Inf. Process. Manag. **56**(5), 1849–1864 (2019). https://doi.org/10.1016/j.ipm.2019.03.005. http://www.sciencedirect.com/science/article/pii/S0306457318306058
4. Baxter, J.: A model of inductive bias learning. J. Artif. Intell. Res. **12**, 149–198 (2000)
5. Changpinyo, S., Hu, H., Sha, F.: Multi-task learning for sequence tagging: an empirical study. arXiv preprint arXiv:1808.04151 (2018)
6. Chen, S., Zhang, Y., Yang, Q.: Multi-task learning in natural language processing: an overview. CoRR abs/2109.09138 (2021). https://arxiv.org/abs/2109.09138
7. Deng, J., Dong, W., Socher, R., Li, L.J., Li, K., Fei-Fei, L.: Imagenet: a large-scale hierarchical image database. In: 2009 IEEE Conference on Computer Vision and Pattern Recognition, pp. 248–255. IEEE (2009)
8. Devlin, J., Chang, M.W., Lee, K., Toutanova, K.: Bert: pre-training of deep bidirectional transformers for language understanding (2018). https://doi.org/10.48550/ARXIV.1810.04805. https://arxiv.org/abs/1810.04805
9. Jung, I., Lim, J., Kim, H.K.: PF-TL: payload feature-based transfer learning for dealing with the lack of training data. Electronics **10**(10), 1148 (2021). https://doi.org/10.3390/electronics10101148. https://www.mdpi.com/2079-9292/10/10/1148
10. Kotonya, N., Toni, F.: Explainable automated fact-checking for public health claims. In: Proceedings of the 2020 Conference on Empirical Methods in Natural Language Processing (EMNLP), pp. 7740–7754. Association for Computational Linguistics, Online (2020). https://www.aclweb.org/anthology/2020.emnlp-main.623
11. Kula, S., Kozik, R., Choraś, M.: Implementation of the BERT-derived architectures to tackle disinformation challenges. Neural Comput. Appl. (2021). https://doi.org/10.1007/s00521-021-06276-0

12. Lekhtman, E., Ziser, Y., Reichart, R.: Dilbert: customized pre-training for domain adaptation with category shift, with an application to aspect extraction. In: Proceedings of the 2021 Conference on Empirical Methods in Natural Language Processing, pp. 219–230 (2021)
13. Li, Y., Jiang, B., Shu, K., Liu, H.: MM-COVID: a multilingual and multimodal data repository for combating COVID-19 disinformation (2020)
14. Lin, Y.H., et al.: Choosing transfer languages for cross-lingual learning. arXiv preprint arXiv:1905.12688 (2019)
15. Mou, L., et al.: How transferable are neural networks in NLP applications? arXiv preprint arXiv:1603.06111 (2016)
16. Pentina, A., Lampert, C.H.: Lifelong learning with non-IID tasks. In: Advances in Neural Information Processing Systems, pp. 1540–1548 (2015)
17. Ramponi, A., Plank, B.: Neural unsupervised domain adaptation in NLP - a survey. CoRR abs/2006.00632 (2020). https://arxiv.org/abs/2006.00632
18. Risdal, M.: Getting real about fake news. Kaggle, Online (2016). https://www.kaggle.com/mrisdal/fake-news
19. Rogers, A., Kovaleva, O., Rumshisky, A.: A primer in BERTology: what we know about how BERT works. Trans. Assoc. Comput. Linguist. **8**, 842–866 (2020). https://doi.org/10.1162/tacla00349. https://aclanthology.org/2020.tacl-1.54
20. Ruder, S.: Neural transfer learning for natural language processing. Ph.D. thesis, NUI Galway (2019)
21. Ruder, S., Bingel, J., Augenstein, I., Søgaard, A.: Sluice networks: learning what to share between loosely related tasks. arXiv preprint arXiv:1705.08142 (2017)
22. Ruvolo, P., Eaton, E.: Ella: an efficient lifelong learning algorithm. In: International Conference on Machine Learning, pp. 507–515 (2013)
23. Szczepański, M., Pawlicki, M., Kozik, R., Choraś, M.: New explainability method for BERT-based model in fake news detection. Sci. Rep. **11**(1), 23705 (2021). https://doi.org/10.1038/s41598-021-03100-6
24. Thrun, S., Pratt, L.: Learning to Learn. Springer, New York (2012). https://books.google.pl/books?id=X_jpBwAAQBAJ
25. Xia, M., Zheng, G., Mukherjee, S., Shokouhi, M., Neubig, G., Awadallah, A.H.: Metaxl: meta representation transformation for low-resource cross-lingual learning. arXiv preprint arXiv:2104.07908 (2021)
26. Yosinski, J., Clune, J., Bengio, Y., Lipson, H.: How transferable are features in deep neural networks? In: Advances in Neural Information Processing Systems, vol. 27 (2014)
27. Zhao, J., Shetty, S., Pan, J.W., Kamhoua, C., Kwiat, K.: Transfer learning for detecting unknown network attacks. EURASIP J. Inf. Secur. **2019**(1), 1 (2019). https://doi.org/10.1186/s13635-019-0084-4. https://jis-eurasipjournals.springeropen.com/articles/10.1186/s13635-019-0084-4

Security SFC Path Selection Using Deep Reinforcement Learning

Shuangxing Deng, Man Li[✉], Qi Guo, and Huachun Zhou

School of Electronic and Information Engineering, Beijing Jiaotong University,
Beijing 100044, China
{21120038,20111018,20120044,hchzhou}@bjtu.edu.cn

Abstract. Traffic flows can be forwarded through different security service functions based on SDN/NFV technology, which constitutes security service function chaining (SFC). However, the current deployed security service function chaining cannot be dynamically adjusted according to the state of the network environment, and cannot adapt to the rapidly changing security requirements. This paper proposes a security SFC path selection scheme based on deep reinforcement learning. The optimal path of security SFC is dynamically selected in real time using the DQN algorithm, according to the features of the traffic entering the SFC and the detection results of the security service functions. The security capability of the SFC is improved and the latency of the SFC is reduced under the optimal path. We design and implemented a prototype system of this scheme, conduct experiments with DDoS detection security function, and compare the proposed DQN algorithm with Q-learning algorithm. The results show that SFC path selection by DQN algorithm can effectively improve the average DDoS attack detection rate and reduce the latency.

Keywords: Security Service · Service Function Chaining · Deep Reinforcement Learning

1 Introduction

Currently, network operators use a large number of dedicated hardware to provide security functions, including deep packet inspection, firewalls and intrusion detection systems, etc. The dedicated equipment is expensive, and the network framework lacks flexibility, manageability and scalability. The paths between security function nodes are inflexible and lack dynamic adaptation to network changes [1].

Network Functions Virtualization (NFV) and Software Defined Network (SDN) technologies have changed the implementation of network security functions and provided a new development direction for solving the above challenges [2]. Based on SDN and NFV technology, security functions are virtualized on a general hardware platform, and different security functions are combined in sequence according to requirements, which constitutes a security service function chain [3].

I. You et al. (Eds.): MobiSec 2022, CCIS 1644, pp. 97–107, 2023.
https://doi.org/10.1007/978-981-99-4430-9_7

The current service function chain relies more on manual configuration. Traffic passes through the security service function in the preset path, and the path cannot be dynamically adjusted according to the change of traffic and the change of the state of the security function, resulting in that the function chain cannot meet the security requirements. This paper proposes a security SFC path selection scheme based on deep reinforcement learning, and uses different types of DDoS detection modules as security service functions for experimental verification. According to the traffic features and the detection results of each DDoS detection module, the DQN algorithm is used to dynamically select the path for the security SFC. The results show that this scheme improves the overall DDoS detection capability and reduces the SFC delay.

The rest of this paper is organized as follows: Sect. 2 presents related works about security service function chain, Sect. 3 explains our proposed system model, Sect. 4 provides experimental verification, and Sect. 5 concludes this paper.

2   Related Work

The network security service has the characteristics of changing security processing requirements, responding quickly according to the security situation, and rapidly deploying related network security services. SFC realizes the combination of security service functions according to security requirements, and achieves the purpose of security protection detection. The dynamic adjustment of the security SFC according to the system state can improve the security capability of the service function chain and avoid the waste of resources caused by unnecessary security functions.

Iffländer et al. [4] propose a framework for the reordering of security service function chaining. The SFC controller collects information to model the system state, uses this information to determine the security function order and dynamically adjusts the order. Li et al. [5] propose a mechanism based on Q-learning to capture the changes of network state and automatically select the security service function chaining, considering the security benefits, service quality, resource cost and the diversity of security service functions. Zolotukhin et al. [6] use reinforcement learning to solve the optimal security function chain problem, and they designed an intelligent defense system that mitigates threats by redirecting network traffic flows and reconfiguring virtual security devices according to the current network state. Feng et al. [7] propose a framework that integrates machine learning and virtualized SFC, and proposed an anomaly detection algorithm based on machine learning, which is used as a service strategy of SFC classifier to guide the classifier to conduct fast traffic classification and subsequent attack flow redirection. Li et al. [8] propose a security service chaining orchestration algorithm with delay awareness and reliability assurance. First, the Q-learning algorithm is used to achieve efficient security service chaining orchestration. Then, the physical nodes of virtual security functions are backed up according to the node importance of virtual security functions. Hantouti et al. [9] propose the deployment of the concept of partial symmetry in SFC for future 5G networks. And they propose an algorithm to dynamically calculate the reverse path for an SFC by including only service functions requiring symmetry. Partial symmetry reduce both the SFC delivery time and the load on VNFs.

The above research considers more about the creation of security SFC paths, and do not consider dynamic adjustment after path deployment, and cannot make decisions based on real-time network status and security service function status. In this paper, we dynamically select paths for security SFC based on traffic features and detection results of security service functions to improve the security capability of SFC.

3   System Model

In this section, we first introduce the overall framework of the security service function chain path selection based on deep reinforcement learning, and then describe how to make the path selection of the security SFC based on the DQN algorithm.

3.1   Framework

Figure 1 shows the overall framework of the system. The system includes an analyzer, a controller, a service function chain, and interfaces between the modules. The analyzer is the core module of the system and is responsible for receiving and saving feedback data from each security service function and the traffic features entering the service function chaining, and analyzing these data through a deep reinforcement learning model to select the best path for the service function chain. The best SFC path is converted into a corresponding high-level path policy and sent down to the controller.

The controller includes the security policy controller and the service function chain controller, which functions to connect the analyzer in the upper layer and the service function chaining in the lower layer. The system is implemented based on SDN technology, and the analyzer cannot directly realize the deployment of SFC path after deriving the best path. Firstly, the security policy controller needs to translate the high-level path policy from the analyzer to the low-level path policy, and the SFC controller configures the corresponding flow table for the forwarding module according to the low-level path policy to complete the actual deployment of the SFC path.

The service function chaining includes the forwarding module and all security service functions, which include intrusion detection system (IDS), firewall, and various types of DDoS attack detection modules. The whole system meets the security requirements through the service function chaining, and the traffic is forwarded between different security functions by the forwarding module, and each security function detects different aspects of the traffic. At the same time, the features of the traffic entering the service function chaining and the feedback results of each security service function are sent to the analyzer through the monitoring interface.

The system runs as follows: when the traffic entering the service function chain changes, the analyzer obtains the new traffic features and the feedback results of the security function through the monitoring interface in time to select the best path for the service function chain by deep reinforcement learning algorithm. After acquiring the new high-level path policy, the security policy controller and the service function chaining controller complete the actual deployment of the best SFC path by configuring the flow table. Our proposed system dynamically selects security SFC paths based on traffic features and detection results to combine security service functions more flexibly and improve the overall detection capability, as well as to avoid unnecessary security functions contained in the SFC paths.

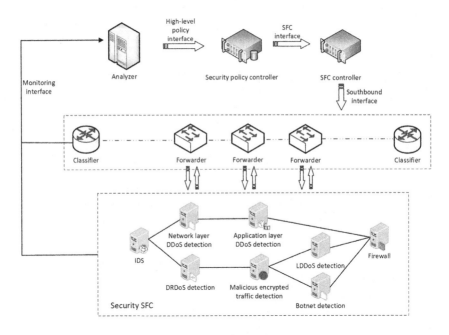

Fig. 1. Security SFC path selection framework

3.2 DQN Based Model

Deep reinforcement learning based algorithms can learn the state of the security SFC and make the corresponding decisions. The path selection process of the security SFC can be considered as Markov Decision Process (MDP), where the agent does not need an exact mathematical model, but only needs to perform actions based on the state and obtain a reward [10].

We use the DQN algorithm [11] to explore the optimal security SFC path under different traffic flows, and the optimal path is defined as the one with the highest overall detection capability and the lowest SFC latency under that path. The higher the detection capability, the higher the proportion of detected malicious traffic to the malicious traffic entering the security SFC, and the detection capability of a certain detection module is defined as shown in Eq. (1). The most important factor affecting the SFC latency is the number of security service functions in the SFC, and the number of security service functions is used in the model to indicate the latency.

$$C = \frac{1}{1 - \frac{T}{A}} \tag{1}$$

where A represents the number of real malicious traffic and T represents the number of detected malicious traffic.

The MDP tuple is shown as follows:

State: Different traffic correspond to different optimal SFC paths. To distinguish the traffic, we select 17 packet-level features of the flows and use them as the first 17 dimensions of the state. The traffic features are shown in Table 1. Statistical features are based on entropy, and also include packet rate, etc. These features can effectively distinguish different kinds of DDoS attack traffic. In the process of constructing security SFC paths, duplicate detection modules do not improve the overall detection capability and lead to an increase in latency. The last 15 dimensions of the state indicate the detection modules already contained in the current path by different values to avoid duplication of detection modules.

Actions: The action set contains all detection modules and exit classifiers. The agent takes one action, which means that the corresponding module is added to the end of the path. If the module selected by the agent is an exit classifier, it means that the security SFC path construction is completed.

Reward: Our proposed system is to select the best path for SFC with the highest overall detection capability and the shortest latency. The reward needs to represent a combination of detection capability and latency, and we use the ratio of the detection capability of the corresponding detection module of the action to the length of the SFC path as the reward. Duplicate detection modules in a security SFC path will not improve the overall detection capability and will result in increased latency due to additional detection. To avoid duplicate detection modules contained in the SFC path, after the agent takes an action, the environment checks if the detection module is already present in the path. If it is present, a negative reward is given. The reward function is defined as shown in Eq. (2).

$$r_s = \begin{cases} \frac{C}{L}, & a\ not\ in\ path \\ -150, & a\ in\ path \end{cases} \tag{2}$$

where C is the detection capability shown in Eq. (1) and L represents the length of the constructed SFC path, i.e., the number of detection modules included in the constructed SFC path.

Table 1. Traffic features

Feature	Description
Packets rate	Number of packets forwarded per second
Bytes rate	Number of bytes forwarded per second
Packet size	Average packet size
Package number variance	Variance of the number of packets per unit time interval
H(TTL)	Entropy of packet survival time TTL
H(TCP Sport)	Entropy of TCP packet source port
H(TCP Dport)	Entropy of TCP packet destination port
H(UDP Sport)	Entropy of the source port of UDP packets
H(UDP Dport)	Entropy of the UDP packet destination port
H(Packet Size)	Entropy of packet size
H(Sip|Dip)	Conditional Entropy of source ip given destination ip
H(Sip|Dport)	Conditional Entropy of source ip given destination port
H(Dport|Dip)	Conditional Entropy of destination port given destination ip
H(Sip)	Entropy of the source IP address
H(Dip)	Entropy of the destination IP address
H(ΔSip)	Entropy of the source IP change in the current time window compared to the previous time window
H(ΔDip)	Entropy of the change in destination IP in the current time window compared to the previous time window

For deep reinforcement learning training, hundreds of rounds of training can be performed in 1s of time. However, the time required to reselect paths for security SFC in a real environment is about 2s. If an agent is used to interact with the real environment, it will lead to hundreds of times increase in training time and there are risks such as system failures that affect training. Therefore, we use an offline approach to train the DQN path selection model. And the model is saved and used for online SFC path selection after the training is completed. Algorithm 1 describes the offline training process of path selection using the DQN algorithm. The process of one round of path selection is as follows. First, a traffic feature is randomly selected and dimensions are added to it to complete the initialization of the state. The evaluation network outputs the action according to the current state s. The environment calculates the reward of the action and modifies the last 15 dimensions of the state s to get the next state s'. The next step updates the evaluation network and keeps cycling until the action is the exit classifier to complete this path selection.

4   Performance Evaluation

We built the system environment shown in Fig. 1 on a server using the VMware vSphere platform. The server CPU model is Intel(R) Xeon(R) CPU E5-2609 v4,

---

Algorithm 1. DQN offline training

Input: Traffic feature set $F = \{f_1, f_2, \ldots, f_n\}$, detection results of each detection module corresponding to the traffic features $D = \{[d_1^1, d_1^2, d_1^3, d_1^4, d_1^5], \ldots, [d_n^1, d_n^2, d_n^3, d_n^4, d_n^5]\}$, initialize the evaluation network $Q(\theta)$, initialize the target network $Q(\theta') = Q(\theta)$, initialize replay memory M

Output: The trained neural network model

1: **for** $episode = 1, \ldots, N$ **do**
2:　　Initialize the path length counter $counter = 0$
3:　　Initialize $done = False$
4:　　Randomly select set of traffic feature f, initialize state $s = [f, 0, \ldots, 0]$
5:　　**while** $done = False$ **do**
6:　　　　$counter = counter + 1$
7:　　　　For the current state s, randomly chose an action with probability ϵ or choose the action a according to the output of the neural network
8:　　　　Modify the last 15 dimensions of the state $s = s'$ according to the action a
9:　　　　Calculate the reward r according to Equation (2)
10:　　　　Store transition (s, a, r, s') in M, and sample random minibatch from M
11:　　　　Update the evaluation network $Q(\theta)$
12:　　　　Copy the parameters of the evaluation network $Q(\theta)$ to the target network $Q(\theta')$ each K episode
13:　　　　**if** $a = exit\ classifier$ **then**
14:　　　　　　$done = True$
15:　　　　**end if**
16:　　**end while**
17: **end for**

---

the virtual machine is running Ubuntu 15.04 system. We use OpenDaylight as the function chain manager, Open vSwitch to implement the forwarder and classifier functions, and Docker containers to virtualize each security service function, with security functions deployed decentralized on server nodes. In our experimental environment, we use five modules including distributed reflection denial of service (DRDoS) detection, network layer DDoS detection, botnet detection, low-rate DDoS (LDDoS) detection, and application layer DDoS detection [12] as security service functions. Each detection module can detect all types of DDoS attacks, but with different detection capabilities. And each module has the highest detection rate when it detects DDoS attacks corresponding to its name compared to other types of DDoS attacks. For convenience, we use DRDoS, Network, Botnet, LDDoS and Application to represent these five DDoS attack detection modules in the path.

We conduct experiments using two types of DDoS attack traffic, DRDoS and LDDoS. For DRDoS, we use one attack host and two servers. The attacker use the Scapy library to send fake requests to the two servers to generate DRDoS attack traffic, including Memcached, TFTP, Chargen, NTP, SNMP, and SSDP. For LDDoS, we use eight hosts, including two routers, four attack hosts, and two web servers. The attack hosts use Slow HTTPTest to send LDDoS attacks to the web server. The LDDoS attacks include slow headers, slow body, shrew, and slow read.

We first collect the attack traffic features and the corresponding detection results of each module to train the DQN model offline. A security SFC path path1 = {Network, DRDoS, LDDoS, Botnet} is preset in the prototype system, and then we let DRDoS attack traffic and LDDoS attack traffic enter the security SFC separately, and use the trained DQN model under the preset path to select the corresponding best path according to the traffic features, and by delivery flow table to modify the actual security SFC path, the paths chosen by the DQN algorithm under DRDoS attack traffic and LDDoS attack traffic are path2 = {Application}, path3 = {Application, LDDoS, Botnet} respectively. To evaluate the performance of the proposed DQN model, we also used the Q-learning algorithm for path selection. The paths selected by the Q-learning algorithm under DRDoS attack traffic and LDDoS attack traffic are path4 = {Application, Network, DRDoS} and path5 = {Application, LDDoS, Botnet, DRDoS}, respectively.

To describe the overall security capability of the security SFC, we define the average DDoS attack detection rate shown in Eq. (3) ,which calculates the average of DDoS attack detection rates of all detection modules under the security SFC path.

$$D_{mean} = \frac{\sum_{i=1}^{n} D_i}{n} \tag{3}$$

where n is the number of DDoS detection modules in the security SFC, D_i is the DDoS attack detection rate of the corresponding detection module, i.e., the ratio of the number of detected DDoS attack traffic to the number of real DDoS attack traffic.

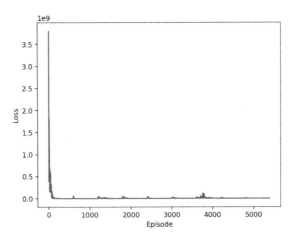

Fig. 2. DQN offline training loss values

Figure 2 shows the change of the loss value of the DQN neural network during the offline training process. It can be seen that the loss value decreases rapidly as the number of training rounds grows. During the learning process, if the reinforcement learning agent randomly selects to parts that were incompletely explored before, it will lead to an increase of the loss value. It leads to fluctuations in the loss value in subsequent training.

Figure 3 shows the variation of the weighted reward value with rounds during the offline training process. Because a negative reward is used to avoid duplicate detection modules in the paths, paths containing duplicate modules are constructed during the exploration process at the beginning of the training, so the weighted reward is mostly negative in the early stage, and the reward tends to stabilize after about 2500 rounds of training. The reward value stabilizes at a high value indicating that the trained DQN model can select the SFC path with the highest overall detection capability and lowest latency for any type of DDoS attack traffic.

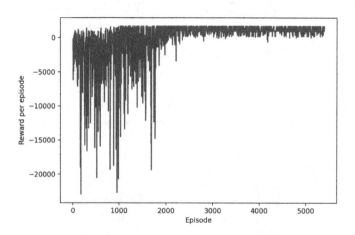

Fig. 3. DQN offline training loss values

Figure 4 shows the latency of different paths of the security service function chain under DRDoS attack traffic and LDDoS attack traffic. Under DRDoS attack traffic, the path latency selected by the DQN model decreases by 40% and 27.9% compared to the defualt path and the path selected by Q-learning, respectively. Under LDDoS attack traffic, the path latency selected by the DQN model decreases by 47% and 13.8% compared to the defualt path and the path selected by Q-learning, respectively.

Figure 5 shows the average DDoS attack detection rate for different paths of the security SFC under DRDoS attack traffic and LDDoS attack traffic. Under DRDoS attack traffic, the average DDoS attack detection rate for the path selected by the DQN model increases by 37% and 9% compared to the default path and the path selected by Q-learning, respectively. Under LDDoS attack traffic, the average DDoS attack detection rate for the path selected by the DQN model increases by 48% and 21% compared to the default path and the path selected by Q-learning, respectively.

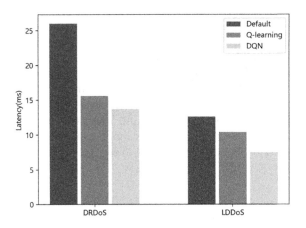

Fig. 4. Security SFC path latency

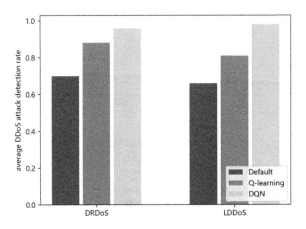

Fig. 5. Average DDoS attack detection rate for different security SFC paths

5   Conclusion and Future Work

In this paper, we present a deep reinforcement learning-based path selection framework for security SFC. The most critical module in this framework is the analyzer, which acquires the features of traffic entering the security SFC and the detection results of each security service function in real time, and selects the best security SFC path based on the trained DQN model. And the actual path of SFC is modified by the controller. We conducted experiments with DDoS detection as a security function, and the results show that the scheme is effective in improving the average DDoS attack detection rate and reducing the latency of the security SFC. In the future, we plan to use deep reinforcement learning models to select paths that contain forks for security SFCs, further improving the flexibility of the combination of security service functions and increasing the security capability of SFC.

Acknowledgments. This paper is supported by National Key R&D Program of China under Grant No. 2018YFA0701604.

References

1. Zhang, J., Wang, Z., Ma, N., Huang, T., Liu, Y.: Enabling efficient service function chaining by integrating NFV and SDN: architecture, challenges and opportunities. IEEE Network **32**(6), 152–159 (2018)
2. Duan, Q., Ansari, N., Toy, M.: Software-defined network virtualization: an architectural framework for integrating SDN and NFV for service provisioning in future networks. IEEE Network **30**(5), 10–16 (2016)
3. Adoga, H.U., Pezaros, D.P.: Network function virtualization and service function chaining frameworks: a comprehensive review of requirements, objectives, implementations, and open research challenges. Future Internet **14**(2), 59 (2022)
4. Iffländer, L., Beierlieb, L., Fella, N., Kounev, S., Rawtani, N., Lange, K.D.: Implementing attack-aware security function chain reordering. In: 2020 IEEE International Conference on Autonomic Computing and Self-Organizing Systems Companion (ACSOS-C), pp. 194–199. IEEE (2020)
5. Li, G., Zhou, H., Feng, B., Li, G., Yu, S.: Automatic selection of security service function chaining using reinforcement learning. In: 2018 IEEE Globecom Workshops (GC Wkshps), pp. 1–6. IEEE (2018)
6. Zolotukhin, M., Kotilainen, P., Hämäläinen, T.: Intelligent IDS chaining for network attack mitigation in SDN. In: 2021 17th International Conference on Mobility, Sensing and Networking (MSN), pp. 786–791. IEEE (2021)
7. Feng, B., Zhou, H., Li, G., Zhang, Y., Sood, K., Yu, S.: Enabling machine learning with service function chaining for security enhancement at 5G edges. IEEE Network **35**(5), 196–201 (2021)
8. Li, W., et al.: Reliability assurance dynamic SSC placement using reinforcement learning. Information **13**(2), 53 (2022)
9. Hantouti, H., Benamar, N., Bagaa, M., Taleb, T.: Symmetry-aware SFC framework for 5G networks. IEEE Network **35**(5), 234–241 (2021)
10. Sutton, R.S., Barto, A.G.: Reinforcement Learning: An Introduction. MIT Press, Cambridge (2018)
11. Van Hasselt, H., Guez, A., Silver, D.: Deep reinforcement learning with double Q-learning. In: Proceedings of the AAAI Conference on Artificial Intelligence, vol. 30 (2016)
12. Li, M., Zhou, H., Qin, Y.: Two-stage intelligent model for detecting malicious DDoS behavior. Sensors **22**(7), 2532 (2022)

Data Sub-sampling Method for Developing Personalized Human Activity Model Based on Incremental Learning

Jeongbin Lee[(✉)], Jaewoong Kang, and Mye Sohn ⓘ

Department of Industrial Engineering, Sungkyunkwan University, Suwon, South Korea
{jim2091,kjw1727,myesohn}@skku.edu

Abstract. This paper proposes a method to conduct data sub-sampling for developing personalized human activity recognition (HAR) model based on incremental learning. The quality of training dataset required to execute incremental learning is a critical factor affecting its performance. To generate a high-quality training dataset, this paper performs two-phase sub-sampling. The first phase discriminates the activity data into the borderline data with a high risk of mislabeling and the non-borderline data with a low risk of mislabeling. To do so, entropy-based distances between the decision boundaries and the activity data are calculated. The second phase separates the correctly labeled borderline data from the entire borderline data. This paper generates the KDE-based probability density function to discover the correctly labeled borderline data and performs binary clustering. Finally, incremental learning is performed to obtain the personalized HAR model using the non-borderline and correctly labeled borderline data. To show the superiority of the proposed method, we conduct experiments on two benchmark datasets named the HAPT and WISDM datasets.

Keywords: Personalized Human Activity Recognition · Incremental Learning · Data Selection

1 Introduction

The advent of incremental learning, which can continuously learn knowledge from new data while retaining most of the previously learned knowledge [1], has made it possible to personalize existing HAR (Human Activity Recognition) models developed without considering the behavioral characteristics of individual users [2]. At this time, personalization of the HAR models using incremental learning means that the decision boundaries or weights of already trained HAR models are shifted or revised appropriately by further utilizing the activity data of specific individuals. However, not all activity data of individuals positively influences the shift of the decision boundary, which is key to personalized HAR models. Furthermore, the influence of the data affecting the shift of the decision boundaries may also not be uniform. Therefore, training datasets for incremental learning must be carefully constructed to enhance the performance of personalized HAR models.

I. You et al. (Eds.): MobiSec 2022, CCIS 1644, pp. 108–121, 2023.
https://doi.org/10.1007/978-981-99-4430-9_8

Data classified by applying an arbitrary classification model can be divided into the following. Although it is ambiguous to be far and near the boundaries, one is data close to the decision boundaries (hereafter, borderline data). They may have been misclassified and consequently are at high risk of mislabeling. The other is data far from the decision boundaries (hereafter, non-borderline data). They have a relatively low risk of misclassification and a low risk of mislabeling. To guarantee the performance of incremental learning, it is required to generate training dataset excluding borderline data as much as possible.

To do so, this paper proposes a method of sub-sampling a training dataset for incremental learning consisting of only good data. The proposed sub-sampling method is conducted in two phases. In the first phase, this paper selects the non-borderline data from the individual activity data. To do so, this paper devises the entropy-based distance metric for calculating between the decision boundaries and the activity data. At this time, not all borderline data negatively affect the shift of the decision boundaries required to get the personalized HAR model. Therefore, it is necessary to identify data that can positively influence the shift of the decision boundaries among the boundary data. To do so, this paper uses Kernel Density Estimation (KDE) and binary clustering to perform refinement on the borderline data. Finally, this paper performs incremental learning on the HAR model using the training data set augmented with refined the borderline data.

This paper is organized as follow. The related works are summarized in Sect. 2. Section 3 offers the overall framework and detailed descriptions of the components. In Sect. 4, the superiority of the proposed framework is proven by experimentation. Finally, Sect. 5 presents the conclusions and further research.

2 Related Works

Incremental learning, which can continuously learn new knowledge from new sample data and maintain the most previously known knowledge, is spotlighted [3]. Recently, research on performing HAR using incremental learning has emerged. The purpose of incremental learning for HAR is to develop a personalized HAR model [4]. At this time, the personalization methods based on incremental learning are classified into the model- and data-based research. The former attempts to personalize the HAR model by adding decision boundaries that can discriminate new activities [5]. In other words, the HAR model is changed by adding decision boundaries for the new activities. The latter attempts to personalize by shifting the decision boundaries of the HAR model using only core data after evaluating the value of new data [6]. At this time, the data is evaluated by human knowledge or by the relationships between the data. The ActiveHAR is representative method for evaluating data using human knowledge [7]. In ActiveHAR, the system asks the users to determine the importance of the data through a Q&A. However, this method carries the risk of introducing individual bias in evaluating the data and is labor-intensive. On the other hand, the method using the relationships between data is first performed clustering on the new data [8]. It assigns different importance to the centroid data and around the centroid data. By doing this, the degree of shift of the decision boundaries for the personalization of HAR can be determined. Still, there is a limitation in that the direction of shift of the decision boundaries cannot be determined. To overcome the limitations, this paper proposes a new method for evaluating the importance of data without human intervention. Incremental learning for developing personalized HAR is performed using important data.

3 Overall Framework

As mentioned above, it is essential to construct an appropriate training dataset to generate a personalized HAR model through incremental learning. To do so, this paper proposes a sub-sampling framework to construct the training datasets for incremental learning. As depicted in Fig. 1, a pre-trained HAR model is required to create the personalized HAR model through incremental learning. However, as the development of the pre-trained model is out of the scope of the paper, this paper assumes that a suitable pre-trained model has already been developed. Prior to a detailed description of each step, the variables to be used throughout this paper are defined as follows.

$\mathbb{X}_i$: i^{th} activity data of the specific user

$F(\cdot)$: arbitrary pre-trained HAR model, $F(\mathbb{X}_i) = \{p_{i1}, \ldots, p_{ic}, \ldots, p_{iM}\}$ where $i > 1$, $c = 1, \ldots, M$, and $0 \leq p_{ic} \leq 1$,

p_{ic}: the probability that $\mathbb{X}_i$ is classified as activity c

θ_c: a misclassification threshold of activity c

The proposed sub-sampling framework comprises two modules, as depicted in Fig. 1.

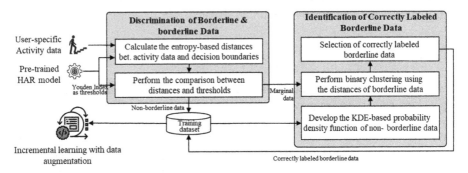

Fig. 1. Data sub-sampling framework for incremental learning

3.1 Sub-sampling of Non-borderline Data

Using the pre-trained HAR model, the human activities are classified. At this time, to perform the personalization of the HAR model, it is important to quality of data. To identify high-quality data, classification is performed using user activity data, and sub-sampling is performed using the classification results. For instance, when there are two activities to classify, data that has a positive effect on incremental learning is non-borderline data, while borderline data can have a negative effect (Fig. 2).

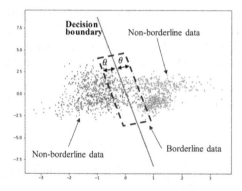

Fig. 2. Type of training data for incremental learning

To generate the training dataset for incremental learning, it first separates the non-boarder line data from the activity data. Given the set of decision boundaries of the pre-trained HAR model, it calculates the distances between the decision boundaries and activity data. At this time, the classification result of the activity data is M-dimensional vector $F(\mathbb{X}_i)$. The distances are calculated using entropy, which varies depending on the deviation of the probability value $(p_{i1}, \ldots, p_{ic}, \ldots, p_{iM})$. For $\mathbb{X}_i$, the smaller (larger) the deviation of $(p_{i1}, \ldots, p_{ic}, \ldots, p_{iM})$, , the larger (smaller) entropy value $E_{\mathbb{X}_i}$. In this light, $\mathbb{X}_i$, which has larger entropy, is likely to be the borderline data, and vice versa. $E_{\mathbb{X}_i}$ is calculated as follows.

$$E_{\mathbb{X}_i} = -\sum_{c=1}^{M} (p_{ic}log(p_{ic})) - \min_{c}(p_{ic}log(p_{ic})) \text{for} \forall i \tag{1}$$

Unlike conventional entropy, $E_{\mathbb{X}_i}$ has a correction term named $\min_{c}(p_{ic}log(p_{ic}))$. It is a device that amplifies the entropy difference between data to facilitate comparison. Since the entropy and distance are inversely related, the distance $(d_{\mathbb{X}_i})$ between $\mathbb{X}_i$ and the decision boundaries is simple calculated as follows.

$$d_{\mathbb{X}_i} = {}^{1}/_{E_{\mathbb{X}_i}} \text{for} \forall \mathbb{X}_i \tag{2}$$

Using $d_{\mathbb{X}_i}$, this paper separates the non-borderline data from the activity data. To so do, thresholds are required to determine whether activity data is the non-borderline or not. As the thresholds for discriminating the non-boundary data, this paper uses the Youden Index (J), which minimizes the misclassification performance in the ROC curve of the HAR model [9]. For all pairs of c and c', we perform the pairwise comparison with p_{ic} and $p_{ic'}$ θ_c and $\theta_{c'}$ $(c, c' \in M)$.

- For all pairs of classes, if there is one class c with $p_{ic} \geq \theta_c$ and the other classes c' is $p_{i_{ic'}} < \theta_{c'}$, then $\mathbb{X}_i$ is classified as class c and assigned to the non-borderline data.
- For all pairs of classes, if there is any combination of $p_{ic} \geq \theta_c$ and $p_{ic'} \geq \theta_{c'}$, then $\mathbb{X}_i$ is assigned to borderline data because it can be misclassified.
- If there is $p_{ic} < \theta_c$, $p_{ic'} \geq \theta_{c'}$ and $p_{ic} > p_{ic'}$, then $\mathbb{X}_i$ may be misclassified into c' although its prediction probability is smaller than the activity c. To resolve the

problem, this paper generates virtual data $\mathbb{X}_v$ with thresholds for each activity as probability values $(F(\mathbb{X}_v) = \{\theta_1, \ldots, \theta_c, \ldots, \theta_M\})$. Finally, this paper compares the distances between $\mathbb{X}_i$ and $\mathbb{X}_v$. If $d_{\mathbb{X}_i}$ is greater than or equal to $d_{\mathbb{X}_v}$, then $\mathbb{X}_i$ is assigned to the non-borderline data. Otherwise, it is assigned to the borderline data.

Finally, using Eqs. (1) and (2), the non-borderline data is identified, and its complement is taken as the borderline data. The activity data $(\mathbb{X})$ is represented as follows.

$$\mathbb{X} = \mathbb{X}^b \cup \mathbb{X}^{nb} \tag{3}$$

where $\mathbb{X}^b$ is a set of the borderline data. $\mathbb{X}^{nb}$ is a set of the non-borderline data and is classified into one of the activities.

3.2 Identification of Correctly Labeled Borderline Data

As mentioned, since not all $\mathbb{X}^b$ negatively affect the decision boundary shifts required for the personalization of the HAR model, $\mathbb{X}^b$ must be differentiated from correctly labeled borderline data $(\mathbb{X}^{cb})$ and other data $(\mathbb{X}^{cb^c})$ to obtain high-performance personalized HAR model. The process of separating $\mathbb{X}^b$ into $\mathbb{X}^{cb}$ and $\mathbb{X}^{cb^c}$ is as follows.

- Generation of the distributions using the non-borderline data by activity ($\mathbb{X}_{a_c}^{nb}$, where $\mathbb{X}^{nb} \equiv \mathbb{X}_{a_1}^{nb} \cup \ldots \cup \mathbb{X}_{a_c}^{nb} \cup \ldots \cup \mathbb{X}_{a_M}^{nb}$): It is impossible to check whether $\mathbb{X}^b$ is $\mathbb{X}^{cb}$ or not, only with $\mathbb{X}^b$. Therefore, we first generate the probability distribution of $\mathbb{X}_{a_c}^{nb}$ that implies the user's c^{th} activity pattern (for $\forall c$). Since the distribution of $\mathbb{X}_{a_c}^{nb}$ cannot be known in advance, Kernel Density Estimation (KDE), which can predict the distribution non-parametrically, is used. The KDE-based probability density function $(\widehat{f_h}(\mathbb{X}_{a_c}^{nb}))$ is derived as follows.

$$\widehat{f_h}\left(\mathbb{X}_{a_c}^{nb}\right) = \frac{1}{N_c} \sum_{i=1}^{N_c} K_h\left(\mathbb{X}_{a_c}^{nb} - E\left(\mathbb{X}_{a_c}^{nb}\right)\right) \text{for} \forall c \tag{4}$$

where K_h is the non-negative kernal function, h is a smoothing parameter, and N_c is the number of cth activity data.

- Perform binary clustering on the activity c's borderline data $(\mathbb{X}_{a_c}^b)$ using $\widehat{f_h}(\mathbb{X}_{a_c}^{nb})$: This paper performs binary clustering to separate only correctly labeled data from borderline data. However, of all the borderline data, the number of borderline data likely to be correctly labeled as activity c is relatively small. In other words, a data imbalance may occur between correctly labeled data and others. To solve the data imbalance, this paper amplifies the borderline data as much as the number of the non-borderline data using $\widehat{f_h}(\mathbb{X}_{a_c}^{nb})$. This paper performs the binary clustering using the amplified borderline data. Using the results of binary clustering, the distribution of borderline data contained in each cluster is generated. Then, each distribution is compared with $\widehat{f_h}(\mathbb{X}_{a_c}^{nb})$. Finally, we take the data of a cluster with distributions more similar to $\widehat{f_h}(\mathbb{X}_{a_c}^{nb})$ as elements of $\mathbb{X}^{cb^c}$. Repeat this process for all activities.

Using $\mathbb{X}^{nb}$ and $\mathbb{X}^{cb^c}$, this paper performs incremental learning o obtain the personalized HAR model.

4 Performance Evaluation

4.1 Experimental Setup

Dataset. This paper demonstrates the superiority of the proposed sub-sampling method using the HAPT dataset [10] and the WISDM dataset [11] as benchmark datasets. The HAPT dataset is a dataset in which three daily actions collected through the inertial sensor built into smartphones and partial actions occurring between them are divided into units of 2.56 s. The WISDM dataset is a dataset that collects six daily actions through sensors built into smartphones. The WISDM dataset has been feature engineering using hand-crafted features. The characteristics of two datasets is summarized in Table 1.

Table 1. Summary of HAPT and WISDM datasets

Dataset	#Instance	#Activity	#Feature	#User	#Data
HAPT	15,534	12	561	30	
Walking					2452
Walking upstairs					2146
Walking downstairs					1974
Sitting					2586
Standing					2846
Laying					2826
Stand to sit					94
Sit to stand					46
Sit to lie					150
Lie to sit					120
Stand to lie					180
Lie to stand					114
WISDM	5,424	6	46	36	
Walking					2082
Jogging					1626
Upstairs					633
Downstairs					529
Sitting					307
Standing					247

To guarantee the generalized learning performance of the HAR model, in this paper, preprocessing was performed as follows. For the HAPT dataset, this paper deleted activity data that occurred in small amounts. In addition, for the WISDM dataset, instead of performing direct preprocessing, the data obtained by processing data samples divided into 10-s units into one feature value was used. Prior to the experiments, the two datasets were partitioned into two kinds of datasets: the training dataset (70%) and dataset for the personalized model (30%). In addition, to analyze the patterns of the two datasets, t-SNE, which maps high-dimensional data to a low-dimensional discriminable space, was applied and visualized in two dimensions as depicted in Fig. 3 and Fig. 4.

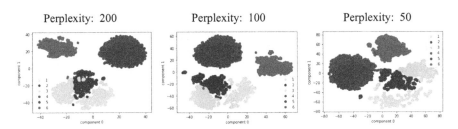

Fig. 3. t-SNE visualization results for the HAPT dataset

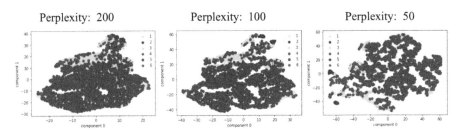

Fig. 4. t-SNE visualization results for the WISDM dataset

In general, the performance of a classifier is strongly influenced by patterns in the data. As shown in Fig. 3, the patterns in the HAPT dataset are spherical and show relatively well-discriminated distributions by activity. Therefore, a classifier sensitive to the density of the sample, like an SVM utilizing a Gaussian kernel may to show good performance. In addition, it is expected that the proposed method can be effectively applied to overlapping activities such as 4 and 5. On the other hand, since the WISDM dataset has too many overlapping samples, it is difficult to classify the activities with general classifiers. In particular, methods for finding an optimal hyperplane according to class discrimination power, such as SVM, is likely to fail in convergence. In summary, the HAPT dataset with simple patterns shows excellent performance no matter which classification model is used. In contrast, the WISDM dataset with class overlapping across the entire domain is a hard case for most classifiers, including the proposed method, to classify.

4.2 Evaluations

This paper performed three experiments to prove the superiority of the proposed method.

Experiment 1. This is an experiment to show the effect of separating $\mathbb{X}_i^{cb}$ from $\mathbb{X}_i^b$. To do so, this paper compared predictive performance of SVM, KNN, and random forest, which are the most widely used classification methods in HAR, as baselines. The pre-trained model for the proposed method is selected using the results of the t-SNE as follows. As the pre-trained model, the HAPT dataset selected SVM and the WISDM dataset selected RF. The experimental results are summarized in Table 2 (precision), Table 3 (recall), Table 4 (F1 Score), and Table 5 (accuracy).

Table 2. Comparison results of precision

Datasets		Baseline models			Personalized HAR ($\mathbb{X}_i^{nb}$ only)	Personalized HAR $\left(\mathbb{X}_i^{nb} \& \mathbb{X}_i^{cb}\right)$
		SVM	*KNN*	*RF*		
HAPT	Walking	0.9757	0.9163	0.9319	0.9802	**0.9805**
	Walking upstairs	0.9173	0.8947	0.8674	0.9279	**0.9316**
	Walking downstairs	**0.9614**	0.8900	0.9191	0.9564	0.9605
	Sitting	0.9177	0.8535	0.8544	**0.9288**	0.9157
	Standing	0.9181	0.8511	0.9051	0.9171	**0.9238**
	Laying	**0.9981**	0.9972	0.9908	0.9958	0.9956
WISDM	Walking	0.0000	0.1324	0.3855	0.5543	**0.5917**
	Jogging	0.6212	0.5857	0.9036	**0.9552**	0.9541
	Upstairs	0.3870	0.5445	0.6941	0.9476	**0.9700**
	Downstairs	0.5839	0.5295	0.6904	0.9654	**0.9699**
	Sitting	0.6500	0.1588	0.4120	0.6539	**0.6842**
	Standing	0.5576	0.5702	0.8036	0.8597	**0.8791**

Table 3. Comparison results of recall

Datasets		Baseline models			Personalized HAR ($\mathbb{X}_i^{nb}$ only)	Personalized HAR $\left(\mathbb{X}_i^{nb} \, \& \, \mathbb{X}_i^{cb}\right)$
		SVM	KNN	RF		
HAPT	Walking	**0.9513**	0.9288	0.9073	0.9433	0.9466
	Walking upstairs	0.9581	0.9127	0.9019	0.9579	**0.9596**
	Walking downstairs	0.9391	0.8545	0.9057	0.9558	**0.9620**
	Sitting	0.9049	0.8174	0.8965	0.8979	**0.9083**
	Standing	0.9255	0.8725	0.8570	**0.9332**	0.9249
	Laying	**1.0000**	0.9975	0.9952	**1.0000**	**1.0000**
WISDM	Walking	0.0000	0.2005	0.4134	0.4581	**0.5271**
	Jogging	0.6824	0.6390	0.9214	**0.9722**	0.9672
	Upstairs	0.6887	0.5107	0.6792	**0.9770**	0.9726
	Downstairs	0.0576	0.4362	0.7017	0.9192	**0.9467**
	Sitting	0.0061	0.0676	0.3958	0.5080	**0.5576**
	Standing	0.8343	0.5785	0.7713	0.9423	**0.9437**

As shown in Table 2–5, the personalized HAR model using $\mathbb{X}_i^{nb}$ and $\mathbb{X}_i^{cb}$ together showed the best precision, recall, F1 Score, and accuracy for almost all activities. In the case of the HAPT data, the low performance of the personalized HAR model in some activities is attributed to the lack of data. This can be resolved by adjusting the hyper-parameter value to increase the amount of non-borderline samples of the proposed method. In the case of the WISDM dataset, it was found that the performance of the proposed method was excellent in all activities. The reason is judged to be that there were many overlapping samples in all activities.

Experiment 2. This experiment was conducted to analyze the effect of the pre-trained model's size of the training dataset for the proposed method on the prediction performance. Using the experimental results, it is possible to evaluate whether the proposed method can show robust prediction performance even when the training dataset is insufficient. It is not easy to collect labeled training data for HAR. Therefore, whether it is possible to develop a robust personalized HAR model using the pre-trained model using a small amount of training dataset is a very important key performance indicator (KPI). To do so, this paper compared the F1 Scores by performing sub-sampling of five sizes on the dataset. The results are summarized in Table 6.

Table 4. Comparison results of F-1 Score

Datasets		Baseline models			Personalized HAR ($\mathbb{X}_i^{nb}$ only)	Personalized HAR $\left(\mathbb{X}_i^{nb}\ \&\ \mathbb{X}_i^{cb}\right)$
		SVM	*KNN*	*RF*		
HAPT	Walking	0.9614	0.9205	0.9158	0.9605	**0.9627**
	Walking upstairs	0.9346	0.9024	0.8826	0.9401	**0.9432**
	Walking downstairs	0.9481	0.8679	0.9112	0.9551	**0.9602**
	Sitting	0.9107	0.8322	0.8739	0.9112	**0.9115**
	Standing	0.9214	0.8597	0.8798	0.9238	**0.9239**
	Laying	**0.9991**	0.9973	0.9929	0.9979	0.9978
WISDM	Walking	0.0000	0.1590	0.3987	0.5007	**0.5569**
	Jogging	0.6478	0.6093	0.9086	0.9635	**0.9606**
	Upstairs	0.4880	0.5120	0.6789	0.9619	**0.9708**
	Downstairs	0.1042	0.4724	0.6890	0.9413	**0.9580**
	Sitting	0.0120	0.0928	0.3946	0.5700	**0.6105**
	Standing	0.6671	0.5718	0.7850	0.8991	**0.9099**

Table 5. Comparison results of accuracy

Datasets		Baseline models			Personalized HAR ($\mathbb{X}_i^{nb}$ only)	Personalized HAR $\left(\mathbb{X}_i^{nb}\ \&\ \mathbb{X}_i^{cb}\right)$
		SVM	*KNN*	*RF*		
HAPT	accuracy	0.9471	0.8993	0.9121	**0.9496**	0.9491
	precision	0.9481	0.9005	0.9115	0.9510	**0.9513**
	recall	0.9465	0.8972	0.9106	0.9480	**0.9502**
	f1-score	0.9459	0.8967	0.9094	0.9481	**0.9499**
WISDM	accuracy	0.5773	0.4935	0.7460	0.8588	**0.8669**
	precision	0.4666	0.4202	0.6482	0.8227	**0.8415**
	recall	0.3782	0.4054	0.6471	0.7962	**0.8191**
	f1-score	0.3198	0.4029	0.6425	0.8061	**0.8278**

Table 6. F-1 scores according to the size of the train dataset

Datasets		100% of train dataset	80% of train dataset	60% of train dataset	40% of train dataset	20% of train dataset
HAPT	Walking	0.9616	0.9560	0.9535	0.9434	0.9379
	Walking upstairs	0.9442	0.9340	0.9373	0.9205	0.9180
	Walking downstairs	0.9581	0.9516	0.9539	0.9456	0.9410
	Sitting	0.9096	0.9032	0.8977	0.8893	0.8806
	Standing	0.9223	0.9171	0.9145	0.9069	0.8972
	Laying	0.9979	0.9964	0.9958	0.9955	0.9950
WISDM	Walking	0.9134	0.9331	0.9129	0.8966	0.8887
	Jogging	0.9674	0.9721	0.9629	0.9583	0.9555
	Upstairs	0.5847	0.6809	0.5981	0.5939	0.5756
	Downstairs	0.5419	0.6554	0.5828	0.5167	0.5492
	Sitting	0.9736	0.9734	0.9758	**0.9392**	**0.7687**
	Standing	0.9486	0.9609	0.9474	0.9392	0.9534

Although the proposed model's performance decreases as the train dataset's size decreases, the change in performance due to data reduction is not significant, even though the entire train dataset is reduced by 20%. It shows that the proposed model is robust. Even if the performance of the pre-trained model is poor, it is proved that there is robustness to lack of information when performing incremental learning using the proposed method. In the sitting activity of the WISDM in bold case, it shown that the performance dropped significantly as the size of the train dataset was reduced from 40% to 20%. It is analyzed that misclassification occurred because the number of $\mathbb{X}_i^{nb}$ was also very small due to too small amount of data, and as a result, the distribution for selecting $\mathbb{X}_i^{cb}$ was not properly generated.

Experiment 3. In the last experiment, the change in performance according to threshold θ, which is the hyper-parameter of the proposed method, was analyzed. For the HAPT dataset, the maximum value of θ for each activity was relatively large, so this paper performed comparing from 1.2θ to 0.4θ. In contrast, due to a large number of overlapping activity data, the WISDM dataset has a very small θ for each activity. Therefore, this paper performed comparing from 1.0θ to 1.8θ. The experimental results are summarized in Table 7 and Table 8.

Table 7. F-1 scores according to the size of thresholds for the HAPT

Datasets		1.2 θ	1.0 θ	0.8 θ	0.6 θ	0.4 θ
HAPT	Walking	**0.9622**	0.9616	0.9613	0.9611	0.9602
	Walking upstairs	0.9381	**0.9442**	0.9403	0.9404	0.9376
	Walking downstairs	0.9531	**0.9581**	0.9559	0.9559	0.9515
	Sitting	0.9049	0.9096	0.9140	0.9137	**0.9147**
	Standing	0.9173	0.9223	**0.9274**	0.9261	0.9253
	Laying	**0.9979**	**0.9979**	**0.9979**	**0.9979**	**0.9979**

Table 8. F-1 scores according to the size of thresholds for the WISDM

Datasets		1.2 θ	1.0 θ	0.8 θ	0.6 θ	0.4 θ
WISDM	Walking	0.9106	0.9098	**0.9139**	0.9080	0.9042
	Jogging	0.9609	0.9611	0.9637	**0.9654**	0.9653
	Upstairs	**0.6036**	0.5847	0.5806	0.5737	0.5699
	Downstairs	0.5397	0.5426	**0.5454**	0.5340	0.5288
	Sitting	0.9712	0.9616	**0.9726**	0.9638	0.9607
	Standing	0.9579	0.9477	**0.9592**	0.9463	0.9464

In the case of walking, walking upstairs, and walking downstairs activities of the HAPT dataset, the best performance is shown near 1.2θ. So, it proved that the proposed threshold θ is appropriate. For laying activities with a low degree of data overlapping, the classification performance using the pre-trained model can be very high. Therefore, even if the training data is slightly changed by variation of the thresholds, the classification performance is not significantly affected. In contrast, sitting and standing activities with a high degree of data overlapping showed high performance at values smaller than the threshold derived using the Youden index. This is considered because the degree of overlap between sitting and standing activities is so severe that the threshold derived using Youden Index is too small to classify them. In the case of the WISDM dataset, it shows the best performance at thresholds that are larger than the suggested thresholds in all data. It is judged that this is a problem due to the degree of severe overlapping of the WISDM dataset and insufficient data for each activity. This is considered a problem caused by the large degree of overlapping of the WISDM dataset and the lack of data for each activity. So, this paper will perform additional research that can determine the weight of the threshold for each activity depending on the shape of the dataset.

5 Conclusion and Future Works

This paper proposes a method to develop the personalize HAR model using incremental learning. To do so, this paper conducts the sub-sampling of non-boundary data from the entire activity data and identifies correctly labeled borderline data from the whole borderline data. In the experiments, it was shown that the proposed method is superior in terms of precision, recall, F1 Score, and accuracy.

Contributions of the paper can be summarized as follows. First, this paper proposes the construction method of the training dataset incremental learning for developing the personalized HAR model. The proposed method avoids human intervention and shifts the decision boundaries considering the direction and degree of the shift at the same time. Second, to improve the accuracy of the personalized HAR model, this paper proposes the two-phase method for generating a training dataset for incremental learning. By doing his, we can discover the optimal decision boundaries for the personalized HAR model.

This research can be extended in several directions. A representative field that can be expanded is cyber security. It is possible to develop a robust model that can respond to irregular cyberattacks by inputting and learning new aspects of attack data into a deep learning model that can detect cyberattacks. We are currently conducting this research.

Acknowledgements. This research is supported by Basic Science Research Program through the National Research Foundation of Korea (NRF) funded by the Ministry of Education, Science and Technology (NRF2019R1A2C1004102).

References

1. Ade, R.R., Deshmukh, P.R.: Methods for incremental learning : a survey. Int. J. Data Mining Knowl. Manag. Process **3**(4), 119–125 (2013)
2. Siirtola, P., Röning, J.: Incremental learning to personalize human activity recognition models: the importance of human AI collaboration. Sensors **19**(23), 5151 (2019)
3. Luo, Y., Yin, L., Bai, W., Mao, K.: An appraisal of incremental learning methods. Entropy **22**(11), 1190 (2020)
4. Vakili, M., Rezaei, M.: Incremental Learning Techniques for Online Human Activity Recognition. arXiv preprint arXiv:2109.09435 (2021)
5. Ordo´nez, F.J., Roggen, D.: Deep convolutional and LSTM recurrent neural networks for multimodal wearable activity recognition. Sensors **16**(1), 115 (2016)
6. Bulling, A., Blanke, U., Schiele, B.: A tutorial on human activity recognition using body-worn inertial sensors. ACM Comput. Surv. (CSUR) **46**(3), 1–33 (2014)
7. Gudur, G.K., Sundaramoorthy, P., Umaashankar, V.: Activeharnet: towards on-device deep Bayesian active learning for human activity recognition. In: The 3rd International Workshop on Deep Learning for Mobile Systems and Applications, pp. 7–12, (2019)
8. Garcia-Ceja, E., Osmani, V., Mayora, O.: Automatic stress detection in working environments from smartphones' accelerometer data: a first step. IEEE J. Biomed. Health Inform. **20**(4), 1053–1060 (2015)
9. Fluss, R., Faraggi, D., Reiser, B.: Estimation of the youden index and its associated cutoff point. Biometrical J. J. Math. Meth. Biosci. **47**(4), 458–472 (2005)

10. Anguita, D., Ghio, A., Oneto, L., Parra, X., Reyes-Ortiz, J.L.: A public domain dataset for human activity recognition using smartphones. In: Proceedings Eur. Symposium Artificial Neural Network (ESANN), p. 3 (2013)
11. Kwapisz, J.R., Weiss, G.M., Moore, S.A.: Activity recognition using cell phone accelerometers. ACM SIGKDD Explor. Newslett. **12**(2), 74–82 (2011)

A Graph Neural Network Detection Scheme for Malicious Behavior Knowledge Base

OuYang Liu[ID], Kun Li[(✉)], Ziwei Yin, and Huachun Zhou

School of Electronic and Information Engineering, Beijing Jiaotong University,
Beijing 100044, China
{21120086,kun_li,20120151,hchzhou}@bjtu.edu.cn

Abstract. Network intelligence has become an important trend in modern communication networks. In the future 6G network, the unrestricted communication between massive heterogeneous terminals will lead to more and more kinds of DDoS attacks, which will become an important factor affecting network security. In this paper, we propose a knowledge base detection scheme for malicious behavior of DDoS attacks based on graph neural networks. First, this paper constructs a malicious behavior knowledge base for a variety of common DDoS attacks. Considering the problem of multi-source heterogeneity under 6G network, this paper proposes a malicious behavior knowledge graph construction algorithm, which constructs a global malicious behavior knowledge graph from both address correlation and time correlation of network services. And the graph attention network is introduced on the basis of the knowledge graph to identify the malicious behaviors occurring in the network. The experimental results show that the detection scheme can enrich the feature representation of malicious behavior nodes. The scheme has a better performance compared with the machine learning scheme, and ultimately reduces the malicious traffic caused by DDoS attacks by more than an order of magnitude.

Keywords: DDoS attack · Malicious behavior knowledge base · Graph neural networks

1 Introduction

Network intelligence is gradually becoming an important trend in the development of 6G networks [1]. Currently, machine learning and deep learning have been deeply applied in the field of network security. Among the various types of network security problems, distributed denial of service attacks have the most serious impact [2]. Distributed denial of service attack (DDoS) refers to the attacker sending a large amount of useless and forged traffic to the target host by controlling a botnet as a way to exhaust the bandwidth or resources of the target host, which finally causes the target host to be unable to provide services to legitimate users [3]. With the growing variety and traffic of DDoS attacks, the

I. You et al. (Eds.): MobiSec 2022, CCIS 1644, pp. 122–133, 2023.
https://doi.org/10.1007/978-981-99-4430-9_9

management and application of massive data has become an urgent problem to be solved.

Knowledge graphs are becoming more and more important as a technique to manage traffic knowledge effectively [4]. Structurally, knowledge graphs exist in the form of directed attribute graphs, and knowledge is organized in the triad of "entity-relationship-entity". Knowledge graph construction mainly includes key technologies such as relationship extraction technology, knowledge fusion technology, entity linking technology and knowledge inference technology [5]. Building a knowledge base of network malicious behaviors in the form of knowledge graph has the advantages of efficient spatial structure storage, effective retrieval capability and timely knowledge update, and can provide effective support for detecting malicious behaviors in the network.

Currently, the field of detecting DDoS attacks is mainly dominated by machine learning or deep learning methods [6]. Compared with traditional machine learning and deep learning methods, graph neural networks have better malicious behavior detection capability by considering the spatial characteristics of sample nodes in the network structure. Traditional machine learning methods build models for training against flow features. While these models tend to achieve good accuracy when trained and evaluated using traffic, they are particularly vulnerable to targeting by attackers. Attackers typically change the characteristics of attack traffic over time to avoid detection. In contrast, graph neural networks can establish a "host-flow-host" topology and adjust this structure in real time according to the communication relationships between hosts in the network to enhance the robustness of algorithm detection.

The major contributions of this paper include: (1) We collect the dataset including normal traffic, network layer DDoS attack traffic, application layer DDoS attack traffic, botnet traffic, low-rate DDoS attack traffic and DRDoS attack traffic. (2) We constructs a knowledge base of malicious behavior based on the knowledge map and Neo4j graph database. (3) We proposes a malicious behavior knowledge graphconstruction algorithm, which constructs a global malicious behavior knowledge graph from both address correlation and time correlation of network services. (4) We propose a malicious behavior detection method based on graph focus network to be used in the network intrusion detection field.

The content structure of this paper is as follows: Sect. 2 discusses the related work. Section 3 presents the details of the proposed framework in this paper. Section 4 details the experiments related to malicious behavior knowledge base construction and detection. Section 5 summarizes the overall work and makes some suggestions for future work.

2   Related Work

Currently, research on the construction aspects of cybersecurity knowledge graphs is gradually increasing. [7] describes the objectives of the web topic structure and web ontology research in earlier studies, and also introduces the way to build a mid-level web security ontology based on time, space, people, events, and network operations, and gives specific recommendations on the overall construction method and future development of the future web ontology architecture. [8] proposes the ONTIDS framework, which uses ontology logic rules written in Semantic Query Enhanced Web Rule Language (SQWRL) to correlate and filter irrelevant alerts. [9] reviewed the basic concepts and definitions of knowledge inference and inference methods for knowledge graphs. The authors classify inference methods into three categories: rule-based inference, distributed representation-based inference, and neural network-based inference. Also, the authors review relevant applications of knowledge graph reasoning and discuss future challenges of knowledge graph reasoning.

The network exists as a form of graph structure with a powerful spatial representation. [10] states that traditional machine learning and deep learning approaches detect DDoS attacks by traffic characteristics. Although these models often achieve good accuracy when tested and evaluated, in practice, attackers change the traffic characteristics at any time to avoid detection. The paper constructs a connectivity graph between hosts and flows, followed by a GNN model to classify the nodes, and the experimental results prove to outperform traditional machine learning methods in the CIC-IDS2017 dataset. The article constructs the global topology between nodes only from a spatial perspective. [11] proposes a graph neural network framework called GLASS, which is a graph learning approach for detecting and identifying distributed denial-of-service attacks in an SDN environment. The authors use spectral clustering to specifically identify compromised entities and also analyze the impact of DDoS attacks on for network performance such as throughput and transmission latency. [12] proposes a data plane programmable SDN detection model based on spatio-temporal graph convolutional networks, which maps the network as a graph. The model can effectively extract the temporal and spatial features of the network state. However, the model does not consider the importance between different nodes. It can be seen that graph neural networks play an important role in knowledge mining of knowledge graphs, so this paper first constructs a malicious behavior knowledge base and proposes a malicious behavior knowledge graph construction algorithm from both spatial and temporal aspects, then introduces graph attention networks to optimize the connection relationship between nodes and finally completes the task of malicious behavior node detection.

3   Design and Application of Malicious Behavior Knowledge Base

3.1   Malicious Behavior Knowledge Base Detection Framework

Considering the difficulty that traditional machine learning and deep learning methods cannot effectively extract structural information in the network, and in order to solve the problem of anomalous traffic diversity in future 6G networks, this paper proposes a malicious behavior knowledge base detection scheme based on graph neural networks. The scheme contains three parts: malicious behavior knowledge base construction, malicious behavior knowledge graph construction and malicious behavior node detection.

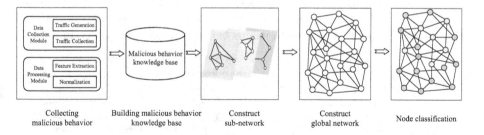

Fig. 1. Malicious behavior knowledge base detection framework

Figure 1 shows the overall framework of the system. Firstly, the traffic data of normal and malicious behaviors in real network environment is collected, after which the stream features of the data are extracted. Then the malicious behavior knowledge base is constructed based on the flow data. After that, we construct sub-networks based on address correlation and time correlation of data services and combine them into a global network. Finally, we transform the malicious behavior detection task into a node classification task and implement malicious behavior detection by graph attention networks. The malicious behavior knowledge base detection scheme proposed in this paper fully takes into account the correlation representation of network traffic in the communication process and enriches the feature representation of current nodes by the neighboring nodes of each traffic, which finally significantly improves the detection capability of malicious behavior.

In this paper, we use hping3 tool and python script to launch multiple types of DDoS attack traffic and normal traffic on the attacking host side. On the attacked host side, we use the Tcpdump packet capture tool to implement. By specifying the capture interval, Tcpdump can periodically capture the traffic and generate the corresponding PCAP file. Then we use the CICFlowMeter tool to obtain the flow characteristics of 83 dimensions of DDoS attack traffic and normal traffic. In order to eliminate the influence of the dimensionality of different features in the dataset, we choose the normalization formula $X = \frac{X - X_{min}}{X_{max} - X_{min}}$ to pre-process the collected data.

The malicious behavior knowledge base is constructed based on the concept of knowledge graph. The malicious behavior knowledge graph exists in the form of a triplet $\langle Entity, Relationship, Attribute \rangle$. Entities have one-way or two-way relationships with each other, and each entity or relationship can have multiple attributes.

Figure 2 illustrates the process of building a malicious behavior knowledge base. It is mainly divided into two preliminary processes: building entities and building relationships, and then building a malicious behavior knowledge base in the form of "entity-relationship-entity". The knowledge base constructed in this paper contains two entities: the attacking host, the attacked host and the malicious behavior node, and the attributes of the host include IP address and device model. The attributes of the host include IP address and device model, and the attributes of the malicious behavior node are the flow characteristics of 83 dimensions. The types of relationships between entities are shown in Table 1.

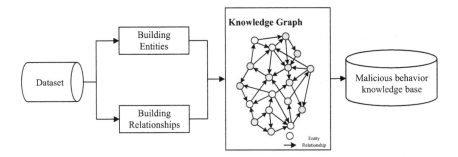

Fig. 2. Malicious behavior knowledge base construction process

Table 1. Inter-entity relationships.

Entity1	Relationship	Entity2
Host	launch	Malicious Behavior Node
Malicious Behavior Node	arrive	Host
Malicious Behavior Node	related	Malicious Behavior Node

3.2   Building Malicious Behavior Knowledge Graph

In order to perform effective correlation analysis of malicious behavior traffic, this paper constructs malicious behavior knowledge graphs G in terms of address correlation and time correlation. $G = (V, E)$ is a directed graph, where $V = \{V_1, V_2, \ldots, V_n\}$ is the set of all malicious behavior nodes to be detected, and N is the number of all nodes in the graph. $E = \{E_{i,j}\}$ denotes the set of edges. Considering that when the attacking host initiates malicious traffic to the attacked host, the characteristics of each malicious traffic will be influenced by other malicious traffic in a short period of time, this paper proposes a new method for constructing malicious behavior knowledge graph based on information such as IP address and timestamp, which can enhance the correlation analysis between nodes expressing malicious traffic.

With Algorithm 1, we can obtain the malicious behavior knowledge graph composed of all nodes in the malicious behavior knowledge base. The malicious behavior knowledge graph can enhance the embedded representation of malicious behavior nodes from address correlation and time correlation. Ultimately, the malicious behavior knowledge graph is fed into the detection model to detect the occurrence of malicious behaviors in the communication network.

Algorithm 1. Malicious behavior knowledge graph construction algorithm

---

Input: Feature matrix of malicious behavior nodes $V = \{V_1, V_2, \ldots, V_n\}$
Output: Malicious behavior knowledge graph $G = (V, E)$
1: Initialize the time difference threshold $t_d = 5s$
2: **Address correlation:** divide the original data set into multiple sub-data sets $S = \{S_1, S_2, \ldots, S_n\}$ based on the source IP address and destination IP address of the stream
3: **for** $i = 1, \ldots, n$ **do**
4:    Get the number of malicious behavior nodes in the sub-dataset $n = length(S_i)$
5:    **for** $j = 1, \ldots, n$ **do**
6:       **for** $k = 1, \ldots, n$ **do**
7:          **Time correlation:** Calculate the absolute value of the time difference between malicious act node i and malicious act node j
8:             $t_s = |t_i - t_j|$
9:             **if** $t_s < t_d$ **then**
10:                $e_{i,j} = 1$, there is a relationship between two malicious behavior nodes
11:             **else**
12:                $e_{i,j} = 0$, there is no relationship between two malicious behavior nodes
13:             **end if**
14:          **end for**
15:       **end for**
16: **end for**
17: Combine multiple sub-networks e into global network E
18: output malicious behavior knowledge graph G

3.3 Malicious Behavior Node Detection Based on Graph Attention Networks

The graph attention network adaptively assigns weights to each neighboring node through an attention mechanism and improves the expressiveness of the model by aggregating the features of its neighbors during the training process. In the malicious behavior detection phase, we introduced the graph attention network [13]. Graph Attention network can learn the characteristic knowledge and structural knowledge of malicious behavior nodes stored in malicious behavior knowledge, and obtain malicious behavior detection nodes.

The set of feature representations of nodes is $h = \{h_1, h_2, \ldots, h_n\}, h_i \in \mathbb{R}^F$, where n denotes the global number of malicious traffic and F denotes the feature dimension of each malicious traffic. The attention interrelationship number $e_{i,j}$ between connected malicious traffic node i and malicious traffic node j is given by

$$e_{i,j} = LeakReLu(\alpha(Wh_i \| Wh_j)) \tag{1}$$

According to formula 1, $W \in \mathbb{R}^{F \times F}$ is a shared linear change matrix that can be learned. This matrix is applied to each malicious traffic node to transform the original feature space into a higher-level feature space to obtain better node representation.

The graph attention network calculates the attention correlation coefficient for each malicious traffic node and its related neighbor nodes, and obtains the normalized mutual attention correlation coefficient $\alpha_{i,j}$ by the sotfmax function.

$$\alpha_{i,j} = softmax(e_{i,j}) = \frac{exp(e_{i,j})}{\sum\limits_{k \in N_i} (e_{i,k})} \tag{2}$$

In the graph attention network, the normalized mutual attention correlation coefficient $\alpha_{i,j}$ indicates the importance of node i for node j. After obtaining the number of mutual correlations of all nodes, we can calculate the representation of node features in the high-level dimensional space.

$$h_i^{l+1} = \sigma(\sum\limits_{j \in N_i} \alpha_{i,j} W h_j^l) \tag{3}$$

According to formula 3, $\sigma(\cdot)$ denotes the activation function used in the current layer. The network in this paper has two layers. The ReLu activation function is selected for the first layer. The softmax function is selected for the second layer to accomplish the classification task.

4   Experimental Results

4.1   Evaluation Metric

To verify the detection quality of different models, we choose the following performance metrics: accuracy, precision, recall and F1. Also, we use the malicious traffic detection capability DC. this metric measures the order of magnitude by which the model can reduce malicious traffic.

$$DC = \frac{1}{1 - \frac{\sum_{i=1}^n T_i}{\sum_{i=1}^n A_i}} \tag{4}$$

According to formula 4, T_i denotes the number of correctly detected flows in traffic class i. A_i denotes the total number of flows for traffic class i.

4.2   Malicious Behavior Knowledge Base Construction Experiment

We collected a total of 101,791 pieces of data in the malicious behavior collection phase. This dataset contains normal traffic data and five types of DDoS attack traffic data [14]. The specific categories and quantities are 45031 normal traffic, 13091 network layer DDoS attack traffic, 16078 application layer DDoS attack traffic, 11089 botnet traffic, 12598 low-rate DDoS attack traffic, and 16502 DRDoS(distributed reflection denial of service) attack traffic.

We choose to use the Neo4j graph database to create the knowledge graph. We first create the host node using the $"CREATE(Label\_Type :$ $Lable\{Property\_Type :"$ $Property\_Value"\})"$ syntax, and then use the

"$LOAD\ CSV$" method to import the collected malicious behavior nodes. Finally, we use the "$CREATE(Start\_Label\_Type) - [r : Relationship\_Type] - >$ (End_Label_Type)" method to create the relationship between the host and the malicious relationships between hosts and malicious behavior nodes. The created knowledge graph is shown in Fig. 3.

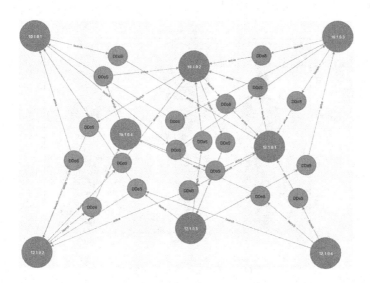

Fig. 3. Knowledge graph between hosts and malicious behavior nodes

4.3   Malicious Behavior Detection Experiment

To ensure the authenticity of the experiments, we use the random distribution method to select 10,000 data from the malicious behavior knowledge base for the experiments, and randomly select 80% of the data as the training set and 20% of the data as the test set. The parameter values of our graph attention network are shown in Table 2. We use Droupout and Early Stopping to prevent overfitting of the network training. Droupout is the percentage of units of neural network units randomly discarded during the training process. Early Stopping is a strategy to stop early during the training process.

Table 2. Network Parameters

Parameter Name	Parameter Value
Learning Rate	0.03
Droupout	0.6
Early Stopping	20
Optimizer	Adam
First layer activation function	Relu
Second layer activation function	Softmax

Our proposed scheme indicates the effect in detecting multiple types of DDoS attacks as shown in Fig. 4. The recall rate of low-rate DDoS attacks and precision and normal traffic is relatively low, which is mainly caused by the fact that the attack rate of low-rate DDoS attacks is slower and more similar to normal traffic, so it causes the malicious behavior detection module to misclassify low-rate DDoS attacks as normal traffic.

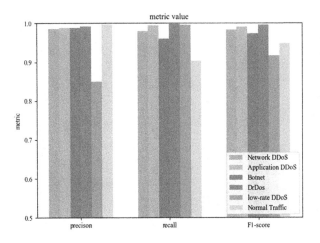

Fig. 4. Experimental result

After getting the specific categories of malicious behavior nodes, we store the detection results into the malicious behavior knowledge base through Cyber statements, and we can update the knowledge graph between hosts and malicious behavior nodes as shown in Fig. 5.

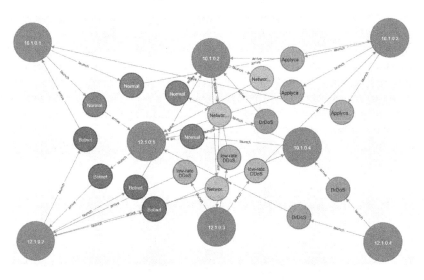

Fig. 5. Knowledge graph update result

4.4   Model Comparison Experiment

To verify the effectiveness of the proposed scheme in detecting malicious behaviors, we compare the detection scheme proposed in this paper with a variety of machine learning-based detection schemes. The details are as follows.

Logistic regression (LR). Logistic regression is a common classification method in the field of DDoS detection. It can quickly perform dichotomous or multiclassification problems. The logistic regression detection method used in this paper adds an additional term with L2 regularization factor of 0.1 for optimization.

Naive Bayes (NB). Naive Bayes is a detection scheme that aims to minimize the probability of misclassification. The method obtains the prior probability of each malicious node based on the data statistics of the knowledge base, and obtains the posterior probability based on the Bayesian formula, which in turn classifies the already nodes.

K-Nearest Neighbor (KNN) algorithm. KNN algorithm uses the idea of nearest neighbor, which means that the class of the current node is determined based on its neighbors. In this paper, the value of K is taken as 6, which represents the total number of categories of malicious behavior nodes in the knowledge base.

Random forest (RF). Random forest is essentially a decision tree based Bagging integrated learning model. Its results are determined by adjudicating the results of multiple decision trees. In this paper, when using the random forest algorithm, the number of random forests n parameter is taken as 20, and the CART algorithm is used for the classification method of each decision tree.

Support vector machine (SVM). The support vector machine algorithm is a supervised classification model with the goal of maximizing the classification interface. In this paper, when using the support vector machine model, the kernel function is chosen as the rbf radial basis kernel function, the penalty factor is taken as 10, and the training is stopped when the error accuracy is less than 0.001.

As can be seen in Table 3, we compare the performance of the proposed method in this paper with five machine learning methods in detecting malicious behavior. From the experimental results, we can see that the scheme used in this paper outperforms the traditional machine learning algorithms in four metrics: accuracy, recall, F1-score and malicious traffic detection capability.

Table 3. Performance comparison of different methods

Method	Precision	Recall	F1-score	DC
LR	0.83	0.84	0.83	6.3
NB	0.81	0.82	0.81	5.6
KNN	0.91	0.93	0.92	14.3
RF	0.89	0.89	0.89	9.1
SVM	0.95	0.94	0.94	16.7
GAT	0.96	0.96	0.96	29.7

In summary, the graph attention network can effectively learn the feature knowledge and network structure of malicious traffic in the malicious behavior knowledge base, and the feature representation of malicious behavior nodes can be strengthened by aggregating the features of neighboring nodes. The experimental results show that the detection scheme used in this paper can classify normal traffic and five typical DDoS attack traffic stored in the knowledge base, and the malicious traffic detection capability reaches 29.7, which successfully reduces the malicious traffic caused by DDoS attacks by more than one order of magnitude.

5   Conclusion and Future Work

Network security has always been an important issue in the field of computer networks. The issue has become more and more visible along with the development of modern communication networks. In the future 6G network field, various artificial intelligence techniques will be incorporated into the network architecture. In this paper, a graph neural network-based knowledge base detection scheme for DDoS malicious behaviors is proposed. The scheme contains two parts: malicious behavior knowledge base construction and malicious behavior detection based on graph neural network. This paper constructs a malicious behavior knowledge base based on Neo4j and Cyber statements, which can be used to collect and store the malicious behavior events of DDoS attacks occurring in the network. The malicious behavior knowledge base not only provides a graphical display effect between hosts and malicious behavior nodes, but also provides effective data support for the malicious behavior detection module. The malicious behavior detection scheme proposed in this paper is based on the graph attention network approach, which aggregates the features of neighboring nodes based on the malicious behavior graph and strengthens the feature representation of the current node. Experimental results show that the detection scheme has superior performance compared with traditional machine learning methods. The knowledge of a single malicious behavior knowledge base is limited. In the future, we will integrate the federated learning scheme to complete the knowledge sharing of multi domain malicious behavior knowledge base, so that the malicious behavior knowledge base can obtain stronger detection capability.

Acknowledgements. This paper is supported by National Key R&D Program of China under Grant No. 2018YFA0701604.

References

1. Yang, H., Alphones, A., Xiong, Z., Niyato, D., Zhao, J., Wu, K.: Artificial-intelligence-enabled intelligent 6G networks. IEEE Network **34**(6), 272–280 (2020)
2. Guo, J., Wang, L.: Learning to upgrade internet information security and protection strategy in big data era. Comput. Commun. **160**, 150–157 (2020)
3. Jing, X., Yan, Z., Pedrycz, W.: Security data collection and data analytics in the internet: a survey. IEEE Commun. Surv. Tutor. **21**(1), 586–618 (2018)

4. Galeano-Brajones, J., Carmona-Murillo, J., Valenzuela-Valdés, J., Luna-Valero, F.: Detection and mitigation of dos and DDoS attacks in IoT-based stateful SDN: an experimental approach. Sensors **20**(3), 816 (2020)
5. Qi, G., Gao, H., Wu, T.: The research advances of knowledge graph. Technol. Intell. Eng. **3**(1), 4–25 (2017)
6. Arshi, M., Nasreen, M., Madhavi, K.: A survey of DDoS attacks using machine learning techniques. In: E3S Web of Conferences, vol. 184, p. 01052. EDP Sciences (2020)
7. Obrst, L., Chase, P., Markeloff, R.: Developing an ontology of the cyber security domain. In: STIDS, pp. 49–56. Citeseer (2012)
8. Sadighian, A., Fernandez, J.M., Lemay, A., Zargar, S.T.: ONTIDS: a highly flexible context-aware and ontology-based alert correlation framework. In: Danger, J.-L., Debbabi, M., Marion, J.-Y., Garcia-Alfaro, J., Zincir Heywood, N. (eds.) FPS - 2013. LNCS, vol. 8352, pp. 161–177. Springer, Cham (2014). https://doi.org/10.1007/978-3-319-05302-8_10
9. Chen, X., Jia, S., Xiang, Y.: A review: knowledge reasoning over knowledge graph. Expert Syst. Appl. **141**, 112948 (2020)
10. Pujol-Perich, D., Suárez-Varela, J., Cabellos-Aparicio, A., Barlet-Ros, P.: Unveiling the potential of graph neural networks for robust intrusion detection. ACM SIGMETRICS Perform. Eval. Rev. **49**(4), 111–117 (2022)
11. Nagaraj, K., Starke, A., McNair, J.: Glass: a graph learning approach for software defined network based smart grid DDoS security. In: ICC 2021-IEEE International Conference on Communications, pp. 1–6. IEEE (2021)
12. Cao, Y., Jiang, H., Deng, Y., Wu, J., Zhou, P., Luo, W.: Detecting and mitigating DDoS attacks in SDN using spatial-temporal graph convolutional network. IEEE Trans. Dependable Secure Comput. **19**(6), 3855–3872 (2021)
13. Veličković, P., Cucurull, G., Casanova, A., Romero, A., Lio, P., Bengio, Y.: Graph attention networks. arXiv preprint arXiv:1710.10903 (2017)
14. Li, M., Zhou, H., Qin, Y.: Two-stage intelligent model for detecting malicious DDoS behavior. Sensors **22**(7), 2532 (2022)

Recent Challenges in a New Distributed Learning Paradigm

Sandi Rahmadika$^{(\boxtimes)}$ ⬤, Bayu Ramadhani Fajri⬤, Geovanne Farell⬤,
Ahmaddul Hadi⬤, and Khairi Budayawan⬤

Department of Electronic Engineering, Universitas Negeri Padang,
Sumatera Barat, Indonesia
{sandi,geovannefarell,dulhadi,khairi}@ft.unp.ac.id, bayurf@unp.ac.id

Abstract. The majority of online transactions between the parties can be reported in real-time publicly by relying on smart contracts (SCs) and federated learning (FL). They are both decentralized and reinforced. By aggregating the gradient values from client devices, FL enables a large number of clients to create deep learning models anonymously. Yet, it lacks an incentive system for the contributing clients. Conversely, since self-executing contracts with immutable data records are resilient to failure, the virtues of SCs can be a tenable solution as an incentive mechanism in the FL system. The clients can claim the rewards by providing a proof transaction function and stating their contribution arbitrarily through SCs. However, because the transactions are made public, directly implementing SCs in the CL system could jeopardize the users' privacy. The observer can deduce the characteristics of the client's resources. Therefore, in this research, we elaborate on the critical points to be taken into account in adopting SCs as an incentive mechanism for the FL environment. We also state an empirical investigation and the open challenges that can address the aforementioned issues and concerns. Eventually, we recapitulate the essential points to be considered in developing a new distributed learning paradigm.

Keywords: Blockchain · Distributed Learning · Federated Learning · Smart Contracts

1 Introduction

A collaborative machine learning technique using dispersed training data is known as federated learning (FL). This machine learning method is a breakthrough because it converts centralized raw data into a decentralized form [1]. In the internet of things (IoT) context, FL can be seen as the result of the convergence of on-device AI, blockchain technology, and edge computing. The number of IoT devices is expected to increase to 10 billion by 2020 and 22 billion by 2025, according to the IoT analytic [2]. On the other hand, according to data, there will be 1 trillion more sensors in use by 2030 [3]. The proliferation

© The Author(s), under exclusive license to Springer Nature Singapore Pte Ltd. 2023
I. You et al. (Eds.): MobiSec 2022, CCIS 1644, pp. 134–144, 2023.
https://doi.org/10.1007/978-981-99-4430-9_10

of connected devices presents new problems for AI, particularly in the field of machine learning. The challenges of assembling datasets from various sources, as mentioned by [4], are one of the main issues facing the development of AI. Additionally, each device contains private data that the parties have access to [5]. In order to address the problems, the Google AI research team launched FL as a method of increasing communication effectiveness in 2016.

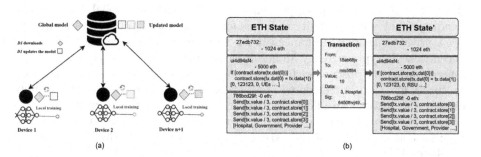

Fig. 1. (a) The FL model in general; (b) State transaction function in Ethereum

With blockchain technology as a core component, Bitcoin has gained popularity as a solution to the flaws in most centralized systems. Without the intervention of a third party (middleman), blockchain carries out the parties' transactions. As a result, blockchain eliminates the centralized system's inherent single point of failure. Since each piece of data recorded in a blockchain is uniquely timestamped by cryptographic procedures, security is built into the system from the start [6]. In other words, attackers cannot alter or hack blockchain data. As a result, researchers have been very interested in exploring how to use the blockchain in other sectors, such as artificial intelligence (AI) scope. Blockchain plays a role in decentralized validating every activity, such as updating and exchanging data, because the number of linked devices is constantly increasing over time, and FL depends on the updated model of the devices (based on local training data). In order to avoid the need for a central mediator, many researchers offer a conceptual model of a jointly federated learning system using blockchain technology as a distributed local model of updated data. Figure 1 presents the FL model in general and the state transaction function in Ethereum SCs. We emphasize the Ethereum virtual machine (EVM), which serves as a compute engine for carrying out blockchain transactions, as the main element of the Ethereum protocol and operation. The EVM, which can store all in-memory values on a stack, has an architecture based on stacks and a unique state transaction function. The EVM uses a 256-bit word size to secure the transactions with native hashing and elliptic curve operations.

The characteristic of blockchain maintains the consistency of distributed ledger and the distribution of rewards created by the blockchain network. The reward in the distributed FL can be seen as an incentive for the nearby network nodes that supply the updated AI model. It is believed that every device comes with built-in local training data. We use the standard federated learning architecture as the decentralized FL modelling strategy. The linked devices computed the updated AI model and uploaded it through the blockchain network for validation by the miners. Nevertheless, a research paper in [7] reveals that embracing blockchain for machine learning faces several challenges regarding security, privacy, and scalability. SCs for FL could be a serious consideration if these technologies are implemented in a system with profoundly confidential data. SCs combined with supplemental protocols can be a reliable method to handle privacy and linkability concerns for decentralized applications, supporting a private incentive mechanism in FL systems. For instance, the well-known decentralized cryptocurrency Monero (trading under the ticker name XMR) has several options to obscure each transaction's details. Therefore, complementary protocols must be implemented specifically. To fill the research gap, we note several points that can affect security, transparency, and privacy-awareness in adopting SCs for the FL environment. Not to mention that the empirical investigation and evaluation of the existing techniques to tackle the issues are also highlighted.

The road map of the paper is organized as follows. Section 2 describes the new paradigm in decentralized approaches consisting FL and SCs. Section 3 presents the motivation of this research. Meanwhile, Sect. 4 provides essential information about decentralised techniques' privacy awareness. Finally, the conclusions are outlined in Sect. 5.

2   A New Paradigm in Decentralized Approaches

This section presents the system's core components consisting of the essential aspect of blockchain technology through Ethereum smart contract, decentralized artificial intelligence (AI) in general, and the implementation of FL in several use cases and objectives.

2.1   The Recent Technology of Trust

Thanks to blockchain technology, trade or service agreements are no longer subject to the administrative requirements of static papers. In the decentralized system, Ethereum SCs develop into automation tools that control intricate transactions. The blockchain was expanded with Turing-Complete smart contracts when Ethereum made its public debut in 2015. Compared to Bitcoin, Ethereum manages more answers and more complicated calculations with a self-evolving code. Ethereum is made up of only recursive, rule-based programming. Therefore, blockchain technology through Ethereum SCs is named The Recent Technology of Trust. Figure 2 presents the latest transactions and blocks of the Ethereum SCs blockchain network recorded on September 9, 2015 (01:47 GMT+7) [8]. The timestamp of ETH SCs is crucial in strengthening the blockchain's legitimacy, transparency, and tamper-resistance. It takes the hash value (0x0a1e363a30 ....) and the number of transactions in Ether (ETH) cryptocurrency. According to a recent study by Kiffer et al. [9], the diversity of smart contracts is made up of exact replicas of other contracts. Since the code is so widely utilized, the smart contracts ecosystem also suffers from a severe lack of diversity. However, as several strategies have emerged, such as combining quantum and cloud computing, and artificial intelligence (AI); thus, the issue is gradually being addressed.

Fig. 2. The latest transactions and blocks of the Ethereum blockchain network.

2.2 Federated Learning with Decentralized Incentive Mechanism

In 2017, the Google AI team introduced distributed machine learning methods that allow people to make private machine learning model improvements without disclosing their training data. The system is known as FL as a solution to increase communication effectiveness and provides a detailed explanation of its design [10]. It is deployed on a mobile keyboard for smart devices that can predict the most likely words or phrases. Since then, additional research has been conducted progressively by focusing on particular aspects like incentive systems for the people involved. The FL strategy allows the clients to carry out a local training model entirely on their own. In this way, the raw data provided by the client is solely used to train and update an existing global model, which is then sent iteratively to the central aggregator [11]. Then, to be used in the subsequent iteration, the central aggregator creates a new global model by combining these updated and trained models collected from the participating clients. This procedure is performed numerous times until the global model reaches a certain level of accuracy. There are no reward mechanisms in place for collaborative learning programs. The biggest concern in such a system is the free-rider issue. Incentives can encourage not only consumers but also compel honest behaviour from them. In line with this, adopting blockchain through ETH SCs as a solution for

FL is a viable option. In terms of the conventional machine learning techniques, the client's training data, which contain private information, are aggregated and centralized on a single server which suffers from a serious privacy leakage risk.

In [12], a recent study on FL and blockchain-based incentive systems was presented. These technologies are used in the internet of things (IoT) edge network field (network edge); Also stated in [13] having a similar goal. Key design elements and incentive mechanisms are successfully implemented overall. The offered solution still has problems with privacy, linkability, and traceability, much like in most earlier experiments. A basic implementation is probably not desired for consumers who possess a lot of sensitive information. The new platforms that have evolved with the special capacities supplied are inappropriate and likely vulnerable to unauthorised observers' monitoring. Therefore, determining the type of blockchain used in the private FL system is also crucial. Another paramount aspect that needs to be carefully considered is the effectiveness of authenticating transactions, especially the method of awarding rewards.

3   Motivation

Previous research has focused on implementing blockchain technology for decentralized learning approaches to achieve the objectives of the rewarding mechanism. Moreover, several mapping studies of FL and SCs have explored the output, throughput, scalability concerns, and security perspective. However, the vast majority of research does not come from a systematic mapping study. Therefore its comprehensiveness and significance remain negligible. By nature, integrating FL and blockchain SCs can provide a tamper-proof incentive mechanism while preserving disputes between parties. On the other hand, blockchain can also be very expensive in the long run due to the cost of mining (proof-of-work consensus), power consumption with numerous environmental consequences, market manipulation, scalability and cybersecurity concerns, competing platforms, and concerns about the lack of a physical form or intrinsic value as described in [14]. Therefore, an investigation on integration between FL and blockchain SCs must be conducted regardless of the benefits provided by those technologies.

Due to the above-mentioned concerns, we present critical points and open challenges in embracing blockchain SCs as a decentralized rewarding mechanism in an FL environment. We have noted several critical matters from many literature reviews that have been selected through rigorous screening, such as the information's grade and correctness, the appropriateness of data, type of publication, and so forth. This paper's ultimate goal is to close the research gap by stating the critical points in embracing SCs in the FL system. This paper also extends current studies on applying blockchain technology to methodologies bonded to federated learning. Despite the fact that the research does not cover in detail all aspects of scalability, blockchain legal and regulatory matters, and so on; however, this paper would preserve practical insights in conceiving appropriate advancement techniques for distributed learning with a decentralized incentive environment.

4 Privacy-Awareness and Linkability Concerns

One of the fascinating technological trends is the emergence of decentralized AI. The development of blockchain use in the field of artificial intelligence has begun. Additionally, this idea has drawn much interest because it has many benefits over standard AI techniques, including training efficiency, low latency, and low power usage. In line with this, blockchain technology's fundamental concept is a chain-shaped data structure known as a chain of blocks [15]. Intuitively, the network connectivity, distributed storage, smart contracts, security mechanisms, and distributed consensus (deciding the status of transactions). The amount of transactions in the Bitcoin blockchain over 10 min is recorded by [16], which provides surprising facts. A total of 522 billion transactions per year equates to 1.4 billion per day, or 9.722.200 transactions per 10 min, or 1.4 billion transactions per day. In a nutshell, many experts have beliefs about the security of blockchain, which shows that blockchain is frequently used.

The practical integration scheme between FL and SCs can be seen in Algorithm 1. When using the FL Stochastic Gradient Descent (SGD) technique, IoT devices send parameters or gradients to the aggregation server $DecServer$. The list of potential devices (constructing FL model) are noted as $POT\_CLI_i -> 1, 2, ..., n$. A new model is created using the device's local training data, and it is subsequently uploaded to the associated blockchain network miners $miner_1, miner_2, ..., miner_n$. A decentralized learning system has no set rules or restrictions on how many miners can join in building the FL model. However, there are some rules for minimum device requirements determined by $DecServer$ in terms of device specification, memory, processor, network bandwidth, and to name a few. The $DecServer$ chooses a predetermined number of miners from the network to be the active miners at random. Once $DecServer$ confirms the validation of the updated FL model, the incentives are propagated to the contributed users via Ethereum smart contracts (ETH cryptocurrency). There are two types of incentives that DecServer provides, namely INC_{user} for the contributed users and INC_{miner} for the ETH SCs miners. INC_{user} is equivalently shared with the users associated with their datasets used to train the FL model.

This section examines a distributed learning incentive mechanism using an Ethereum smart contract to address the problems with intermediaries in centralized incentive schemes. However, as this system exposes user gradient values to the public via the smart contract, there are issues if it is used for sensitive data, such as health-related data, as highlighted in [18]. With certain presumptions, the observer can employ an active and passive inference attack to impose training data through gradient values that violate privacy. To understand the specifics of the FL model setting, we advise the reader to consult our earlier work in [19], and [20] both outline more similar assaults and problems. Figure 3 illustrates an inference membership attack that could infer the properties of users' training data in an FL environment. With certain assumptions, the

Algorithm 1. FL [17] with SCs in a General Form. GBS: global batch size; CLI: index idx of the users; BAT: local minibatch size, LnR is learning rate, $DecServer$ aggregation server

---

1: **procedure** DECSERVERUPDATED:
2:   $DecServer$ screening POT_CLI *DecServer screening the potential clients*
3:   **for** every round $rnd = 1, 2, 3, ...$ **do**   *number of rounds could be diverse*
4:     $POT\_CLI \leftarrow \max(GBS \cdot POT\_CLI_i, startfrom1, 2, ...)$
5:     **for** each client $idx \in POT_n$ **in parallel do**
6:       $P\omega_r nd^i \leftarrow$ ClientUpdate(i, POT_t) *for all $->$ updated model is based on POT_GLB*
7:     **end for**
8:     $POT\_updated \leftarrow \frac{1}{rnd} \sum_{idx \in POT\_n} POT^{idx}_{updated}$
9:     $S_{vr} \leftarrow P\omega_{t+1} = P\omega + r_t P\omega_u$ *DecServer derives a new model*
10:   **end for**
11: **end procedure**
12: **procedure** ETH SCs INCENTIVE$(INC_{user}, INC_{miner})$ *incentivized*
13:   $DecServer$ gathers the list of users $POT\_CLI_1, ..., POT\_CLI_{idx}$
14:   Active $miner_1, miner_2, ..., miner_n$ *a group of miners*
15:   **for** $miner_1, miner_2, ..., miner_n \in FL$; $DecServer$ **do**
16:     $DecServer \quad \leftarrow$ CheckTransaction   conducted   by POT_CLI
      DecServer has the list of users
17:     *Other miners validated the result till it gets confirmed*
18:     INC_{user} are distributed to $POT\_CLI_i, startfrom1, 2, ...$ *the rewards are distributed to the users*
19:     INC_{miner} are   distruted   to $miner_1, miner_2, ..., miner_n$
      the reward for the miners
20:   **end for**
21: **end procedure**

---

observer can capture the FL training information output. The observer can calculate the value difference between the updated gradient of the users' training. The authors in [21] introduced the membership inference in earlier work, which reveals unexpected information about users' training data as shown in Fig. 3 (bottom). While the primary objective of FL is to maintain user privacy, the adversary plans to reveal training data. Data leaking puts the system at risk as a whole. Therefore, healthcare-related data from *Yelp-health* (yelp.com/dataset) and *FourSquare* data have been incorporated to evaluate and examine the membership inference attack. Both sets of data are assessed by choosing 30,000 well-known places for *FourSquare* and the 5,000 most popular terms for *Yelp-health*, respectively. In conclusion, this sort of attack generates more false positives as batch sizes increase.

Regarding privacy awareness in integrating FL and blockchain SCs, supplementary protocols can be a plausible solution to solve transparency in SCs transactions since the SCs expose the detailed transaction publicly (the users' activities are noticeable). Recent research in [22] provides a *used-model-only* service to obscure the FL feature while users conduct the training activities. This

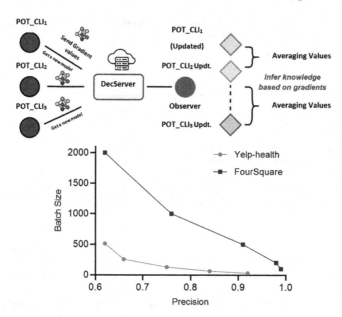

Fig. 3. Inference membership attack in an FL inferring the knowledge of the gradient values.

use case is designed for users who wish to use the model without expecting rewards from model providers or *DecServer* due to an insufficient number of the dataset and any other reasons. Furthermore, the works are extended by preserving an unlikable rewarding ETH for contributed users associated with their datasets. The amount of Ether received by users is linear to the number of data used during training. Intuitively, in the event of *used-model-only*, the users can still benefit from using FL models provided by the system without revealing their identities vividly. At first glimpse, these techniques could provide a viable solution, especially for privacy and linkability issues. Nevertheless, the existing schemes still suffer from a hard fork (radical change) in the Ethereum network, where the entire blockchain network must update the network radically (difficult to achieve perfectly). In the meantime, Table 1 shows how digital assets (cryptocurrencies) were valued using the International Financial Reporting Standards (IFRS) report. This report can be a compass for future decisions in merging FL and blockchain ETH cryptocurrencies.

FL promises to make more data available for improvement. As a result, implementing FL is not without its difficulties. While efforts have been made to improve FL's effectiveness and accuracy, security and transparency remain the two major obstacles. Numerous FL models may be customized to meet needs, such as horizontal FL, vertical FL, and federated transfer learning, to mention a few. Each model has advantages and disadvantages when used in a blockchain setting. Not all blockchain systems and security mechanisms are appropriate for the FL setting. The following are the recent challenges of the integration of FL and SCs:

Table 1. Cryptocurrencies (digital assets) are valued in accordance with International Financial Reporting Standards (IFRS).

Notation	Standard	Assessment	IFRS Acceptance
MRS 7	Flow of funds statement	Currency and its equivalents	X
MSFI 9	Financial instruments (assets that can be traded)	Digital assets at a fair price (profit or loss)	X
MRS 40	Investments in real estate (with its natural resources)	Land and building investments	X
MRS 16	Property, plant, and equipment (PP & E)	PP & E physical or tangible long-term assets	X
MRS 38	Intangible assets	identifiable non-monetary asset	✓
MRS 2	Supply	Supply	Under certain conditions (conditionally)

- The number of training models and samples are not spread equally. The FL system cannot assume that most users would have the same quantity of the local training model because it uses an aggregating server (DecServer).
- Since the FL process is iterative, it is challenging to control the users participating. Briefly, users' communication continues throughout iteration until the process is successful. However, in real-world applications, the users are not entirely engaging in the FL process, which reduces the learning quality for a number of practical reasons.
- Through the devices of millions of users, the data is distributed with a severe lack of performance or quality regularity. If it happens on a significant scale, it will be complicated. The methods for updated data collection must be flexible enough to adapt to the dynamic environment. The constancy of each party has an impact on the AI model's quality as well.
- Non-identical propagation. It may be understood that several users may produce non-identical propagations of information. A model could be trained using the same data distribution that is used to make predictions, thanks to FL. However, because it is private, it is not an excellent notion to directly gather this data since it affects security and transparency.
- The security and transparency concerns such as the inference attacks [23] and model poisoning [24]. Protecting the privacy of the users' data is the primary consideration for FL. Even though the information is not exposed, it can be seen. Repeated model weight updates can uncover characteristics that are not general to the data but particular to individual contributors. Both the server-side and the user-side can execute this inference attack. Additionally, potential risks include errant users introducing backdoor functionality or launching Sybil attacks [25] to contaminate the global model. In this situation, the additional processing time for the Sybil detection mechanism [26] must be considered.

5 Conclusion

Recent challenges in a new distributed learning with a decentralized incentive mechanism were explored in this research. We have elaborated a comprehensive benchmark of consideration in embracing blockchain technology through Ethereum Smart Contract in the federated learning environment. Furthermore, we have highlighted several well-known existing techniques to overcome the privacy issues in federated learning by stating several critical points for future research. We believe that adding more security protocols to protect FL and Ethereum SCs transactions would be the most exciting way to address privacy and transparency issues in decentralized systems among the possible methods and approaches to further this research. The present schemes offer a variety of privacy strategies, but the linkability problems inside the systems are outside the scope of this discussion; therefore, these points become crucial. This study is anticipated to offer fresh perspectives for more in-depth research in the area of decentralized learning. Future research on the performance, latency, scalability, and comparison of various blockchain and FL systems with diverse security methods built into the design would be an intriguing area to focus on. For this purpose, sustainability and efficiency might be increased while considering a wide range of encryption protocols and blockchain platforms.

References

1. Casino, F., et al.: Blockchain-based food supply chain traceability: a case study in the dairy sector. Int. J. Prod. Res. **59**(19), 5758–5770 (2021)
2. IoT analytics. https://iot-analytics.com/state-of-the-iot-update/. Accessed 17 Aug 2022
3. Marjani, M., et al.: Big IoT data analytics: architecture, opportunities, and open research challenges. IEEE Access **5**, 5247–5261 (2017)
4. Mamoshina, P., et al.: Converging blockchain and next-generation artificial intelligence technologies to decentralize and accelerate biomedical research and healthcare. Oncotarget **9**(5), 5665 (2018)
5. McMahan, B., Moore, E., Ramage, D., Hampson, S., et al.: Communication-efficient learning of deep networks from decentralized data. In: International Conference on Artificial Intelligence and Statistics (AISTATS) (2017)
6. Kim, H.M., Laskowski, M.: Toward an ontology-driven blockchain design for supply-chain provenance. Intell. Syst. Account. Finance Manag. **25**(1), 18–27 (2018)
7. Salah, K., Rehman, M.H.U., Nizamuddin, N., Al-Fuqaha, A.: Blockchain for AI review and open research challenges. IEEE Access **7**, 10127–10149 (2019)
8. Blockchain Explorer. The latest transaction and blocks of eth smart contracts (2022). https://www.blockchain.com/explorer. Accessed 15 Sept 2022
9. Kiffer, L., Levin, D., Mislove, A.: Analyzing ethereum's contract topology. In: Proceedings of the Internet Measurement Conference 2018, pp. 494–499. ACM Digital Library (2018)
10. Bonawitz, K., et al.: Towards federated learning at scale: system design. arXiv preprint arXiv:1902.01046 (2019)

11. Firdaus, M., Rahmadika, S., Rhee, K.-H.: Decentralized trusted data sharing management on internet of vehicle edge computing (IoVEC) networks using consortium blockchain. Sensors **21**(7), 1–20 (2021)
12. Khan, L.U., et al.: Federated learning for edge networks: resource optimization and incentive mechanism. IEEE Commun. Mag. **58**(10), 88–93 (2020)
13. Qu, Y., Pokhrel, S.R., Garg, S., Gao, L., Xiang, Y.: A blockchained federated learning framework for cognitive computing in industry 4.0 networks. IEEE Trans. Ind. Inform. **17**, 2964–2973 (2020)
14. Seuwou, P., Adegoke, V.F.: The changing global landscape with emerging technologies and their implications for smart societies. In: Handbook of Research on 5G Networks and Advancements in Computing, Electronics, and Electrical Engineering, pp. 402–423. IGI Global (2021)
15. Rahmadika, S., Rhee, K.-H.: Reliable collaborative learning with commensurate incentive schemes. In: 2020 IEEE International Conference on Blockchain (Blockchain), pp. 496–502. IEEE (2020)
16. Blockchain transaction report. https://worldpaymentsreport.com. Accessed 5 June 2019
17. McMahan, H.B., Moore, E., Ramage, D., Arcas, B.A.Y.: Federated learning of deep networks using model averaging. arXiv:1602.05629 (2018)
18. Kumar, P., Garg, S., Singh, A., Batra, S., Kumar, N., You, I.: MVO-based 2-D path planning scheme for providing quality of service in UAV environment. IEEE Internet Things J. **5**(3), 1698–1707 (2018)
19. Rahmadika, S., Rhee, K.-H.: Enhancing data privacy through a decentralised predictive model with blockchain-based revenue. Int. J. Ad Hoc Ubiquitous Comput. **37**(1), 1–15 (2021)
20. Chen, R., Guo, J., Wang, D.C., Tsai, J.J., Al-Hamadi, H., You, I.: Trust-based service management for mobile cloud IoT systems. IEEE Trans. Netw. Serv. Manag. **16**(1), 246–263 (2018)
21. Melis, L., Song, C., De Cristofaro, E., Shmatikov, V.: Exploiting unintended feature leakage in collaborative learning. In: 2019 IEEE Symposium on Security and Privacy (SP), pp. 691–706. IEEE (2019)
22. Rahmadika, S., Rhee, K.-H.: Unlinkable collaborative learning transactions: privacy-awareness in decentralized approaches. IEEE Access **9**, 65293–65307 (2021)
23. Melis, L., Song, C., De Cristofaro, E., Shmatikov, V.: Inference attacks against collaborative learning. CoRR, abs/1805.04049 (2018)
24. Bhagoji, A.N., Chakraborty, S., Mittal, P., Calo, S.: Analyzing federated learning through an adversarial lens. CoRR, abs/1811.12470 (2018)
25. Bagdasaryan, E., Veit, A., Hua, Y., Estrin, D., Shmatikov, V.: How to backdoor federated learning. CoRR, abs/1807.00459 (2018)
26. Fung, C., Yoon, C.J.M., Beschastnikh, I.: Mitigating sybils in federated learning poisoning. CoRR, abs/1808.04866 (2018)

Cryptography and Data Security

Theoretical and Deep Learning Based Analysis of Biases in Salsa 128 Bits

S.K. Karthika[✉] and Kunwar Singh

Department of of Computer Science and Engineering, National Institute of Technology, Tiruchirappalli, TamilNadu 620015, India
karthika231188@gmail.com, kunwar@nitt.edu

Abstract. Salsa, designed by Daniel J. Bernstein is one of the finalists candidate of eSTREAM projects in 2005. It is a well known stream cipher and it gained its popularity when the most used stream cipher RC4 was subjected to multiple cryptanalytic techniques. The stream cipher Salsa comes in two versions - 128 bits and 256 bits depending upon the size of the seed key. Salsa has went through various key recovery attacks up to its 8-th round where most of the attacks were focused on Salsa 256 bits. There are many more prevalent experimental attacks on Salsa while leaving space for theoretical analysis. Theoretical analysis helps in spotting the feature that subjects the cipher to attack and thus can be used to design a better cipher that is resistive to attacks. Dey et al. [1] have theoretically analyzed the cause of distinguishers in Salsa 256 bits and Chacha 256 bits that occur in experimental attacks. Motivated by this work, in this paper, we have theoretically analyzed differential attack on Salsa 128 bits up to four rounds and mathematically proved the probabilities of the observations. Also, our theoretical analysis results of Salsa 128 bits are on par with the experimental results. As an extension of this work and to find more accurate distinguishers for round 4 and higher rounds, we are working on the idea to find neural distinguisher in Salsa 128-bits based on the model proposed by Gohr in CRYPTO 2019 [2].

Keywords: Stream Cipher · Salsa · Cryptanalysis · Differential attack · Theoretical analysis · Deep Learning

1 Introduction

Stream ciphers are symmetric key cryptosystems that encrypts data one bit or one byte at a time. The main objective of stream ciphers is to compute long pseudo-random sequence from a short random stream. The long pseudo-random sequence is called as keystream and the short random stream is the Secret key (Seed). The challenging part in any stream cipher is to generate keystream that looks like a random stream. Reusing a secret key to encrypt more than one message will make it vulnerable to attacks. At the same time, generating new secret key for each set of message is practically impossible. The solution to these issues is the use of Initialization Vector (IV). All the modern stream ciphers use

© The Author(s), under exclusive license to Springer Nature Singapore Pte Ltd. 2023
I. You et al. (Eds.): MobiSec 2022, CCIS 1644, pp. 147–164, 2023.
https://doi.org/10.1007/978-981-99-4430-9_11

IV as part of keystream generation. The IVs are public variables that differ for each encryption and are generally randomizers. Using the same key, different messages can be encrypted just by varying the IVs. In this way, same secret key can be used for different messages. The security of a stream cipher is based on the idea that, the adversary cannot distinguish the keystream generated by the stream cipher from a random stream.

Salsa is a software oriented stream cipher designed by Daniel J. Bernstein in 2005 [3]. When the renowned stream cipher RC4 was subjected to various cryptanalytic techniques, eSTREAM project was announced. In the eSTREAM project, four hardware and four software oriented stream ciphers were shortlisted. Salsa is one of the finalists in software category of eSTREAM projects. The variant of Salsa called the Chacha was adopted by GOOGLE in its security protocols. Due to the increasing popularity of Salsa and Chacha, these became a topic of interest to cryptanalysis. The first attack on Salsa was done by Paul Crowley in 2005 [4]. Crowley imposed differential cryptanalysis on salsa reduced to 5-th round. In INDOCRYPT 2006, Fischer et al. performed a key recovery attack on 6 round salsa and also observed non-randomness at round 7 [5]. Later, Tsunoo et al. found a bias in 4 round salsa which they further exploited to recover key in the 8-th round with a low computational complexity [6]. In this work, we tend to analyze the reason behind distinguishers caused by differential attacks on Salsa 128 bits. The process is as follows - A single bit in input (IV) is changed and its impact on the results after certain number of rounds are analyzed. The results are compared with the results of the unmodified input. At each stage, the changes are analyzed probabilistically.

Motivation: In recent days, internet based mobile devices are predominant when it comes to simple and fast communication. These mobile devices with internet access are slowly replacing many activities that could be done in personal computers. When compared to personal computers, mobile devices are restricted to resources and have power constraints. Also, mobile devices when used for communication, demands security protocols that consume less resources and power without compromising security. This need has lead way to the research field lightweight cryptography. Among the cryptographic primitives, stream ciphers are the efficient ones in terms of simplicity and speed. The stream ciphers which gives uncompromising security with limited resources and power consumption are called lightweight stream ciphers. The widespread use of lightweight stream ciphers in different power constrained environments like mobile devices has motivated us to explore it in the light of cryptanalysis.

Contribution: Dey et al. in [7,8] have analyzed the reason for forward bias that leads to distinguishers in lightweight stream cipher Salsa. To the best of our knowledge, this is the first ever theoretical analysis on Salsa differential attack. Recently Dey et al. [1] proposed theoretical analysis of Salsa and Chacha 256 bits. Motivated by this, we have theoretically analyzed Salsa 128 bits upto four rounds and our theoretical analysis is on par with experimental results.

In CRYPTO 2019, Gohr [2] proposed a Deep Learning based differential cryptanalysis on the block cipher Speck. In his analysis, he found that neural distinguishers were more accurate than traditional method of finding distinguishers using difference distribution table. Using the model given by Gohr, we are attempting to find neural distinguishers in the stream cipher Salsa 128-bits. With this model, finding distinguishers for higher rounds with high accuracy is possible.

Paper Outline: The paper is organized as follows - Preliminaries about Salsa and Differential attack in Sect. 2, general probability results in Sect. 3, mathematically observed biases in Salsa 128 bits with proof in Sect. 4, theoretical and experimental result comparison in Sect. 5, related work in Sect. 6, followed by a brief summary to deep learning based differential cryptanalysis in Sect. 7 and lastly conclusion and future work in Sect. 8.

2 Preliminaries

2.1 Salsa

Salsa contains three main functions - the hash function, the expansion function and an encryption function where the hash function is the core of salsa. The hash function takes in 64 byte input and produces a 64 byte output. The 64 byte input is considered as 16 words each of size 4 bytes. The 16 words are categorized as 8 words of key, $\{k_1, k_2, \cdots, k_8\}$, 4 words of IV (Initialization Vector), $\{IV_1, IV_2, IV_3, IV_4\}$, and 4 constant words, $\{c_1, c_2, c_3, c_4\}$. The salsa version of being it 128 bits or 256 bits depends on the key type that is chosen. The 8 key words constitute to 256 bits and if the initial key is 128 bits, it will be added to itself to make it 256 bits i.e., the keys K_5, K_6, K_7, K_8 are same as K_1, K_2, K_3, K_4 respectively. The words of salsa are denoted as,

$$W = \begin{pmatrix} W_1 & W_2 & W_3 & W_4 \\ W_5 & W_6 & W_7 & W_8 \\ W_9 & W_{10} & W_{11} & W_{12} \\ W_{13} & W_{14} & W_{15} & W_{16} \end{pmatrix} = \begin{pmatrix} C_1 & K_1 & K_2 & K_3 \\ K_4 & C_2 & IV_1 & IV_2 \\ IV_3 & IV_4 & C_3 & K_5 \\ K_6 & K_7 & K_8 & C_4 \end{pmatrix}$$

These words are processed in columns and rows. In odd number of round, the columns are processed and in the even number of rounds, the rows are processed. In each column and row processing, a function called 'quarterround' function is employed. The quarterround, column round and row round are denoted as follows,

Quarterround: The quarterround takes a 4 word sequence as input and outputs a 4 word sequence. If $W = (W_1, W_2, W_3, W_4)$ is the input to quarterround, then $quarterround(W) = (S_1, S_2, S_3, S_4)$ where,

$$S_2 = W_2 \oplus ((W_1 + W_4) \lll 7)$$
$$S_3 = W_3 \oplus ((S_2 + W_1) \lll 9)$$
$$S_4 = W_4 \oplus ((S_3 + S_2) \lll 13)$$
$$S_1 = W_1 \oplus ((S_4 + S_3) \lll 18)$$

Columnround: Let the input to the column round function be $W = (W_1, W_2, \cdots, W_{16})$. The column round for the 16 word salsa matrix is given as,

$$(S_1, S_5, S_9, S_{13}) = quarterround(W_1, W_5, W_9, W_{13})$$
$$(S_6, S_{10}, S_{14}, S_2) = quarterround(W_6, W_{10}, W_{14}, W_2)$$
$$(S_{11}, S_{15}, S_3, S_7) = quarterround(W_{11}, W_{15}, W_3, W_7)$$
$$(S_{16}, S_4, S_8, S_{12}) = quarterround(W_{16}, W_4, W_8, W_{12})$$

Rowround: Let the input to the row round function be $W = (W_1, W_2, \cdots, W_{16})$. The row round for the 16 word salsa matrix is given as,

$$(S_1, S_2, S_3, S_4) = quarterround(W_1, W_2, W_3, W_4)$$
$$(S_6, S_7, S_8, S_5) = quarterround(W_6, W_7, W_8, W_5)$$
$$(S_{11}, S_{12}, S_9, S_{10}) = quarterround(W_{11}, W_{12}, W_9, W_{10})$$
$$(S_{16}, S_{13}, S_{14}, S_{15}) = quarterround(W_{16}, W_{13}, W_{14}, W_{15})$$

2.2 Differential Attack

The idea of differential attack is to observe how the change in input affects the output. This attack traces the input difference to find a distinguisher in the cipher. This attack is generally a chosen-plaintext attack. The assumption in this work regarding differential attack is that the adversary is accessible to the IV bits. In this paper, a differential attack on Salsa 128 bits is analyzed theoretically. The idea of analysis is as follows - Two 16 word sequences W and W' are taken where W' has one bit different from W. Each word is composed of 32 bits, indexed from 0 to 31. The difference is given at 31st bit in the eighth word of W'. This implies, when W and W' are XORed, only the 31st bit of the eighth word in the result will be as 1. Both the word sequences are subjected to Salsa round functions and the differences are traced. Probabilities of the similarities of the outputs are compared and analyzed. If the computed probability is varying from 0.5, then the output is considered to be distinguishable and thus proving the non-randomness of the cipher.

3 Probabilistic Results

3.1 Basic Notations

The following are the notations used in this paper,

1. W_i indicates a word with number i.
2. $W_i[n]$ denotes n^{th} bit of W_i.
3. $W_i^r[n]$ denotes n^{th} bit of W_i at round r.
4. $Pr[E]$ indicates the probability of occurrence of an event E.

5. Let $\lambda_w[n] = Pr(W[n] = W'[n])$ denote the event that n^{th} bit of W and W' are equal.
6. Let $\bar{\lambda}_w[n] = Pr(W[n] \neq W'[n])$ denote the event that n^{th} bit of W and W' are different.
7. Let $\Phi(W[n], k)$ denote the event that for any pair of words (W, W'), the bits from n to k are complemented exactly.
8. Let $\bar{\Phi}(W[n], k)$ denote the event that for any pair of words (W, W'), the bits from n to k are complemented at the least.

3.2 Proved Results

Herewith we have stated a Lemma and two theorems which will be used in Salsa analysis.

Lemma 1. *Let X and Y be two independently chosen random 32 bit numbers. Let Y' be a 32 bit number that differs exactly at one bit position (let it be n) as to Y. Consider $Z = X + Y \bmod 2^{32}$ and $Z' = X + Y' \bmod 2^{32}$. Now, for any $k \geq 0$ such that $n + k \leq 31$, the probability that Z and Z' differ at $(n + k)^{th}$ bit is $\frac{1}{2^k}$.*

The proof of this Lemma is available in [9].

Theorem 1. *Let X and Y be two independently chosen random single bit numbers. Let X' and Y' be two single bit numbers such that $Pr(X = X') = p$ and $Pr(Y = Y') = q$. Let $Z = X + Y$ and $Z' = X' + Y'$. Then the probability that $Pr(Z = Z')$ is given as*

$$pq + (1 - p)(1 - q) \ if \ c = c'$$
$$p(1 - q) + q(1 - p) \ if \ c \neq c'$$

Theorem 2. *Let X and Y be two independently chosen random $n-$bit numbers. Let X' and Y' be two $n - bit$ numbers such that $Pr(X[n] = X'[n]) = p_i$ and $Pr(Y[n] = Y'[n]) = q_i$ for $0 \leq n \leq 31$. Let $c[n]$ be the carry generated at position n in $Z = X + Y$ and $c'[n]$ be the carry generated at position n in $Z' = X' + Y'$. Then,*

$$Pr\left(c_{i+1} \neq c'_{i+1}\right) = Pr\left(c_i \neq c'_i\right) \cdot \left(1 - p - q + \frac{3pq}{2}\right) + Pr\left(c_i = c'_i\right) \frac{(1 - pq)}{2}$$

Theorems 1 and 2 are proved in [7].

4 Bias in Salsa 128 Bits

The input to Salsa 128 bits is 4 words of IV values, 4 words of Constants and 8 words of key bits where a 4 word (128 bits) key stream is added to itself to make it

8 words (256 bits) key stream. In [7] and [1], the authors have analyzed the biases observed in Salsa 256. Since, in salsa 128 bits, the keys are repeated twice, there will be changes in biases too. Therefore, in this work, we have analyzed the biases in Salsa 128 bits using similar approach as in [1]. Let $W = (W_1, W_2, \cdots, W_{16})$ be the original input and $W' = (W'_1, W'_2, \cdots, W'_{16})$ be the one bit modified input. The difference is given at 31-st bit of the eighth word and the biases are observed up-to four rounds of Salsa 128 bits.

4.1   Observations of Round 1

In round 1, the computation is done column wise. The quarterround applied to the first three columns of W and W' does not show any difference in output since the inputs are same. The input difference to W' was given at the last column i.e., 31-st bit of W'_8. The observations of the last column are as follows,

- $W'^1_4 = W'^0_4 \oplus ((W'^0_{16} + W'^0_{12}) \lll 7)$: This computation does not involve W'^0_8 and thus there is no change observed.
- $W'^1_8 = W'^0_8 \oplus ((W'^0_4 + W'^1_{16}) \lll 9)$: The addition does not show any difference. The difference in output occurs during XOR operation. Since the input contains a difference at 31-st bit of W'^0_8, this difference remains at 31-st bit of W'^1_8.
- $W'^1_{12} = W'^0_{12} \oplus ((W'^1_8 + W'^1_4) \lll 13)$: W'^1_4 does not have any difference and W'^1_8 has difference at 31-st bit. So addition result has difference at 31-st bit and the difference does not propagate to the left since it is the last bit. During left rotation, this difference gets shifted to 12-th bit. Since W'^0_{12} does not have any change, the difference remains at 12-th bit of W'^1_{12}.
- $W'^1_{16} = W'^0_{16} \oplus ((W'^1_{12} + W'^1_8) \lll 18)$: W'^1_{12} has difference at 12-th bit and W'^1_8 has difference at 31-st bit. These differences shift to positions 30 and 17 respectively during 18 bit left rotation and remains in the same position at W'^0_{16} after XOR.

Thus, at the end of round 1, W' has differences at 4 bit positions $W'^1_8[31]$, $W'^1_{12}[12]$, $W'^1_{16}[17]$, $W'^1_{16}[30]$.

4.2   Observations of Round 2

Theorem 3. *At the end of round 2,*

1. $Pr([W^2_{13}[5] = W'^2_{13}[5]]) = 0$
2. $Pr([W^2_{13}[6] = W'^2_{13}[6]]) = 0.5$
3. $Pr([W^2_{13}[24] = W'^2_{13}[24]]) = 0$
4. $Pr[\Phi(W^2_{13}[24], k)] = \frac{1}{2^k}$ *for* $1 \leq k \leq 7$
5. $Pr([W^2_{13}[7-23] = W'^2_{13}[7-23]]) = 1$

Proof. The first quarterround function of last row is,

$$W_{13}'^{2} = W_{13}'^{1} \oplus ((W_{16}'^{1} + W_{15}'^{1}) \lll 7)$$

Part 1: There is no change in $W_{15}'^{1}$ and there are two bits difference in $W_{16}'^{1}$ i.e., $W_{16}'^{1}[17]$ and $W_{16}'^{1}[30]$. During addition of $W_{15}'^{1}$ and $W_{16}'^{1}$, the changes are reflected in the bit positions 17 and 30. The 30th bit propagates to 5th bit during 7 bit left rotation. Therefore the probability that the bits at position 5 in W_{13}^{2} and $W_{13}'^{2}$ at the end of round 2 is 0.

Part 2: During addition, the change in 30th bit may propagate to its left with probability $\frac{1}{2^{k}}$. In this case, the propagation is only to the 31st bit and this, when left rotated by 7 bits, will go to 6th bit. Therefore, the probability that the sixth bit of output changes is $\frac{1}{2^{1}} = 0.5$.

Parts 3,4,5: In case of the difference in 17th bit, the 7 bit left rotation shifts the difference to bit position 24. Thus, the probability that 24th bit of W_{13}^{2} and $W_{13}'^{2}$ are same is 0. According to Lemma 1, this difference propagates up to k bits and is given as,

$$\Phi_{13}^{2}[24 + k] = \frac{1}{2^{k}} \text{ for } 1 \leq k \leq 7$$

The remaining bits in positions 7 to 23 are unchanged and thus the probability that they are equal is 1. The XOR operation does not produce any change since there is no difference in $W_{13}'^{1}$.

Theorem 4. *At the end of round 2,*

1. $\lambda_{14}^{2}[29] = 0.875$
2. $\lambda_{14}^{2}[30] = 0.9375$
3. $\lambda_{14}^{2}[31] = 0.9687$
4. $Pr([W_{14}^{2}[9 - 13] = W_{14}'^{2}[9 - 13]]) = 1$
5. $Pr([W_{14}^{2}[16 - 25] = W_{14}'^{2}[16 - 25]]) = 1$

Proof. The second quarterround for the last row is,

$$W_{14}'^{2} = W_{14}'^{1} \oplus ((W_{13}'^{2} + W_{16}'^{1}) \lll 9)$$

Parts 1,2,3: The difference at 17th bit of $W_{16}'^{1}$ reflects in the 17th bit of addition result and propagates to the next left bits with probability $\frac{1}{2^{k}}$ (Lemma 1). Therefore, $\bar{\lambda}_{Sum}[21] = \frac{1}{2^{(21-17)}} = 0.0625$. This means, $\lambda_{Sum}[21] = 0.9375$ This difference, when rotated 9 bits left, propagates to $W_{14}'^{2}[30]$ and XOR does not cause any change since there is no difference in $W_{14}'^{1}$. Similarly it can be proved that $\lambda_{Sum}[20] = 0.875$ and $\lambda_{Sum}[22] = 0.9687$. This difference reflects in $W_{14}'^{2}[29]$ and $W_{14}'^{2}[31]$ respectively.

Part 4,5: $W_{13}'^{1}$ has changes in 5th bit, 6th bit and from 24th bit as in Theorem 3. All the differences in the sum of $W_{13}'^{1}$ and $W_{16}'^{1}$ are seen between the bit positions 5, 6 and 17 to 31. The bits in positions 0 to 4 and 7 to 16 are unchanged. This when rotated to left by 9 bits, reflect in bit positions 9 to 13 and 16 to 25. Therefore, the bit positions from 9 to 13 and 16 to 25 in W_{14}^{2} are unchanged.

Theorem 5. *At the end of round 2,*

1. $\lambda^2_{15}[12] = 0.9612$
2. $\lambda^2_{15}[11] = 0.9235$
3. $\lambda^2_{15}[10] = 0.8515$
4. $Pr([W^2_{15}[0-4] = W'^2_{15}[0-4]]) = 1$
5. $Pr([W^2_{15}[22-26] = W'^2_{15}[22-26]]) = 1$
6. $Pr([W^2_{15}[29-31] = W'^2_{15}[29-31]]) = 1$

Proof. The third quarterround for the last row is,

$$W'^2_{15} = W'^1_{15} \oplus ((W'^2_{14} + W'^2_{13}) \lll 13)$$

Parts 1,2,3: From Theorem 3, we have $\Phi^2_{13}[24+k] = \frac{1}{2^k}$ for $0 \le k \le 7$. Therefore, for k=7,

$$\lambda^2_{13}[31] = 1 - \frac{1}{2^{(31-24)}} = 0.9921.$$

Also, from Theorem 4, we have $\lambda^2_{14}[31] = 0.9687$. Let $Sum[31] = W'^2_{13}[31] + W'^2_{14}[31]$, $\lambda^2_{13}[31] = 0.9921$ be p and $\lambda^2_{14}[31] = 0.9687$ be q. Applying Theorem 1,

$$\lambda_{Sum}[31] = pq + (1-p)(1-q) = 0.9612$$

After shifting it 13 bits to the left and XOR with W'^1_{15}, this difference propagates to $W'^2_{15}[12]$. Similarly $W'^2_{15}[11] = 0.9235$ and $W'^2_{15}[10] = 0.8515$ can be proved.

Parts 4,5,6: As in Theorem 3, the bits in positions 7 to 23 of W'_{13} are unchanged and as in Theorem 4, the bits in positions 9 to 13 and 16 to 25 of W'^2_{14} are unchanged. Thus, the common unchanged bit positions when these two words are added are 9 to 13 and 16 to 23. When rotated by 13 bits to the left, this is reflected in bit positions, 22 to 26, 29 to 31 and 0 to 4.

Theorem 6. *At the end of round 2,*

1. $\lambda^2_{16}[30] = 0.1073$
2. $\lambda^2_{16}[29] = 0.8605$
3. $Pr([W^2_{16}[22-25] = W'^2_{16}[22-25]]) = 1$

Proof. The fourth quarterround for the last row is,

$$W'^2_{16} = W'^1_{16} \oplus ((W'^2_{15} + W'^2_{14}) \lll 18)$$

Part 1: Let $Sum' = W'^2_{14} + W'^2_{15}$. The twelfth bit of Sum' will be XORed with 30th bit of W'^1_{16}, i.e.,

$$W'^2_{16}[30] = W'^1_{16}[30] \oplus Sum'[12].$$

At the end of round 1, there was a difference at $W'^1_{16}[30]$. Therefore, $\lambda^1_{16}[30] = 0$. During addition of $W'^2_{14} + W'^2_{15}$, let us consider the bits 12, 11 and 10. The 12th, 11th and 10th bit of W'^2_{14} does not have any difference so far. Therefore,

$$\lambda^2_{14}[12] = p_{12} = 1$$
$$\lambda^2_{14}[11] = p_{11} = 1$$
$$\lambda^2_{14}[10] = p_{10} = 1$$

From Theorem 5 we have,

$$\lambda_{15}^2[12] = q_{12} = 0.9612$$
$$\lambda_{15}^2[11] = q_{11} = 0.9235$$
$$\lambda_{15}^2[10] = q_{10} = 0.8515$$

Since we consider only bits $10, 11$ and 12, ignore the carry from the 9th bit. Therefore, $Pr(c[10] = c'[10]) = 1$. Using Theorem 2, compute $Pr(c[11] = c'[11])$ as,

$$Pr(c[11] = c'[11]) = 1 - Pr(c[10] \neq c'[10])$$
$$= 1 - 0.07425 = 0.92575$$

Similarly,

$$Pr(c[12] = c'[12]) = 1 - Pr(c[11] \neq c'[11])$$
$$= 1 - 0.07425 = 0.92575$$

$$Pr(c[12] \neq c'[12]) = 0.07425$$

Let $Sum[12] = W_{14}^2[12] + W_{15}^2[12]$ and $Sum'[12] = W_{14}'^2[12] + W_{15}'^2[12]$. Now,

$$\lambda_{Sum}[12] = Pr(Sum[12] = Sum'[12])$$
$$= Pr(c[12] = c'[12])Pr((Sum[12] = Sum'[12])$$
$$|(c[12] = c'[12])) + Pr(c[12] \neq c'[12])Pr((Sum[12] = Sum'[12])|(c[12] \neq c'[12]))$$

Using Theorem 1, we can find $Pr((Sum[12] = Sum'[12])|(c[12] = c'[12])) = 0.9612$ and $Pr((Sum[12] = Sum'[12])|(c[12] \neq c'[12])) = 0.0388$. Substituting these values to find $\lambda_{Sum}[12] = Pr(Sum[12] = Sum'[12])$, we get $\lambda_{Sum}[12] = 0.8927$. Therefore,

$$\bar{\lambda}_{Sum}[12] = 1 - 0.8927 = 0.1073.$$

This difference at $Sum[12]$ will be XORed with $W_{16}'^1[30]$ due to 18 bit left rotation. We already know that $\bar{\lambda}_{16}^1[30] = 0$. Therefore, $W_{16}'^2[30] = 0.1073$.

Part 2: The eleventh bit of Sum' will be XORed with 29th bit of $W_{16}'^1$, i.e.,

$$W_{16}'^2[29] = W_{16}'^1[29] \oplus Sum'[11].$$

The $Pr(Sum[11] = Sum'[11])$ can be computed as shown in part a. We find $\lambda_{Sum}[11] = Pr(Sum[11] = Sum'[11]) = 0.8605$. When $Sum'[11]$ is left shifted by 18 bits, it is XORed with $W_{16}'^1[29]$. So far, there is no difference observed at $W_{16}'^1[29]$. Therefore, the difference at $Sum[11]$ is reflected in $W_{16}'^2[29]$ and thus $\lambda_{16}^2[29] = 0.8605$.

Part 3: From Theorems 4,5 we know that the bits in positions 9 to 13 and 16 to 25 of $w_{14}'^2$ and bits in positions 0 to 4, 22 to 26 and 29 to 31 of $w_{15}'^2$ are unchanged. The common bits positions in these two that are unchanged are bits in positions 22 to 25. This reflects in sum and when shifted to left by 18 bit positions, this is observed in bit positions 8 to 11. Further, after XOR, since there are no changes in these positions in $w_{16}'^1$, the bits in positions 8 to 11 are unchanged in $w_{16}'^2$.

Theorem 7. *At the end of round 2,*

1. $Pr(W_{12}^2[12] = W_{12}'^2[12]) = 0$
2. $Pr[\Phi(W_9'^2[21], k)] = \frac{1}{2^k} \ for \ 0 \le k \le 10.$

Proof. Part 1: The first quarterround function of the third row is,

$$W_{12}'^2 = W_{12}'^1 \oplus ((W_{11}'^1 + W_{10}'^1) \lll 7)$$

There is no difference in $W_{11}'^1$ and $W_{10}'^1$ at the end of round 1. There is a difference at $W_{12}'^1[12]$ and this reflects in $W_{12}'^2[12]$. Therefore, $Pr(W_{12}^2[12] = W_{12}'^2[12]) = 0$.
     Part 2: The second quarterround function of the third row is,

$$W_9'^2 = W_9'^1 \oplus ((W_{12}'^2 + W_{11}'^1) \lll 9)$$

From the above result, we know that $W_{12}'^2[12]$ has a difference. During addition with $W_{11}'^1$, this difference propagates to the left with probability $\frac{1}{2^k}$ (Lemma 1). With 9 bit left rotation, this difference shifts to 21st bit and propagates to its left. Since $W_9'^1$ does not have any difference, this difference reflects in $W_9'^2$. Therefore,

$$Pr[\Phi(W_9'^2[21], k)] = \frac{1}{2^k} \ for \ 0 \le k \le 10.$$

Theorem 8. *At the end of round 2,*

1. $\lambda_{10}^2[28] = 0.875$
2. $\lambda_{10}^2[29] = 0.9375$
3. $\lambda_{10}^2[30] = 0.9688$
4. $\lambda_{10}^2[31] = 0.9844$
5. $Pr([W_{10}^2[13 - 24] = W_{10}'^2[13 - 24]]) = 1$

Proof. The third quarterround function of third row is,

$$W_{10}'^2 = W_{10}'^1 \oplus ((W_9'^2 + W_{12}'^2) \lll 13)$$

     Parts 1 - 4: From Theorem 7, we know that $W_{12}'^2[12]$ has a difference. $W_9'^2[12]$ does not have any difference. When $W_{12}'^2[12]$ and $W_9'^2[12]$ are added, the difference at 12th bit propagates to the left with probability $\frac{1}{2^k}$. From this we have,

$$\lambda_{Sum}[15] = 1 - \frac{1}{2^{(15-12)}} = 0.875$$

This difference, after the 13 bit left rotation and XOR, reflects in $W_{10}'^2[28]$. Similarly, the probabilities of $\lambda_{10}^2[29]$, $\lambda_{10}^2[30]$ and $\lambda_{10}^2[31]$ can be proved.
     Part 5: From Theorem 7, it is evident that there is a difference in $W_9'^2$ and $W_{12}'^2$ from bit positions 21 to 31 and 12 respectively. During addition, the changes may propagate and reflect in bits from 12 to 31. The bits in positions 0 to 11 are unchanged. During 13 bit left rotation and after XOR with $W_{10}'^1$ (No initial difference observed in this word), this is observed in bit positions 13 to 24 of $W_{10}'^2$.

Theorem 9. *At the end of round 2,*

1. $Pr([W_7^2 = W_7'^2]) = 1$
2. $Pr([W_8^2[31] = W_8'^2[31]]) = 0$

Proof. Part 1: The first quarterround of second row is,

$$W_7'^2 = W_7'^1 \oplus ((W_6'^1 + W_5'^1) \lll 7)$$

There are no changes observed in $W_6'^1$, $W_5'^1$ and $W_7'^1$ after round 1. Thus W_7^2 and $W_7'^2$ are same.

Part 2: The second quarterround of second row is,

$$W_8'^2 = W_8'^1 \oplus ((W_7'^2 + W_6'^1) \lll 9)$$

There are no changes observed in $W_7'^2$ and $W_6'^1$. Therefore, there are no changes after addition of these two and 9 bit left rotation. At the end of round 1, there was a difference at 31st bit of $W_8'^1$. This reflects after the XOR and is observed in 31st bit of $W_8'^2$. Thus, the probability that $W_8^2[31] = W_8'^2[31]$ is 0.

Theorem 10. *At the end of round 2,*

1. $Pr(W_5^2[12] = W_5'^2[12]) = 0$
2. $Pr(W_6^2[17] = W_6'^2[17]) = 0$
3. $Pr(W_6^2[30] = W_6'^2[30]) = 0$

Proof. Part 1: The third quarterround of second row is,

$$W_5'^2 = W_5'^1 \oplus ((W_8'^2 + W_7'^2) \lll 13)$$

At the end of round 1, there was a difference at $W_8'^1[31]$. $W_7'^1$ and $W_5'^1$ does not have any difference. The difference at $W_8'^1[31]$ reflects in the 31st bit of the sum and shifts to bit position 12 during 13 bit left rotation. Since $W_5'^1$ does not have any difference, the change at position 12 reflects at $W_5'^2[12]$. Thus the $Pr(W_5^2[12] = W_5'^2[12]) = 0$.

Part 2: The fourth quarterround of second row is,

$$W_6'^2 = W_6'^1 \oplus ((W_5'^2 + W_8'^2) \lll 18)$$

From Theorem 9 we know that there is a difference at $W_8'^2[31]$ and from above proof we know that there is a difference at $W_5'^2[12]$. When $W_5'^2$ and $W_8'^2$ are added, the differences are reflected at 31st bit and 12th bits. During 18 bit left rotation, the differences are observed at bit positions 17 and 30. Since $W_6'^1$ does not have any change, after the XOR, the changes are observed in bit positions 17 and 30 of $W_6'^2$.

4.3   Observations of Round 3

Theorem 11. *At the end of third round,*

1. $Pr(W_{10}^3[24] = W_{10}'^3[24]) = 0$
2. $Pr(W_{10}^3[5] = W_{10}'^3[5]) = 0$
3. $\lambda^3{}_{10}[i] = \begin{cases} 0.875 \ for \ i=28 \\ 0.9375 \ for \ i=29 \\ 0.9688 \ for \ i=30 \\ 0.9844 \ for \ i=31 \end{cases}$

Proof. The first quarterround of column 2 is,

$$W_{10}'^3 = W_{10}'^2 \oplus ((W_6'^2 + W_2'^2) \lll 7)$$

Part 1: There is a change observed at $W_6'^2[17]$ in Theorem 10. This, after addition with $W_2'^2$ and 7 bit left rotation, is observed in bit position 24 and is reflected after XOR in $W_{10}'^3[24]$.

Part 2: There is a change observed at $W_6'^2[30]$ in Theorem 10. This, after addition with $W_2'^2$ and 7 bit left rotation, is observed in bit position 5 and is reflected after XOR in $W_{10}'^3[5]$.

Part 3: From Theorem 8, we have $\lambda_{19}^2[28] = 0.875$, $\lambda_{10}^2[29] = 0.9375$, $\lambda_{10}^2[30] = 0.9688$ and $\lambda_{10}^2[31] = 0.9844$. This, after the XOR with left rotated sum, is observed in $W_{10}'^3$.

Theorem 12. *At the end of third round,*

1. $\bar{\lambda}_{14}^3[7] = 0.9688$
2. $\bar{\lambda}_{14}^3[8] = 0.5$
3. $\lambda^3{}_{14}[i] = \begin{cases} 0.875 \ for \ i=29 \\ 0.9375 \ for \ i=30 \\ 0.9687 \ for \ i=31 \end{cases}$

Proof. The second quarterround of column 2 is,

$$W_{14}'^3 = W_{14}'^2 \oplus ((W_{10}'^3 + W_6'^2) \lll 9)$$

Part 1: From Theorem 10 we have, $\lambda_6^2[30] = 0$ and thus let p=0. From Theorem 11 we have, $\lambda_{10}^3[30] = 0.9688$ and thus q=0.9688. Applying Theorem 1,

$$\lambda_{Sum}[30] = pq + (1-p)(1-q) = 0.0312$$

Therefore $\bar{\lambda}_{Sum}[30] = 1 - 0.0312 = 0.9688$. This after 9 bit left rotation and XOR, reflects in bit position 7 of $W_{14}'^4$. Therefore, $\bar{\lambda}_{14}[7] = 0.9688$.

Part 2: From Theorem 10 we have a change in bit position 30 of $W_6'^2$ and this may propagate to left with probability $\frac{1}{2^k}$. From this we have, $\lambda_6^2[31] = 0.5$ (for k=1) and thus let p=0.5. From Theorem 11 we have, $\lambda_{10}^3[31] = 0.9844$ and thus q=0.9844. Applying Theorem 1,

$$\lambda_{Sum}[31] = pq + (1-p)(1-q) = 0.5$$

Therefore $\bar{\lambda}_{Sum}[31] = 1 - 0.5 = 0.5$. This after 9 bit left rotation and XOR, reflects in bit position 8 of $W_{14}'^4$. Therefore, $\bar{\lambda}_{14}[8] = 0.5$.

Part 3: From Theorem 4, we have $\lambda_{14}^2[29] = 0.875$, $\lambda_{14}^2[30] = 0.9375$, and $\lambda_{14}^2[30] = 0.9687$. This, after the XOR with left rotated sum, is observed in $W_{14}'^3$.

Theorem 13. *At the end of third round,*

$$\lambda^3{}_2[i] = \begin{cases} 0.8281 \ for \ i=10 \\ 0.9102 \ for \ i=11 \\ 0.954 \ for \ i=12 \end{cases}$$

Proof. The third quarterround of column 2 is,

$$W_2'^3 = W_2'^2 \oplus ((W_{14}'^3 + W_{10}'^3) \lll 13)$$

From Theorem 12 we have,

$$\lambda_{14}^3[29] = 0.875 = p_{29}$$
$$\lambda_{14}^3[30] = 0.9375 = p_{30}$$
$$\lambda_{14}^3[31] = 0.9687 = p_{31}$$

From Theorem 11 we have,

$$\lambda_{10}^3[29] = 0.9375 = q_{29}$$
$$\lambda_{10}^3[30] = 0.9688 = q_{30}$$
$$\lambda_{10}^3[31] = 0.9844 = q_{31}$$

Let $Sum = W_{14}'^3 + W_{10}'^3$. Using Theorem 1, we can calculate $\lambda_{Sum}[29]$ as,

$$\lambda_{Sum}[29] = p_{29}q_{29} + (1 - p_{29})(1 - q_{29}) = 0.8281$$

This after 13 bit left rotation and XOR, reflects in bit position 10 of $W_2'^3$. Similarly we can prove for other bit positions.

Theorem 14. *At the end of round 3,*

1. $\lambda_4^3[4] = 0.8605$
2. $\lambda_4^3[5] = 0.1073$
3. $Pr(W_4^3[19] = W_4'^3[19]) = 0$

Proof. The first quarterround of column 4 is,

$$W_4'^3 = W_4'^2 \oplus ((W_{16}'^2 + W_{12}'^2) \lll 7)$$

From Theorem 6 we have $\lambda_{16}^2[29] = 0.8605$ and $\lambda_{16}^2[30] = 0.1073$. This, after addition and 7 bit left shift, reflects in bit positions 4 and 5 of the sum. Also, from Theorem 7 we have, $Pr(W_{12}'^2[12] = W_{12}'^2[12]) = 0$. This, after addition and 7 bit left shift, reflects in bit position 19 of the sum. Since $W_4'^2$ does not have any change, XORing does not affect the changes and the observed changes in bit positions 4,5 and 19 of the sum are seen in the same bit positions of $W_4'^3$.

4.4 Observations of Round 4

Theorem 15. *At the end of round 4,*

1. $\lambda_2^4[11] = 0.7957$
2. $\lambda_2^4[12] = 0.1434$

Proof. The first quarterround of row 1 is,

$$W_2'^4 = W_2'^3 \oplus ((W_1'^3 + W_4'^3) \lll 7)$$

From Theorem 14 we have, $\lambda_4^3[4] = 0.8605$ and $\lambda_4^3[5] = 0.1073$. This reflects in the addition with $W_1'^3$ (No change observed in bit positions 4 and 5). During 7 bit left rotation, the change is shifted to bit positions 11 and 12. From Theorem 13 we have, $\lambda_2^3[11] = 0.9102$ and $\lambda_2^3[12] = 0.954$. Let $p_{11} = \lambda_2^3[11] = 0.9102$ and $q_{11} = \lambda_{Sum}^3[11] = 0.8605$. By applying Theorem 1, we can compute $\lambda_2^4[11]$ as,

$$\lambda_2^4[11] = p_{11}q_{11} + (1 - p_{11})(1 - q_{11}) = 0.7957$$

Similarly, let $p_{12} = \lambda_2^3[12] = 0.954$ and $q_{12} = \lambda_{Sum}^3[12] = 0.1073$. We can compute $\lambda_2^4[12]$ as,

$$\lambda_2^4[12] = p_{12}q_{12} + (1 - p_{12})(1 - q_{12}) = 0.1434$$

5 Theoretical and Experimental Result Comparison

We have compared the theoretical results obtained in this work with experimental results. In Sect. 4, we have theoretically analyzed Salsa 128 bits probabilistically. Those results are compared with experimental results. The experiments were conducted with 2^{21} random sets of IVs and the results are computed using probability. We have depicted the results of each bit of words up-to 4 decimal digits. The comparative results are shown in Table 1. Table 1 shows that theoretical analysis is on par with experimental results.

6 Related Work

A correlation attack based differential cryptanalysis technique was introduced in [10] by Aumason et al. at FSE 2008 with the idea of exploiting neutral bits of Salsa. This is the first attempt using neutral bits and is claimed to attack 7 rounds salsa. This attack was later improved by Ishiguro et al. in [11] with distinguisher containing two bit difference. This distinguishing attack was imposed on 9 round Salsa. The Probabilistic Neutral Bit (PNB) based attack proposed by Aumasson et al. in [10] was improved in [12] as new distinguishing attack called as Chaining distinguishers. This distinguisher focused on column and row analysis. Mouha et al. in [13] have worked on exploring optimal differential characteristics in Adding, Rotating and XORing operations and thereby applying it on Salsa. Maitra et al. in [14] have revisited the existing cryptanalytic techniques on Salsa and have improved it by choosing optimal parameters thereby reducing the complexity to $2^{247.2}$ which is less than the existing works. Maitra further extended this work in [15] where he chose IVs based on the keys and improved the attack complexity as 2^{239}. In [16], Choudhuri et al. have shown how to choose output bits combinations to improve the biases for 6 round Salsa. In 2017, Dey et al. [9] proposed a new algorithm for PNB (Probabilistic Neutral Bits) construction in Salsa and has claimed it to be 2.27 times faster than the existing algorithm. Deepthi et al. in [17,18] have revisited cryptanalysis on Salsa and Chacha presented by Maitra et al. in [14] and have attacked 128 bit Salsa with complexity 2^{111}.

Table 1. Theoretical and Experimental result Comparison

Output Bits	Theoretical Result	Experimental Result
$\lambda_{14}^2[29]$	0.8750	0.8760
$\lambda_{14}^2[30]$	0.9375	0.9385
$\lambda_{14}^2[31]$	0.9687	0.9678
$\lambda_{15}^2[10]$	0.8515	0.8586
$\lambda_{15}^2[11]$	0.9235	0.9345
$\lambda_{15}^2[12]$	0.9612	0.9600
$\lambda_{16}^2[29]$	0.8605	0.8638
$\lambda_{16}^2[30]$	0.1073	0.1102
$\lambda_{10}^2[28]$	0.8750	0.8821
$\lambda_{10}^2[29]$	0.9375	0.9359
$\lambda_{10}^2[30]$	0.9688	0.9690
$\lambda_{10}^2[31]$	0.9844	0.9865
$\lambda_{10}^3[28]$	0.8750	0.8774
$\lambda_{10}^3[29]$	0.9375	0.9376
$\lambda_{10}^3[30]$	0.9688	0.9694
$\lambda_{10}^3[31]$	0.9844	0.9841
$\lambda_{14}^3[29]$	0.8750	0.8763
$\lambda_{14}^3[30]$	0.9375	0.9368
$\lambda_{14}^3[31]$	0.9687	0.9694
$\lambda_2^3[10]$	0.8281	0.8305
$\lambda_2^3[11]$	0.9102	0.9137
$\lambda_2^3[12]$	0.9540	0.9556
$\lambda_4^3[4]$	0.8605	0.8614
$\lambda_4^3[5]$	0.1073	0.1077
$\lambda_2^4[11]$	0.7957	0.7960
$\lambda_2^4[12]$	0.1434	0.1438

7   Summary of Deep Learning Based Differential Cryptanalysis on Salsa 128-Bits

Gohr, in CRYPTO 2019, introduced deep learning based differential crypt-analysis on the block cipher speck to find neural distinguishers. The author observed that the accuracy of neural distinguisher is better than the accuracy of traditional distinguisher. Gohr's Deep Neural Network (DNN) contains three blocks - the initial convolution block, residual block and the classification block.

For training the neural network on salsa 128-bits, we use the DNN proposed by Gohr. First we create a data set of ciphertext pairs out of which half the ciphertext pairs are derived from plaintext pairs with random input difference (random pair) and remaining half the ciphertext pairs are derived from plain-text pairs with fixed input difference (real pair). The neural network is trained on the ciphertext pairs data set. Then, this trained neural network is tested to find whether it is able to correctly classify random ciphertext pairs from real ciphertext pairs.

The first block of the neural distinguisher is the initial convolution block. This block has a one dimensional convolution neural network (1D-CNN) with kernel size 1, a batch normalization process and a Rectified Linear Unit (ReLU) function. The second block of the neural network is the residual block and this block contains two 1D-CNNs with kernel size 3 and each of it is followed by a batch normalization process and lastly a ReLU activation function. The last block of the neural network is the classification block and this block contains three perceptron layers with batch normalizations between them and lastly has a sigmoid function to give scores to the ciphertext pairs. If the score for the ciphertext pair is in the range 0 to 1. If the ciphertext pair score is more than 0.5, then the corresponding ciphertext pair is classified to have come from a real pair, else, the ciphertext pair is classified to have come from a random pair.

In consideration to this neural network based differential cryptanalysis on salsa 128-bits, we are in the phase of data set creation. It is well known that for any deep learning based analysis, data set creation is the difficult and time consuming part. Once the data set creation phase is complete, we will use 80% of the data to train the neural network and use the remaining 20% for testing. The presence of distinguishers in round 4 and above can be found using this neural network with percentage of accuracy.

8   Conclusion and Future Work

There are many existing experimental attacks against different ciphers whereas there are a very few works in literature that focuses on theoretical analysis. Analyzing an attack theoretically gives the wisdom of reason for the biases that occur in differential attacks. Experimental analysis helps in finding the vulner-able parts of a cipher while a theoretical analysis gives us an understanding of what makes the cipher vulnerable. In this work, we have theoretically analyzed differential attack on Salsa 128 bits and observed the biases due to the difference.

We have also mathematically proved the observations up to 4 rounds of Salsa and compared the theoretical results with experimental results. A deep learning based differential cryptanalysis will give new light on finding distinguishers for higher rounds in stream ciphers.

Acknowledgement. This research was undertaken as part of the project "Research and Development of Lightweight Stream ciphers" funded by Department of Science and Technology [DST/ICPS/ CPS-Individual/2018/951(G)].

References

1. Dey, S., Sarkar, S.: A theoretical investigation on the distinguishers of salsa and chacha. Discret. Appl. Math. **302**, 147–162 (2021)
2. Gohr, A.: Improving attacks on round-reduced Speck32/64 using deep learning. In: Boldyreva, A., Micciancio, D. (eds.) CRYPTO 2019. LNCS, vol. 11693, pp. 150–179. Springer, Cham (2019). https://doi.org/10.1007/978-3-030-26951-7_6
3. Bernstein, D.J.: Salsa20 specification. estream project algorithm description (2005)
4. Crowley, P.: Truncated differential cryptanalysis of five rounds of salsa20. Cryptology ePrint Archive (2005)
5. Fischer, S., Meier, W., Berbain, C., Biasse, J.-F., Robshaw, M.J.B.: Non-randomness in eSTREAM candidates Salsa20 and TSC-4. In: Barua, R., Lange, T. (eds.) INDOCRYPT 2006. LNCS, vol. 4329, pp. 2–16. Springer, Heidelberg (2006). https://doi.org/10.1007/11941378_2
6. Kubo, H., Suzaki, T., Tsunoo, Y., Saito, T., Nakashima, H.: Differential cryptanalysis of salsa20/8. In: Workshop Record of SASC, vol. 28 (2007)
7. Dey, S., Sarkar, S.: Proving the forward bias of salsa. In: Workshop on Coding and Cryptography (2019)
8. Dey, S., Sarkar, S.: Proving the biases of salsa and chacha in differential attack. Des. Codes Crypt. **88**(9), 1827–1856 (2020)
9. Dey, S., Sarkar, S.: Improved analysis for reduced round salsa and chacha. Discret. Appl. Math. **227**, 58–69 (2017)
10. Aumasson, J.-P., Fischer, S., Khazaei, S., Meier, W., Rechberger, C.: New features of Latin dances: analysis of Salsa, ChaCha, and Rumba. In: Nyberg, K. (ed.) FSE 2008. LNCS, vol. 5086, pp. 470–488. Springer, Heidelberg (2008). https://doi.org/10.1007/978-3-540-71039-4_30
11. Ishiguro, T., Kiyomoto, S., Miyake, Y.: Latin dances revisited: new analytic results of Salsa20 and ChaCha. In: Qing, S., Susilo, W., Wang, G., Liu, D. (eds.) ICICS 2011. LNCS, vol. 7043, pp. 255–266. Springer, Heidelberg (2011). https://doi.org/10.1007/978-3-642-25243-3_21
12. Shi, Z., Zhang, B., Feng, D., Wu, W.: Improved key recovery attacks on reduced-round Salsa20 and ChaCha. In: Kwon, T., Lee, M.-K., Kwon, D. (eds.) ICISC 2012. LNCS, vol. 7839, pp. 337–351. Springer, Heidelberg (2013). https://doi.org/10.1007/978-3-642-37682-5_24
13. Mouha, N., Preneel, B.: Towards finding optimal differential characteristics for arx: Application to salsa20. Cryptology ePrint Archive (2013)
14. Paul, G., Maitra, S., Meier, W.: Salsa20 cryptanalysis: new moves and revisiting old styles. Cryptology ePrint Archive (2015)

15. Maitra, S.: Chosen IV cryptanalysis on reduced round ChaCha and Salsa. Discret. Appl. Math. **208**, 88–97 (2016)
16. Choudhuri, A.R., Maitra, S.: Significantly improved multi-bit differentials for reduced round salsa and ChaCha. IACR Trans. Symm. Cryptol. 261–287 (2016)
17. Deepthi, K.K.C., Singh, K.: Cryptanalysis for reduced round salsa and ChaCha: revisited. IET Inf. Secur. **13**(6), 591–602 (2019)
18. Deepthi, K.K.C., Singh, K.: Cryptanalysis of Salsa and ChaCha: revisited. In: Hu, J., Khalil, I., Tari, Z., Wen, S. (eds.) MONAMI 2017. LNICST, vol. 235, pp. 324–338. Springer, Cham (2018). https://doi.org/10.1007/978-3-319-90775-8_26

Blind Decryption and Private Information Delivery

Akihiro Yamamura[✉]

Department of Mathematical Science and Electrical-Electronic-Computer
Engineering, Akita University, 1-1 Tegata-Gakuen, Akita 010-8502, Japan
`yamamura@ie.akita-u.ac.jp`

Abstract. We analyze the privacy protection scheme given by Bao,
Deng and Feng which is a cryptographic protocol similar to oblivious
transfer and private information retrieval schemes. Their scheme is based
on a commutative family of ciphers. We point out several security flaws
caused by use of an inadequate commutative family of ciphers. Moreover,
we remedy the defects by proposing a new scheme that is regarded as
an extension of their scheme. We use an approach different from them;
we formalize a double encryption and blind decryption scheme employing
the ElGamal encryption algorithm and apply it to realize a private information delivery scheme which is an extension of the privacy protection
scheme.

Keywords: Blind Decryption · Privacy Protection Scheme ·
Commutative Cipher · ElGamal

1 Introduction

Privacy is an important factor of mobile security related to e-commerce, e-
business, e-government, and e-health services. In these electronic services, privacy issues attract attention because many users have concern about how their
private data are used. In particular, mobile devices are ubiquitous with edge
computing technology. The technology allows service providers to use information obtained for knowledge-discovery in databases and keep an eye on consumers
activities on markets. Given large data collections of person-specific information,
providers can mine data to learn patterns, models, and trends that can be used
to provide personalized services such as recommendation system for consumers.
The potential benefits of data mining are substantial, but the collection and
analysis of sensitive personal data such as health care or financial activities also
creates concerns about privacy, data security, and intellectual property rights. In
particular, emergence of cloud services and edge computing give a big impact on
mobile computing and so reducing communication complexity of any protocol is
an inevitable task for mobile computing systems.

Our motivation comes from the data management in the ubiquitous network, in particular, retrieving encrypted data. There are many cryptographic
techniques to attain these security and privacy goals. Oblivious transfer and

I. You et al. (Eds.): MobiSec 2022, CCIS 1644, pp. 165–179, 2023.
https://doi.org/10.1007/978-981-99-4430-9_12

private information retrieval schemes are most fundamental technologies among them. These are inevitable to construct more complex security systems so that users secretly retrieve data of their choice from databases even though the communication complexity is not really practical. Bao, Deng, and Feng introduce a new technique for the same purpose using commutative symmetric key ciphers in [1]. It is called a *privacy protection scheme*. Later, an asymmetric key cipher is introduced for this purpose in [2]. In this paper, we analyze their commutative family of ciphers and we propose a concept of *private information delivery* that extends the that of the privacy protection scheme to remedy the defects and gain more flexibility.

In our scheme, the database is encrypted by the database provider's encrypted key and each user has to ask the database provider to decrypt it in the way that the service provider does not know which data the service provider is decrypting. This implies that we are using the technique of blind decryption. In our approach, the database is encrypted and publicized and this reduce the communication complexity of both directions; query and reception of data. In our scheme, a user (called a sender) can deliver a data through the database server to another user (called a receiver) and neither the sender nor the database server get any information on the data This makes a big difference to the existing schemes. This is extremely ideal to ubiquitous setting where wireless transmission is limited and required to reduce the amount of data transmission.

1.1 Oblivious Transfer and Private Information Retrieval

Suppose that n is the number of the data in the database and k is the size of group element in the data retrieval schemes. The we summarize these approaches as follows. Clearly our scheme is suitable to application in which data transmission is limited such as RFID embedded systems because communication complexity of our method is much smaller than the others. In particular, if the number of data is large, then the communication complexity of the other two will gets large whereas the communication complexity of ours does not depend on the number of data.

In traditional information retrieval, two parties (often called a *database server* and a *user*) participate in the protocol, where a sender keeps a database secretly and a receiver wishes to obtain information in the database without telling the sender which data he wants. These are denoted as **D** and **U**, respectively.

Oblivious Transfer (OT) refers to several types of two party protocols, where one party, the sender, transmits part of its input to another party, the chooser, in a way that protects both parties: the sender is assured that the chooser does not get more information than it is entitled, and chooser is assured that the sender does not learn which part of the inputs it received. The notion of *1-out-of-2 oblivious transfer* (OT_1^2 for short) was introduced in [10], as generalization of Rabin's concept of OT [18]. Brassard, Crépeau, and Robert in [4] generalized the notion further to *1-out-of-N oblivious transfer* (OT_1^N) under the name *all-or-nothing disclosure* (ANDOS). Tzeng discuss an efficient 1-out-n oblivious transfer in [21].

Private Information Retrieval (PIR) *schemes* [5,7–9] allow a user to access a database consisting of N data $m_1, m_2, \ldots, m_N$ (usually data are just a bit) and read any elements without a database manager learning which element was accessed. The emphasis in PIR is on communication complexity which must be $o(N)$. PIR schemes do not protect the owner of the database, because they do not prevent the user from learning more than a single element. A PIR scheme where a user does not learn more than a single data is called a *Symmetric* PIR (SPIR) [12]. See [11] for more information.

1.2   Blind Decryption

The concept of *blind decryption* is introduced by Micali [15] for fair cryptosystems to make trustees oblivious. Blind decryption is further developed by Sakurai and Yamane [19] for protecting user's privacy in electronic commerce and further developed in Green [13]. Sakurai and Yamane's approach is similar to that of Bao, Deng and Feng. A similar concept for signature scheme was introduced by Chaum [6] before the introduction of blind decryption; it is a digital signature in which the content of a message is disguised before it is signed by the signer and can be implemented using standard public key signing schemes like RSA and DSA. Micali's blind decryption scheme is based on RSA encryption and Sakurai and Yamane's blind decryption scheme is based on ElGamal encryption. In the blind decryption scheme, participants are Alice and Bob; we suppose Bob has a pair of public and private key and Alice has a ciphertext encrypted by Bob's public key and then Alice wishes to get a plaintext of the ciphertext without letting Bob know either the ciphertext or the plaintext.

The blind decryption scheme based on RSA encryption is described as follows. Suppose Bob's pair of public and secret key is (e, d) using a composite $n = pq$, where p and q are large primes. Alice has a ciphertext $c = m^e$ of a plaintext m encrypted by Bob's public key e. Alice chooses a random number $s \in (\mathbb{Z}_n)^*$, computes $x = s^e c$ and sends it to Bob. Bob computes $y = x^d$ and send it back to Alice. Note that $y = x^d = (s^e c)^d = (s^e m^e)^d$. Alice computes $y s^{-1} = (s^e m^e)^d s^{-1} = s^{ed} m^{ed} s^{-1} = sms^{-1} = m$ and can obtain m without letting Bob aware of c or m.

The blind decryption scheme based on ElGamal encryption is described in [19]. Suppose Bob's pair of public and private key is (g^b, b) using a primitive generator g of a cyclic group which is a public information. Alice has a ciphertext $(g^r, g^{br} m)$, where r is chosen randomly by Bob. Alice chooses a random number s, computes $x = (g^r)^s = g^{sr}$ and sends it to Bob. Bob computes $y = x^b = (g^{sr})^b = g^{srb}$ and sends it to Alice. Alice computes $z = y^{s^{-1}} = (g^{srb})^{s^{-1}} = g^{br}$ and computes $(g^{br} m) z^{-1} = g^{br} m g^{-br} = m$.

2   Privacy Protection Scheme

Bao, Deng, and Feng introduce an efficient privacy protection scheme for e-commerce of digital goods that is analogous to a private information retrieval and an oblivious transfer in [1]. Their scheme is constructed based on a commutative family of symmetric key ciphers.

2.1 Basic Scheme Using Blind Decryption

Blind decryption can be applied to construct a private protection scheme as Sakurai and Yamane claim in [19]. We show how blind decryption is utilized to construct a privacy protection scheme.

Step 1. The database server $\mathbf{D}$ encrypts the data $m_1, m_2, \ldots, m_n$; $\mathbf{D}$ chooses n secret keys $d_1, d_2, \ldots, d_n$ for an efficient symmetric key cipher $E(\,,\,)$, say, AES. $\mathbf{D}$ encrypts m_i by d_i using E and obtain the ciphertexts $c_i = E(d_i, m_i)$ for each $i = 1, 2, 3, \ldots, n$. Suppose s is the private key for $\mathbf{D}$ of an encryption algorithm $enc(\,,\,)$ which can be decrypted blindly such as RSA or ElGamal. $\mathbf{D}$ encrypts the secret keys d_i by s, that is, $h_i = enc(s, d_i)$. We suppose $d_1, d_2, \ldots, d_n$ belong to the space of messages of $enc(\,,\,)$ Then $\mathbf{D}$ publicizes the list

$$(h_1|c_1, \quad h_2|c_2, \quad \ldots, \quad h_n|c_n)$$

Every user has an access to this publicized list.

Step 2. Suppose the user $\mathbf{U}$ wishes to obtain one of the data (say the jth data m_j). First $\mathbf{U}$ gets $h_j|c_j$ from the publicized list and computes a query $Q(h_j)$. Then $\mathbf{U}$ sends the query $Q(h_j)$ to $\mathbf{D}$.

Step 3. Receiving the *query* $Q(h_j)$, the database server $\mathbf{D}$ computes $dec(s, Q(h_j))$ by decrypting blindly. It is called the *response* to the query and denoted by $R(Q(h_j))$. Then $\mathbf{D}$ sends $R(Q(h_j))$ back to $\mathbf{U}$.

Step 4. The user $\mathbf{U}$ computes d_j from the response Y. Then $\mathbf{U}$ decrypts the ciphertext c_j using d_j and obtain m_j. Note that $\mathbf{U}$ has access to the list $(h_1|c_1, \ h_2|c_2, \ \ldots, \ h_n|c_n)$, which makes a difference from usual oblivious transfer and private information retrieval.

Note that $\mathbf{D}$ gets no information on h_j because computing Y from $Q(h_j)$ is blind decryption. RSA and ElGamal encryption can be employed to realize a basic scheme using blind decryption. The scheme enjoys the properties below.

- $\mathbf{U}$ obtains the message m_j when the protocol ends
- $\mathbf{U}$ obtains no information on any other data m_i
- $\mathbf{D}$ gets no information on h_j nor m_j after the protocol ends
- Eavesdropper of the protocol gets no information on any data

We illustrate data flow and computation done by each participants is illustrated in Fig. 1.

$$\begin{array}{cc}
\textbf{U} & \textbf{D}
\end{array}$$

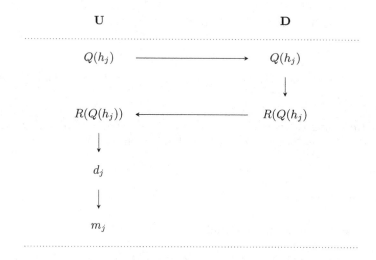

Fig. 1. Privacy protection scheme using blind decryption

2.2   Scheme Using Commutative Family of Ciphers

A commutative family of symmetric key ciphers is employed by Bao, Deng, and Feng to construct a privacy protection scheme in [1]. We consider a family $\{enc(k, \cdot) \mid k \in K\}$ of encryption algorithms with the set K of keys, where $enc(k, \cdot)$ is an encryption algorithm with a secret key k of the message space M onto M. The encryption algorithm $enc(k, \cdot)$ may be either a symmetric key cipher or an asymmetric key cipher. A family $\{enc(k, \cdot) \mid k \in K\}$ is called *commutative* if we have

$$enc(k_i, enc(k_j, m)) = enc(k_j, enc(k_i, m))$$

for any m in M and any $k_i, k_j \in K$. Obviously, stream ciphers which are one-time pad using a pseudorandom generator form a commutative family of symmetric key ciphers. We suppose $\{enc(k, \cdot) \mid k \in K\}$ is a commutative family of symmetric key ciphers hereafter. Blind decryption is easily implemented for a commutative family of ciphers. A privacy protection scheme can be constructed following the basic scheme in Sect. 2.1.

Step 1. The database server $\mathbf{D}$ encrypts the data $m_1, m_2, \ldots, m_n$; $\mathbf{D}$ chooses n secret keys $d_1, d_2, \ldots, d_n$ for an efficient symmetric key cipher E, say, AES. $\mathbf{D}$ encrypts m_i by d_i using E and obtain the ciphertexts $c_i = E(d_i, m_i)$ for each $i = 1, 2, 3, \ldots, n$. Suppose s is the private key for $\mathbf{D}$ of the commutative family $\{enc(k, \cdot) \mid k \in K\}$, where $s \in K$. $\mathbf{D}$ encrypts the keys d_i by s, that is, $h_i = enc(s, d_i)$. Then $\mathbf{D}$ publicizes the list

$$(h_1|c_1, \quad h_2|c_2, \quad \ldots, \quad h_n|c_n)$$

Step 2. Suppose the user $\mathbf{U}$ wishes to obtain one of the data (say the jth data m_j). First $\mathbf{U}$ gets $h_j|c_j$ from the publicized list, encrypts h_j by his secret key x

and then obtains $W = enc(x, h_j)$. Note that

$$W = enc(x, h_j) = enc(x, enc(s, d_j)) = enc(s, enc(x, d_j))$$

because the family $\{enc(k, \cdot) \mid k \in K\}$ is commutative. Then **U** sends the cipher-text W to **D** as a query.

Step 3. Receiving the query W, the database server **D** blindly decrypts W by his private key s and obtains $Y = dec(s, W)$. We note that

$$Y = dec(s, enc(s, enc(x, d_j))) = enc(x, d_j).$$

Then **D** sends Y to **U**.

Step 4. The user **U** decrypts Y and obtains

$$dec(x, Y) = dec(x, enc(x, d_j)) = d_j.$$

Then **U** decrypts the ciphertext c_j using d_j and obtain m_j as $m_j = D(d_j, c_j)$, where D is the decryption algorithm for E. Note that **U** has access to the list $(h_1|c_1, h_2|c_2, \ldots, h_n|c_n)$, which makes a difference from usual oblivious transfer protocols and private information retrieval schemes.

2.3   Commutative Family of Symmetric Key Ciphers by Bao, Deng, and Feng

To realize a privacy protection scheme blind decryption, Bao, Deng, and Feng introduce a concrete commutative family of symmetric key ciphers in [1]. Their encryption algorithm is given below. We points out several defects of the schemes.

Let $p = 2q+1$, where p and q are large primes. A secret key s is an odd integer in $\mathbb{Z}_{2q}$ other than q. An encryption function $enc(s, \cdot)$ of the set of messages $\mathbb{Z}_p$ onto itself is defined as follows. For any message $M \in \mathbb{Z}_p$, the encryption is given by

$$enc(s, M) = M^s \pmod{p}$$

It is easy to see that the family is commutative.

Since s belongs to $\mathbb{Z}_{2q}$, s is odd and $s \neq q$, s and $2q$ are coprime. Therefore, there exists an integer t such that

$$st = 1 \pmod{2q}.$$

We should note that $2q = p - 1$. Then t corresponds to s and these two integers form secret keys. The decryption of a ciphertext C is given by

$$dec(t, C) = C^t \pmod{p}.$$

We touch on several issues regarding security and privacy although we do not fully discuss vulnerability. Recently privacy issues are getting more and more demanding. Users wish to use on-line service secretly and safely. In addition to confidentiality, users also desire stronger privacy property such as unlinkability. The unlinkability refers to the security function that hides history of services used. This violates the linkability of user's history of services. In the case of a privacy protection scheme, a user $\mathbf{U}$ can obtain the data of his choice, however, if $\mathbf{U}$ once again tries to retrieve the same data using the same secret key, then the database server $\mathbf{D}$ gets to know that $\mathbf{U}$ is trying to get exactly same data even though $\mathbf{D}$ cannot know which data $\mathbf{U}$ is obtaining. Because the commutative family of symmetric key ciphers by Bao, Deng, and Feng is deterministic, a ciphertext is always the same for any plaintext. Therefore, it is critical to use a distinct secret key for each data transaction. However, changing keys is a severe demand for each user because this requires a user to generate a secret key t from s using Euclidean algorithm and so it is not always possible. Therefore, the symmetric key cipher given by Bao, Deng, and Feng does not satisfy need of unlinkability.

2.4   Commutative Asymmetric Key Ciphers by Bao, Deng, Feng, Guo and Wu

Bao, Deng, Feng, Guo and Wu claim that asymmetric key ciphers, that is, public key cryptosystems are suitable to realize the privacy protection scheme because it prevents total compromise due to exposure of secret keys in [2]. Therefore, they introduce a concrete example of a commutative family of asymmetric key cryptosystems. We remark that a blind decryption using standard cryptosystems like RSA and ElGamal can be employed following the basic scheme in Sect. 2.1. Unfortunately, their proposal is inappropriate to realize the privacy protection scheme. As a matter of fact, their scheme contains many shortcomings. They claim that their proposed algorithm is an asymmetric key encryption in the sense that keys for encryption and decryption are distinct, however, it is not a public key cryptosystem in more essential sense as we point pout below.

   The commutative asymmetric key ciphers by Bao, Deng, Feng, Guo and Wu algorithm in [2] are described below. Let p and q be large primes. Suppose d is an odd integer. Then p, q and d are secret information. Let $n = pq$ and e be the integer such that $ed = 1 \pmod{q-1}$. Then, n and e are made public. A plaintext is an integer $M \in \mathbb{Z}_q^*$. We define an encryption function $enc(e, \ )$ by

$$enc(e, M) = M^e \pmod{n}$$

The decryption function $dec(d, \ )$ is given as follows:

$$dec(d, C) = C^d \pmod{q}$$

for a ciphertext C. It is easy to see encryption algorithms are commutative. First of all, plaintexts must satisfy the condition $0 < M < q$ and so this restriction leaks a partial information on the private information q, which is an undesirable property.

We discuss more essential defect of applying this encryption algorithm in the privacy protection scheme in Subsect. 2.1. As a matter of fact, the algorithm does not match the privacy protection scheme. Every user $\mathbf{U}$ and the database server $\mathbf{D}$ must share the same system parameters to generate legitimate pairs of public and private keys. If the user $\mathbf{U}$ uses the pair (e, d) of public and private key, then $\mathbf{U}$ first chooses d and then computes e or vice versa. To compute e satisfying $ed = 1 \pmod{q - 1}$ using Euclidean algorithm, $\mathbf{U}$ must know q and consequently the factorization of n. Therefore, every user $\mathbf{U}$ and the database server $\mathbf{D}$ must know the values p and q. It implies that every participants in the scheme can derive anybody's pair of public and private keys. It follows that each user $\mathbf{U}$ can decrypt ciphertext encrypted by $\mathbf{D}$, which totally compromises the privacy protection scheme. Therefore, the encryption algorithm given by Bao, Deng, Feng, Guo and Wu does not satisfy the desired property to realize the privacy protection scheme in Subsect. 2.1. This defect can be eliminated by employing a trusted third party to join the scheme and make all pairs of public and private keys for users and the database server and keep p and q secret to anybody else. However, allowing a third trusted party causes the big brother problem which is undesirable to any privacy sensitive system. This pitfall is caused by the condition that secret keys are shared to make a pair of public and private keys. Therefore, the algorithm given by Bao, Deng, Feng, Guo and Wu is not an asymmetric key encryption algorithm in a rigorous sense.

3   Private Information Delivery

We have seen that the scheme by Bao, Deng, and Feng suffers from vulnerabilities because of inappropriate choice of commutative encryption algorithms. We realize a private protection scheme using blind decryption of public key cryptosystem different from that of [1,2]. As a matter of fact, using ElGamal encryption we extend the scheme and propose a concept of a *private information delivery* scheme in which a sender and a receiver may be different parties.

In oblivious transfer, private information retrieval and the privacy protection schemes, only two participants are involved in the protocols; a *database server* $\mathbf{D}$ and a *user* $\mathbf{U}$. Let us now consider a new scheme where the party requesting a data and the party receiving the data are different. In this setting, three players are involved in the protocol; a *sender*, a *receiver* and a *database server* (written as $\mathbf{S}$, $\mathbf{R}$ and $\mathbf{D}$, respectively). As the privacy protection scheme, a database server $\mathbf{D}$ maintains the list of the encrypted data

$$(h_1|c_1, \quad h_2|c_2, \quad \ldots, \quad h_n|c_n)$$

where $h_i = enc(s, d_i)$ and d_i are secret keys to encrypt the data $m_1, m_2, \ldots, m_n$, that is, $c_i = Enc(d_i, m_i)$ for each i. A sender $\mathbf{S}$ wishes to send one of the data m_i to a receiver $\mathbf{R}$ without letting $\mathbf{D}$ know which data is sent. We apply the method of double encryption and blind decryption so that $\mathbf{R}$ can obtain d_i and then decrypt c_i to gain m_i.

3.1   Basic Scheme Using Double Encryption and Blind Decryption

We propose a *double encryption and blind decryption scheme* to realize a private information delivery as described in the scenario above. Let h be a ciphertext of a plaintext d encrypted by **D**'s public key p_D, that is, $h = enc(p_D, d)$. Suppose that a sender **S** wishes to send one of the data m_i to a receiver **R**. Then **S** encrypts h by **R**'s public key p_R. The ciphertext $enc(p_R, h)$ which is equal to $enc(p_R, enc(p_D, d))$ is called a *query* for h and denoted by $Q(h)$. Note that it is a double encryption of a plaintext d encrypted by p_D and next p_R. The query $Q(h)$ is sent to **D**. Then **D** is asked to decrypt $Q(h)$ blindly and sends the resulting data $dec(s_D, Q(h))$ where s_D is a private key of **D**, called a *response* and denoted by $R(Q(h))$, to **R**. Then **R** can decrypt the response and obtain the plaintext d. We require that **S** gets no information on d and that **D** does not obtain any information on either c or d. Such scheme is constructed by double encryptions and blind decryption.

If all of the three parties **S**, **D** and **R** are honest, **R** can obtain the data d as **D** specified, whereas **D** obtains no information on d. We illustrate data flow and computation done by each participants is illustrated in Fig. 2.

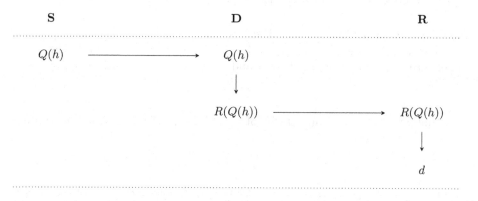

Fig. 2. Private information delivery

Note that $h = enc(p_D, d)$, $Q(h) = enc(p_R, h)$ and $R(Q(h)) = dec(s_D, Q(h))$, where s_D is the **D**'s private key. We summarize the properties enjoyed by the scheme as follows.

- **S** obtains no information on any data
- **D** gets no information on h nor d after the protocol ends
- **R** obtains d after the protocol ends
- Eavesdropper of the protocol gets no information on any data

We may regard the query $Q(h)$ as a double encryption of a plaintext d and the response $R(Q(h))$ as a blind decryption of the first encryption. It is not trivial to decrypt blindly the double encryption. We discuss how to realize such a scheme in the next section.

3.2   Double Encryption and Blind Decryption Scheme Using ElGamal

We realize a double encryption and blind decryption scheme using ElGamal encryption algorithm. The goal of the scheme is that $\mathbf{R}$ receives a ciphertext of a plaintext d using ElGamal encryption through $\mathbf{D}$ from $\mathbf{S}$ provided that $\mathbf{S}$ possesses only a ciphertext of d encrypted by $\mathbf{D}$'s public key.

Initialization
Our scheme is based on the ElGamal encryption algorithm and so the system parameters are same as those of ElGamal. Let G be a cyclic group. We suppose that the order of G is a large prime p. A generator g of G is chosen as a system parameter and made public. The receiver $\mathbf{R}$ keeps the pair

$$(g^x, x)$$

of the public key and the private key where x belongs to $\mathbb{Z}_p^*$.

Encrypted data: first encryption
Suppose $\mathbf{D}$'s private key s is chosen from $\mathbb{Z}_p^*$. Then g^s is the public key of $\mathbf{D}$. Therefore, the pair of the public key and the private key of $\mathbf{D}$ is given by

$$(g^s, s).$$

A plaintext d, which is an element of G, is encrypted by ElGamal encryption algorithm using $\mathbf{D}$'s public key;

$$(g^t, g^{st}d)$$

where t is randomly and uniformly chosen from $\mathbb{Z}_p^*$ and must be kept secret. Let us denote the ciphertext by h, that is, $h = (g^t, g^{st}d)$.

Query: second encryption
Suppose that $\mathbf{S}$ wants to send the data d to $\mathbf{R}$ through $\mathbf{D}$. Then $\mathbf{S}$ computes a query $Q(h)$ as follows. First, $\mathbf{S}$ chooses randomly and uniformly u and v from $\mathbb{Z}_p^*$. The query $Q(h)$ is formed by g^u, $g^{ux}g^t$, g^v, $g^{vx}g^{st}d$ with the recipient identification information $\mathbf{R}$;

$$Q(h) = (g^u, g^{ux}g^t, g^v, g^{vx}g^{st}d, \mathbf{R}).$$

We should note that both $(g^u, g^{ux}g^t)$ and $(g^v, g^{vx}g^{st}d)$ are ciphertexts of the plaintexts g^t and $g^{st}d$ by ElGamal encryption algorithm using the public key g^x of $\mathbf{R}$, respectively, with randomly chosen u and v. Then $\mathbf{S}$ sends the query $Q(h)$ to $\mathbf{D}$.

Response: blind decryption
Receiving the query $Q(h)$, **D** computes

$$((g^{ux}g^t)^s)^{-1}g^{vx}g^{st}d = g^{vx-usx}d$$
$$(g^u)^s = g^{us}$$

and computes the response $R(Q(h))$ consisting of g^v, g^{us}, $g^{vx-usx}d$

$$R(Q(h)) = (g^v,\ g^{us},\ g^{vx-usx}d)$$

and sends it to **R**. We note that $(g^{v-us}, g^{(v-us)x}d)$ may be regarded as a ciphertext of d by ElGamal encryption using **R**'s public key g^x where $v - us$ may be considered as randomly chosen from $\mathbb{Z}_p^*$. Therefore, the response $R(Q(h))$ is a ciphertext of ElGamal encryption using the public key of **R**.

Retrieval
Receiving the response $R(Q(h))$, **R** computes

$$((g^v)^{-1}(g^{us}))^x g^{vx-usx}d = d$$

and obtains the data d.

We show the data flow and computation done by each participant of the scheme in Fig. 3.

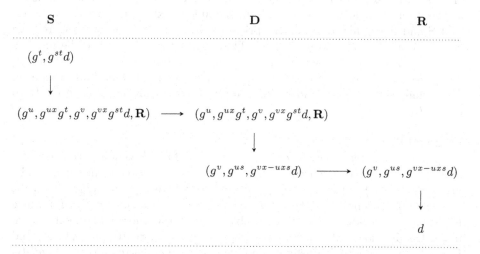

Fig. 3. Double encryption and blind decryption scheme using ElGamal

3.3   Security Analysis

We discuss security and privacy issues of the double encryption and blind decryption scheme using ElGamal provided that each participant and the database server behave honestly.

Correctness

If **S** and **D** follow the protocol honestly, then **R** obtains d as we have seen above.

Privacy for S

Privacy issue on **S** is that no information on the ciphertext that **S** asks **D** to decrypt blindly and send its response to **R** is leaked to **D**. The database server **D** cannot distinguish a query $Q(h_1)$ for the ciphertext h_1 of a plaintext d_1 and a query $Q(h_2)$ for the ciphertext h_2 of a plaintext d_2 because the query $Q(h_1)$ and $Q(h_2)$ are ciphertexts of ElGamal encryption and ElGamal encryption is indistinguishable against the chosen plaintext attack under the decision Diffie-Helman assumption.

Confidentiality of plaintext

Confidentiality of the plaintext requires that no information on the plaintext is leaked to anybody although it may happen that a ciphertext itself exposed. In particular, the private key s of **D** and the random number t must not be exposed. Obviously, nobody can obtain any information on d as long as ElGamal encryption algorithm is semantic secure. It is impossible for **R** to obtain information on **D**'s public key s or t from $R(Q(h))$ which consists of $g^v, g^{us}, g^{vx-uxs}d$ as far as the discrete logarithm problem is intractable. Next let us consider the case that **S** and **R** collude to obtain the private key s of **D**. Note that **S** and **R** have $g^v, g^{us}, (g^x)^{v-us}$ and also g^x and g^u. They can obtain g^{xus}. Since the discrete logarithm problem is intractable, it is infeasible to obtain s from g^{xu} and $(g^{xu})^s$. Therefore, **S** and **R** have no clue to get s. We remark that no information on t is included in $R(Q(h))$ and so information theoretically intractable for **R** to obtain t.

Unlinkability

Suppose **S** sends two queries $Q(h_1)$ and $Q(h_2)$ to **D**. It is required that nobody other than **S** can notice whether the ciphertexts h_1 and h_2 coincides or not. The first query $Q(h_1)$ is $(g^{u_1}, g^{u_1x}g^t, g^{v_1}, g^{v_1x}g^{st}d_1)$ where h_1 is a ciphertext of d_1. Likewise, the second query $Q(h_2)$ is given by $(g^{u_2}, g^{u_2x}g^t, g^{v_2}, g^{v_2x}g^{st}d_2)$. Since ElGamal encryption is indistinguishable against the chosen plaintext attack under the decision Diffie-Helman assumption, the ciphertexts $(g^{u_1}, g^{u_1x}g^t)$ and $(g^{u_2}, g^{u_2x}g^t)$ are indistinguishable and similarly the ciphertexts $(g^{v_1}, g^{v_1x}g^{st}d_1)$ and $(g^{v_2}, g^{v_2x}g^{st}d_2)$ are indistinguishable. Hence, **D** cannot distinguish $Q(h_1)$ and $Q(h_2)$.

Anonymity

Since a query $Q(h)$ includes information on the receiver **R**, the scheme does not enjoy the property of anonymity, that is, $\mathbf{D}$ knows who sends a query and who receives a data. To realize anonymous property that $\mathbf{D}$ does not know who is a sender and who is a receiver after the protocol ends, it is necessary to add some more mechanism to make the scheme anonymous. On the other hand, the receiver $\mathbf{R}$ does not know who sends the data to $\mathbf{R}$ just because $R(Q(h))$ consists of $g^v, g^{us}, g^{vx-usx}d$, however, these data include no information on $\mathbf{S}$ as u and v are random numbers. We can make the scheme so that $\mathbf{R}$ can get to know who asks $\mathbf{D}$ to send the response just by adding the identity information of the sender $\mathbf{S}$ to the query and the data delivery set.

Computation
Computations of $\mathbf{S}$, $\mathbf{D}$ and $\mathbf{R}$ are bounded above by a polynomial in the security parameter, that is, the size of the prime p. We remark that sizes of data d do not affect computation complexity of the scheme.

3.4   Realization of Private Information Delivery

It is easy to see that a private information delivery scheme can be constructed applying a double encryption and blind decryption scheme. The database server $\mathbf{D}$ maintains a list $(h_1|c_1, \ h_2|c_2, \ \dots, \ h_n|c_n)$, where h_i is the ciphertext $(g^{t_i}, g^{st_i}d_i)$ of the secret key d_i and c_i is the ciphertext $Enc(d_i, m_i)$, where t_i is randomly and uniformly chosen and $Enc(\ ,\ )$ is an efficient symmetric key cipher. A query and a response is computed as double encryption and blind decryption to obtain the secret key d_i.

If $\mathbf{S}$ and $\mathbf{R}$ coincide, the scheme can be applied to realize a private data protection scheme. Therefore, the private information delivery scheme exceeds the functionality of that of a privacy protection scheme. For the private information delivery scheme, the property of the public key cryptosystem is essential and inevitable, on the other hand, the privacy protection scheme does not require the property of the public key cryptosystem.

4   Conclusion and Future Work

The scheme in Sect. 3 does not enjoy anonymity for users $\mathbf{S}$ and $\mathbf{R}$ against the database server $\mathbf{D}$. It may be plausible that $\mathbf{S}$ and $\mathbf{R}$ want to hide their identity from $\mathbf{D}$. On the other hand, $\mathbf{D}$ provide service in exchange for payment by $\mathbf{S}$ and $\mathbf{R}$ while $\mathbf{D}$ does not mind who pay for it. Therefore, $\mathbf{D}$ provide service for anybody who pay even though the identity of the person is not known to $\mathbf{D}$. An *anonymous authentication scheme* (or anonymous group identification scheme) is a protocol that allows a member called a prover of a group to convince a verifier that she is a member of the group without revealing any information about her. So this is an interactive proof; the protocol consists of two parties, the prover and the verifier, and the prover convinces the verifier that she knows a secret without revealing itself. There are several such schemes to attain such anonymous authentication such as [3, 14, 16, 17, 20, 22, 24, 26]. These techniques can be applied to make the scheme anonymous. It may also plausible to use asymmetric key encryption algorithms that are different form the existing algorithm, for example [23,25] for realizing anonymity. We will discuss more on this topic in the future.

References

1. Bao, F., Deng, R.H., Feng, P.: An efficient and practical scheme for privacy protection in the e-commerce of digital goods. In: Won, D. (ed.) ICISC 2000. LNCS, vol. 2015, pp. 162–170. Springer, Heidelberg (2001). https://doi.org/10.1007/3-540-45247-8_13
2. Bao, F., Deng, R., Feng, P., Guo, Y., Wu, H.: Secure and private distribution of online video and some related cryptographic issues. In: Varadharajan, V., Mu, Y. (eds.) ACISP 2001. LNCS, vol. 2119, pp. 190–205. Springer, Heidelberg (2001). https://doi.org/10.1007/3-540-47719-5_17
3. Boneh, D., Franklin, M.: Anonymous authentication with subset queries. In: ACM Conference on Computer and Communications Security, pp. 113–119 (1987)
4. Brassard, G., Crepeau, C., Robert, J.-M.: All-or-nothing disclosure of secrets. In: Odlyzko, A.M. (ed.) CRYPTO 1986. LNCS, vol. 263, pp. 234–238. Springer, Heidelberg (1987). https://doi.org/10.1007/3-540-47721-7_17
5. Cachin, C., Micali, S., Stadler, M.: Computationally private information retrieval with polylogarithmic communication. In: Stern, J. (ed.) EUROCRYPT 1999. LNCS, vol. 1592, pp. 402–414. Springer, Heidelberg (1999). https://doi.org/10.1007/3-540-48910-X_28
6. Chaum, D.: Blind signatures for untraceable payments. In: Chaum, D., Rivest, R.L., Sherman, A.T. (eds.) Advances in Cryptology, pp. 199–203. Springer, Boston, MA (1983). https://doi.org/10.1007/978-1-4757-0602-4_18
7. Chor, B., Gilboa, N.: Computationally private information retrieval (extended abstract). In: Proceedings of the Twenty-Ninth Annual ACM Symposium on Theory of Computing. pp. 304–313. STOC 1997, Association for Computing Machinery (1997)
8. Chor, B., Goldreich, O., Kushilevitz, E., Sudan, M.: Private information retrieval. In: Proceedings of IEEE 36th Annual Foundations of Computer Science, pp. 41–50 (1995). https://doi.org/10.1109/SFCS.1995.492461
9. Chor, B., Goldreich, O., Kushilevitz, E., Sudan, M.: Private information retrieval. J. ACM **45**(6), 965–981 (1998)
10. Even, S., Goldreich, O., Lempel, A.: A randomized protocol for signing contracts. Commun. ACM **28**, 637–647 (1985)
11. Gasarch, W.I.: A survey on private information retrieval (2004)
12. Gertner, Y., Ishai, Y., Kushilevitz, E., Malkin, T.: Protecting data privacy in private information retrieval schemes. In: Proceedings of the Thirtieth Annual ACM Symposium on Theory of Computing, pp. 151–160. STOC 1998 (1998). https://doi.org/10.1145/276698.276723
13. Green, M.: Secure blind decryption. In: Catalano, D., Fazio, N., Gennaro, R., Nicolosi, A. (eds.) PKC 2011. LNCS, vol. 6571, pp. 265–282. Springer, Heidelberg (2011). https://doi.org/10.1007/978-3-642-19379-8_16
14. Lee, C.H., Deng, X., Zhu, H.: Design and security analysis of anonymous group identification protocols. In: Naccache, D., Paillier, P. (eds.) PKC 2002. LNCS, vol. 2274, pp. 188–198. Springer, Heidelberg (2002). https://doi.org/10.1007/3-540-45664-3_13

15. Micali, S.: Fair public-key cryptosystems. In: Brickell, E.F. (ed.) CRYPTO 1992. LNCS, vol. 740, pp. 113–138. Springer, Heidelberg (1993). https://doi.org/10.1007/3-540-48071-4_9

16. Nakazato, J., Wang, L., Yamamura, A.: Privacy enhancing credentials. In: Cervesato, I. (ed.) ASIAN 2007. LNCS, vol. 4846, pp. 55–61. Springer, Heidelberg (2007). https://doi.org/10.1007/978-3-540-76929-3_6

17. Nyang, D., Yamamura, A.: More efficient threshold signature scheme in gap Diffie-Hellman group. IEICE Trans. Fundam. Electron. Commun. Comput. Sci. **E92-A**, 1720–1723 (2009)

18. Rabin, M.O.: How to exchange secrets with oblivious transfer (2005). Harvard University Technical report 81 talr@watson.ibm.com 12955. Accessed 21 Jun 2005

19. Sakurai, K., Yamane, Y.: Blind decoding, blind undeniable signatures, and their applications to privacy protection. In: Anderson, R. (ed.) IH 1996. LNCS, vol. 1174, pp. 257–264. Springer, Heidelberg (1996). https://doi.org/10.1007/3-540-61996-8_45

20. Santis, A., Crescenzo, G., Persiano, G.: Communication-efficient anonymous group identification. In: Proceedings of the 5th ACM Conference on Computer and Communications Security, pp. 73–82. CCS 1998, Association for Computing Machinery (1998)

21. Tzeng, W.-G.: Efficient 1-out-n oblivious transfer schemes. In: Naccache, D., Paillier, P. (eds.) PKC 2002. LNCS, vol. 2274, pp. 159–171. Springer, Heidelberg (2002). https://doi.org/10.1007/3-540-45664-3_11

22. Viet, D.Q., Yamamura, A., Tanaka, H.: Anonymous password-based authenticated key exchange. In: Maitra, S., Veni Madhavan, C.E., Venkatesan, R. (eds.) INDOCRYPT 2005. LNCS, vol. 3797, pp. 244–257. Springer, Heidelberg (2005). https://doi.org/10.1007/11596219_20

23. Yamamura, A.: Homomorphic encryptions of sums of groups. In: Boztaş, S., Lu, H.-F.F. (eds.) AAECC 2007. LNCS, vol. 4851, pp. 357–366. Springer, Heidelberg (2007). https://doi.org/10.1007/978-3-540-77224-8_41

24. Yamamura, A., Kurokawa, T., Nakazato, J.: Threshold anonymous group identification and zero-knowledge proof. In: Pieprzyk, J., Ghodosi, H., Dawson, E. (eds.) ACISP 2007. LNCS, vol. 4586, pp. 370–384. Springer, Heidelberg (2007). https://doi.org/10.1007/978-3-540-73458-1_27

25. Yamamura, A., Kurosawa, K.: Generic algorithms and key agreement protocols based on group actions. In: Eades, P., Takaoka, T. (eds.) ISAAC 2001. LNCS, vol. 2223, pp. 208–218. Springer, Heidelberg (2001). https://doi.org/10.1007/3-540-45678-3_19

26. Yamamura, A., Saito, T.: Private information retrieval based on the subgroup membership problem. In: Varadharajan, V., Mu, Y. (eds.) ACISP 2001. LNCS, vol. 2119, pp. 206–220. Springer, Heidelberg (2001). https://doi.org/10.1007/3-540-47719-5_18

Using Machine Learning for Detecting Timing Side-Channel Attacks in SDN

Faizan Shoaib$^{(\boxtimes)}$ ⓘ, Yang-Wai Chow ⓘ, Elena Vlahu-Gjorgievska ⓘ, and Chau Nguyen ⓘ

School of Computing and Information Technology, University of Wollongong,
Wollongong, Australia
`fs984@uowmail.edu.au`

Abstract. Software-Defined Networking (SDN) is a networking technology that allows for the programming and efficient management of networks. Due to the separation of the data plane and the control plane, SDN is prone to timing side-channel attacks. The adversary can use timing information to obtain data about the network such as flow tables, routes, controller types, ports, and so on. The focus of current mitigation strategies for timing side-channel attacks is largely on minimizing them through network architectural changes. This adds considerable overhead to the SDNs and makes establishing the origin of the attack a challenge. In this paper, we propose a machine learning-based approach for detecting timing side-channel attacks and identifying their source in SDNs. We adopt the machine learning methodology for this solution since it delivers faster and more accurate output. As opposed to conventional methods, it can precisely detect timing side-channel activity in SDN and determine the attacker's origin. Because this security solution is intended to be used in association with SDN, its architecture ensures that it has a low impact on network traffic and resource consumption. The overall design findings indicate that our method is effective in detecting timing side-channel attacks in SDN and accurately identifying the attacker's machine.

Keywords: software-defined network · side-channel attack · machine learning-based detection

1 Introduction

Conventional networking has been replaced by Software-Defined Networking (SDN) to a great extent. Tech giants such as Google, Microsoft and Facebook have embraced SDN for their public cloud-based network services. SDN technology is being used by mobile core networks to optimise mobile network connectivity. To provide 5G mobile internet at high speeds, next-generation mobile networks are using SDNs. As the adoption of SDN in telecommunications networks and datacentres increases, it introduces multitudinous security challenges

I. You et al. (Eds.): MobiSec 2022, CCIS 1644, pp. 180–194, 2023.
https://doi.org/10.1007/978-981-99-4430-9_13

that hinder its deployment and execution. SDN has proven vulnerable to a variety of attacks, including Advanced Persistent Threats (APT), Denial of Service (DoS), Distributed Denial of Service (DDoS), and Man-In-The-Middle (MITM) attacks. Many techniques have been proposed to mitigate these attacks efficiently. Existing research on SDN security is primarily focused on implementing security controls on the SDN controller or utilizing specialized apps on the application layer, such as pre-defined firewall applications. Also, the present work is more focused on attack prevention rather than detection of attack activities or adversary's source identification.

One of the rising apprehensions for SDNs is 'timing side-channel attacks'. In these attacks, the adversary exploits a system using timing information, which might result in the leakage of information about the overall system. These threats can also escalate to multistage attacks, which can exhaust the system's resources. The isolation of the control plane and the data plane in SDN renders it vulnerable to timing side-channel attacks. Timing side-channels have a substantial impact on SDNs. They are used to disclose information such as routing information, Access Control Lists (ACLs), flow table entries, and so on. Using this information, more severe systemic repercussions can be triggered. Traditional networking implements both the control and data planes on physical infrastructure such as routers or switches. As a result, traditional networks are not vulnerable to timing attacks. Due to these architectural differences between SDN and traditional networks, timing side-channel attacks have been overlooked when integrating SDN. Nonetheless, researchers have highlighted this as a potential impediment to SDN adoption [18]. Only a few techniques for preventing timing attacks have been developed and applied to date. Although these strategies can reduce time side-channels in SDN, they fall short of identifying the adversary's location or detecting timing probe activity in the network.

In this paper, we present an innovative approach for detecting timing side-channel attacks in SDNs. This technique uses a customized dataset and random forest algorithm to correctly predict a timing probe activity in SDN. To obtain the most recent network topology and flow table, this solution connects an API to the controller. The approach takes advantage of this data to pinpoint the attack's origin. With the adoption of our solution, an adversary's attempt to conduct a timing side-channel attack will be promptly identified and will alert the network administrator. Additionally, the malicious host's MAC address, IP address, and Openflow switch port will be known to the network administrator. The implementation, in contrast to earlier work, is light and has little influence on the SDN environment. Unlike traditional methodologies, our strategy is based on machine learning for high accuracy and rapid identification of timing attacks. It uses its resources for data gathering, learning, training, prediction, and monitoring at all stages of the machine learning process. As a result, the SDN experiences negligible impact. The findings show that our solution detects timing side-channel attacks in SDNs proactively and efficiently.

2   Related Work

Extensive research has been conducted to improve the security and performance of SDNs. This has generally been accomplished by introducing distinctive components in the topology or making design improvements to existing architectures. Some of these research projects are based on vulnerabilities discovered in SDN protocols, while others reveal the limitations of its capabilities. There is numerous research that provides strategies to patch these vulnerabilities and overcome constraints. The amount of research on SDN security demonstrates the significance of this topic in communication and datacenter networks.

Several studies have demonstrated security challenges and solutions in SDNs. Ahmad et al. [1] highlighted security challenges faced by 5G mobile networks when integrating with SDN. Joberto et al. [14] suggested an intrusion detection system-based security architecture for detection and response in SDNs. Manu et al. [13] employed flow monitoring to create an intrusion-tolerant SDN architecture. Nicolas et al. [16] recently introduced SYNAPTIC, which was originally designed to automatically certify security chains in SDN. Later, the same technique was leveraged to present a security policy checker for SDN-based networks [17].

Many systems have been successfully attacked with timing side-channel attacks. [9] demonstrates the use of timing-based side-channel attacks against hardware and software systems. Timing side-channel attacks in systems-on-chip were investigated by Martha et al. [19]. They demonstrated how side-channel attacks with precise timing could allow an attacker to collect processor information. To identify control system abnormalities, Dunlap et al. [7] also introduced timing-based side-channel assaults.

In SDN, timing side-channel detection has not received much attention. The majority of the work is devoted to the prevention of such attacks. Yoon et al. [22] presented detailed research on threats faced by SDN. The authors describe data leakage in the data plane as attacks based on packet Round-Trip Timings (RTT). To evaluate communication patterns and scan the network, the attacker computes a control path delay. Conti et al. [6] proposed the "Know Your Enemy" attack in a similar study. This attack exploits temporal expertise to acquire knowledge about an SDN network's configuration. The proposed countermeasure in this work routes all traffic through the solution, resulting in an increased RTT for all traffic. Timing probing packets are used in [23] to discover the parameters of data plane events and control plane parameters. The proposed approach in this study relies on heavy flow-insertion processes and makes use of the calculation and queueing resources of the switch, resulting in data rate limitations. Timing side-channels attacks in SDNs were also demonstrated by Liu et al. [12]. They suggest that network information might be gleaned from the delay that is introduced when a packet is routed to the controller. Hou et al. [8] recommended postponing the flow installation at random more recently, doing so to mask the timing discrepancy between numerous requests. In this solution every time the host MAC address is modified, the flow installation operation is delayed. MAC address spoofing has not been considered by the authors. In a short period, an attacker can counterfeit and use a range of MAC addresses. Also, Arsalan et al. [2] presented a solution for timing assaults in Vehicular Ad Hoc Networks.

To detect timing channel attacks in SDN, Anyi Liu et al. [11] proposed a solution. Although the results show that the solution can detect timing channels in an SDN cloud, it can be argued that the attacker can choke the resources of the cloud. It also lags the ability to identify the Virtual Machine used by the adversary. [15] uses machine learning techniques to address the timing side-channel in the Internet of Things (IoT). The results show that this method can be used to identify timing side-channels in IoT. Deep learning and machine learning approaches have also been used with SDN to resolve DDoS and other attacks [5]. These techniques have yet to be proven for detecting timing side-channel activity in a SDN.

In one of our recent research projects [20], we presented a security solution "Netkasi". It used response randomization techniques to prevent an SDN environment from timing side-channel attacks. Because "Netkasi" was mainly focused on prevention rather than detection, the network administrator had limited visibility into the attacker's origins. The existing methods for mitigating timing side-channel attacks mostly rely on switching and controller processing resources, which have an adverse effect on the network's performance. Most of the conventional techniques also have processing bottlenecks due to the placement and design of the proposed solution. Moreover, the existing approaches are incapable of detecting timing probe activity or identifying the source of the attacker. The method proposed in this paper addresses these concerns by offering a solution based on timing activity detection and by offering the ability to locate the adversary. This is a machine learning-based peripheral solution that relies on its own compute and processing resources rather than causing overhead on the Openflow switch or SDN controller. Its architecture ensures that it has minimum computational constraints. The solution ensures great precision and low false positives as it is based on cutting-edge machine learning algorithms. It has no discernible effect on overall network performance.

3   Proposed Solution

Timing side-channel attacks, unlike the other types of attacks, can be carried out at a slow pace. As a result, they are distinct and difficult to detect. Detection and source identification techniques for other attacks are often based on packet flow rate and packet type. In timing attacks, the adversary can leverage legitimate probing packets to determine the Round-Trip Time (RTT) and compromise a network. Therefore, detecting such attacks or a timing probe cannot be accomplished through traditional detection approaches based on traffic rate, packet size, or type.

Machine learning is a component of Artificial Intelligence (AI) that allows software applications to become even more effective at forecasting without explicitly programming them to do so. Machine learning algorithms forecast newoutput

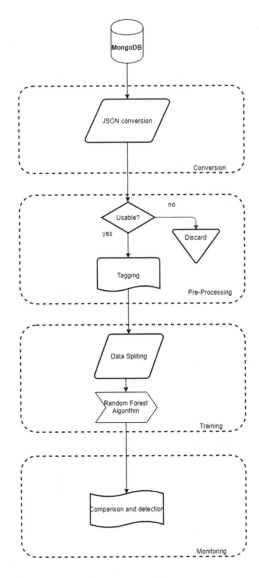

Fig. 1. Implementation of Solution

values using historical data as input. These characteristics make this technology an excellent choice for detecting timing side-channel assaults. The machine learning model is fed the features of a timing probe activity, and the prediction model assesses whether future packets are attack probes or normal traffic. We use machine learning for building this solution because of its ability to predict output accurately and efficiently.

SDN offers the centrally managed programming of network functionality by software applications that use APIs. A SDN's application layer facilitates network integration with proprietary and open source network applications and automation tools. We leverage this layer for the integration of our machine learning based solution with SDN. The solution also connects to the controller to get visibility about the entire SDN topology.

The solution is intended to receive incoming packets (Packet-Ins) from any SDN environment, sample them, and check for timing probe activity. It anticipates the timing attack attempts using an algorithm trained on a historical dataset. Along with each received packet, the solution extracts information about the source of each packet. This is done by attaining the flow tables from all the switches connected to the SDN topology. Later, this information is used to locate the source of the adversary. The output of our solution depicts the timing attack probing activity and accurately displays the origin of this activity. The network administrator can use this output to take further action based on the source machine. These actions can be to deny, allow or monitor further. The innovative method for integrating SDN and machine learning make the approach an efficient way of detecting timing probes and determining the source of the attacks.

3.1   Implementation of Solution

The presented solution is primarily located on the application layer of the SDN. A listener application "Listener API" is used to connect an SDN controller with the solution. This is a Southbound SDN API which means that it has the ability to extract information from the controller and the underlying Openflow switching layer. This API is designed to receive a copy of selective incoming requests to the controller. These are all the requests having an unknown destination MAC address. It also fetches the network topology, switch port, MAC and IP addresses along with the flows. On East, this API connects to the database of the solution. It stores the information from the SDN environment in the database. Figure 1 depicts the implementation model of the proposed approach.

We deploy MongoDB [4] as the database for this solution. MongoDB is a non-SQL database application that works with JSON (JavaScript Object Notation) format and optional schemas. The MongoDB is populated by a listener application which operates within the SDN topology. This forms a dataset. Normal 'non-attack' traffic is generated in the SDN environment including ICMP, HTTP and traffic on TCP and UDP ports. All requests and flows are recorded in the DB. Next, probe traffic is generated in the same network which includes 'arping', Nmap and others to simulate a timing attack. These are also recorded in the same dataset.

Next, the raw data is converted into a usable form for the machine learning steps. We convert all flows and host information in the DB to JSON type which makes it usable by a machine learning model. After getting this data in raw JSON format it will go through the pre-processing stage. This step ensures that the raw data has proper formatting and is in a usable form for machine learning stages. Following are the key functionalities performed at this filtration stage:

- Removes excessive fields from the dataset.
- Removes LLDP requests from the broadcast traffic.
- Identifies existing and non-existing flows in the switch table.
- Identifies table hit and table miss attempts.
- Segregation of request type: TCP, UDP, ARP, IPv4.
- Application of logic for selective tagging of the samples.

Once we have the pre-processed data, we train our machine learning model. The training module is based on a random forest algorithm [21]. We select this algorithm as it creates multiple decision trees during training stage and delivers the mean of predicted class at output. It builds trees based on multiple samples of data and uses average to improve its accuracy. Also, random forest is more accurate than the decision making trees. In this step, the dataset is used to train the machine learning model and divided into two parts, for training and testing. The classifiers for the random forest algorithm are applied at this stage. Following are the components of this stage:

- Confirmation of usable data.
- Normalization of dataset.
- Scaling of dataset.
- Split data in to train and test datasets.
- Application of random forest classifiers.
- Prediction model.

When we have a working dataset, we are ready for the monitoring step. In this step the monitoring module compares the live traffic with the existing model. By matching the samples and using anomaly detection techniques it identifies the timing side-channel activity. By live traffic monitoring enables the monitoring module to identify the source of the attack.

3.2   Dataset

To date, the data set with timing side-channel attack footprints in a SDN environment is not available. This prompted us to construct our dataset. We set up a 'listener' application with RYU controller. 'listener' in a python-based RYU application receives selective network flows and records them in the MongoDB. This application ensures that the topology information about the network is sent to the DB. It also extracts the source IP, source MAC, destination IP, and destination MAC with the timestamps of all packet-in requests. It can identify a UDP and TCP request. The switch name and switch port originating the request is also monitored and sent to the DB.

For creating the dataset, we run the simulation and run legitimate traffic patterns using a script. This includes netstat, HTTP, ICMP and traffic on various TCP and UDP ports. In this step, we ensure that all the switches have current flows and know the topology of the network. The flows added by the controller will be legitimate. The Mongo DB shows the number of samples collected.

Next, we run the attack probes which are a combination of attack ping scanning, broadcast traffic and Nmap scan traffic. We generate timing probes using a script. This action also creates several samples in MongoDB. To attain a useful number of samples in the Dataset we repeat these steps multiple times. MongoDB collects all the samples in raw form. After successfully attaining samples for the dataset, we convert them to JSON format and use this dataset in our machine learning model.

3.3   Pre-processing

After the conversion of the dataset into a usable format, we pre-process the data based on the samples. For any machine learning process, this is an essential step. It aids in preparing the raw data for the machine learning model by cleaning, arranging, and structuring it. We develop a python application for preprocessing which takes the JSON data as input from the previous step for preprocessing. This step includes splitting and tagging the data samples. The samples are marked as malicious timing probes on in this process based on the algorithm mentioned in the next section.

3.4   Algorithm

The classification of samples is based on the packets with non-existing destination MAC addresses. Algorithm used for classification and tagging of the timing attack samples at the pre-processing stage is shown in Algorithm 1. We pick ten samples at a time and check the number of samples with unknown destination MAC addresses. Packets with unknown MAC addresses are sent to the controller and are mirrored to the database. In every ten samples, if eighty percent of the samples coming from one source are with unknown destination MAC we tag this as timing probe.

3.5   Training

Once we have the pre-processed data, we train our machine learning model. The training module is based on random forest algorithm. Random forest is a learning method for classification, regression and other problems that functions by creating several decision trees at training time [21]. In this step, the dataset is used to train the machine learning model. The classifiers for the random forest algorithm are applied at this stage. Also, the dataset is scaled, normalized, and formatted at this stage.

3.6   Monitoring

For this step, we set up the same network topology as we did for the dataset. We design and run a monitoring application to link the existing machine learning model with the incoming traffic. To contemplate timing side-channel attacks, we use a timing probe script from one of the hosts connected to the network. We run the probe from the host 10 times and get a testing sample count each time. The results in the further section show that our model correctly identifies the presence of timing side-channel attacks in SDNs. For each test, our console also displays the mac and IP address of the host machine which is generating the timing attack.

Algorithm 1: Classification algorithm for attack packets

N = Number of samples with no destination MAC addresses. T = Total
Number of collected samples.
$i = N$;
$t = T$;
$n \leftarrow 10$;
$p \leftarrow 0.8$;
if $i > 0$ **then**
    if $t \leq n$ **then**
        $s = i/t$;
        if $s \geq p$ **then**
            tag;
        else
            return;
        end
    else
        return;
    end
else
    pass;
end

---

4   Experiment

We use Mininet [10] as a base simulator for this experiment, which is installed on a Linux-based virtual machine. Mininet is a software emulator that allows you to simulate a vast network on a single system. A custom SDN Network topology is created using python as shown in Fig. 2. The topology uses a remote controller. At the time of execution, this topology is imported into Mininet with a remote controller. We use RYU [3] as an SDN controller. The RYU SDN controller is installed on a separate Linux virtual machine. On the application layer, RYU Controller is used with customized python-based applications.

In the threat model, it is assumed that the adversary has gained control of one of the hosts connected to the network. The attacker's goal is to launch a timing side-channel attack using probe packets to extract as much information about the system as possible. In this experiment, the adversary aims to find out the timing difference between the responses of various timing probes. Timing probe packets are specially created packets that the attacker uses to find out

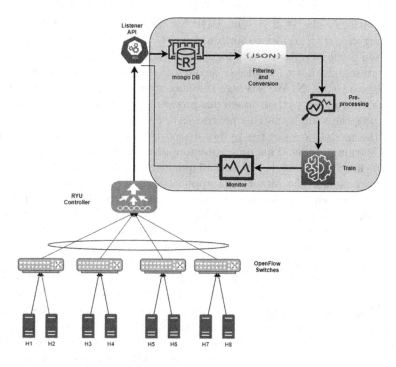

Fig. 2. Network Topology

timing statistics. These packets are transmitted with the intention of finding out how long the controller takes to process data. We use a variety of timing probe packets in our experiment, such as Ping (ICMP), Netstat, Arping, Nmap scans, etc. These are commonly utilized as timing probes in timing side-channel attacks.

The network topology includes four OpenFlow switches. Each of them is connected to the remote RYU Controller. Each OpenFlow switch is connected to two host machines. To contemplate traffic congestion on links, each link between host and switch in the topology has been programmed to have 2 milliseconds (ms) delay. The RYU applications enable the controller to install flows on all the switches. With the RYU controller, we run an application to handle the Spanning tree and the ARP requests in the network topology. For the solution, we created a listener application 'Listener API'. This application is designed to integrate with the RYU controller and the database. The Listener API forwards selective 'Packet Ins' to MongoDB. MongoDB is installed on a Linux machine and acts as a database for our model. For Pre-processing, Training and Monitoring stages we developed three separate python applications respectively. The network topology is presented in Fig. 2.

After setting up the custom topology, we start the first stage of this experiment. We ran multiple traffic patterns using scripts on multiple hosts in the topology. These include the timing probe packets and normal traffic. We extensively use utilities like TCP Netcat, UDP Netcat, ICMP (Ping), Netstat, Nmap and Arping etc. with scripts to form a dataset. The listener selects the 'packet Ins' and sends the samples to the MogoDB. In total 60649 samples were collected in this dataset. To use this dataset in our machine learning model we convert these samples to JSON. We leverage the 'mongoexport' feature for this step. In the next step, run our python-based pre-processing application. We clean, structure and tag the samples in this process. After this stage, the dataset is ready to train the model. We use the python-based training application to train our machine learning model. This pre-processing gives us 42489 samples.

For the monitoring stage, we clear all queues and reset the topology. We start the topology again. The Monitoring application is a python-based application which integrates with our machine learning model and the listener API. We run the network topology again and start the monitoring application. The monitor application is also programmed to determine the source of the attack and it correctly identifies the IP and MAC address of the adversary host. Additionally, it identifies the host by revealing information about the switch and port that the host is connected to. To simulate a realistic network, we use a script to run background traffic. During the experiment's twelve hours, we launch the timing probe multiple times, varying the number of attacks each time. We keep track of the number of attack samples, which are shown in Table 1. We run the attempts in numerous instances to verify the solution's competence and to account for the variation in background traffic. To extract the results, we make use of MongoDB and the attributes of the Monitor application.

The Monitor application detects the timing side-channel probe activity successfully. It accurately identifies the source of the timing probe. The results in Table 1 show that there is a very low number of false positives.

5   Results

As seen in Fig. 3, the results from the experimentation show that our approach shows a high level of accuracy against a large number of timing attack samples. There were only a small number of timing attack attempts which were not detected (false negatives) by the solution. Also, the results in Fig. 4 show that the increase in the number of attack attempts at any point in time increases the number of false positives.

The overall results for all attack attempts are shown in Table 1. This shows that our model learning approach to detect the timing side-channel attacks in SDNs is accurate and effective. The precession, recall and F1-score in Table 2 depict the correct decision-making capabilities of the presented solution.

6   Discussion

The outcomes show that the machine learning-based approach that has been presented is adequate for detecting a time side-channel attack in SDNs. For this experiment, we trigger the attack probes after certain intervals. This ensured that

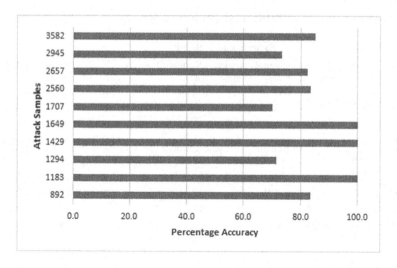

Fig. 3. Attack Samples and Percentage Accuracy

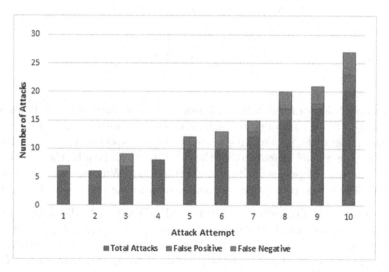

Fig. 4. False Positives and False Negatives

the background traffic varies every time we launched the probes. The advanced machine learning techniques and the listener application certify that the solution is efficient and not detectable. The following are some of the distinguishing features of the solution.

Machine Learning Based Solution. Our approach is distinctive in the way it combines SDNs with machine learning detection techniques. Our method is unique and distinctive because it combines SDNs with machine learning techniques for detection. Existing techniques for the solution of timing side-channel

Table 1. Experimental Results

Dataset:Training		Attack and Experimental			Results				
Total Samples	Trained Samples	Total Samples	Normal Samples	Attack Samples	Number of Attacks	Detected	False Negatives	False Positives	Accuracy
60649	42489	6273	5381	892	6	5	1	0	0.83
60649	42489	9902	8473	1429	8	8	0	0	1.00
60649	42489	17794	15234	2560	12	10	2	1	0.83
60649	42489	19101	17452	1649	10	10	0	2	1.00
60649	42489	22134	20951	1183	6	6	0	0	1.00
60649	42489	28088	25431	2657	17	14	3	1	0.82
60649	42489	28466	27172	1294	7	5	2	0	0.71
60649	42489	31343	29636	1707	10	7	3	0	0.70
60649	42489	36328	32746	3582	20	17	3	3	0.85
60649	42489	38471	35526	2945	15	11	4	2	0.73

Table 2. Precession Recall and F1-Score

Precision	Recall	F1-Score
0.94	0.85	0.89

attacks in SDN add a fixed delay to selected requests or downward flows [6,23]. They use the SDN controller to segregate requests into queues. The queue is given priority and the probe is responded to after a specific delay. An adversary can exploit the queueing features of these solutions and choke the controller by sending a stream of packets within a short period. Whereas, in our approach, the solution remains unrevealed by silently monitoring real-time SDN traffic.

Independence of Openflow Switch and SDN Controller. Because it is a peripheral setup, our solution may be connected to any SDN controller or switch. Between the controller and switch, the flow channel will have no effect. The attack vectors used in this analysis are based on the events in the SDN architecture. We anticipate that any SDN setup with hardware or software switches will benefit from this approach.

Dataset Updates. The results depict that the dataset is sufficient, and the tagging process shows a high level of accuracy. It can be argued that the dataset created during this experimentation is static and cannot be updated. The collection of data from a network to MongoDB is a quick process. However, further stages to make this data usable i.e., pre-processing and training are time-consuming and require a lot of computing resources. We suggest updating this dataset on the addition or removal of an Openflow switch to the network or after a set period.

7   Conclusion and Future Work

Our solution represents a peripheral security solution to detect timing side-channel attacks in SDNs and identify the origin of such attacks. Its implementation reflects minimal overhead in the SDN environment. Implementation of machine learning techniques and source detection methodologies used with SDN to discover timing attacks are some of the novel features of this work. These characteristics also make our solution invisible to the adversary. As seen from the results, the proposed method shows a negligible number of false positives and false negatives. This shows that the solution is a reliable and practical approach for the detection of timing side-channel attacks in SDNs.

The expense of having independent computing resources comes with the solution, even though it does not significantly increase network overhead. In future work, we will automate the process of dataset updating so that it is updated when a topology change is triggered in the network. We will also test the dataset with other classification techniques like logistic regression and support vector machines.

References

1. Ahmad, I., Kumar, T., Liyanage, M., Okwuibe, J., Ylianttila, M., Gurtov, A.: Overview of 5g security challenges and solutions. IEEE Commun. Stand. Mag. **2**(1), 36–43 (2018)
2. Arsalan, A., Rehman, R.A.: Prevention of timing attack in software defined named data network with vanets. In: 2018 International Conference on Frontiers of Information Technology (FIT), pp. 247–252. IEEE (2018)
3. Asadollahi, S., Goswami, B., Sameer, M.: Ryu controller's scalability experiment on software defined networks. In: 2018 IEEE International Conference on Current Trends in Advanced Computing (ICCTAC), pp. 1–5. IEEE (2018)
4. Banker, K., Garrett, D., Bakkum, P., Verch, S.: MongoDB in action: covers MongoDB version 3.0. Simon and Schuster (2016)
5. Boukria, S., Guerroumi, M.: Intrusion detection system for SDN network using deep learning approach. In: 2019 International Conference on Theoretical and Applicative Aspects of Computer Science (ICTAACS), vol. 1, pp. 1–6. IEEE (2019)
6. Conti, M., De Gaspari, F., Mancini, L.V.: A novel stealthy attack to gather SDN configuration-information. IEEE Trans. Emerg. Top. Comput. **8**(2), 328–340 (2018)
7. Dunlap, S., Butts, J., Lopez, J., Rice, M., Mullins, B.: Using timing-based side channels for anomaly detection in industrial control systems. Int. J. Crit. Infrastruct. Prot. **15**, 12–26 (2016)
8. Hou, J., Zhang, M., Zhang, Z., Shi, W., Qin, B., Liang, B.: On the fine-grained fingerprinting threat to software-defined networks. Futur. Gener. Comput. Syst. **107**, 485–497 (2020)
9. Karimi, E., Fei, Y., Kaeli, D.: Hardware/software obfuscation against timing side-channel attack on a GPU. In: 2020 IEEE International Symposium on Hardware Oriented Security and Trust (HOST), pp. 122–131. IEEE (2020)
10. Kaur, K., Singh, J., Ghumman, N.S.: Mininet as software defined networking testing platform. In: International Conference on Communication, Computing & Systems (ICCCS), pp. 139–42 (2014)

11. Liu, A., Chen, J.X., Wechsler, H., et al.: Real-time timing channel detection in an software-defined networking virtual environment. Intell. Inf. Manag. **7**(06), 283 (2015)
12. Liu, S., Reiter, M.K., Sekar, V.: Flow reconnaissance via timing attacks on SDN switches. In: 2017 IEEE 37th International Conference on Distributed Computing Systems (ICDCS), pp. 196–206. IEEE (2017)
13. Manu, B., Koundinya, A.K.: Intrusion tolerant architecture for SDN networks through flow monitoring. In: 2017 2nd International Conference on Computational Systems and Information Technology for Sustainable Solution (CSITSS), pp. 1–5. IEEE (2017)
14. Martins, J.S., Campos, M.B.: A security architecture proposal for detection and response to threats in SDN networks. In: 2016 IEEE ANDESCON, pp. 1–4. IEEE (2016)
15. Sahu, K., Kshirsagar, R., Vasudeva, S., Alzahrani, T., Karimian, N.: Leveraging timing side-channel information and machine learning for IoT security. In: 2021 IEEE International Conference on Consumer Electronics (ICCE), pp. 1–6. IEEE (2021)
16. Schnepf, N., Badonnel, R., Lahmadi, A., Merz, S.: Automated verification of security chains in software-defined networks with synaptic. In: 2017 IEEE Conference on Network Softwarization (NetSoft), pp. 1–9. IEEE (2017)
17. Schnepf, N., Badonnel, R., Lahmadi, A., Merz, S.: Synaptic: a formal checker for SDN-based security policies. In: NOMS 2018–2018 IEEE/IFIP Network Operations and Management Symposium, pp. 1–2. IEEE (2018)
18. Scott-Hayward, S., Natarajan, S., Sezer, S.: A survey of security in software defined networks. IEEE Commun. Surv. Tutor. **18**(1), 623–654 (2015)
19. Sepulveda, M.J., Diguet, J.P., Strum, M., Gogniat, G.: NOC-based protection for SOC time-driven attacks. IEEE Embed. Syst. Lett. **7**(1), 7–10 (2014)
20. Shoaib, F., Chow, Y.W., Vlahu-Gjorgievska, E.: Preventing timing side-channel attacks in software-defined networks. In: 2021 IEEE Asia-Pacific Conference on Computer Science and Data Engineering (CSDE), pp. 1–6 (2021). https://doi.org/10.1109/CSDE53843.2021.9718377
21. Wikipedia contributors. Random forest – Wikipedia, the free encyclopedia (2022). Accessed 15 Sep 2022
22. Yoon, C., et al.: Flow wars: systemizing the attack surface and defenses in software-defined networks. IEEE/ACM Trans. Netw. **25**(6), 3514–3530 (2017)
23. Zhang, M., et al.: Control plane reflection attacks and defenses in software-defined networks. IEEE/ACM Trans. Netw. **29**(2), 623–636 (2020)

A Token-Based Access Control Mechanism for the Internet of Things Using Blockchain

Yuzheng Yang⑩, Zhe Tu$^{(\boxtimes)}$, Haoxiang Song, and Huachun Zhou

School of Electronic and Information Engineering, Beijing Jiaotong University,
Beijing 100044, China
{21120151,zhe_tu,20120099,hchzhou}@bjtu.edu.cn

Abstract. The traditional access control model faces the problems of coarse granularity and poor management, and its centralized implementation architecture also leads to the emergence of security problems such as single point of failure and information leakage. In response to this problem, this paper proposes a token-based access control mechanism and uses blockchain technology for distributed implementation. In our scheme, the access control process consists of three steps: Policy upload, Token request and Resource request. It takes the token as the credentials of user access permissions as well as realizes fine-grained resource allocation and permission management through token control. In addition, we use blockchain technology for distributed implementation, which alleviates the security risks brought by the centralized architecture. The performance evaluation results show that the model can achieve reliable permission allocation and management and control the access request processing delay within 1 s.

Keywords: token-based access control · blockchain · smart contract

1 Introduction

With the continuous development of Internet of Things and mobile communication technology, 'Internet of Everything' has greatly accelerated the collection, analysis and sharing of information in the Internet [1]. However, heterogeneous access requirements and growing data information will bring serious security problems such as data leakage, malicious tampering of information, excessive access and illegal access [2]. In addition, the existing centralized network implementation architecture cannot meet the requirements of decentralization and transparency of information management [3]. Therefore, how to build a reliable access control system and implement it through a distributed network architecture has become an important research topic in the field of Internet of Things.

The existing access control research is mainly based on several common access control models, such as the role-based access control model (RBAC), attribute-based access control model (ABAC) and capability-based access control model

© The Author(s), under exclusive license to Springer Nature Singapore Pte Ltd. 2023
I. You et al. (Eds.): MobiSec 2022, CCIS 1644, pp. 195–206, 2023.
https://doi.org/10.1007/978-981-99-4430-9_14

(CapBAC) [4]. However, they cannot provide a truly fine-grained, manageable and efficient mechanism to adapt to the heterogeneous data characteristics and short-term authorization requirements of IoT networks. In addition, traditional access control usually verifies the access permissions of entities by centralized institutions, and faces security threats such as single point of failure [5]. Therefore, this paper proposes a token-based access control model, which takes 'token' as the credential of user permissions, generates corresponding tokens for users according to the specific resource operation permissions they need for each access request, instead of providing users with all the permissions they can operate at once, so as to achieve a more fine-grained permission assignment, and realizes manageable authorization mode by controlling the validity, expiration time and usage times of the token. In addition, this paper uses blockchain technology to build a distributed architecture to achieve secure and transparent distributed access control, and uses smart contracts to achieve access decisions to alleviate the problem of inefficient processing of resource devices.

The content structure of this paper is as follows: The second section discusses the related work. The third section describes the process of token-based access control model and blockchain smart contract functions. The fourth section introduces the implementation process of token-based access control method and tests its performance. The fifth section summarizes the whole work.

2   Related Work

Access control is an important means of controlling resources, which plays an important role in resource authorization management and data privacy protection. The key of access control is to limit the user's access to resources. The current popular access control methods are: role-based access control (RBAC), attribute-based access control (ABAC) and capability-based access control (CapBAC). [6] proposed RBAC model, which uses the concept of role to simplify the allocation of access permissions, that alleviates the problem of poor flexibility of traditional access control, but it will cause the problem of role explosion in the face of massive access. [7] proposed a more flexible ABAC, ABAC is an extension of RBAC, which requires access to the subject to provide more other attributes, such as subject attributes, object attributes, resource attributes and environmental attributes, making its system configuration more flexible. However, ABAC still cannot provide a manageable mechanism to flexibly control the allocation and revocation of access permissions. [8] proposed a capability-based access control system CapBAC, which first proposed the concept of 'token' to map permissions into passable capability tokens. However, CapBAC is a distributed access control implemented by lightweight devices in IoT, which leads to the problem that the system is less secure because the devices are vulnerable to attacks. [9] provides a more detailed description of the token based access control method. The general data structure of the access control token is given and the feasibility of the system is demonstrated by simulation experiments, but it focuses more on the theoretical introduction of various variants of the token application and lacks specific descriptions in a practical application environment.

In terms of access control system implementation architecture, traditional access control mainly relies on the authorization of centralized decision-making entities, which easily leads to security problems such as single point of failure. Blockchain has natural security advantages in the field of access control due to its distributed, decentralized and tamper-proof characteristics [10]. [11] proposed a blockchain-based RBAC model, which uses blockchain to store user-role, role-role mapping rules and access control policies. However, the above model still has the problem of poor management. [12] proposed a blockchain-based decentralized federal access control system, BlendCAC, which is similar to CapBAC in that it uses tokens as credentials for permissions, with the difference that it uses smart contracts to implement distributed token registration, propagation, and revocation operations.

This paper proposes a token-based access control mechanism, which generates tokens for users based on specific resource operation permissions to solve the problem of coarse-grained resource allocation in traditional access control, and achieves manageable authorization by controlling the validity, expiration time and usage times of the token. This paper uses blockchain to realize distributed architecture and uses smart contracts to make access control decisions, which improves the security, reliability and efficiency of the system.

3   Token-Based Access Control

3.1   System Model

The token-based access control system model is shown in Fig. 1. The system consists of four subjects:

- **User**: The subject who needs to obtain resource permissions and initiate access requests.
- **Resource owner**: The subject who owns the resources, each Resource owner has one or more resources, can upload, delete and modify and access control policies to the blockchain through the Gateway.
- **Gateway**: Gateway is the manager of the domain and also the node that constitutes the blockchain. By invoking the blockchain smart contract, it processes the Resource owner's access control policy related requests and the User's token requests and resource requests.
- **Blockchain**: Maintain distributed ledgers for each blockchain node, record User, policy, and token information, and perform access control judgment operations. It includes three smart contracts t_uinfo, t_policy and t_token to process User information, access control policy and token related requests, respectively.

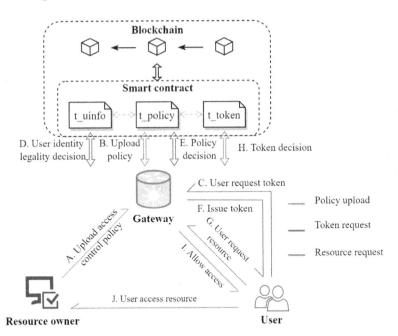

Fig. 1. Token-based access control system model

3.2   Token-Based Access Control Mechanism Process

The key idea of the token-based access control is to translate User access permission to resources into a specific token, and Users can access resources with the legal token. The access control process can be divided into three parts: Policy upload, Token request and Resource request, which correspond to Step A-B, Step C-F and Step G-J in Fig. 1, respectively. Each part will be described in detail below.

Policy Upload. As shown in Step A-B of Fig. 1, the system performs the policy upload first.

Step A: The Resource owner sends the access control policy to the Gateway. $policy := \{OID\_resX, [op, (UID), (role), (IP), (loca), period]\}$, in which OID_resX represents Resource owner and its resource name corresponding to the policy, op represents an operation allowed by the resource, and the remaining fields represent the conditions to be satisfied for the operation of the resource: (UID) represents the restricted User identity set, $(role)$, (IP) and $(loca)$ represent the role set, IP address set and geographic location set of the licensed User, respectively, $period$ represents the time period that the resource is allowed to access.

Step B: The Gateway uploads the access control policy to the blockchain by invoking the $uppolicy()$ in the smart contract t_policy.

The system can also perform policy deletion and modification operations, and the corresponding functions are: *deletepolicy()* and *modifypolic()*, which are similar to the upload policy operation. The difference is that the policy content needs to be provided for deletion or modification.

Token Request. The Token request is shown in Step C-F of Fig. 1. The User sends the token request to the Gateway. After receiving the request, the Gateway invokes the smart contract to determine the legality of the User identity and makes a policy decision based on the predefined access control policy. If the decision condition is met, the token is generated and granted to the User. It is important to emphasize that, unlike traditional access control where all the user's permissions are determined at once, in our system, the User's request will contain the permissions it needs to obtain, and the system will generate a token for the user based on this specific permission, thus avoiding over-authorization and achieving fine-grained access control. Details of the Token request process are shown in Fig. 2.

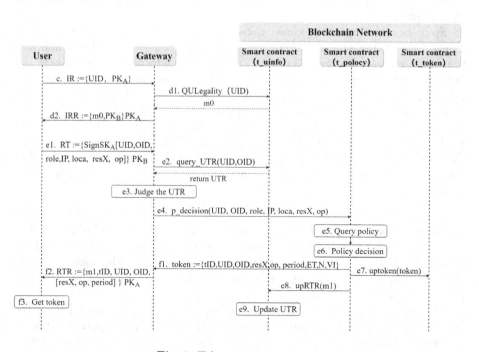

Fig. 2. Token request process

Step C: c) The User sends identity legality decision request IR to the Gateway before requesting the token. $IR := \{UID, PK_A\}$, which includes the User identity UID and the User public key PK_A.

Step D: The system performs User identity legality decision. d1) After receiving the IR, the Gateway invokes the $QULegality()$ in the smart contract

t_uinfo to determine the legality of the User identity and get the result $m0$. d2) The Gateway returns the identity legality decision result IRR to the User, $IRR := \{m0, PK_B\}PK_A$, which includes $m0$ as well as the Gateway public key PK_B, and is encrypted using PK_A.

Step E: The system performs Policy decision. e1) The User sends the request token message RT to the Gateway. $RT := \{SignSK_A[UID, OID,$ $role, IP, loca, resX, op]\}PK_B$, which contains User information and is signed by SK_A and encrypted by PK_B. e2) After receiving the RT, the Gateway queries the User token reputation value UTR by invoking the $query\_UTR()$ in the smart contract t_uinfo according to UID and OID. e3) Judge the UTR. If the reputation value is low, the request is rejected. e4) Policy decision by invoking the $p\_decision()$ in smart contract t_policy. e5) Query if the policy exists. e6) Determine whether the policy requirements are satisfied and get the token request result $m1$. e7) Save the token on the chain by invoking the $uptoken()$ in the smart contract t_token. e8) Save the token request result by invoking the $upRTR()$ of the smart contract t_uinfo. e9) Calculate UTR based on the result. If the UTR is less than the identity threshold, the system will restrict the User identity legality.

Step F: The system issues token for the User. f1) If the requirements are satisfied, a token is generated and the token information is returned to the Gateway. The token information is: $token :=$ $\{tID, UID, OID, resX, op, period, ET, N, VI\}$, in which, tID represents the token unique identity, ET represents the token expiration time, N represents usage times of the token, and VI represents the token validity identifier. f2) The Gateway sends the request token result RTR to the User, $RTR := \{m1, tID, UID, OID, [resX, op, period]\}PK_A$, which includes $m1$ and part of the token content, and use PK_A to encrypt these messages. f3) The User extracts the token information from the RTR and can then perform Resource request operations via the token.

Resource Request The Resource request is shown in Step G-J of Fig. 1. The User can continue to submit the resource request after holding the token, and the Gateway will grant the User the required permissions after the token decision, thus allowing the User to access the resources. Details of the Resource request process are shown in Fig. 3.

Step G: g) The User need to submit request resource message RR to the gateway before accessing resources. $RR := \{UID, OID, resX, op, tID\}PK_A$.

Step H: The system performs Token decision. h1) After the Gateway receives the RR, it invokes the $t\_decesion()$ in the smart contract t_token to perform the token decision. h2) In the decision process, first query whether the token exists based on tID, and then query whether the token is valid based on ET, VI and N. h3) After querying a valid token, query the User resource reputation value URR by invoking the $query\_URR()$ in the smart contract t_uinfo according to the UID and OID. h4) Judge the URR. If the URR is lower than the threshold, the resource request is rejected and the token is set to invalid (set the VI to

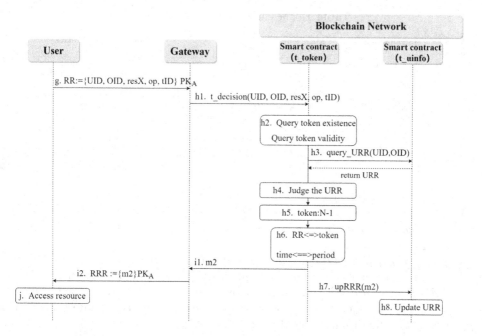

Fig. 3. Resource request process

F). h5) If URR is higher than the threshold value, the usage times of token N is subtracted by 1. h6) Determine whether the token contains the resources and operations requested by the User and whether the current time period is within the *period*. h7) Save the resource request result by invoking the $upRRR()$ of the smart contract t_uinfo. h8) Calculate URR based on the result.

Step I: The system returns the request resource result to the User. i1) The smart contract returns the result $m2$ to the Gateway. i2) The Gateway encrypts $m2$ to get the request resource result RRR, $RRR := \{m2\}PK_A$, and sends it to the User.

Step J: j) The User receives the RRR and can access resource if it passes the resource request.

3.3 Smart Contract

The access control mechanism contains three smart contracts t_policy, t_uinfo and t_token to handle requests related to access control policy, User information and token respectively, and is used as a medium of interaction from the Gateway to the blockchain to store related information on the chain. The contents of the smart contract are shown in Table 1.

Table 1. The contents of smart contract

Smart contract	Introduction	Main functions	Format of saved data
t_uinfo	Save User information and access control results.	$QULegality(UID)$; $query\_UTR(UID, OID)$; $query\_URR(UID, OID)$; $upRTR(m1)$; $upRRR(m2)$	UserInfo{UID, Legality, RT_record, RR_record, URR, UTR}
t_policy	Save access control policy information and perform policy decision.	$uppolocy(policy)$; $deletepolicy(OID\_resX)$; $modifypolicy(OID\_resX, item, CRY)$; $p\_decision(UID, OID, role, IP, loca, resX, op)$	policy{OID_reX, op, UID, role, IP, local, period}
t_token	Save token information and perform token decision.	$uptoken(token)$; $t\_decision(UID, OID, resX, op, tID)$	token{tID, UID, OID, resX, op, period, ET, N, VI}

(1) Smart contract t_uinfo

- $QULegality(UID)$: Invoked by the Gateway to determine if the User's current identity is legality.
- $query\_UTR(UID, OID)$, $query\_URR(UID, OID)$: Invoked by the Gateway or smart contract t_token to query the User's reputation value.
- $upRTR(m1)$, $upRRR(m2)$: Invoked by smart contract t_policy or t_token to save token request and resource request result, and also update UTR and URR according to access control result.

(2) Smart contract t_policy

- $uppolocy(policy)$:Invoked by the Gateway to save the access control policy on the blockchain.
- $deletepolicy(OID\_resX)$, $modifypolicy(OID\_resX, item, CRY)$: Invoked by the Gateway to delete or modify the access control policy. Where item and CRY are the entries to be modified and the modified content, respectively.
- $p\_decision(UID, OID, role, IP, loca, resX, op)$: Invoked by the Gateway to make a policy decision during the token request process. If the User meets the policy requirements, the token is generated and the $uptoken()$ in t_token is invoked to save the token.

(3) Smart contract t_token

- $uptoken(token)$: Invoked by the smart contract t_policy to save the token on the blockchain.
- $t\_decision(UID, OID, resX, op, tID)$: Invoked by the Gateway to make the token decision during the Resource request. If the policy decision is passed then the User is allowed to access the resource.

4   Performance Evaluation

In this paper, we build a distributed architecture with the use of Hyperledger Fabric 1.4.3 to implement the token-based access control model. First, the blockchain architecture is built on 9 virtual machines, where three virtual machines are used as orderer nodes for transaction sequencing and each virtual machine is involved in blockchain ledger maintenance as a peer node. The virtual machine with the orderer node is simulated as the Gateway, and the other 6 virtual machines are simulated as Users and Resource owners, respectively. Then, smart contracts *t_uinfo*, *t_policy* and *t_token* on User information, policies and tokens are written using Go 1.11.5 and deployed to the blockchain. Use python 3.8.10 to write interaction scripts and allocate them to the virtual machines corresponding to the Gateway, Resource owner and User.

4.1   Access Control Model Functional Tests

The model is implemented according to the token-based access control mechanism process in Subsect. 3.2 of this paper. As shown in Fig. 4, the operations and results of blockchain processing of Policy upload, Token request, and Resource request can be observed through the smart contract log output.

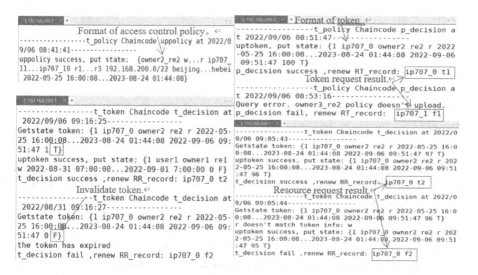

Fig. 4. Smart contract log output

According to the token format, we can find that the system generates tokens in units of specific resource operation permissions, and when a user performs resource access, the system will only grant a specific resource to the user based on its token content and deny other resource requests from the user. This prevents over-assignment of permissions and enables fine-grained access control. In addition, the token specifies the token expiration time and usage times of the token. As can also be observed in Fig. 4, when the usage times of the token N are reduced to 0, the system will automatically invalidate the token, and subsequent accesses by the User holding the token will be denied. Therefore, the control of tokens enables the timely recovery of permissions and achieves manageable access control.

4.2   Access Control Model Performance Tests

In this subsection, we test the performance of the token-based access control model by testing the total number of token requests and resource requests processed by the system at different times (as shown in Fig. 5) and comparing the total delay of 200 token requests or resource requests processed by the system with different proportion of normal requests (as shown in Fig. 6).

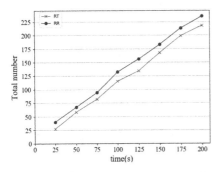

Fig. 5. Total number of token requests and resource requests processed at different times.

Fig. 6. Processing delay of 200 requests with different percentage of normal requests.

Figure 5 illustrates the capability of the access control system as evidenced by the total number of requests processed by the system in a given time period. Taking the case of 75s as an example, the system can process 82 token requests or 94 resource requests in 75s, which shows that the system has high efficiency and can control the access request processing delay within 1 s, and the efficiency of processing resource requests is higher than that of token requests. In addition, it can be concluded from the curve trend in the figure that the processing capacity of the system does not decrease significantly as the total duration increases. Figure 6 illustrates the difference in delay between the system processing normal and abnormal requests based on the total delay in processing the same requests with different proportion of normal requests. The results show that the total delay for processing the same number of access control requests decreases when the percentage of normal requests decreases for both token requests and resource requests, from which it can be concluded that the system requires a higher delay for processing normal requests than for abnormal requests, because in the access control process, once the user does not satisfy a certain access control requirement, the system rejects the request in time and omits the subsequent determination process.

5   Conclusion

This paper investigates the access control issue in the IoT, for which we proposed a token-based access control mechanism, and uses the Hyperledger Fabric blockchain platform for distributed implementation. The token-based access control mechanism conceptualizes user permissions as 'tokens' and achieves manageable and fine-grained access control through token control. It also enhances the security of the access control system by using the decentralized and transparent features of blockchain. This paper builds a blockchain platform based on Hyperledger fabric architecture for system implementation, proving the granularity and manageability of the model, and prove that the system has advantages in processing capacity by performance testing, and can control the access request processing delay within 1 s.

Acknowledgement. This paper was supported in part by the National Key R & D Program of China under Grant No. 2018YFA0701604, and in part by the Fundamental Research Funds for the Central Universities under Grant No. 2021YJS012.

References

1. Chopra, K., Gupta, K., Lambora, A.: Future internet: the internet of things-a literature review. In: 2019 International Conference on Machine Learning, Big Data, Cloud and Parallel Computing (COMITCon), pp. 135–139. IEEE (2019) Location (1999)
2. Alaba, F.A., Othman, M., Hashem, I.A.T., Alotaibi, F.: Internet of Things security: a survey. J. Netw. Comput. Appl. **88**, 10–28 (2017). https://doi.org/10.1016/j.jnca.2017.04.002
3. Shen, X.S., Liu, D., Huang, C., Xue, L., Yin, H., Zhuang, W., et al.: Blockchain for transparent data management toward 6G. Engineering **8**, 74–85 (2022). https://doi.org/10.1016/j.eng.2021.10.002
4. Zhang, Y., Wu, X.: Access control in internet of things: a survey. arXiv preprint arXiv:1610.01065 (2016)
5. Ammar, M., Russello, G., Crispo, B.: Internet of Things: a survey on the security of IoT frameworks. J. Inf. Secur. Appl. **38**, 8–27 (2018). https://doi.org/10.1016/j.jisa.2017.11.002
6. Cugini, J., Kuhn, R., Ferraiolo, D.: Role-based access control: features and motivations. In: Proceedings of the Annual Computer Security Applications Conference, Los Alamitos, Calif, (1995). https://doi.org/10.1145/266741.266758
7. Hu, V.C., Kuhn, D.R., Ferraiolo, D.F., Voas, J.: Attribute-based access control. Computer **48**(2), 85–88 (2015). https://doi.org/10.1109/MC.2015.33
8. Gusmeroli, S., Piccione, S., Rotondi, D.: A capability-based security approach to manage access control in the internet of things. Math. Comput. Model. **58**(5–6), 1189–1205 (2013). https://doi.org/10.1016/j.mcm.2013.02.006
9. Gan, G., Chen, E., Zhou, Z., Zhu, Y.: Token-based access control. IEEE Access **8**, 54189–54199 (2020). https://doi.org/10.1109/ACCESS.2020.2979746
10. Li, W., Meng, W., Liu, Z., Au, M.: Towards blockchain-based software-defined networking: security challenges and solutions. IEICE Trans. Inf. Syst. **103**(2), 196–203 (2020). https://doi.org/10.1587/transinf.2019INI0002

11. Sun, S., Chen, S., Du, R.: Trusted and efficient cross-domain access control system based on blockchain. Sci. Program. **2020**(10), 1–13 (2020). https://doi.org/10.1155/2020/8832568

12. Xu, R., Chen, Y., Blasch, E., Chen, G.: Blendcac: a blockchain-enabled decentralized capability-based access control for IoTs. In: 2018 IEEE International conference on Internet of Things (iThings) and IEEE green computing and communications (GreenCom) and IEEE cyber, physical and social computing (CPSCom) and IEEE Smart Data (SmartData), pp. 1027–1034. IEEE (2018). https://doi.org/10.1109/Cybermatics_2018.2018.00191

Cyber Security

DyBAnd: Dynamic Behavior Based Android Malware Detection

Shashank Jaiswal[1], Vikas Sihag[1], Gaurav Choudhary[2(✉)], and Nicola Dragoni[2]

[1] Department of Science, Technology and Forensics, Sardar Patel University of Police, Security and Criminal Justice, Jodhpur, India
`spu19cssj@policeuniversity.ac.in, vikas.sihag@policeuniversity.ac.in`
[2] DTU Compute, Technical University of Denmark, 2800 Kongens Lyngby, Denmark
`gauch@dtu.dk, ndra@dtu.dk`

Abstract. Android is the most popular widely accessible smartphone operating system, yet its permission declaration and access control systems cannot detect malicious activities. Advanced malware uses cutting-edge obfuscation techniques to mask its true intentions from scanning engines, and traditional malware detection approaches are no longer effective in such cases. In this paper we propose DyBAnd, an Android malware detection approach based on Multilayer Perceptron, a neural network-based model for recognising dynamic malware activity. DyBAnd makes use of behavioural characteristics gleaned via dynamic analysis of a program running in an emulated environment, allowing it to detect malicious code in real time environment. The proposed system is tested against 17,341 contemporary applications from various domains, including Banking, Riskware, Adware, SMS, and Benign. Experimental results show that DyBAnd detects malware with a 98.98% accuracy and a false positive rate of 1.02%, significantly higher than Linear Programming. DyBAnd also outperforms conventional machine learning techniques.

Keywords: Android · Malware Detection · Machine Learning

1 Introduction

Android OS accounts for 72.26% of the world's smartphones, representing de facto the most popular operating system for mobile devices and static smart devices[1]. This attracts cyber crooks that prey on the privacy and security of users. 98% of mobile malware targets Android devices, with roughly 24000 malicious mobile applications being banned every day[2]. Due to its open environment, Android is the mobile platform that has been attacked the most by malware that aims to steal personal information or control the user's devices. Furthermore,

---

[1] https://www.statista.com/statistics/330695/number-of-smartphone-users-worldwide/ [June 12, 2022].
[2] https://purplesec.us/resources/cyber-security-statistics/ [June 12, 2022].

© The Author(s), under exclusive license to Springer Nature Singapore Pte Ltd. 2023
I. You et al. (Eds.): MobiSec 2022, CCIS 1644, pp. 209–219, 2023.
https://doi.org/10.1007/978-981-99-4430-9_15

Android features a number of third-party application shops, making it simple for fraudsters to repackage Android apps with harmful code.

Android malware detection uses two approaches: static and dynamic analysis. Static analysis disassembles malware into source code, from which certain features can be retrieved. Malware is tracked in an isolated environment during dynamic analysis. Machine learning methods have been utilized in both ways to develop classification models by training classifiers with malware datasets, and characteristics gathered from static or dynamic analysis. Static analysis is low-weighted and provides extensive code coverage. Dynamic analysis keeps track of an application's behavior and technical indicators while running. Advanced malware does not respond well to static analysis. Application hardening techniques easily defeat pattern matching and statistically based detection engines. The efficiency of machine learning solutions is determined by characteristics collected from both malicious and authentic data. Due to its automated feature extraction from raw data for categorization, they have been demonstrated to be useless against complicated malware in the actual world. The learned classification models are then utilized to identify and categorize dangerous programs into their respective families [1].

To elude anti-malware detection, malware researchers are employing cutting-edge application stealth methods such as complex code obfuscation and protection mechanisms [2,3]. The generic process of Android application Malware detection is shown in Fig. 1. However, advanced malware does not respond well to static analysis. Existing approaches for malware detection are not fully capable of identifying advanced malware, and application hardening techniques easily defeat pattern matching and statically based detection engines [4,5].

Contribution of the Paper: In this paper we propose DyBAnd, an advanced Android malware detection method based on dynamic behaviour of an application. DyBAnd is based on a semi-supervised learning approach termed backpropagation to train a feed-forward Artificial Neural Network (ANN) based model Multilayer Perceptron (MLP). MLP differs from a linear perceptron in that it has many layers and non-linear activation. The attributes that may be retrieved from the network log, system call's log, and system binder's log files of Android applications are used in dynamic analysis of the machine learning-based approach to recognize dynamic malware activity. The main contribution of the paper can be summarised as follows:

- We propose DyBAnd, an Android application dynamic behavior based malware detection approach
- We identify the optimum hidden layer configuration for MLP based detection
- We compare DyBAnd against existing state of the art malware detection approaches, showing it's novelty in terms of accuracy and false positive rate.

Outline of the Paper. Section 2 covers related work. Section 3 and 4 present DyBAnd and experimental results, respectively. Section 5 concludes the paper.

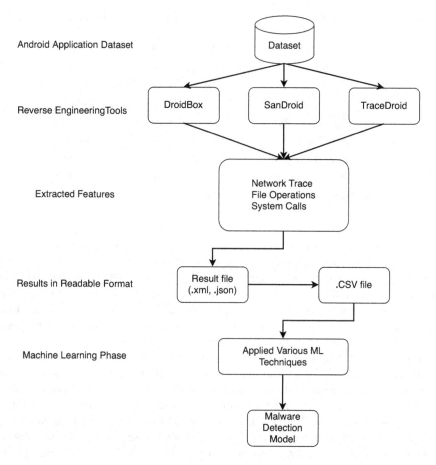

Fig. 1. The stepwise process of Android application Malware detection.

2   Related Works

This section briefly examines recent research on malware detection on Android utilizing dynamic analysis-based feature capture and deep learning-based classification methods. By deconstructing the program without executing it, static analysis-based Android malware detection retrieves program elements like API calls, intents, and permissions. To detect Android malware, academic and industrial researchers employ machine learning methods such as Naive Bayes, Simple Vector Machine, Decision Tree, and k-NN [6]. On the other hand, deep learning is a subset of machine learning that tries to accurately and efficiently extract high-level characteristics from raw data [7]. A comparison of Android malware detection approaches is shown in Table 1.

The advantages of the static analysis detection technique include code coverage and rapid feature extraction. Obfuscation techniques including class encryption, renaming, reflection, and API hiding are adopted to get around it. The

Table 1. The state of the art summary of Android Malware Detection Methods.

Year	Paper	Technique	Model	Result
2014	Yuan et al. [8]	Hybrid	DBN	96.00%
2016	Hou et al. [9]	Static	Auto Encoder	93.68%
2017	Bacci et al. [2]	Dynamic	CNN	90.00%
2019	Xiao et al. [10]	Dynamic	CNN	98.16%
2019	Alzaylaee et al. [11]	Dynamic	NN	97.80%
2020	Mahdavifar et al. [12]	Dynamic	CNN	97.84%
2021	Sihag et al. [13]	Dynamic	NN	98.08%
2021	DyBAnd	Dynamic	MLP	98.98%

dynamic detection technique (i.e., an application is run in a controlled environment using dynamic analysis) can discover obfuscated or dynamically loaded code parts that escape static analysis. Emulated user interactions are required for an Android application running in an emulated environment during automated dynamic analysis. Stateless input generation tools such as Dynodroid [14], Monkey[3], ACTEve [15], and PUMA [16] are used to simulate interactions.

Droid-Sec [17] was the first deep learning framework for Android malware detection, and it employed a static and dynamic methodology to extract 200 characteristics from a small number of applications. DroidDetector was created to expand on this. Deep4MalDroid suggested a deep learning-based Linux system call-based detection solution. By interpreting one device call sequence of Android malware as a statement, Xiao et al. [10] employed two LSTM language models to train malware and benign samples. They compute the sequence's similarity score and employ the two qualified networks to identify an APK under examination.

Bacci et al. [2] used a real-world device to monitor system calls that were then fed into a CNN. By incorporating monitoring functions into an application. Alzaylaee et al. [11] introduced DL-Droid, which leverages DynaLog, a dynamic analytic framework, to produce dynamic features. For high code coverage, it employs a stateful input-generating approach. Hou et al. [9] proposed AutoDroid, which used static analysis to feed API call features. They tested a number of deep learning networks and discovered that DBN performed the best in the specific situation.

3 DyBAnd

In this Section, we describe the main idea behind DyBAnd as well as the experimental setup for evaluating the approach's performance in an emulated environment. To detect whether an Android app is harmful or benign, we first run the program's Android Application Package (APK) file in an emulated environment [13]. The emulator's logs are parsed and preprocessed to provide a feature

---

[3] https://developer.android.com/studio/test/monkey.html [June 12, 2022].

vector representation of the program [18]. The deep learning model is trained using this feature vector. The training model is compared to the testing dataset for malware identification, and Neurons in MLP calculate a smooth variant of this. Figure 2 depicts an architectural diagram of MLP.

$$\vec{x} \mapsto f_{log}(w_0 + \langle \vec{w}, \vec{x} \rangle)$$

with

$$f_{log}(z) = \frac{1}{1 + e^{-z}}$$

f_{log} is called logistic function

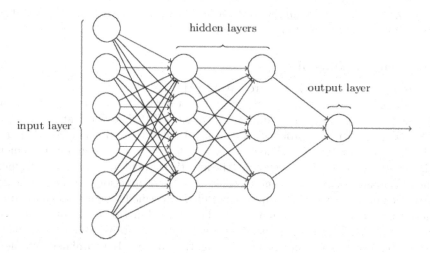

Fig. 2. Architectural Diagram of MLP.

DyBAnd is based on four major modules, as described below.

Dynamic Analysis

In the literature, there are several solutions based on static and dynamic analysis. The advantages of static analysis include code coverage and rapid feature extraction. To get around it, obfuscation techniques including class encryption, renaming, reflection, and API hiding are deployed. Dynamic analysis executes an application in a controlled environment (emulator or real device). Obfuscated or dynamic loaded code segments evaded during static analysis can be detected using dynamic approach. A dynamic analysis methodology is used to extract Android OS interactions from an application sample. The sample is executed in an emulated environment to log application activity in dynamic analysis. Copperdroid [19] is used to recreate remote procedure call and inter-process communication interactions as well as Android-specific objects. System call tracking, binder analysis, network traffic collection, and composite behavior interaction were all reported in detail in the logs. We utilize DroidBot[4], a stateful tool for controlling the emulator to produce user interactions.

Feature Extraction and Preprocessing

We evaluate binder information, system calls, and network logs during feature extraction to acquire behavioral insight. The logs, as mentioned above, are in JSON format and were extracted during dynamic analysis. JSON log files for each APK file are processed and converted into .csv for further analysis to extract the features. As a result, a feature vector representing all low-level behavioral data is created. Datasets of feature vectors are normalized using image creation and label encoding, further processed, transformed, and reshaped to get the normalized dataset. Rescaling data to a mean of zero and a standard deviation of one (unit variance) is standardization.

Deep Learning Classifier

The normalized feature vectors are put into Multilayer Perceptrons in the learning module. We use the StandardScaler() that standardizes a feature by removing the mean and then scaling to unit variance and MLPClassifier that maps input data sets onto a set of appropriate outputs. For all of the hidden layers, there are multiple activation functions like identity (no-op activation, useful for implementation of a linear bottleneck), logistic (the logistic sigmoid function), tanh (hyperbolic tan function), and relu (the rectified linear unit function). However, we get the best result with relu. We employ the ReLU (Rectified Linear Unit) activation functions, that returns $f(x) = \max(0, x)$. The ReLU function does not simultaneously stimulate all of the neurons. As a result, some neurons' weights and biases are not updated throughout the backpropagation process. In neural network models that predict a multinomial probability distribution, we train the Multilayer Perceptrons (Riskware, Benign, SMS, Adware, and Banking). Various Multilayer Perceptrons models were examined in terms of the number of hidden layers and neurons. The model was trained for 100 epochs. The model was optimized using Adam, the stochastic gradient-based optimizer, a replacement optimization approach. On relatively large datasets, Adam performs brilliantly in training time and validation score (with thousands of training samples or more).

Datasets and Evaluation Metrics

For testing, 20% of the dataset samples were chosen by random state. The confusion matrix was used to assess the performance efficacy of the classifier model. We also compare our approach with KNN, Support Vector Machine, Naive Bayes, Random Forest, Decision Tree, and Convolutional Neural Network, all popular machine learning algorithms. We used an Android application dataset CICMal-Droid2020[5] of 17,341 samples to test our research and compare it to other standard techniques. Their classification of the data sample is shown in Table 2.

---

[4] https://github.com/honeynet/droidbot [June 12, 2022].

[5] https://www.unb.ca/cic/datasets/maldroid-2020.html [June 12, 2022].

The dataset was created using samples from various sources, and it comprises Benign, Riskware, Banking, SMS, and Adware programs from a range of categories. A boxplot chart representing size distribution in different classes of the considered dataset is shown in Fig. 3. It can be observed that benign samples and riskware malware samples have wide filesize distribution compared to other malware classes. Malware filesize distribution is a collection of samples in all malware classes (Adware, Banking, Riskware, and SMS).

Table 2. CICMalDroid2020 dataset: APK sample distribution

	Category					
	Adware	Banking	Riskware	SMS	Benign	Total
#	1,253	2,100	2,546	3,904	1,795	11,598

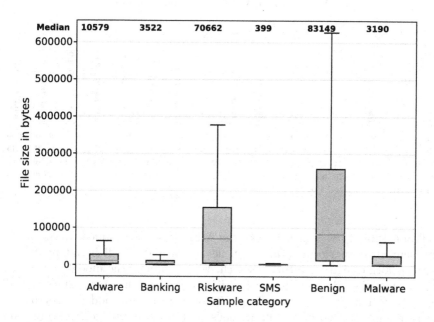

Fig. 3. Comparison of file size distribution of samples belonging to different classes.

4 Experimental Results

Experiments were run on an Intel Core i5-9300H 2.4 GHz CPU computer with 16 GB RAM and Ubuntu 20.04 LTS operating system. The CopperDroid emulator was used during dynamic analysis to generate network logs, system calls, and a system binder and set up to give an example application in a real-world environment. Before running the program in a clean state, the IMEI number, IMSI number, contact information, SMS, etc., were all changed. Our MLP model has input layer neurons that are the same size as the feature vector, fine-tuned hidden layers, neurons, and a single output layer for family classification. For an ideal layout, the number of hidden neurons and hidden layers are adjusted. We trained our model for a batch size of 500 with 100 epochs sizes of randomly picked samples during the learning process.

The classification loss function is a function that calculates how much information is. Logarithmic loss, or log loss, measures a classifier's accuracy by penalizing incorrect classifications. Increasing the accuracy of the classifier by reducing the Log Loss is effectively the same thing. The loss function for both the training and testing sets lowers as the epoch values increase, as seen in Fig. 4. The final value of log loss for the training curve is relatively low for both segments of the trials.

Table 3. DyBAnd Classification Metrics

Hidden Layers	2				3					4				
# Neurons	[100,100]	[200,100]	[200,200]	[400,400]	[100,100,100]	[200,200,200]	[400,400,400]	[400,300,200]	[400,200,200]	[100,100,100,100]	[200,200,200,200]	[400,400,400,400]	[400,300,200,100]	[400,200,200,100]
Precision	98.30	98.28	**98.66**	98.52	98.51	98.56	97.87	98.39	97.63	98.33	98.56	97.42	98.18	98.55
Recall	97.94	97.76	**98.88**	95.53	97.92	98.75	97.90	98.64	98.37	98.44	98.70	97.42	98.35	98.75
F-Measure	98.11	98.01	98.76	98.52	98.19	98.65	**98.87**	98.50	97.96	98.37	98.62	97.40	98.26	98.64
Accuracy	98.32	98.26	**98.98**	98.75	98.49	98.85	98.03	98.74	98.37	98.61	98.79	97.70	95.49	98.85
Error Rate	1.68	1.74	**1.02**	1.25	1.51	1.15	1.97	1.26	1.63	1.39	1.21	1.30	1.51	1.15

From Table 3, we can say that the MLP with two hidden layers of [200, 200] neurons outperforms other deep networks, and it will be adopted as the deep network design for future research. While running the model, it is noticed that the model's efficiency rises at first with the growth in epoch values and then begins to decrease after a point. To put it another way, the model starts to match the training data too well. The model's performance will decline, and model execution time will increase if the model's overfitting threshold is not found. In the worst-case situation, resource depletion will occur. Overfitting will result in the generalization of training data and incorrectly detected malware instances in the confusion matrix. When using the model.fit() method, the EarlyStopping parameter is set to 3 to solve this problem. This option keeps track of training results and, if it is activated, it will put a halt to it. Our MLP architecture's malware detection performance is examined. Figure 4 depicts the accuracy of our method's training and test datasets throughout 100 epochs and 500 batches. As expected, as the number of epochs increases, the accuracy steadily improves.

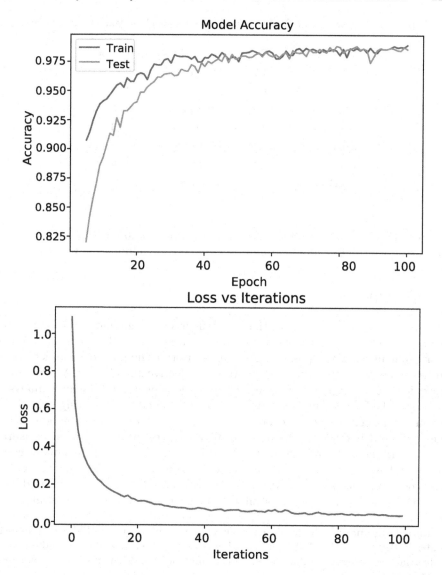

Fig. 4. Average accuracy and loss of DyBAnd vs total number of iterations for training and test samples.

The weighted average accuracy of our approach is 98.98% with an F1-score of 98.76% and a false positive rate of 1.02%. As shown in Table 4, we compare the performance of the proposed MLP-based solution with existing machine learning methodologies. We compared the performance of KNN, Naive Bayes, Simple Vector Machine, Decision tree, Random Forest, Convolutional neural network with the suggested technique on the test data. MLP beats machine learning techniques, as seen in the Table. In the Table, the proposed methodology is

Table 4. Comparison of DyBAnd with popular machine learning classifiers.

Method	Error Rate	F-Measure	Accuracy
KNN	4.74	83.67	95.26
Naive Bayes	7.16	79.30	92.84
SVM	5.40	89.28	94.60
Decision Tree	2.87	92.18	97.13
Random Forest	3.1	91.38	96.89
CNN	2.16	96.54	97.84
DyBAnd	*1.02*	97.80	98.98

compared to current state-of-the-art machine learning approaches. Our technique produces promising results and may be improved by adding many features.

5   Conclusion

Malware detection and classification is a difficult challenge that requires identifying and selecting different features from malware samples. The process becomes more difficult when the program uses obfuscation techniques to avoid detection. In this paper we have proposed DyBAnd, an effective and efficient Android malware detection system based on a multilayer perceptron and dynamic analysis. We tested DyBAnd using the CICMalDroid2020 dataset, extracting behavioral features and comparing it to other state of the art malware detection methods. DyBAnd is quick to execute and allows to prioritize mitigation measures by defining the malware's category. The collection encompasses five major categories of Adware, Banking, SMS malware, Riskware, and Benign, and comprises the most comprehensive dynamic feature sets ever gathered. For malware detection, DyBAnd has been demonstrated to be effective and 98.98% accurate.

Acknowledgement. This work has been supported by project TRANSACT funded under H2020-EU.2.1.1. - INDUSTRIAL LEADERSHIP - Leadership in enabling and industrial technologies - Information and Communication Technologies (grant agreement ID: 101007260).

References

1. Sihag, V., Prakash, S., Choudhary, G., Dragoni, N., You, I.: DIMDA: deep learning and image-based malware detection for Android. In: Singh, P.K., Wierzchoń, S.T., Chhabra, J.K., Tanwar, S. (eds.) FTNCT 2021. LNEE, vol. 936, pp. 895–906. Springer, Singapore (2022). https://doi.org/10.1007/978-981-19-5037-7_64
2. Bacci, A., Bartoli, A., Martinelli, F., Medvet, E., Mercaldo, F.: Detection of obfuscation techniques in Android applications. In: Proceedings of the 13th International Conference on Availability, Reliability and Security, pp. 1–9 (2018)

3. Sihag, V., Vardhan, M., Singh, P.: BLADE: robust malware detection against obfuscation in Android. Forensic Sci. Int. Digit. Invest. **38**, 301176 (2021)
4. Sihag, V., Choudhary, G., Vardhan, M., Singh, P., Seo, J.T.: PICAndro: packet inspection-based Android malware detection. Secur. Commun. Netw. **2021** (2021)
5. Borana, P., Sihag, V., Choudhary, G., Vardhan, M., Singh, P.: An assistive tool for fileless malware detection. In: 2021 World Automation Congress (WAC), pp. 21–25. IEEE (2021)
6. Gyamfi, N.K., Goranin, N., Čeponis, D., Čenys, A.: Malware detection using convolutional neural network, a deep learning framework: comparative analysis. J. Internet Serv. Inf. Secur. **12**(4), 102–115 (2022)
7. Park, J., Shim, H., Vu, L.N., Jung, S.: Android adware detection using soot and CFG. J. Wirel. Mob. Netw. Ubiquit. Comput. Dependable Appl. (JoWUA) (4), 94–104 (2022)
8. Yuan, Z., Lu, Y., Wang, Z., Xue, Y.: Droid-Sec: deep learning in Android malware detection. In: Proceedings of the 2014 ACM Conference on SIGCOMM, pp. 371–372 (2014)
9. Hou, S., Saas, A., Ye, Y., Chen, L.: DroidDelver: an Android malware detection system using deep belief network based on API call blocks. In: Song, S., Tong, Y. (eds.) WAIM 2016. LNCS, vol. 9998, pp. 54–66. Springer, Cham (2016). https://doi.org/10.1007/978-3-319-47121-1_5
10. Xiao, X., Zhang, S., Mercaldo, F., Hu, G., Sangaiah, A.K.: Android malware detection based on system call sequences and LSTM. Multimed. Tools Appl. **78**(4), 3979–3999 (2019). https://doi.org/10.1007/s11042-017-5104-0
11. Alzaylaee, M.K., Yerima, S.Y., Sezer, S.: DL-Droid: deep learning based Android malware detection using real devices. Comput. Secur. **89**, 101663 (2020)
12. Mahdavifar, S., Ghorbani, A.A.: Application of deep learning to cybersecurity: a survey. Neurocomputing **347**, 149–176 (2019)
13. Sihag, V., Vardhan, M., Singh, P., Choudhary, G., Son, S.: De-LADY: deep learning based Android malware detection using dynamic features. J. Internet Serv. Inf. Secur. **11**(2), 34–45 (2021)
14. Machiry, A., Tahiliani, R., Naik, M.: Dynodroid: an input generation system for Android apps. In: Proceedings of the 2013 9th Joint Meeting on Foundations of Software Engineering, pp. 224–234 (2013)
15. Anand, S., Naik, M., Harrold, M.J., Yang, H.: Automated concolic testing of smartphone apps. In: Proceedings of the ACM SIGSOFT 20th International Symposium on the Foundations of Software Engineering, pp. 1–11 (2012)
16. Hao, S., Liu, B., Nath, S., Halfond, W.G.J., Govindan, R.: PUMA: programmable UI-automation for large-scale dynamic analysis of mobile apps. In: Proceedings of the 12th Annual International Conference on Mobile Systems, Applications, and Services, pp. 204–217 (2014)
17. Cai, H., Meng, N., Ryder, B., Yao, D.: DroidCat: effective Android malware detection and categorization via app-level profiling. IEEE Trans. Inf. Forensics Secur. **14**(6), 1455–1470 (2018)
18. Sihag, V., Swami, A., Vardhan, M., Singh, P.: Signature based malicious behavior detection in Android. In: Chaubey, N., Parikh, S., Amin, K. (eds.) COMS2 2020. CCIS, vol. 1235, pp. 251–262. Springer, Singapore (2020). https://doi.org/10.1007/978-981-15-6648-6_20
19. Tam, K., Fattori, A., Khan, S., Cavallaro, L.: CopperDroid: automatic reconstruction of Android malware behaviors. In: NDSS Symposium 2015, pp. 1–15 (2015)

The Enhancement of FlexE Network Performance Based on Network Calculus Theory

Kaiqiang Gao[1], Zhihui Wang[1], Juan Pan[1(✉)], Yuhang Pang[1], Lei Wei[2], and Song Jiang[3]

[1] China Electric Power Research Institute Co., Ltd., Nanjing, China
panjuan2022@126.com
[2] State Grid Jiangsu Electric Power Co., Ltd., Nanjing, China
[3] Information and Telecommunication Branch, State Grid Jiangsu Electric Power Co., Ltd., Nanjing, China

Abstract. The Fine Granularity Unit (FGU) refines the granularity of hard slicing from 5 Gbps of Flexible Ethernet (FlexE) to 10 Mbps, which can meet the bearing needs of differentiated service such as small bandwidth, high isolation, and high security in scenarios. Taking the collection and control class data about power service as examples, we first analyze the typical service of FlexE as 10M slicing service, time slot allocation, time slot cross-configuration, and traffic configuration scheme. Then the topology scheme of FlexE slicing network is designed, and the characteristics of different topologies are analyzed. The carrying services of protection paths are studied, and the network performance indexes are tested and analyzed based on the network calculus theory.

Keywords: FlexE · Network calculus · Energy scenario

1 Introduction

Internet plays a very serious role, and research on new network technologies has always been a hot spot [1]. Compared with high-speed mobile networks with inflexible interaction, unreliable connection, and generally inefficient computing [2], the construction of the Energy Internet requires all kinds of staff to be online in real time, comprehensively monitor the power grid data and equipment status, fully realize the reliable control of power grid equipment, and finally share production and consumption information. Flexible Ethernet (FlexE) is a new technology led by the Optical Internetworking Forum (OIF), an international standards organization, that reuses the existing IEEE 802.3 Ethernet physical layer standard and adds FlexE to the MAC and PCS layers. MAC layer and PCS

The paper is funded by the science and technology project of the headquarters of State Grid Corporation of China. The project name is "Research on Key Technologies of FlexE Flexible Ethernet Technology Application in Energy Internet" (No: 5700-202118377A-0-0-00).

layer to achieve network flexibility, multi-rate, and rigid interface features. Its Bonding, Channelization, Sub-rating shown in Fig. 1 and other features can be well interfaced with IP/Ethernet technology to provide a slicing isolation mechanism based on the ethernet physical interface, which is the focus of technology selection for carrying multiple services of the Energy Internet.

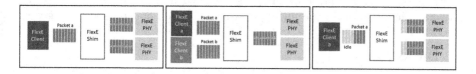

Fig. 1. Bonding, Channelization, and Sub-rating

Nowadays, Industrial Internet needs to make the best decisions on equipment selection, computing, and spectrum resource allocation [3]. Specifically for the power industry in Fig. 2, the grid business that can be carried by FlexE network slicing technology mainly includes main network differential protection, distribution network differential protection, distribution network automation and precise load control, and provide technical support for network collaboration [4]. In the future, there is an urgent need to realize precise control of various types of loads, adapt to the new grid model with ultra high voltage as the backbone and coordinated development of power grids at all levels; realize monitoring and inspection of important corridors of power grids at all levels, introduce new operation methods of visualization, real-time and leaning; realize two-way interaction of users and fine management of electricity consumption, and carry out a new type of operation based on "Internet +" new business model [5]. The future development of power business, IoT business and broadband business coexist, the number of terminal concurrency will reach 100,000 levels, the demand for milliseconds of latency, reliability requirements of 99.999%, the business bearing capacity of the Energy Internet has put forward higher requirements [6].

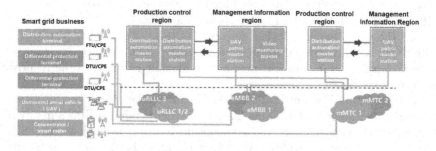

Fig. 2. The Smart Grid Service Architecture

Facing the Industrial Internet of things, this paper focuses on the FlexE technology of the third generation bearer network, simulates the three-layer topology of the FlexE technology bearer network based on the network calculus theory, and analyzes the network topology performance. The second part of this paper introduces FlexE technology and network topology technology; In the third part, the network calculus theory and the actual FlexE service are analyzed; In the fourth part, the three-layer topology is designed and simulated based on the network calculus tool; In the fifth part, the conclusion and prospect are given.

2   Background

2.1   FlexE Technology

In 2011, the Optical Internetworking Forum (OIF), established the FlexE research group, and the FlexE 2.0 standard was officially released at the OIF 2018 Q3 meeting [7]. The International Organization for Standardization OIF launched a study on flexible Ethernet technology in March 2015 and officially released the FlexE 1.0 standard in March 2016. In addition to the OIF standards working group, standards organizations including the IETF and BBF have also initiated standardization work related to FlexE, and the BroadBand Forum launched the "Network Services in IP/MPLS Network using Flex Ethernet" standards project in May 2017. The BBF launched the "Network Services in IP/MPLS Network using Flex Ethernet" standards project in May 2017. Internet Engineering Task Force (IETF) launched the development of the FlexE control plane standard, the goal is to combine the IETF's IP/MPLS technology to extend FlexE from the interface technology into an end-to-end technology that can provide port-level hard isolation effects to achieve network fragmentation, large customer dedicated lines and other technical solutions [8].

In addition to major standards organizations, major vendors around the world have also conducted in-depth research on FlexE technology. In May 2017 Ceres exhibited the world's first complete FlexE 1.0 solution. In June 2017, ZTE demonstrated FlexE Tunnel technology based on FlexE on site for the first time in Shanghai; on September 25, 2018, Huawei, together with China Telecom, officially released the "White Paper on Flexible Ethernet Technology". In January 2019, together with the authoritative consultancy Heavy Reading, ZTE officially released the white paper "FlexE Embraces 5G Bearer". In addition to this, the white paper also provides a In September 2019, China Unicom, together with Huawei, completed the network entry test of Flexible Ethernet in the IP private line scenario in Xiongan New Area.

In 2021, China Unicom proposed the Slicing Packet Network (SPN) small granularity technology. FGU (Fine Granularity Unit) inherits SPN's highly efficient Ethernet core and integrates fine-grained slicing technology into SPN's overall architecture to provide a low-cost, fine-grained, hard-isolated, small granularity bearer pipe. The small granularity slicing capability of SPN bearer network will be a key force to facilitate the deployment of 5G+ vertical industry and private line applications in government and enterprises.

2.2   Network Topology Technology

The network topology models of common rules are the following, star, ring, bus, tree, and mesh [9]. A mixture of the above topologies is usually used in real networks, i.e. hybrid topologies. This kind of network can adopt distributed access control strategy to coordinate data transmission [10]. As the scale of the network continues to expand and the structure becomes more complex, the hierarchical management of the network can solve the dilemma that the overall maintenance is becoming more and more difficult. The entire network is usually divided into multiple levels according to different management levels, and the managers at different levels are only responsible for managing the network at this level, while the network managers at the higher levels are responsible for the mutual coordination among the lower levels.

For power grid services, star network topology can basically meet the requirements of protection and control functions and has a large application scale. At the same time, star network itself is easy to expand, and is more suitable for large-scale networking. In small-scale networking, ring network can be used to ensure network reliability. As shown in Fig. 3, the core layer and distribution layer of the power grid use star network topology to facilitate protection and control and ensure reliability. The access layer uses star network topology to access large-scale services and ensure the flexibility of expansion.

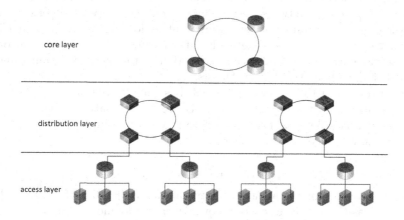

Fig. 3. Three Layers Network Topology

In this way, different levels of network managers can focus on the management of their own networks, and the core managers no longer have to think about trivial details. Such network hierarchy improves the efficiency of network management and makes network management more effective. In addition, computer networks are also hierarchical in nature, with different network devices working at different levels, such as routers at the network layer, switches at the data link layer, and hubs at the physical layer. So this leads to different management needs, managers sometimes need to display network topology on the network layer and sometimes need to display topology on the link layer, so topology discovery needs to explore different levels of network information.

3 FlexE Modeling Theory

3.1 Network Calculus Analysis

Network calculus is a deterministic queuing theory based on nonlinear algebra, that is now widely used in computer network modeling and performance analysis, especially providing an effective tool for computing definite bounds on end-to-end performance parameters such as latency and backlog.

The research work of network algorithm can be divided into theoretical research and applied research. The object of theoretical research is the mathematical model of network algorithm, which is the foundation of network algorithm to be widely used. Each step of theoretical research can lead to a large number of practical applications. Since network algorithm is an interdisciplinary research field and involves more mathematical theories, the progress of theoretical research is slow compared with applications [11].

In general, network algorithms as a network performance analysis tool are classified as deterministic network algorithms or stochastic network algorithms. Deterministic network algorithms are relatively simple and aim to obtain the worst-case bounds on network performance. Stochastic network algorithms aim to provide random quality of service guarantees for the network, taking into account the random bursts of network data streams, self-awareness and other characteristics, as well as the access congestion of the network channel due to physical channel fading and other factors.

In network algorithms, flows are modeled as cumulative functions. The accumulation curve A ≥ the departure curve D needs to be satisfied and is used to model that a data flow cannot leave before it arrives. Define $\alpha(t)$ as the arrival curve of a flow, which at any moment is:

$$A(t) - A(s) \leq \alpha(t - s) \tag{1}$$

Service curves provide a way to represent the availability of resources [12]. Define $\beta(t)$ as the service curve of a flow, which at any moment is:

$$D(t) - A(s) \geq \beta(t - s) \tag{2}$$

Given some arrival and departure curves A and D, the difference between curves A and D at moment t is defined as b(A, D, t). d(A, D) is the network time delay caused by curves A and D.

The network algorithm uses the minimum additive algebra [13]. The relationship between the output cumulative curve and the input cumulative curve is as follows:

$$D(t) \geq inf_{0 \leq u \leq t}\{A(u) + \beta(t - u)\} = (A \otimes \beta)(t) \tag{3}$$

In the network algorithm, inf represents the lower exact bound of the taken value, and $\otimes$ is the minimum plus rollup operator. The formula relates the output accumulation curve to the input accumulation curve through the service curve. Furthermore, the sending process can be considered the next hop's arrival process, and the output accumulation curve D(t) can be bounded by the next hop's arrival curve $\alpha'(t)$, which are related as follows:

$$\alpha'(t) = sup_{u \geq 0}\{\alpha(t+u) - \beta(u)\} = (\alpha \oslash \beta)(t) \tag{4}$$

Sup represents the upper exact bound on the value taken, and $\oslash$ is the network algorithm's minimum plus deconvolution operator.

3.2   FlexE Service Performance Modeling

Take intelligent distribution business analysis as an example. Intelligent distribution communication network needs to meet the requirements of advanced distribution automation, distribution network protection, and distribution.

The communication requirements for services such as formal energy access, precise load control, and distribution network equipment operation status monitoring are shown in Table 1.

This topology design refers to the star topology of the data communication network and the ring network topology of the SDH/OTN transmission network. In the context of the Energy Internet, the intelligent distribution service line is a mega network that requires a three-layer architecture network for data transmission, as illustrated in Fig. 3.

The core layer gathers high-speed networks, which constitute the high-speed switching skeleton of the network. Core router plays a very important role in the three-layer network. The core layer should have the following characteristics: reliability, efficiency, redundancy, fault tolerance, manageability, adaptability, low latency, etc. The core layer needs to use switches with higher bandwidth, such as Gigabit Ethernet switches. The core layer switch uses the load balancing function and the control function to maintain the network environment. It bears and gathers the whole network's data, so how to design the core layer and how to reasonably plan and arrange the network equipment are very important. Core switches need a lot of money, and the intelligent power distribution system with large geographical coverage, large user scale and large number of networks is suitable for a ring-type structure where multiple switching centers exist but only two adjacent points are interconnected.

The convergence layer connects the access layer and the core layer. In order to relieve the pressure on the core layer, the flow transmitted to the switch needs to converge first. The aggregation layer must have a strong data processing capability, cannot lose the data from the access layer, and must successfully input it to the core layer. Therefore, the aggregation layer switches need strong routing and forwarding functions. The aggregation layer has multiple functions, such as address filtering, security protection, workgroup access, route virtualization, policy implementation, etc. In order to effectively isolate each domain and network

Table 1. Specific communication requirements for intelligent power distribution services.

Service type	Service name	Communication requirements		
		delay	bandwidth	reliability
Control	Intelligent distributed distribution automation	≤15 ms	≤2 Mbps	99.999%
	Precise load control	≤200 ms	≤2 Mbps	99.999%
	Distributed energy regulation	≤3 s	2 Mbps	99.999%
Collect	Low voltage centralized reading	≤2 s	1–2 Mbps	99.9%
	Power station patrol robot	≤200 ms	4–10 Mbps	99.9%
	UAV patrol inspection of power distribution route			
	Video integrated monitoring of power distribution room			
	Mobile site construction operation control		20–100 Mbps	
	Comprehensive application of emergency site ad hoc network			

segment, the aggregation layer generally uses a three-layer switch with a virtual function. The convergence layer has a channel protection mechanism, generally using a ring structure, which can provide uplink to the core layer and ensure the rapid self-healing and recovery of the communication network.

The access layer accesses the local terminal equipment. In the access layer, the number of base stations is small, providing high-speed bandwidth for services. The access layer generally uses a layer 2 common switch to reduce infrastructure investment. The part that connects or accesses the network directly to users is called the access layer. The access layer switch has low overhead and a large number of ports. It is only for the terminal to access the network. Therefore, the cost-effective switch is selected. The interface of the access layer needs plug and play, and is easy to use and maintain. Here, the access layer is accessed mainly by devices related to intelligent power distribution. From the feeder communication network level, 100M bandwidth optical fiber with star network topology and network optimization strategy can basically meet the demand for protection and control functions; the application scale of star network is larger than that of ring network, in addition, because the star network itself is easy to expand, it is more suitable for the scenario of an intelligent power distribution system.

4   FlexE Network Topology Performance Simulation

4.1   Experimental Environment Setup

We calculate the worst-case performance upper bound in the network algorithm framework based on Python module [14]. The simulation is shown in Fig. 4. Smart grid distribution services are divided into two classes, acquisition and control, which will be accessed by two switches at the access layer, and at the aggregation into a ring of four switches used, and the services are aggregated and fed to one switch at the core layer.

Since the typical service granularity of FlexE is 10M, the minimum flow is 10M. There are three classes of services within the control, all with 2M bandwidth, which can be arranged in a 10M granularity with a 2M interval for each service. Each collection class with less than 10M of bandwidth is arranged in a 10M granularity. Services with more than 10M bandwidth use multiple 10M granularity. Therefore, the bandwidth of the entire acquisition service is N × 10M, and N is generally greater than 10.

Since the bandwidth of the collection class service far exceeds that of the control class service, the bandwidth of the collection class service is shunted and converged from both sides of the distribution layer ring to reduce the pressure on the switch. When the distribution layer link fails, a protection mechanism is adopted, and all services are converged in a straight line. Finally, they converge at one switch in the core layer.

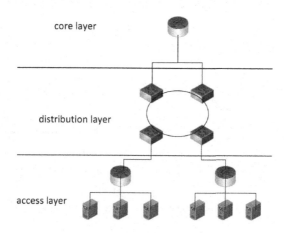

Fig. 4. The Simulation Topology

In the simulation, three flows are designed with 10M granularity, 10M, 50M and 50M. 10M bandwidth flow is the control class service, and 50M bandwidth flow is the collection class service. One 10M control class service flow and one 50M acquisition class service flow pass through the same path at the distribution layer, and the other 50M acquisition class service flow takes another path and finally converges to a switch at the core layer. The initialization of flow 0 is 50M, flow 1 is 50M, and flow 2 is 10M. Switches are defined as servers, access layer switches are server 0 and server 1. Distribution layer switches are server 2, server 3, server 4, and server 5. Core layer switches are server 6. The core layer switches are server 6.

4.2   Analysis of Experimental Results

The simulation diagram of the topology network is shown in Fig. 5. The utilization rate is defined as the ratio of the input bandwidth to the design flow bandwidth. The top left graph represents the backlog of different utilization flow 0 at core layer switch server 6, the top right graph represents the backlog of different utilization flow 1 at core layer switch server 6, the top left graph represents the backlog of different utilization flow 0 at core layer switch server 6, the bottom left graph represents the backlog, and the lower left graph represents the latency of the three flows across the network. Two analysis methods are used. Separate Flow Analysis (SFA), curves are labeled as SFA. Determine boundary analysis, curves are labeled as Flows.

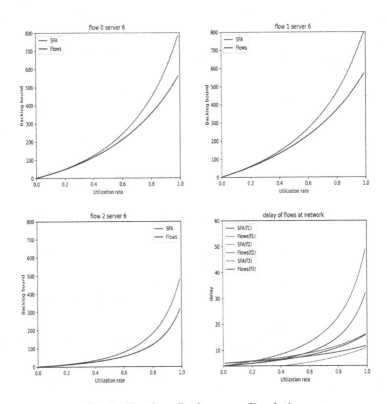

Fig. 5. Topology Performance Simulation

From the graph, flow 0 and flow 1 have a bandwidth of 50M, but flow 1 and flow 2 take the same path, so the backlog at server 6 is slightly larger than low 0. Since the bandwidth of flow 2 is 10M, the backlog is significantly lower than that of flow 0 and flow 1 when the utilization is high. It can be seen from the delay graph of three flows in the network that flow 0 and flow 1 are relatively close, while flow 2 has a large delay. This is because flow 1 and flow 2 take the same path, but flow 1 has a larger bandwidth, and the switch server on the path needs to do processing on flow 1's large amount of traffic when forwarding, so flow 0 has a larger latency.

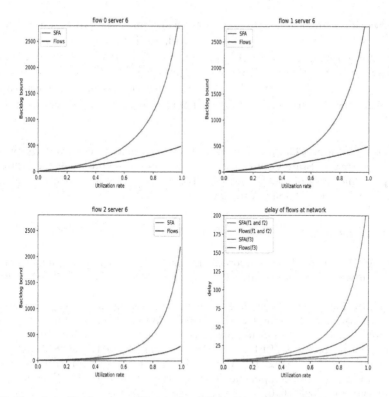

Fig. 6. Topology Performance Simulation When Distribution Layer Link is Faulty

Figure 6 shows the topology network simulation diagram when the aggregation layer link fails. Then flow 0 and flow 1 take the same path, and since flow 0 and flow 1 have the same bandwidth, the curves are the same. Since all three flows take the same path at the aggregation layer, the backlog and delay of the whole network are very large. At utilization greater than 0.7, the backlog of flows and the delay in the network rise rapidly.

5   Conclusion

The power communication network is an important infrastructure to support the development of the smart grid, ensuring the security, real-time, accuracy, and reliability of various power services. The power communication network for power generation, transmission, and substation is called the backbone communication network, which has achieved full coverage of fiber-optic dedicated network in China. The power communication network for power distribution and consumption is called terminal access network, which has the characteristics of multiple points and wide area coverage. Therefore, smart distribution and utility networks need to be combined with FlexE technology to realize ubiquitous, flexible, economic, and reliable connections. Optical fiber with star network topology and network optimization strategy can basically meet the protection and control function requirements, and the star network itself is easy to expand, which is more suitable for the scenario of intelligent power distribution system. Through the above analysis, the FlexE network topology with its three layers structure is suitable for power scenarios. FlexE's 10M particle size mechanism is superior. The FlexE-based third-generation carrier network will shine in the Industrial Internet.

Acknowledgement. The paper is funded by the science and technology project of the headquarters of State Grid Corporation of China. The project name is "Research on Key Technologies of FlexE Flexible Ethernet Technology Application in Energy Internet" (No: 5700-202118377A-0-0-00).

References

1. Zhang, W., et al.: Deep reinforcement learning based resource management for DNN inference in industrial IoT. IEEE Trans. Veh. Technol. **70**(8), 7605–7618 (2021)
2. Song, F., Li, L., You, I., Shui, Yu., Zhang, H.: Optimizing high-speed mobile networks with smart collaborative theory. IEEE Wirel. Commun. **29**(3), 48–54 (2022)
3. Zhang, W., et al.: Optimizing federated learning in distributed industrial IoT: a multi-agent approach. IEEE J. Sel. Areas Commun. **39**(12), 3688–3703 (2021)
4. Song, F., Ai, Z., Zhang, H., You, I., Li, S.: Smart collaborative balancing for dependable network components in cyber-physical systems. IEEE Trans. Ind. Inf. **17**(10), 6916–6924 (2020)
5. Zhou, X., Wang, F., Ma, Y.: An overview on energy internet. In: 2015 IEEE International Conference on Mechatronics and Automation (ICMA), pp. 126–131. IEEE (2015)
6. Song, F., Zhu, M., Zhou, Y., You, I., Zhang, H.: Smart collaborative tracking for ubiquitous power IoT in edge-cloud interplay domain. IEEE Internet Things J. **7**(7), 6046–6055 (2019)
7. Flex Ethernet: Implementation agreement. IA# OIF-FLEXE-01.0 (2016)
8. Song, F., Yu-Tong Zhou, Yu., Wang, T.-M.Z., You, I., Zhang, H.-K.: Smart collaborative distribution for privacy enhancement in moving target defense. Inf. Sci. **479**, 593–606 (2019)
9. BICSI: Network Design Basics for Cabling Professionals, pp. 0885–8950. McGraw-Hill Professional (2002)
10. Song, F., Ai, Z., Zhou, Y., You, I., Choo, K.-K.R., Zhang, H.: Smart collaborative automation for receive buffer control in multipath industrial networks. IEEE Trans. Ind. Inform. **16**(2), 1385–1394 (2019)
11. Jiang, Y., Liu, Y., et al.: Stochastic Network Calculus, vol. 1. Springer, London (2008). https://doi.org/10.1007/978-1-84800-127-5
12. Bouillard, A., Jouhet, L., Thierry, E.: Service curves in network calculus: dos and don'ts. Ph.D. thesis, INRIA (2009)
13. Zippo, R., Stea, G.: Nancy: an efficient parallel network calculus library. arXiv preprint arXiv:2205.11449 (2022)
14. Bouillard, A.: Stability and performance bounds in cyclic networks using network calculus. In: André, É., Stoelinga, M. (eds.) FORMATS 2019. LNCS, vol. 11750, pp. 96–113. Springer, Cham (2019). https://doi.org/10.1007/978-3-030-29662-9_6

Security Consideration of Each Layers in a Cloud-Native Environment

Youngsoo Kim[(✉)], Cheolhee Park, and Yong-yoon Shin

Electronics and Telecommunications Research Institute, 218 Gajeong-Ro, Yuseong-Gu, Daejeon 34129, Republic of Korea
{blitzkrieg,chpakr0528,uni2u}@etri.re.kr

Abstract. With the advent of 5G environments, the importance of 'Cloud Native' is increasing. Cloud native refers to an approach to building and running applications that utilizes a cloud computing delivery model instead of an on-premise data center. Cloud-native takes full advantage of the cloud's advantages, including scalability, buildability, manageability, and unlimited on-demand computing power. To this end, it adopts a microservices structure, dividing the application into as few units as possible and having these granular units run as containers. In addition, cloud-native systems aim to reduce productivity, business agility, and cost by introducing a devops strategy and agile methodology for immediate service execution and frequent and continuous upgrade according to market and service demands, and applying it to software development. In this regard, containers which is a core component of cloud native can produce advantages in efficiency and scalability, as virtualized objects are light and can be executed quickly. However, security may be relatively weak compared to virtual machines with independent operating systems. In this paper, we explore security threats and solutions for container platforms, focusing on 'cloud native security' defined by the Cloud Native Computing Foundation.

Keywords: Cloud-native · Container · Virtualization · Edge Security

1 Introduction

With the advent of 5G environments, the importance of "Cloud Native" is increasing. As the 5G mobile communication business shifts towards a service-oriented approach, the mobile communication networks are evolving to be more agile and flexible, allowing for rapid development, distribution, and expansion. This evolution is facilitated by the adoption of Software Defined Networking (SDN) and Network Function Virtualization (NFV) technologies, with a focus on cloud computing technology for 5G Core. Moreover, the traditional hardware-oriented network structure is being replaced by software-based virtual network functions (VNFs) and cloud-native network functions (CNFs).

The NFV structure offers improved service agility compared to the traditional equipment-oriented structure, but to deliver 5G network-based services, network virtualization performance needs to be improved, and automation-based NF creation, distribution, and expansion needs to be enhanced. This is why 5G mobile operators are

I. You et al. (Eds.): MobiSec 2022, CCIS 1644, pp. 231–242, 2023.
https://doi.org/10.1007/978-981-99-4430-9_17

paying attention to the concept of Cloud Native. In this structure, VNFs are divided into micro-services based on function/characteristics, which are loaded and distributed in containers. A container is a package that bundles the micro-service, related libraries, binaries, and configuration information, and can run as a virtual application on the host OS without the need for a hypervisor or guest OS. As a result, containers are lighter and faster than VMs, improving virtualization performance.

However, containers may have relatively weak security compared to VMs with independent operating systems. In particular, there is a risk of malicious code infection or abnormal image inflow due to frequent and continuous image updates, as well as the possibility of a container control authority takeover attack due to arbitrary container authority manipulation. Moreover, there is also a risk of data manipulation or leakage through open API vulnerabilities of MEC applications. In this paper, we explore security threats and solutions for container platforms, focusing on 'cloud native security' defined by the Cloud Native Computing Foundation.

The rest of this paper is organized as follows. Section 2 examines each security threat by dividing the cloud native environment into cloud, cluster, container, and code layers. Section 3 describes countermeasures against security threats for each layer discussed in Sect. 2, and Sect. 4 concludes the paper.

2   Cloud Native Security Threats

The following table shows security threats of each layers like cloud, cluster, container and code in cloud native environments (Table 1).

Table 1. Security Threats in 4Cs

Cloud-layer Security Threats	Cluster-layer Security Threats
• Wrong configuration • Automation • Host OS component vulnerabilities • User access control • increased attack surfaces • Kernel sharing • Host OS file system tampering	• Poorly separated network traffic between containers • Mixing of workload importance levels • Improper administrative access • Poor account management • Cluster node trust • Orchestrator vulnerabilities • Cluster network complexity
Container-layer Security Threats	Code-layer Security Threats
• Container runtime vulnerabilities • Poor container runtime configuration • Container application vulnerabilities • Malicious behavior of container through network access • Incorrect inter-container traffic segregation • Rogue containers • Poor hardware resource management • Kernel data leaks • Resource exhaustion attacks	• Malware embedded in images • Cleartext secret embedded in images • Out-of-data image vulnerabilities • Improper image configuration • Use of unverified images • Insecure communication channel between images and image registries • Out-of-date images in image registries • Insufficient authentication and authorization

2.1 Cloud-Layer Security Threats

Although the cloud has many advantages such as flexible IT infrastructure management, excellent service scalability, traffic control through auto-scaling, and rapid infrastructure introduction, it is exposed to new security threats according to the cloud environment. Cloud-based resources are very complex and dynamic, and there is a risk of data leakage, which is a prime target for cyberattacks, such as through misconfiguration or improper modification. Poor management of physical resources, data, systems, or access can cause problems with personal identification and credentials. In addition, the cloud environment is a structure that is easy to hijack accounts through phishing, so it can be a target for hackers, and insider threats are always present. Several vulnerabilities in the user interface and API may provide an attacker with an easy way to steal user or employee accounts. If administrators cannot fully control and manage the infrastructure due to a complex cloud environment, the control plane may become vulnerable and problems may arise from using unauthorized applications or misusing authorized applications. In addition, Meta-structure, which means the boundary between cloud service providers and customers, contains various information related to system protection, so that unauthorized access of customers can be detected through API calls. However, conversely, there is a risk of exposing sensitive information such as logs and audit system data.

Wrong Configuration. Various cloud architectures exist and environment configuration for them also requires specialization, so they can be exposed to security threats due to incorrect configuration. For example, if many services and applications are set to be exposed to the Internet, many bots and attackers can use it to perform RCE (Remote Code Execution) or use it for cryptocurrency mining. **Host OS Component Vulnerabilities.** Basic system components such as cryptographic libraries and primitives related to process calls may have vulnerabilities. In this case, it can affect all containers and applications running using those components on the host. **Increased Attack Surface.** Due to virtualization and decentralization, methods for attackers to access and attack vulnerabilities are also diversifying compared to the existing environment. The larger the attack surface, the more likely an attacker is to find and access vulnerabilities, and the host OS and running containers can be compromised. **Kernel Sharing.** Even if a container-only OS is used, which has relatively few attack points compared to general-purpose OS, since the kernel is shared, there are more attack points between objects than the hypervisor. That is, the level of isolation by the container runtime is not as high as the hypervisor. In addition, if there is a vulnerability in the kernel, an attacker can easily exploit the vulnerability inside the container to damage the host kernel, so a container running in the shared kernel may be vulnerable.

2.2 Cluster-Layer Security Threats

In a cloud environment, a cluster consists of nodes running containerized applications. The worker node hosts the pods that make up the application workload, and the control plane manages the worker nodes and pods in the cluster. In order to provide basic security of the cluster-layer, it is necessary to control access to the API server, which is the orchestrator control plane, and to restrict direct access to *etcd*, which is the main data store of the orchestrator.

Poorly Separated Network Traffic Between Containers. In a container environment, traffic between containers is routed on a virtual network, and the orchestrator is responsible for the management. Existing network security tools that do not consider the container environment target encrypted packets between hosts, so they cannot understand container traffic. An encrypted network to ensure confidentiality provides safety, but it is difficult to apply the monitoring function for network traffic management, so it is not easy to identify traffic anomalies. In addition, when applications of different importance use the same virtual network, if the application of lower importance is compromised by a network attack, the attacker can perform malicious actions on the application of high importance through the shared network, which may cause the network itself to be in dangerous status. **Mixing of workload importance levels.** If the orchestrator applies the default settings, it allocates workloads based on resource allocation efficiency rather than importance. In this case, workloads with different levels of importance or sensitivity of usage data can be deployed together. For example, deploying sensitive data processing containers on critically vulnerable web servers increases the risk of compromise. **Cluster node trust.** In a container environment, it is necessary to maintain trust between the orchestrator and other container components. This is the case when an unauthorized host joins the cluster and runs containers, or when communication between orchestrators, DevOps personnel, administrators, and hosts is not encrypted or does not perform authentication. Also, if all nodes in the cluster share a public key-private key pair required for authentication, if one host is compromised, the entire cluster is at risk. **Orchestrator Vulnerabilities.** Vulnerabilities in orchestrators can lead to privilege escalation, container escape and denial of service attacks. By exploiting the vulnerability of the orchestrator, an attacker can execute arbitrary commands in the pod through privilege escalation, and can perform malicious actions by changing the node's privilege to that of the entire cluster. And, since the symbolic link can be resolved by the host before it is mounted on the container, an attacker can access the directory outside the container. This can lead to race condition attacks and create or overwrite files outside of the container. Additionally, the Orchestrator API server is vulnerable to distributed denial of service attacks through ping flood and reset flood attacks. Also, because input YAML files are not properly validated, parsing maliciously crafted YAML files can consume excessive CPU and memory, leading to DoS attacks.

2.3   Container-Layer Security Threats

Container Runtime Vulnerabilities. Container runtime vulnerabilities allow an attacker to compromise container isolation or escape from a container and gain access to the host file system. If *containerd*, a high-level container runtime, inadvertently exposes the *containerd-shim* API to a container that shares the host network namespace, an attacker with root privileges in that container can execute arbitrary commands on the host through the *containerd-shim* socket and this can disable container isolation. Even in the case of *runC*, which is a low-level container runtime, it is vulnerable to *symlink* exchange attacks, so an attacker can bind the host file system to the container by requesting a seemingly harmless container configuration. If a container is started and *runC* is mounted inside a volume shared with another container that performs a *symlink* exchange attack, you can trick *runC* into mounting it outside the container root filesystem by replacing the mount target with a symbolic link [4]. **Poor container runtime configuration.** If the administrator does not properly configure the options of the container runtime, the security level of the system can be relatively low. For example, a container runtime daemon configured to listen on remote TCP sockets without authentication could be exploited by an attacker to create new maliciously privileged containers and take control of the host. Even if the daemon only listens on local UNIX sockets, if an unauthorized user is added to a group, this UNIX socket can be exploited to create a privileged container to escalate privileges (Table 2).

Table 2. Security Threats caused by poor container runtime configuration

Excessive allowance of container system calls
In case of system call in Linux container host it should not be allowed except for items for safe operation of container. If too many system calls are allowed other containers and the host OS can be harmed through the compromised container
Run container privileged mode
When running in privileged mode, the container gains root privileges to access all devices on the host, which can affect all other containers running on the host OS
Allow file system changes through containers
If you allow a host's sensitive directory to be mounted by a container, a compromised container could maliciously change the underlying functional control path of the host OS and, through escalation of privilege, attack other containers running on the host and the host itself
Runtime resources isolation settings
The container runtime provides execution commands to support Linux namespaces, such as PID namespace, UTS namespace, IPC namespace, network namespace, and user namespace. However, the container runtime can allow containers to share host namespaces by specifying parameters as hostnames, which can circumvent Linux namespace isolation and weaken container security
Runtime resource constraints
The container runtime provides execution instructions to support Linux *cgroups* with respect to resource limits such as CPU shares, memory limits, and device read/write speed limits. It is desirable to use as many *cgroups* as possible to defend against resource exhaustion attacks by malicious container users
Security configuration
The container runtime provides security options commands to allow the user to specify additional security configurations, such as enforcing the MAC (Mandatory Access Control) mechanism, preventing the acquisition of new privileges, and configuring the *seccomp* profile

Container Application Vulnerabilities. Even if a container runs in a secure environment, a flaw in the running application can damage the container. Well-known application vulnerabilities can also occur in container environments, and when a container is compromised, it can be exploited in various ways, such as unauthorized access to sensitive information or attacks on other containers or host OS. For example, an application having a *slowloris* vulnerability on the Apache server can be utilized in a DoS attack to inhibit container availability. **Malicious behavior of containers through network access.** A malicious container can put other resources in the container environment at risk by accessing other containers or hosts, identifying vulnerabilities through methods such as network scanning and providing them to attackers. **Incorrect inter-container traffic segregation.** If traffic between containers is not separated correctly, a compromised container can perform man-in-the-middle attacks against other containers. A compromised container can also make other containers obsolete or severely degrade performance through traffic flooding.

2.4 Code-Layer Security Threats

A container image consists of binaries, packages, and related components required to deploy a container environment, and these binaries and packages may contain vulnerabilities. Several studies have shown that many vulnerabilities exist in commercial container images, and the number of vulnerabilities in images stored in verified image repositories is increasing every year [5, 6]. In addition to these software vulnerabilities, container images can contain many intentionally injected malicious software. Such malware can be used to attack other containers or the host OS.

Malware Embedded in Images. Since the malicious code included in the image has the same function as other components, it can be used to attack other containers or host OS in a container environment. Base layers and other images of unknown origin included in the image should be thoroughly verified before use. **Cleartext secret embedded in images.** When the application is packaged as an image, the DB connection string, SSH private key, X.509 private key, etc. can be stored as plain text in the file system of the image. In this case, anyone with permission to access the image can obtain this secret by parsing the image and edit it and abuse it, so it can be a big security threat. **Out-of-data image vulnerabilities.** Vulnerabilities are more likely to be discovered if the latest updates to the components contained within the image and used to run specific applications are not made. In a container environment, software updates are made upstream from the image itself and then redeployed. Therefore, if the image used to create a container has a vulnerability, the container is highly likely to perform malicious actions targeting other containers or the host OS. For example, in the case of the Shellshock vulnerability, which infected most Linux systems, an application running in a container attacks another container through remote code execution [7]. **Insecure communication channel between images and image registries.** If a secure communication channel is not established between the image and the registry, confidentiality cannot be guaranteed and there is a risk of exposing sensitive information or secrets in the image. They can also be vulnerable to man-in-the-middle attacks that intercept network traffic to obtain credentials and send malicious or obsolete images to the orchestrator. **Insufficient authentication and**

authorization. The image registry may store images used to run sensitive applications or access sensitive data. Therefore, if the authentication and authorization process is insufficient, it can lead to loss of intellectual property or expose important application-related technologies to attackers. In general, users often trust that valid and verified software is stored in the image registry, so if the image registry is compromised, the container and host that receives and uses the image may also be compromised.

3 Countermeasures for Cloud Native Security Threats

3.1 Countermeasures for Cloud-Layer Security Threats

Security Requirements When Configuring Infrastructure. In the cloud environment, all access to the orchestrator control plane is not allowed by default, and it is necessary to control only through the network access control IP list for cluster management purposes. The network access to the node should be configured to allow connection only from the control plane of the specified port, and the node should be configured to allow connection of the node port and the *loadbalancer* type of container orchestrator service. For orchestrator access to the Cloud Provider API, it is desirable for each cloud provider to configure a policy on the cluster that grants different permissions to the control plane and node, and only minimal permissions to related resources. Data storage access is limited to only the control plane, and data storage is used through TLS depending on the configuration. And it is desirable to keep all storage encrypted as much as possible, including data storage that contains a lot of sensitive information and maintenance information for the entire cluster. **Host OS component vulnerabilities.** All software components of the host OS should be updated regularly to keep them up to date. The latest updates to the kernel and container runtime components are particularly important. The latest update is very important because it sometimes adds additional defenses and functions related to security in addition to simply fixing vulnerabilities. It is possible to redeploy a new instance of the OS with only the necessary updates, but for more sophisticated operation, it is desirable to update the entire system. In addition, the host OS should be operated in an immutable manner, in which data or state is not continuously stored in the host and there is no application-level dependency by the host. Instead, by packaging and distributing applications with dependencies on all components in containers, the host can operate in an almost stateless manner while reducing the attack surface. **Increased attack surface.** You can reduce the attack surface by using a container-only OS that hosts containers, uses a read-only file system, and is specifically designed to disable other services and features. If a container-only OS is not available, ensure that the host running the container runs only the container and the host OS does not run unnecessary system services that increase the attack surface. In addition, not only the container runtime but also the lower-level components of the host are continuously checked for vulnerabilities and critical updates. **Kernel sharing.** To prevent safety degradation due to differences in importance, container workloads are grouped on a host according to importance, and containerized workloads and non-containerized workloads are separately executed by host. By separating containerized tasks into a container dedicated host, protection measures optimized for container protection can be established and applied. Research on namespaces specialized for security that is different from the existing ones is also in progress. Y. Sun et al. proposed security namespace, which allows containers to autonomously control security mechanisms such as integrity measurement architectures and MAC frameworks, and P. R. Sampat proposed a novel kernel namespace mechanism called CPU namespace, which creates scrambled virtual CPU maps to separate CPU information [8][9]. Since all virtual namespace CPUs are mapped to physical CPUs, both the control interface and the display interface can recognize the CPU namespace.

3.2 Countermeasures for Cluster-Layer Security Threats

Security Requirements When Configuring Clusters. First, for orchestrator API access control, it is desirable to encrypt all API traffic through TLS and perform API authentication through authentication mechanisms such as certificates, tokens, and LDAP servers to be used by API servers and clients when installing clusters. In addition, it is necessary to check whether API calls are approved by user group or role using RBAC to determine whether access rights are violated. Second, you need to restrict the way objects behave in clusters and resources with policies. For example, it is necessary to limit the capacity of resources assigned to the namespace such as CPU, memory, disk, Pod, and volume, limit the permission level of containers, and prevent the containers from loading unwanted kernel modules. In addition, for network access control, it is necessary to restrict the pods that can access the pods and ports of the namespace, and to control the nodes that the pods want to access. Third, it is necessary to limit access to etcd, enable audit logs, and shorten the life cycle of infrastructure credentials to reduce the exposure to attack as much as possible to prevent cluster damage. In addition, when integrating with a third party, it is necessary to analyze the suitability of the requested permission required for extension, apply the orchestrator security update immediately, and carefully analyze the vulnerability report to prepare. **Poorly separated network traffic between containers.** The orchestrator should be set up to separate network traffic into individual virtual networks according to their importance. For example, it is recommended to separate multiple public applications to share one virtual network and internal applications that handle sensitive information to use a different virtual network. **Mixing of workload importance levels.** Orchestrators need to be set up to split clusters according to their importance. It is desirable to group containers according to their respective purpose, relative importance, and threat level, and ensure that only containers with the same purpose, importance, and threat run on a specific host. Using multiple physical servers for this segmentation is recommended, but even using a modern hypervisor is powerful enough to mitigate this risk. Separating containers in this way makes it difficult for an attacker to perform reconnaissance after infiltrating one server, attack other containers of similar importance, or access other servers. In such an environment, data management is also very important. It should be ensured that data used or generated in containers of similar importance cannot be used in containers of different importance. In large environments with hundreds of hosts and thousands of containers, this separation can also serve as a layer for DID (Defense in Depth). Organizations can isolate containers inside a hypervisor by separating hosting zones or networks, and can isolate network traffic so that traffic of applications with a specific priority is separated from traffic of applications with different priorities. **Cluster node trust.** It is necessary to configure so that a secure environment is provided for all applications that the orchestrator runs. The orchestrator must securely include nodes in a cluster, ensure that nodes have a unique persistent identity for the entire lifecycle, and be able to manage a list of connection states between nodes. When designing an orchestrator, it is necessary to consider fault tolerance to ensure that if a specific node is compromised, it can be detached and removed from the cluster without affecting the safety of the entire cluster. **Orchestrator Vulnerabilities.** The primary way to combat orchestrator vulnerabilities is to configure a secure orchestration environment. The CIS (Center for Internet Security) presented the orchestrator setting guidelines by dividing them into control plane components such as master nodes, API servers, controller managers, and schedulers, worker nodes, and policies [10]. In addition, recently, NSA (National Security Agency) and CISA (Cybersecurity and Infrastructure Security Agency) have presented practical measures for security, access control, auditing, and upgrade of pod and cluster networks [11].

3.3 Countermeasures for Container-Layer Security Threats

Security Requirements when Configuring Containers. It is important to check the latest update status of containers and whether they contain vulnerabilities. It is necessary to check whether there is any problem in the image and the application running in the container using various commercial tools. You also need to make sure that the running container is using an image from a known source or known image repository. It is important to maintain trust in the container content, such as through an image signing tool. Also, when using a container with permission to use the root function of the host system, safety problems may occur. Therefore, only a user with the minimum OS permission required to perform the task should run the container. **Poor container runtime configuration.** The basic way to deal with container vulnerabilities is to configure a secure container environment. The CIS presented container configuration guidelines by classifying them into host OS (Linux), Docker daemon, container image, and container runtime [12]. Organizations need to introduce and apply automation tools including processes for continuously evaluating and actively implementing the settings of the entire environment based on these guidelines. It also uses MAC (Mandatory Access Control) technology that allows only certain files, paths, and processes in the host OS layer to access container applications, allowing containers to access only certain files, processes, and network sockets, and preventing compromised containers from affecting hosts or other containers [13]. **Container application vulnerabilities.** In order to detect vulnerabilities in container applications, it is necessary to implement and apply tools designed in consideration of the scale and change rate of the container environment. These tools should have the ability to automatically create each security profile by learning and analyzing the behavior of container applications to detect and prevent anomalies in container applications, such as running processes different from existing patterns or sending traffic to unexpected destinations. In addition, monitoring through the tool becomes very easy by allowing the container to run as a read-only root file system so that only specifically defined directories can be isolated. With a read-only file system, if a container is damaged, all tampering can be isolated to this particular location and easily separated from the rest of the application, enabling rapid recovery without compromising the entire environment. **Malicious behavior of containers through network access.** In order to prevent a single malicious container from exposing other resources to risk, controls must be implemented at least at the perimeter of the network so that the container cannot send traffic to networks of different importance. However, since virtual encrypted traffic is generated between containers and container IPs are dynamically assigned by the orchestrator and constantly changed according to load balancing, organizations must use a combination of traditional network equipment and application-aware network tools. Application-aware tools should be able to see the traffic between containers and dynamically create traffic filtering rules based on the characteristics of the application. And, it should be able to automatically determine the appropriate container network surface and detect network anomalies.

3.4 Countermeasures for Code-Layer Security Threats

Static code analysis is one of the fastest and best ways to detect security problems within code. It is recommended to include one or more static analysis tools in the development pipeline, which identifies unsafe coding practices each time a developer commits a new code. It is also desirable to perform automated scans and checks regularly to test common application program attacks such as SQL injection, Cross Site Scripting (XSS), and Cross Site Reference Forger (CSRF). On the other hand, most cloud-native applications consist of libraries or code with third-party dependencies created by third parties, making it difficult to verify with common static analysis tools. Therefore, it is recommended to use a dependency check tool to identify old or vulnerable libraries.

Malware Embedded in Images. The basis for reducing the damage caused by malicious code contained in images is to thoroughly verify the base layer and other images of unknown origin included in the images before using them. For malicious code that is not filtered during image verification, there is a method to continuously monitor the container image through malicious code patterns and behavior analysis methods based on actual attacks. **Cleartext secret embedded in images.** Secrets should not be stored in the container image, but should be provided dynamically during execution. The orchestrator provides secure confidential storage outside of the container image and the deployment process for confidential processing. For example, if a particular web application container tries to access a particular string in a database, the orchestrator allows only that web application to access this database connection string prevents it from being stored on disk, and provides secrets to the web application whenever it is deployed. **Out-of-data image vulnerabilities.** A vulnerability management tool suitable for the container model is required. These tools must be integrated with the lifecycle of the image, such as the deployment process, registry, and runtime, and have visibility into vulnerabilities by layer, such as the image layer, application framework layer, and custom software layer. The organization needs to configure the tool so that the process can proceed only for images that meet the vulnerability and setting policy at each stage of the deployment process. **Insecure communication channel between images and image registries.** If a secure communication channel is not formed between the image and the registry, sensitive information or secret in the image may be exposed, so it is necessary to ensure that only trusted endpoints such as orchestrator and container runtime can exchange data with the registry and encrypt data during transmission. **Insufficient authentication and authorization.** All access to write to the registry must be authenticated, so that only trusted personnel can add images to the registry. For the registry where important images are stored, all accesses to read the images must be recorded. Also, ensure that only images that have been signed by the person in charge and that have passed vulnerability checks and compliance assessments can be stored in the registry to prevent vulnerable or misconfigured images from proceeding to the next level or being deployed.

4   Concluding Remarks

In this paper, the cloud native environment is divided into four layers: cloud, cluster, container, and code layer, each security threat is examined, and the countermeasures for each security threat are described.

First of all, in order to reduce the attack surface, it is desirable to use a container-only host OS that is explicitly designed to run only containers with most services and functions disabled, and has a read-only file system and system hardening applied. And, by grouping containers according to purpose, importance, and threat state, even if an attacker penetrates one group, it is necessary to obtain a defense-in-depth effect that makes it difficult to additionally penetrate another group while preventing the remaining data from being exposed. In addition, since the server on which the application container runs may vary depending on resource availability at the time of execution, it is necessary to introduce a container-specific vulnerability management tool and process, not the existing vulnerability detection solution, to accurately identify vulnerabilities. Since these tools and processes are designed in consideration of both SW vulnerabilities and settings of the image, they can detect vulnerabilities inside containers, unlike existing tools. Meanwhile, HW ROT (Root of Trust) stores the host's firmware, SW, and configuration data. Before booting the host, the stored measured value and the current measured value are compared to determine whether the host is trusted. By extending the HW-based trust chain to the OS kernel and OS components, trust verification for boot mechanisms, system images, container runtimes, and container images is possible. Finally, it is necessary to utilize a container-native security solution that can monitor the container environment and accurately detect abnormal/malicious activities inside.

Here, the requirements for solutions/tools dedicated to container environments and environment settings by security administrators and commercial security solutions/tools are mainly described, and detailed countermeasures for the latest vulnerabilities and attack methods are continuously being studied.

As various services are activated in the 5G environment, it is expected that the related security threats will increase further. In particular, research on cloud-based security threats that occur in various layers in various layers should be continuously researched.

Acknowledgements. This work was supported by Institute of Information & communications Technology Planning & Evaluation (IITP) grant funded by the Korea government (MSIT) (No.

2020–0-00952, Development of 5G Edge Security Technology for Ensuring 5G+ Service Stability and Availability).

References

1. Netmanias, Evolution to 5G: Cloud Native. https://www.netmanias.com/ko/post/blog/14631/5g-sdn-nfv/evolution-to-5g-cloud-native-1
2. CNCF Cloud Native Definition v1.0. https://github.com/cncf/toc/blob/master/DEFINITION.md
3. Kubernetes, Overview of Cloud Native Security. https://kubernetes.io/docs/concepts/security/overview/
4. Red Hat Customer Portal, Symblic Exchange Attack (CVE-2021–30465) (2021). https://access.redhat.com/security/vulnerabilities/RHSB-2021-004
5. Shu, R., Gu, X., Enck, W.: A study of security vulnerabilities on docker hub ser. CODASPY 2017, pp. 269–280 New York, NY, USA (2017)
6. Socchi, E.: A deep dive into docker hub's security landscape-a story of inheritance? Master's thesis (2019)
7. NIST, CVE-2014–6271 Detail, National Vulnarability Database (2021). https://nvd.nist.gov/vuln/detail/cve-2014-6271
8. Sun, Y., Safford, D., Zohar, M., Pendarakis, D., Gu, Z., Jaeger, T.: Security namespace: making linux security frameworks available to containers. In: 27th USENIX Security Symposium (USENIX Security 18). USENIX Association, pp. 1423–1439 (2018)
9. Sampat, P.R.: Introduce cpu namespace. https://lwn.net/Articles/872507/
10. Center for Internet Security, CIS Kubernetes Benchmark (2020). https://www.cisecurity.org/benchmark/kubernetes
11. NSA and CISA, Kubernetes hardening guidance (2021)
12. Center for Internet Security, CIS Docker Benchmark (2020). https://www.cisecurity.org/benchmark/docker/
13. Security Enhanced Linux (SELinux). https://selinuxproject.org/page/Main_Page

Shannon Entropy Mixing Cumulative Sum Algorithm for DoS/DDoS Detection and Defense

Shih-Ting Chiu[1], Heru Susanto[2], and Fang-Yie Leu[1,3]([✉])

[1] Department of Computer Science, Tunghai University, Taichung 407224, Taiwan
{G08350023,leufy}@thu.edu.tw
[2] Center for Innovative Engineering, Universiti Teknologi, Malaysia, Brunei
heru.susanto@utb.edu.bn
[3] Emergency Response Management Center, Ming Chuan University, Guishan, Taoyuan, Taiwan

Abstract. Nowadays, 5G networks has gradually entered human's everyday lives. But network services re quested by users continuously grow. On the other hand, hackers can be found everywhere. Our information systems and network devices connected to the Internet may be attacked at any moment. Currently, 5G networks request security mechanisms to automatically detect DoS/DDoS attacks. Many systems have been proposed. But, none focuses on defending 5G networks against DoS/D DoS attacks. In other words, those 5G systems cannot effectively protect their users and facilities from DoS/DDoS attacks. Thus, this research proposes a network autonomous security system, named Detection and Defense of DoS/DDoS on 5G (DDD5G) which analyzes 5G network traffics and deter mines whether a protected system is under DoS/DDoS attack or not by using Shannon entropy (SE) and/or a mixed model. The latter mixes Shannon entropy and Cumulative Sum Algorithm (CUSUM) to further enhance a system's security level. Basically, Shannon entropy adopts entropy derived from normal traffic at time intervals as the threshold and compares it with entropy of other time intervals, denoted by T, to detect whether there are intrusions and attacks in T or not, while the CUSUM collects traffic and checks to see whether it exceeds the predefined thresholds or not to determine if this system is under attack. We also evaluate performance of these two methods. After simulating the DDD5G on MiniNet, we confirm that the proposed system based on the two mentioned algorithms can effectively self-detect and defend DoS/DDoS attacks without the need of human intervention.

Keywords: 5G · 5G Security · DoS/DDoS · Flash Event · Entropy · Shannon Entropy · Cumulative Sum Algorithm

1 Introduction

In our everyday lives, the degree of dependence on high-tech services continues increasing. High-tech applications make our lives easier, and make people in the world close to each other. Correspondingly, malicious behaviors done by hackers are constantly

I. You et al. (Eds.): MobiSec 2022, CCIS 1644, pp. 243–253, 2023.
https://doi.org/10.1007/978-981-99-4430-9_18

enhanced. Their motivations are usually demonstrating a considerable level of IT ability, showing themselves having a sense of technical achievement (e.g., through firewall vulnerability of a government office, successfully attack the government's web sites, and so on), or carrying out malicious purposes (e.g., paralyzing corporate servers to achieve criminal acts, such as extortion), Many types of network attacks have been commonly used by hackers to penetrate or intrude network systems. Among them, Denial of Service (DoS) [1] inappropriately occupies a system or shares its resources, such as: CPU, network, hard disk, etc. The behaviors that interfere with the normal operation of a system all belongs to this type of attacks. Distributed Denial-of-Service attack (DDoS) [2] usually adopts BOTs as a springboard to attack one or several target computers in a centralized control manner.

Computers in the Bots send a large amount of network packets in a distributed manner to consume the resources of the target network or system. In recent years, the frequencies that hackers attack network systems have been hugely increased. Even 3GPP R15 and 5G SA (Stand-alone) have defined better security facilities for 5G networks, like increasing service domain security and strengthen ing user authorization procedure, hackers may still illegally track user's location and information. R16 and R17 provide more secure capabilities, e.g., the service-based architecture (SBA), to enhance the security of data transmission [3]. Further, the high user capacity and high transmission rate of 5G networks not only lead to high traffic demands, but also force our systems facing toward serious security threats.

Therefore, this research proposes a network autonomous security system, called Detection and Defense of DoS/DDoS on 5G (DDD5G for short), which analyzes 5G network traffic to detect whether the protected system X is under DoS/DDoS attack or not by using Shannon entropy (SE) and Cumulative Sum Algorithm (CUSUM). To achieve this, the DDD5G provides means of self-determinate mitigation. When X is being attacked, besides detection, it can also reduce the impact on users by disconnecting the attacking connections. Our experiments demonstrate that functions of the DDD5G are feasible, and it can effectively defend against DoS/DDoS attacks without the need of human intervention.

This paper is organized as follows. Section 2 briefly reviews related literature of this study. Section 3 introduces the function of the DDD5G. System simulation and verification are presented and discussed in Sect. 4, respectively. Section 5 concludes this study and addresses our future work.

2 Related Work

This section briefly describes related work of this study.

2.1 DoS/DDoS Detection

In recent years, several studies proposed ways to enhance 5G security [4–6]. Liang et al. [4] presented a software-defined-security architecture for SDN-based 5G networks. This architecture adopts a centralized controller which communicates with the SDN controller to provide mobile users with flexible and network-aware security services.

Hong et al. [5] introduced the concept of dynamic threshold for DoS/DDoS mitigation a in SDN environment. Through the characteristics of SDN, a feasible detection and defense approach on DoS/DDoS attacks was designed. It dynamically calculates the entropy of the traffic collected from the environment of a target network, i.e., a dynamic threshold is derived from the traffic, to judge whether or not the environment is under DoS/DDoS attacks; Sahoo et al. [6] proposed a 5G network, in which its SDN controller collects traffic information. From this information, it derives General Entropy to detect DoS/DDoS attacks.

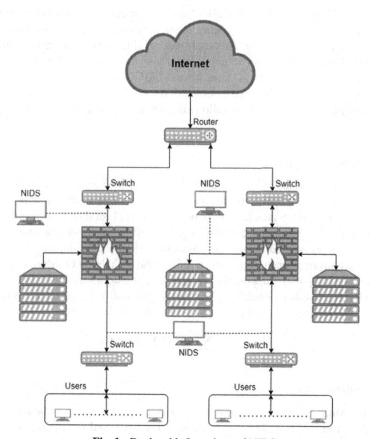

Fig. 1. Deployable Locations of NIDS.

2.2 Network Intrusion Detection System (NIDS)

Network intrusion Detection systems (NIDSs) detect attacks by analyzing packet traffic of each network segment. The advantage is that it does not increase the burden for the servers in the network segment. Figure 1 is a referential example showing deployable locations of NIDS in a network. It can be installed at the place between the server and the firewall or between the firewall and the Internet. If we choose the latter, the location is exactly the throat point of the network. All attack packets from the Internet will go through it. For the former, all packets that violate the firewall policies of the firewall are discarded so as to reduce the burden of NIDS, i.e., NIDS can focus on the detection and analysis of attacks. It can also be protected by the firewall to reduce the chance of being attacked.

2.3 5G Edge Computer and 5GC

Mobile Edge Computer (EC) is usually placed near users so as to serve nearby users, thus reducing the long transmission delay due to long-distance transmission, and shortening the system's response time. This study places Edge Computers on the input/output ports of a switch so that users can enjoy faster and more accurate security protection services when transferring data. 5G Core Network (5GC) consists of 5G control function infrastructure, usually installed in the computer room. The main function is user authentication and operation control. It also allows users to access other networks through 5GC settings.

2.4 Shannon's Entropy

In this study, entropy value of a network's traffic is calculated and checked to see whether the value exceeds the set threshold or not. If yes, it further verifies whether it is true positives, i.e., DoS/DDoS attack, or false positives, i.e., Flash Events. If it is the former, corresponding and appropriate defensive actions will be taken, or a warning message will be issued to system administrators. Shannon [7] called the degree of information uncertainty as information entropy, which reflects the probability of different degrees of uncertainty in the system. Suppose there is a discrete random variable $x = x_1, x_2, x_3, \ldots$, x_n, which has n distinct values. Let $p(x_i)$ be the probability that the random variable's value is x_i. The entropy H(x) of the random variable x is defined as

$$H(x) = - \sum_{i=1}^{n} p(x_i) \, log_2 \, p(x_i) \tag{1}$$

2.5 Cumulative Sum

Cumulative Sum (CUSUM) Algorithm [8] detects the time point when traffic starts abnormal in a relatively stable data sequence. The abnormal time point is defined as the mean or mean square deviation of the entire sequence which changes significantly affecting the stability of the traffic. When the traffic on the network is greater than the predefined threshold H which is greater than the average value M_0 of the usual traffic, the CUSUM algorithm starts accumulating these values that exceed H. When the accumulated value SUM (see Eq. (2)) is greater than the pre-defined critical value T, it is determined that the system currently suffers from DoS/DDoS attacks. Where x_j is the average traffic in time interval j.

$$Sum = \sum_{j=1}^{i} \left(\overline{x}_j - H \right) \tag{2}$$

3   DDD5G System Architecture

The following describes the functions of the DDD5G.

3.1   Defense Mechanisms

Figure 2 shows the architecture of the DDD5G system. The black lines are data paths, while the red lines are control paths. In this study, we also compare the performance of Shannon entropy and the mixed model. The latter integrates entropy calculation and CUSUM, when packets, denoted by P1, are sent from mobile phones to the base station. e.g., B, and B transmits P1 to a switch, e.g., S, S duplicates P1, denoted by P2, and sends P2 to EC via S's traffic tapping for intrusion detection. If the detection discovers that traffic is abnormal, it is further determined whether this is an attack or not. If yes, the DDD5G notifies the SDN controller to update the flow entry or entries of the flow table in S. S will drop all packets sent by the nodes delivering P1, denoted by IPs, to protect the underlying system. If it is Flash Event, S continues forwarding the packets sent by these IPs to their destinations. The packets received from the systems outside the protected one, e.g., Internet, are also detected by the DDD5G. In other words, all packets delivered through S will be detected.

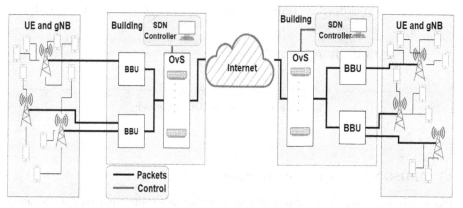

Fig. 2. Architecture of DDD5G Network Defense Mechanism.

3.2   DDD5G of Shannon Entropy IDD Algorithm

In the DDD5G, the intrusion-detection and Defense (IDD) algorithm that employs Shannon Entropy is shown in Fig. 3. It first collects the normal traffic in a time interval of t_0 seconds and calculates the Shannon Entropy as the threshold Ep th. It continues collecting incoming packets in a time interval of t_1 seconds and calculates their Shannon Entropy, denoted by $E(t_1)$. If Ep th $> E(t_1)$, it is considered that traffic is abnormal. The DDD5G immediately collects traffic in a time interval t_2 which in this study is 5 s and calculates the entropy for t_2, denoted by $E(t_2)$. If $E(t_1) <$ Ep th, i.e., traffic both in t_1 and

t_2 are abnormal, the DDD5G considers that there is a DoS/DDoS attack. The source IP is then transferred to the abnormal index to issue an alarm for defense. After receiving the alarm, the SDN controller sets Action field of the Flow table in S for the source IP(s) to "Drop" the packets they send, these IPs are recorded by traffic tapping. If $E(t_1)$ ¡ Ep th and $E(t_2)$ < Ep th, we consider traffic in t_1 is a flash event so that the packets sent by this source IP can continue their travel.

DDD5G

Let Ep_th be the flow entropy in time interval t_0 as the threshold

Let $E(t_1)$ be the flow entropy in t_1 time interval

Let $E(t_2)$ be the flow entropy in t_2 time interval

If Ep_th > $E(t_1)$ then

/* do judge abnormal type */

    If Ep_th > $E(t_2)$ then

        { print(" suffer DoS/DDoS");

          do drop flow issued by these IPs sending abnormal traffic}

    else

        print("Flash Event");

Fig. 3. Shannon Entropy IDD Algorithm.

3.3 DDD5G Mixed Model IDD Algorithm

Shannon Entropy is also employed in Fig. 4. We inherit some parameters of Shannon Entropy, e.g., Ep th, $E(t_1)$ and $E(t_2)$. When the flow is sent, CUSUM starts accumulating the traffic that exceeds H where H is larger than the average traffic, denoted by M_0, of the system normal traffic. The accumulated traffic, denoted by CS1 begins increasing. In this study, the CUSUM threshold CS th is set to 1MB. When Ep > $E(t_1)$ and CS th < CS1, it is considered that there is a DoS/DDoS attack. When Ep th > $E(t_1)$ or CS th < CS1, but not both, it is judged as "maybe abnormal" and the Flash Event will be verified. The procedure is that, the judge value CS2 starts accumulating the amount of traffic T which exceeds its traffic threshold H, i.e., T = current traffic – H. When CS2 > CS th and Ep th > $E(t_2)$, it will be judged as a DoS/DDoS attack. Otherwise, we consider it is a Flash Event. The method reduces occurrence of misjudgment.

DDD5G mix model .

Let Ep_th be the flow entropy in time interval t_0 as the threshold

Let $E(t_1)$ be the flow entropy in t_1 time interval

Let $E(t_2)$ be the flow entropy in t_2 time interval

Let CS_th be the threshold set by user

Let CS1 be the flow sum in time interval t_1

Let CS2 be the flow sum in time interval t_2

If (Ep_th > $E(t_1)$ and CS_th > CS1) or (CS_th < CS1 and Ep_th < $E(t_1)$)then

    If Ep_th > $E(t_2)$ or CS_th < CS2 then

        print(" suffer DoS/DDoS") ;

        do drop flow issued by these IPs sending abnormal traffic ;

    else

        print("Flash Event")

        do continue forwarding flow issued by these source IPs ;

Fig. 4. DDD5G Mixed Model IDD Algorithm.

4 Experiment and Validation

The following experiment is used to verify network autonomous security of the DDD5G. First, the server is attacked with a single large flow; second, the server is attacked with multiple small flows.

4.1 Attack Layout

We simulate DoS/DDoS attacks on the Mininet, The RYU as the SDN controller to control UEs and switches (i.e., UPF), requesting UEs to send UDP flooding to attack victims. Network traffic is monitored by Sflow agent.

4.2 Experimental Platform

We build the experimental topology shown in Figure 5 on Mininet. 3 hosts as traffic senders are employed.

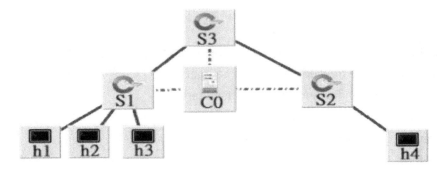

Fig. 5. Experimental topology.

4.3   Functional Verification and Result Comparison

First, we initialize network flow and acquire a calculated threshold TH. When the normal packets are sent, and their entropy value is greater than TH, the packets are continually forwarded. When considering that it is a DoS/DDoS attack, the protected system starts discarding the packets sent by these source IPs for defending. The Y-axes of the following figures are throughputs (Byte per second) and X-axes are time lines. Flooding simulation on Shannon Entropy is shown in Figure 6. When test started at the 29th second, the DDD5G is triggered. At the 48th second, attack is mitigated. The attack lasts about 19 s.

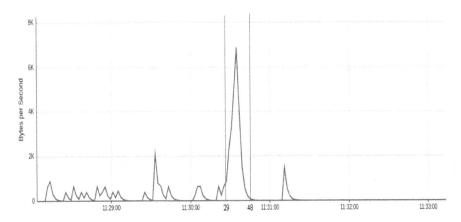

Fig. 6. Experimental results of flooding when Shannon Entropy is used.

The mixed model is employed in the same environment. Which is attacked by flooding. As shown in Figure 7, when cumulative value is higher than the predefined threshold, the DDD5G starts to defend Flooding at the 25th second and mitigate at the 39th second, lasting about 14 s. The performance of mixed is better than that when Shannon Entropy is employed only.

In the second experiment, the iperf pressure test is utilized as attack traffic. The experimental results on Shannon Entropy are shown in Figures 8. At the 58th second, the DDD5G is triggered. The attack was mitigated at about the 70th second. Taking about 12 s. Experimental results of mixed model are shown in Figures 9, Test begins at the 8th second, the DDD5G is triggered and the attack is mitigated at about the 21th second, consuming about 13 s. It is clear that the difference is insignificant.

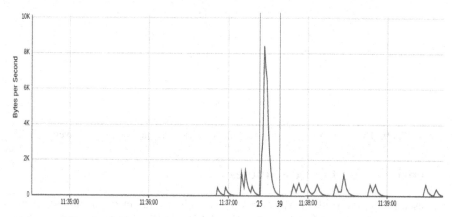

Fig. 7. Experimental results of flooding when Mixed model is utilized.

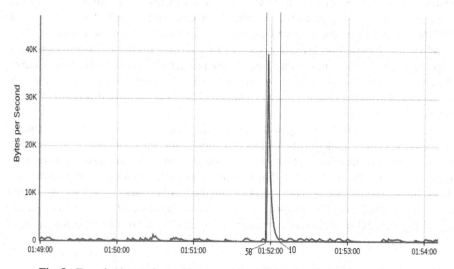

Fig. 8. Experiment results on Shannon Entropy when iperf pressure test is given.

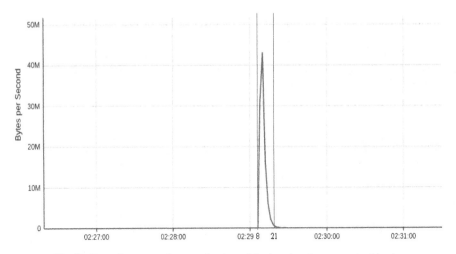

Fig. 9. Experiment results on mixed model when iperf pressure test is given.

5   Conclusion and Future Studies

This research compares the performance of two algorithms in the same architecture and network environment in which the DDD5G is employed to autonomously detect DoS/DDoS. Detecting DoS/DDoS attacks by using only Shannon Entropy or Shannon-Entropy-mixed-Cumulative-Sum allows normal network users to continue receiving network services from the protected system. After discovering DoS/D DoS attack, the DDD5G blocks attack packets with the switch the nearest to attack sources (e.g., UE), thereby mitigating the hurt to the attacked victim. Experiments show that both algorithms inspect packets by collecting traffic entering the protected system, the Shannon Entropy algorithm used by the DDD5G sometimes fails to detect the flooding attack traffic; The mixed model with the features of CUSUM can effectively improve this drawbacks and increase detection rates.

Actually, we are still working on this project. In the future, we will focus on the mixed model as the system malicious-behaviors detection frame work with which we can adopt different detection approaches to do their experiments on it. We will also expand it in the applications of network slicing so that we can detect the DoS/DDoS attacks on network slices. Since when a slice is under attacks, from the whole system viewpoint, the system works in a normal case. We would also like to derive the reliability model and behavior model for DDD5G so that users can realize its reliability and behaviors before using it. This constitutes our future studies.

Acknowledgments. This study is financial support in part by Ministry of Science and Technology, Taiwan under the grants MOST 108–2221-E-029–009 and MOST 109–2221-E-029–017-MY2.

References

1. Denial of Service(DOS), Wikipedia. https://en.wikipedia.org/wiki/Denial-of-serviceattack

2. Distributed Denial-of-Service attack(DoS/DDoS). wikipedia. https://en.wikipedia.org/wiki/Denialof-serviceattack
3. 5G security, IMT-2020(5G) promotion China Academy of Information and Communications Technology. https://pdf.dfcfw.com/pdf/H3AP202112141534538451.pdf?1639501401000.pdf
4. Liang, X., Qiu, X.: A software defined security architecture for SDN-based 5G network. In: 2016 IEEE International Conference on Network Infrastructure and Digital Content (IC-NIDC), pp. 17–21 (2016). https://doi.org/10.1109/ICNIDC.2016.7974528
5. Hong, G.-C., Lee, C.-N., Lee, M.-F.: Dynamic threshold for DoS/DDoS. mitigation in SDN environment. In: 2019 Asia -Pacific Signal and Information Processing Association Annual Summit and Conference (APSIPA ASC), pp. 1–7 (2019). https://doi.org/10.1109/APSIPAASC47483.2019.9023229
6. Sahoo, K.S., Sahoo, B., Vankayala, M., Dash, R.: Detection of control layer DoS/DDoS attack using entropy metrics in SDN: an empirical investigation. In: 2017 Ninth International Conference on Advanced Computing (ICoAC), pp. 281–286, December 2017
7. A Gentle Introduction to Information Entropy. https://machinelearningmastery.com/what-is-informationentropy/
8. CUSUM. https://en.wikipedia.org/wiki/CUSUM

IoT Application and Blockchain Security

Enhanced MQTT Method with IoT Data Priority Controls for Scalability and Realiability on Early Landslide Warning System

Noriki Uchida[1]([✉]), Shigeyuki Endo[1], Tomoyuki Ishida[1], Hiroaki Yuze[2], and Yoshitaka Shibata[3]

[1] Fukuoka Institute of Technology, 3-30-1 Wajirohigashi, Fukuoka Higashi-ku, Fukuoka 811-0214, Japan
n-uchida@fit.ac.jp
[2] University of Shizuoka, 52-1 Yada, Suruga-ku, Shizuoka 422-8526, Japan
[3] Iwate Prefectural University, 152-52 Sugo, Takizawa 020-0693, Iwate, Japan

Abstract. Recent catastrophic landslide disasters in Japan have highlighted the need for a quick and reliable warning system. The Early Landslide Warning System, which utilizes many IoT sensors, is considered effective in observing landslides. However, the number of IoT connections and the accuracy of the sensors still need to be improved, especially when compared to conventional survey methods. Therefore, this paper proposes the Enhanced MQTT method for the Early Landslide Warning System, and the proposed method improves connectivity, reduces latency, and minimizes transmitting errors by assigning priority values to IoT data. In detail, the proposed method first assigns the priority value to the user property field in the MQTT header according to the abnormality of the observed IoT data. Secondly, the proposed priority value stores the IoT data in the broker node's priority queues. Finally, the IoT data is asynchronously transmitted to the publisher from the high-priority queue. Then, this paper reports the experiments of the Enhanced MQTT methods by the prototype system, and the effectivity and the future studies are discussed in the paper.

Keywords: Early Landslide Warning System · Disaster Information System · IoT · Wireless Networks · MQTT

1 Introduction

Recent catastrophic landslide disasters such as the Atami landslide disaster in the July of 2021 [1] have highlighted the need for a quick and reliable warning system in Japan. Actually, the Atami landslide disaster hits Atami city, Shizuoka in Japan, where is a famous hot spring resort, and the sudden landslide caused 27 people's death, 580 evacuators, and 136 damaged houses [1]. Japan consists of many mountain areas on the island, and some catastrophic landslides have also happened by heavy rain or considered defective construction. Thus, these impacts cause the demands to prepare for quick and smooth emergency response measures against the landslide disaster in Japan.

© The Author(s), under exclusive license to Springer Nature Singapore Pte Ltd. 2023
I. You et al. (Eds.): MobiSec 2022, CCIS 1644, pp. 257–267, 2023.
https://doi.org/10.1007/978-981-99-4430-9_19

Then, hazard maps of landslides in Japan are being prepared rapidly across the country. However, conventional survey methods are considered to have some limitations. Typically, maps are created through geological surveys using boring tests or radio waves, which can be costly and time-consuming. Additionally, the surveys must be conducted nationwide and the hazard maps lack a real-time alert function.

In contrast, the Early Landslide Warning System (ELWS) incorporating IoT sensors is being studied, particularly in tropical countries. Previous studies [2, 3] have proposed the use of IoT sensors for real-time detection of landslides to prevent catastrophic damage to humans. However, the studies [4, 5] also pointed out some subjects with using IoT sensors in the ELWS. Firstly, the IoT network needs to be scalable to cover wide mountainous areas with numerous IoT sensors. Although MQTT (Message Queueing Telemetry Transport) [6], a commonly used IoT transport protocol, is designed for small data transmissions with many connections, it struggles with the scalability of numerous IoT connections [7]. Secondly, the MQTT protocol lacks reliability as it does not prioritize emergent data [7, 8]. Additionally, IoT sensors, which are often made with low-cost microcomputer boards like Arduino, are susceptible to breakage and the data provided from IoT sensors may not be accurate.

Therefore, this paper proposes the Enhanced MQTT method [9] for the Early Landslide Warning System considered with scalability and reliability of ELWS, and the proposed method improves connectivity, reduces latency, and minimizes transmitting errors by assigning priority IDs to IoT data.

In the followings, the proposed ELWS is outlined in Sect. 2, while Sect. 3 explain the conventional MQTT and the proposed Enhanced MQTT method. Section 4 presents the implementations of the prototype system. Then, the experimental results of the proposed methods using a prototype system are presented in Sect. 5, and finally, Sect. 6 provides conclusions and future researches in this paper.

2   Proposed Early Landslide Warning System

The purposes of the proposed ELWS is to increase the scalability of the IoT network connections and the reliability of transmitting emergency data from IoT sensors. Figure 1. in this paper presents the proposed ELWS.

Figure 1 Illustrates the proposed ELWS that IoT sensors such as gyro, temperature, and soil moisture sensors are deployed on slopes in mountainous areas, and that they are connected by the LPWA (Low Power Wide Area) wireless network such as the 920 MHz LoRa radio band [10]. The data collected by these sensors is transmitted to the IP network via the IoT gateway, and any signs of an impending landslide are detected through analysis of the sensor values in disaster servers. If a potential landslide is detected, an alert is sent to users through the cellular system.

However, as previously suggested, scalability issues, such as the number of wireless connections, and reliability, such as the accuracy of landslide detections, are significant concerns for ELWS using IoT sensors. Although the original MQTT is optimized for small data transmissions with numerous connections, the previous studies [5, 7] have shown that the support for affordable wireless connections is limited to only a few hundred devices and that it lacks priority functions. To enhance the scalability of the

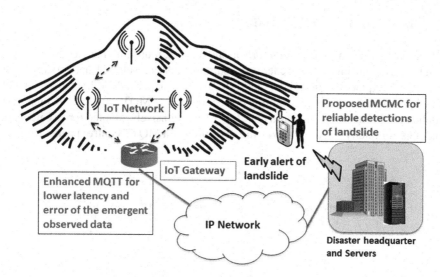

Fig. 1. Proposed Early Landslide Warning System

proposed ELWS to cover vast mountain areas, it is necessary to improve the wireless connectivity between IoT sensors and the IoT gateway. Additionally, it is also essential to enhance the network quality, such as reducing delay and transmission errors of the critical landslide data, to increase the reliability of the system.

Therefore, this paper proposes the Enhanced MQTT method [9] that prioritizes observed abnormal values to increase the wireless connections, to reduce transmission errors, and latency for emergency data from IoT sensors. While conventional MQTT is designed for IoT networks with small data transmissions, such as the 920 MHz LoRa radio, previous studies [7, 8] have pointed out the limitations of MQTT with hundreds of wireless connections or transmission errors due to the overload of the broker node. Therefore, the proposed method introduces priority values for MQTT messages related to emergency landslide detections.

Besides, as previously mentioned, the IoT sensors, which are often made with low-cost microcomputer boards like Arduino, are susceptible to breakage. Thus, it is necessary to consider redundancy with many IoT devices. Moreover, the data from IoT sensors may not be accurate compared with conventional geological surveys using boring tests or radio waves. Therefore, considering with reliability of the system, the proposed ELWS considers applying the abnormal detection method such as the MCMC (Markov Chain Monte Carlo) [11] with numerous IoT sensors in future works. In this method, the location and the accelerometer's threshold values are calculated by the Gaussian distribution point from the previous values. Therefore, landslide detections are estimated by many IoT sensors of location, temperature, and accelerometer considering the wide area, and it is considered to increase the reliability of the landslide alert in real time.

3 Enhanced MQTT Method

IoT devices are often used to monitor various sensors, requiring many connections but with low data transmission and energy consumption. As a result, IoT networks typically utilize low-frequency radio bands, such as 920 MHz with a bandwidth of approximately 250 kbps, and lightweight transmitting protocols, such as MQTT or CoAP (Constrained Application Protocol) [8]. In particular, MQTT is extensively adopted for IoT networks due to its simplicity. Figure 2 shows the structures of a MQTT control packet [6].

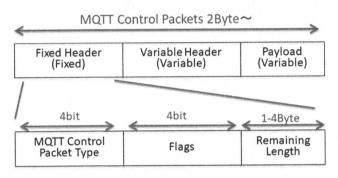

Fig. 2. MQTT Control Packet Structure

Unlike TCP packets, which have headers larger than 20 bytes, the minimum size of an MQTT header is only 2 bytes. According to Fig. 2, the MQTT packet consists of a minimal 2 bytes fixed header, a variable header, and a payload. The fixed header is always present in all MQTT packets, but the variable header and the payload are not always present. Moreover, the fixed header consists of the 4 bits MQTT control packet type, the 4bits flags, and the remaining length. Here, the MQTT control packets type commands the transmission controls between IoT sensors and an IoT gateway, such as CONNECT (bit: 0001), CONNAK (bit: 0010), and PUBLISH (bit: 0011). Then, if the MQTT control packet is 0011(PUBLISH), the next flag field can control the QoS (Quality of Service) levels from QoS0 to QoS2. However, this QoS level is used to retransmit an MQTT message if there is a transmission error between an IoT sensor and an IoT gateway. This function needs to be fixed for the transmission priority of the important data for warning landslides. Therefore, the priority functions for the emergent observed data from numerous IoT sensors are needed for original MQTT controls.

Furthermore, MQTT is specifically designed for IoT networks that follow a publisher-subscriber messaging model, where subscribers request the sensor data from the publishers through the broker node.

In original MQTT, publisher nodes transmit the observed sensor values to the broker node using round-robin routing in LoRa network, and the data is stored in the broker in IP network. Subscribers then request the relevant data using the topic field in the MQTT messages, and receive the selected data from the broker node. However, when hundreds of publisher nodes send to the broker, transmission errors may occur due to the broker becoming overwhelmed by excessive connections. Besides, the QoS function of MQTT cannot deal with the abnormal observed values from IoT sensors because it supports only the number of retransmissions in IP network.

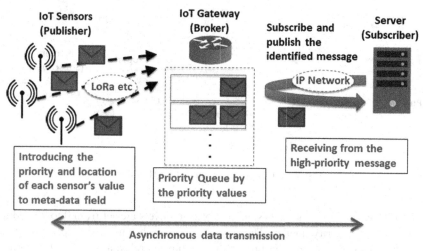

Fig. 3. Enhanced MQTT Method

Therefore, the proposed Enhanced MQTT method introduces the following functions as shown in Fig. 3. The proposed method first assigns the priority value to the user property field in the MQTT header according to the abnormality of the observed IoT data. Secondly, the proposed priority value stores the IoT data in the broker node's priority queues. Then, the subscriber subscribes the messages from the high-priority queue, and the broker publishes the identified data from the high-priority queue. Finally, these data transmissions are asynchronously proceeded from the publisher to the subscriber via the broker.

4   Prototype System

To realize the proposed method, the implementations were confirmed by the GO programming language on the Arduino and the Raspberry PI. Figure 4 shows the main implemented functions in the prototype system.

As shown in Fig. 4, the original MQTT allows users to add metadata fields to the MQTT message, including the topic and the user property fields. The MQTT Topic is comprised of one or more levels separated by forward slashes, such as "/Japan/Tokyo/Temperature." This information is used when the subscribers subscribe to specific data from the broker, and the broker publishes the selected data from its queue to the subscriber. In MQTT version 5.0 and later, the user property field was added, enabling users to add additional user-defined information, such as data format information, geological information, and device resource analysis, to broaden the application scenarios.

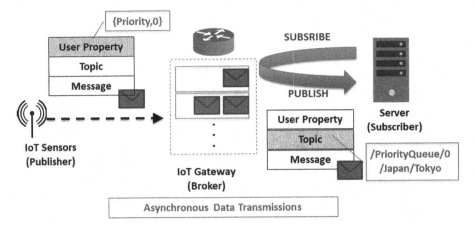

Fig. 4. Functions of Enhanced MQTT Method

Therefore, in the prototype system, the priority levels are set from 0 to 99 and used for the broker's priority queues. The subscriber subscribes to specific priority queues, as illustrated in Fig. 4, and the broker then publishes relevant data to the publisher. Data transmissions are confirmed asynchronously in the prototype system to prevent transmission errors, which often occur in the original MQTT protocol due to broken IoT sensors or increased traffic.

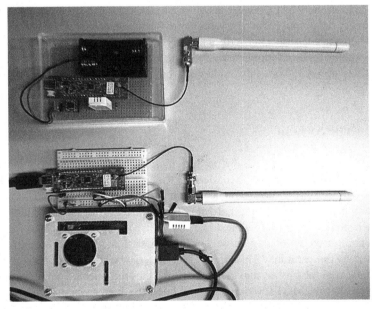

Fig. 5. Prototype System of IoT Sensors (IoT sensor is above. IoT gateway is bottom)

The implemented prototype system of the publisher is shown in Fig. 5 based on Green House GH-EVARDLRB (Arduino Bootloader Atmega328PB, LoRa GH-WM92LRA (920 MHz)), 3-axis accelerometer (Akizuki KXR94–2050), temperature and humidity sensor (Osoyoo DHT11), and soil moisture sensor (DFRobot SEN0193). The broker was also implemented by Raspberry PI 4B (8MB). Also, ambient [12] is used as the subscriber for the restoration and the visualization of observed IoT data via the IoT broker.

5   Experiments

The effectiveness of the proposed Enhanced MQTT was evaluated through experiments, the specifications of which are outlined in Table 1. In these experiments, virtual IoT devices were created using Raspberry PI and Ducker, and the proposed functions implemented in these virtual devices were evaluated.

The experiments compared the average latency and the number of wireless connections of the observed data for the Enhanced MQTT (eMQTT) and the original MQTT with varying numbers of IoT sensors. In each experiment, three message priority levels were set in a balanced ratio for each message from the IoT sensors.

Table 1. Experimental Specifications

IoT Sensor (publisher)	100−500 virtual devices by Ducker in Raspberry PI 4B
IoT Gateway (broker)	Raspberry PI 4B (8 GB, 1 Gbps ethernet)
Server (subscriber)	Raspberry PI 4B (8 GB, 1 Gbps ethernet)
Number of IoT sensors	100−500 (by Ducker)
Number of publish messages	500 from each IoT sensor
Message size	90 Byte
Priority levels	3(High, Mid, Low)
Ratio of priority messages	(High:Mid; Low) = 1:1:1

The average latency results are presented from Fig. 6 to Fig. 8. First, Fig. 6 presents the delay results in high-priority IoT data varying from 100 to 500 IoT devices.

According to Fig. 6, the average latency of high-priority messages is about 0.25 s at the 100 IoT sensors with the Enhanced MQTT method, while the latency with the original MQTT is about 5.0 s. Besides, the difference in the latency increases with the increasing number of IoT sensors, and the difference becomes almost 1.2 s at the 500 IoT devices. Actually, since the MQTT shows high data transmission errors at the 500 IoT devices, as shown in Fig. 9, most of the high-priority could not be delivered to the broker in the experiments. Therefore, from comparing the results in high-priority messages, it can be concluded that the proposed Enhanced MQTT method dramatically reduces the latency of IoT data transmission.

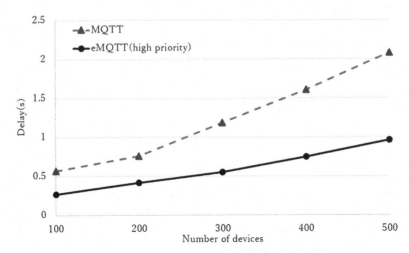

Fig. 6. Results of Average Latency for High-priority Messages

Secondly, Fig. 7 presents the average latency of middle-priority messages. The results also show that the proposed method reduces the average latency of the middle-priority messages from IoT sensors. Although the differences in the latency become smaller than high-priority messages since these messages are transmitted to the broker after the high-priority messages, the difference is about 0.7 s of the latency.

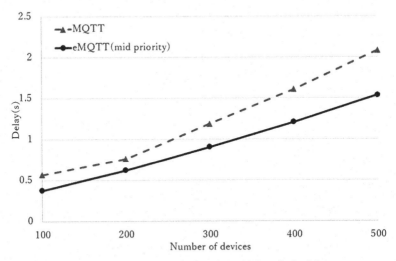

Fig. 7. Results of Average Latency for Middle-priority Messages

Figure 8 shows the average latency of low-priority messages, where the Enhanced MQTT method slightly outperforms the original MQTT. This improvement can be attributed to the asynchronous data transmission used by the Enhanced MQTT, compared to the synchronous transmission used by MQTT. The round-robin routing and synchronous transmission from publisher to broker and then to subscriber in MQTT can lead to a lower performance for low-priority messages. Thus, the proposed method proves to be effective even for low-priority messages.

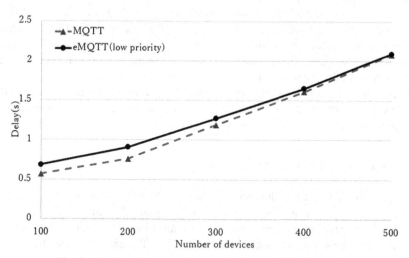

Fig. 8. Results of Average Latency for Low-priority Messages

As the conclusions of the average latency of the proposed method from Fig. 6 to Fig. 8, it is pointed out that the proposed method is well worked to improve the latency.

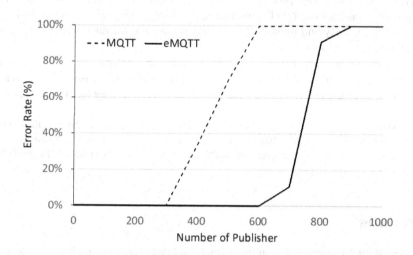

Fig. 9. Major Functions of Enhanced MQTT Method

Also, Fig. 9 shows the results of the data transmission errors varying from 100 to 1000 IoT devices using the same scenarios as the previous experiments. The figure shows the data transmission error rate, including the high, middle, and low priority messages varying the number of IoT sensors.

As shown in Fig. 9, the MQTT has transmission errors from around 300 IoT devices and reaches a 100% error rate at 600 IoT devices. On the other hand, the Enhanced MQTT method has transmission errors from around 600 IoT devices and reaches a 100% error rate at 900 IoT devices. These results highlight a significant improvement in wireless connections with the proposed method.

In conclusion, compared to the conventional MQTT, the proposed Enhanced MQTT method significantly improves the latency and reduces the data transmission error rate, particularly in high and middle-priority messages.

6 Conclusion and Future Works

Recent catastrophic landslide disasters in Japan have highlighted the need for a quick and reliable warning system, and the Early Landslide Warning System, which utilizes many IoT sensors, is considered effective in observing landslides. However, in the system, it is considered that the scalability, such as the number of IoT connections, and the reliability, such as the sensors' accuracy, need to be improved.

Therefore, this paper proposes the Enhanced MQTT method for the Early Landslide Warning System, and the proposed method improves connectivity, reduces latency, and minimizes transmitting errors by assigning priority values to IoT data.

Then, this paper presented the implementations of the prototype system, and the experimental results of the prototype system were reported. The results show that, compared to the conventional MQTT, the proposed Enhanced MQTT method significantly improves the latency and reduces the data transmission error rate, particularly in high and middle-priority messages.

Now, the authors are working on implementing the Enhanced MCMC method to improve accuracy by using many observed values with IoT sensors. Moreover, the implantations of the ELWS for the field experiments are working for future works.

Acknowledgments. This paper is an extended version of a publication presented at the 6th International Symposium on Mobile Internet Security (mobisec2022), held from December 15–17, 2022. Also, this work was supported by JSPS KAKENHI Grant Numbers JP19K04972 and JP22K04643.

References

1. Pref. Shizuoka: Damages Reports by Atami Landslide Disaster on 2021 https://www.pref.shi zuoka.jp/kinkyu/r3_atami_dosyasaigai.html. Accessed 2022
2. Sofwan, A., Sumardi, Ridho, M., Goni, A.: Najib wireless sensor network design for landslide warning in IoT architecture. In: 2017 4th International Conference on Information Technology, Computer, and Electrical Engineering (ICITACEE), pp. 280–283. IEEE (2017). https://doi.org/10.1109/ICITACEE.2017.8257718

3. Fatimah, P., Irawan, B., Setianingsih, C.: Design of landslide early warning system using fuzzy method based on android. In: 2020 12th International Conference on Information Technology and Electrical Engineering (ICITEE), pp. 350–355. IEEE (2020). https://doi.org/10.1109/ICITEE49829.2020.9271676

4. Riasetiawan, M., Prastowo, B.N., Putro, N.A.S., Dhewa, O.A., Baktiar, F.Y.: G-Connect: real-time early warning system for landslide data monitoring. In: 2019 6th International Conference on Instrumentation, Control, and Automation (ICA), pp. 127–130. IEEE (2019). https://doi.org/10.1109/ICA.2019.8916747

5. Kim, Y.S., Lee, H.H., Kwon, J.H., Kim, Y.S., Kim, E.J.: Message queue telemetry transport broker with priority support for emergency events in Internet of Things. Sens. Mater. **30**(8), 1715–1721. M Y U Scientific Publishing Division (2018). https://doi.org/10.18494/SAM.2018.1864

6. Oasis: Mqtt version 5.0. https://docs.oasis-open.org/mqtt/mqtt/v5.0/os/mqtt-v5.0-os.html. Accessed 2022

7. Putra, A.D., et al.: Development of slope deformation monitoring system based on tilt sensors with low-power wide area network technology and its application. J. Civ. Struct. Heal. Monit. **11**(4), 1037–1053 (2021). https://doi.org/10.1007/s13349-021-00494-9

8. Mishra, B., Kertesz, A.: The use of MQTT in M2M and IoT systems: a survey. IEEE Access **8**, 201071–201086. IEEE (2020). https://doi.org/10.1109/ACCESS.2020.3035849

9. Uchida, N., Endo, S., Ishida, T., Yuze, H., Shibata, Y.: Proposal of early landslide warning system considering scalability and reliability with emergent IoT data priority. In: The 6th International Symposium on Mobile Internet Security (MobiSec2022), pp. 1–7. Republic of Korea Article (2022)

10. Semtech.com, lora and lorawan: Technical overview. https://lora-developers.semtech.com/documentation/tech-papers-and-guides/lora-and-lorawan/. Accessed 2022

11. Uchida, N., Fukumoto, M., Ishida, T., Shibata, Y.: Static body detecting methods by locational and rotational sensors on smartphone for dtn based disaster information system. In: Barolli, L., Amato, F., Moscato, F., Enokido, T., Takizawa, M. (eds.) WAINA 2020. AISC, vol. 1150, pp. 605–613. Springer, Cham (2020). https://doi.org/10.1007/978-3-030-44038-1_56

12. AmbientData Inc.: Ambient. https://ambidata.io. Accessed 2022

Blockchain-Based Terminal Access Control in Software Defined Network

Bingcheng Jiang, Qian He[✉], Qi Pan, and Mingliu He

Guilin University of Electronic Technology, Guilin 541004, China
heqian@guet.edu.cn

Abstract. Software-Defined Networking (SDN) decouples the traditional network system into a data plane, control plane and application plane, making the network as flexible and convenient as software, and improving the innovation capability of the network. However, SDN networks lack effective access control methods for terminal access, making it challenging to perform fine-grained access control and management when terminals access SDN networks, increasing the risk of being attacked. In this paper, we design an SDN-based network architecture to provide secure terminal access, which includes an SDN network control layer, data forwarding layer and terminal layer. Based on Programming Protocol-independent Packet Processors (P4) and blockchain, the access control of the terminal in the SDN network is implemented to ensure SDN network security and service quality. Experimental results show that the proposed method achieves fine-grained secure authentication of terminals in SDN networks.

Keywords: Software-Defined Networking (SDN) · Blockchain · Authentication · P4

1 Introduction

With the popularity of cloud computing and the Internet of Things (IoT), a large number of terminals need to be connected via the Internet in order to provide relevant services for upper-layer applications. According to the statistics of IDC (Internet Data Center), by 2030, the number of IoT device connections is predicted to reach about 20 billion in China. Faced with a large number of terminal access, The current network architecture bears great challenges [1,2]. However, the traditional network architecture suffers from complex structural coupling and dull access control management, making the network vulnerable to attacks by malicious endpoints.

In contrast, SDN can achieve optimal allocation of network resources and quality of service improvement. SDN is a network architecture that separates the network's control plane and data plane, enabling network administrators to program network behaviour through software applications [3]. This separation of control and data planes makes it possible to centrally manage and configure

© The Author(s), under exclusive license to Springer Nature Singapore Pte Ltd. 2023
I. You et al. (Eds.): MobiSec 2022, CCIS 1644, pp. 268–279, 2023.
https://doi.org/10.1007/978-981-99-4430-9_20

the network, allowing for more efficient use of network resources and improved quality of service (QoS) [4]. With SDN, network administrators can dynamically allocate network resources based on application requirements, traffic patterns, and user demands. This means that critical applications can be given higher priority over less important ones, ensuring that they receive the necessary network resources to function optimally. SDN also makes it easier to manage network traffic, monitor network performance, and quickly respond to changing network conditions.

However, the security of SDN networks is an urgent research topic [5], in which the open and untrustworthy network environment allows attackers to use forged user identities or with the help of attacked terminals for the purpose of attacking the network [6]. At the same time, SDN controllers lack access control mechanisms for terminal access and cannot achieve the function of authenticating terminals. Therefore, attackers use this feature to access malicious terminals to SDN networks and thus achieve theft and tampering of normal traffic in the network. In addition, how to guarantee the security of the access control policy for terminal access and the traceability of terminal information are also issues worth studying. The main work of this paper consists of the following.

1. We designed a blockchain-based terminal access control system in software-defined networking, including the SDN network control layer, data forwarding layer and terminal layer.
2. To address the lack of an effective access control method for terminal access in SDN networks, a terminal access control method based on SDN and blockchain is proposed. This method uses the unique identification of terminal attributes in the network, takes the IP packet Options field as the access control medium, and introduces the Attribute-Based Access Control, ABAC (attribute-based) and P4 (Programming Protocol-independent Packet Processors) programmable technology to realize the function of controllable terminal access to the SDN network. Experimental results show that the proposed method achieves fine-grained secure access authentication for terminals in the SDN network.

2   Related Work

Access control is a crucial area of research in SDN, and several approaches have been proposed to address this challenge. Porras et al. [7] present a security enforcement kernel that manages the permissions of applications in Floodlight, but it is limited to a specific controller. Phan et al. [8] constructed an access control scheme for SDN northbound, introducing the B-DAC framework to provide decentralized authentication and fine-grained access control for northbound interfaces, which assists administrators in managing and protecting critical resources. Charu et al. [9] propose a three-level policy language and fine-grained permission management to secure APIs sharing in a multi-tenant SDN network, but it requires complex manual permission configuration. Kammoun et al. [10] proposed a new SDN architecture based on IoT trust management and access control through a predefined trust management algorithm to calculate the terminal trust value and prevent malicious devices from accessing the network based on this trust value. However, this scheme does not consider the security of the access control policy, which may lead to policy leakage. Weng et al. [11] utilize broadcast encryption to provide scalable and dynamic access control for SDN-based vehicular network applications, but it relies on a centralized security module. Charu et al. [12] designed a scalable, efficient and cost-effective network architecture that not only meets the changing needs of users but also increases the access of IoT devices by embedding network elements in software instead of dedicated hardware, making it easy to rent them from the pool of available devices and thereby enabling rapid device access. Matias et al. [13] proposed FlowNAC, an access control scheme for SDNs, which can grant users access to the network based on the user's requested target, achieving a fine-grained access control function. However, this scheme is time-consuming and relies on third-party authorization for data flow access, which has a certain probability of insecurity.

In the above literature, some schemes consider the access control policy but the access control policy is single, not enough fine-grained, and does not consider the security of the access control strategy. At the same time, it does not consider how to reduce the access time overhead, which may lead to large authentication overhead, policy tampering and other problems.

3   System Model

3.1   System Architecture

In this paper, we design a blockchain-based terminal access control system in software-defined networking. As shown in Fig. 1, the system is divided into three layers from top to bottom, with the top layer being the SDN network control layer, the second layer being the data forwarding layer, and the third layer being the terminal layer.

SDN Control Layer. This layer contains the blockchain service and Floodlight controllers, where the blockchain service provides services for the controllers, and in the subsequent part of this paper, the blockchain-related functional interface is encapsulated as RestFul service, which provides services such as terminal access authentication to the controller, and the specific functions of the blockchain and controllers are shown below.

1. Firstly, the ABAC model is implemented using smart contract technology. Secondly, the device attribute information or the terminal under a certain SDN controller domain is stored through the device contract. Then, the network administrator invokes the policy contract through the RestFul service to execute the policy-adding operation. Finally, the controller queries the blockchain whether the current terminal has the right to access the SDN network, and the access contract returns the query result to the controller.

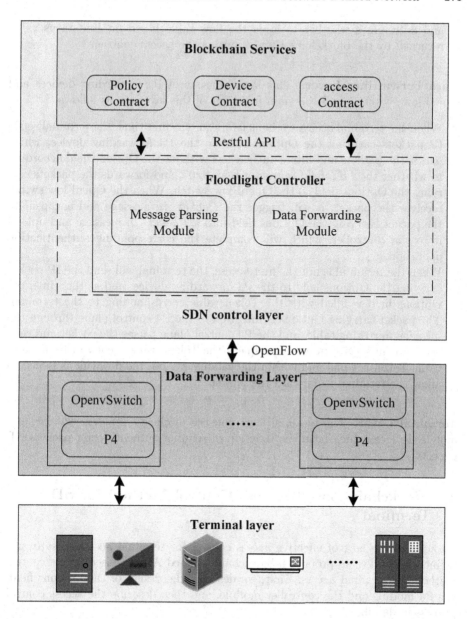

Fig. 1. System architecture

2. When the terminal connects to the SDN network for the first time, the controller receives the *Packet_in* message from the OpenFlow switch, parses the message and gets the Options field value. At the same time, it uses the Options field value to construct an attribute-based access request to the blockchain

and determines whether to issue the flow table based on the status value returned by the blockchain after executing the access contract.

Data Forwarding Layer. This layer consists of P4 forwarding devices and OpenFlow switches, and the main functions of this layer are as follows.

1. When the terminal access to the network for the first time, the terminal sends IP packets carrying the Options field to the P4 forwarding device, which parses the packets and filters out packets without the Options field according to whether the IHL field is greater than $0x05$, and forwards the packets carrying the Options field to the OpenFlow switch. When the OpenFlow switch receives the packet, it will trigger the $Packet\_in$ message and encapsulate the packet carrying the Options field into a $Packet\_in$ message and upload it to the controller, which will complete the corresponding authentication operation.
2. When the terminal is not the first access, the terminal will send the IP packet carrying the Options field to the P4 forwarding device, and at this time, the Options field is filled with the Token value corresponding to the terminal. The packet carrying Options is mirrored to the P4 control plane through the message mirroring table, and the P4 control plane parses the packet and calls the RestFul service interface to query the Token value cached in Redis, and if the Token is equal and within the validity period, the flow rule is issued to allow the terminal to forward the packet.

Terminal Layer. The terminal layer consists of clients, servers, switches and mobile devices, which have the function of sending authentication packets (IP packets).

4   Blockchain-Based Access Control Method for SDN Terminal

To address the lack of effective access control for terminal access in software-defined networks, we propose a blockchain-assisted ABAC-based access control method for terminal access. First, we describe the design of the Options field, the P4 module and the controller module, and then describe the access control process in detail.

4.1   Options Field

To facilitate fast access to the terminal, this paper programs the options field of IP packets, encapsulating the set of attributes required by the AAR into the *Verification_ Token* field in the Options field of the IP header. The P4 forwarding device filters packets without the Options field to enable fast and secure access to the network by the endpoint. The Options field design is shown in Fig. 2 and consists of an 8-bit group options code field and a *Verification_ Token* verification field in accordance with RFC791 [14].

The *Verification_ Token* field is 280 bits long and takes up 35 bytes. The *Verification_ Token* field has two functions.

- On first-time access by the terminal, the set of attributes sent by the terminal is written into the *Verification_ Token*, filtered in the P4 forwarding device and the filtered packets are forwarded to the controller via OpenvSwitch.
- On non-first access, the Token obtained for the first time is stored in *Verification_ Token*, packets without the Options field are filtered in the P4 forwarding device and packets carrying the Options field are mirrored to the P4 control plane for parsing. At the same time, the Token corresponding to the terminal is obtained from Redis for comparison. If the two are consistent and the Token is within the validity period, a flow rule is issued in P4 to allow the packet to be forwarded; otherwise, access is denied.

4.2 P4 Module

In P4, the main logical composition of the code consists of four parts: the header, the parser, the match-action table and the control program. Among these, the header section contains mainly Ethernet and IP header definitions. When the packet arrives at the P4 forwarding device, the parser parses the packet to obtain the value corresponding to each protocol. The header code for the Options field is defined in this paper as follows.

$$headeripv4\_option\_t\{$$
$$bit < 1 > copyFlag;$$
$$bit < 2 > optClass;$$
$$bit < 5 > option;$$
$$bit < 280 > Verification\_Token;$$
$$\}$$

After defining the header, the next step is to use the parser to identify the valid sequences in the header and packet. In this design, *ipv4_ option_ t* is added to

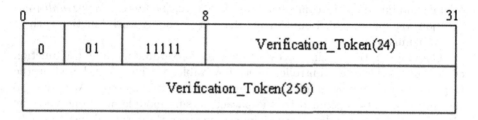

Fig. 2. The Design of options field

ipv4, so the packet is parsed in the order *Ethernet, ipv4, ipv4_ option_ t*. Because IP packets carry the Options field, those with an *IHL* value greater than *0x05*. This paper uses the *IHL* field to filter packets that do not carry the Options field. This field is also used to implement the corresponding processing logic during first-time and non-first-time access.

4.3   Controller Module

Message Parsing Module. The main function of the message parsing module is to parse *Packet_in* messages sent by OpenvSwitch, parse and verify whether the terminal has access permissions. The specific steps are as follows:

When the P4 forwarding device sends a packet with the Options field to OpenvSwitch, the switch cannot perform the corresponding action, encapsulates the received packet as a *Packet_in* message and sends it to the Floodlight controller. At the same time, in the controller, a thread is invoked in the Message parsing module to listen for *Packet_in* messages from the OpenvSwitch switch. When the thread detects a *Packet_in* message arriving, it will be parsed in this module. Among them, the *OFMessage* interface is used to determine the message packet, and according to the *"eth.getEtherType() == EthType.IPV4"* condition, the payload and Options value of the *IPV4* data packet can be obtained. The Options value returns a Byte type array, and the elements in the array are traversed and converted to String type.

In the design process of the Options field in the front of this article, the length of the *Verification_Token* field was defined, so by intercepting a specified number of characters, the submitted attributes can be obtained. The controller uses the subString method to intercept the option value, constructs the current terminal's AAR request through the intercepted value, sends the request to the blockchain access contract through the encapsulated RestFul service to verify whether the terminal has permission to access the network, and returns the response result, which is used by the data forwarding module for judgment.

Data Forwarding Module. The main function of the data forwarding module is to determine whether the terminal has the right to access the SDN network based on the response results from the packet parsing module and to implement the function of table flow installation or rejection of terminal access. By reading the relevant source code functions in the Floodlight controller Forwarding module and based on the controller's business logic, the *processPacketInMessage* function was found, which implements the corresponding work function such as flow table installation.

Therefore, in the design process of the data forwarding module, the function of judging whether the controller issues flow tables to the switch based on the response results can be implemented by overriding this method. According to the response status obtained by the packet parsing module after querying the blockchain, the overridden method judges whether the terminal has the right to access the SDN network. If the response result is "200", it means that the terminal has the right to access the SDN network. The Floodlight controller will execute the function of installing flow tables and allow the terminal's traffic to be forwarded normally. Otherwise, the installation of flow tables will be rejected and an error message will be returned.

4.4   Terminal Access Control Process

Terminal access control has three main parts. In this section, the implementation steps of each part will be explained in detail.

Registration Phase

1. The terminal and the devices under the SDN controller domain submit attributes to the attribute management center, and the attribute management center calls the RestFul service to execute the device contract with the submitted attribute set and store the attributes on the blockchain.
2. The administrator obtains the set of attributes submitted by the terminal or the device under the controller domain through the device contract. Then, the access control policy is formulated for the terminal access to the SDN network based on AG_{S_i}, AG_{O_j}, AG_{P_k}, AG_{E_n}. Among them, the Token value corresponding to the terminal is generated in the process of formulating the access control policy, and the Token value is generated by encrypting the relevant attributes in the access control policy. These operations are done in the chain to ensure that the Token is not tampered with. At the same time, the administrator signs this access control policy to ensure its validity of the access control policy.
3. After the administrator defines the ACP, the access control policy is added, deleted, changed and checked through the RestFul service of the operation policy contract.

Authentication Phase. The blockchain executes the access contract, verifies that the terminal AAR request is sent by the controller, and returns the response to the SDN controller (C0).

1. First, the terminal encapsulates the attribute set into the IP packet Options field. When the message arrives at the P4 forwarding device, the P4 forwarding device parses the packet and quickly filters the messages without the Options field according to the IHL field value. At the same time, the packets carrying the Options field are forwarded to the OpenvSwitch switch connected to it. The switch encapsulates the packets carrying Options into $Packet\_in$ messages and forwards them to C0. C0 parses the $Packet\_in$ packets, gets the value of Options, and uses the parsed Options value to construct the AAR request of the terminal to the blockchain access contract.
2. The blockchain verifies whether the AAR request constructed by C0 satisfies the ACP, and if so, generates a response status code and returns it to C0. At the same time, C0 sends the flow table to OVS, allows the terminal traffic

to be forwarded, and caches the Token value generated by the terminal corresponding to the access control policy with the key as the terminal ID and value as the Token value in Redis and the blockchain. The Token value in Redis is consistent with the Token on the blockchain, and when the Token on the chain changes, it will be synchronized to Redis in real-time. If the AAR request does not satisfy the access control policy, the blockchain returns an error message to C0.

Access Phase. If the terminal's connection is interrupted for external reasons, two situations will occur when it is accessed again: first-time access and non-first-time access.

1. For first-time access, the terminal needs to do the same operations as in the authentication phase.
2. For non-first-time access, the terminal adds the Token value obtained for the first time to the Options field of the IP packet and initiates an access request to the SDN network. First, when the packet carrying the Options field arrives at the P4 forwarding device, the P4 forwarding device parses the packet and filters out the packets without the Options field in the IP packet using the IHL field. Then, the packet is mirrored to the P4 control plane through the to_cpu action, and the P4 control plane parses the Options field value and queries the corresponding Token value to Redis through the RestFul service. If the corresponding Token value is queried and is within the validity period, a function similar to the $Packet\_in$ message is implemented in the P4 control plane, and the flow table is distributed in the control plane to allow the terminal to join the SDN network. Otherwise, IP packets carrying Options are resent to C0, which realizes terminal access to the SDN network after the operation of the authentication stage.

5   Experimental Analysis

5.1   Experimental Environment

In this paper, we use Mininet to simulate the network environment and conduct related experiments. In this experiment, a virtual network topology of one Floodlight controller node, three OpenvSwitch switches, two P4 forwarding devices and two terminals are built, and the experimental topology diagram is shown in Fig. 3.

Hyperledger Fabric is a modular and extensible open-source system for deploying and operating authorized blockchains. The data in Hyperledger Fabric only allows different institutions in the system to read, write and send transactions. It is characterized by fast transaction speed, partial decentralization, strong controllability and low transaction costs. This paper builds a terminal access control prototype based on Hyperledger Fabric.

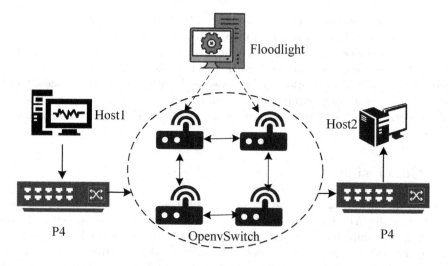

Fig. 3. Network Topology

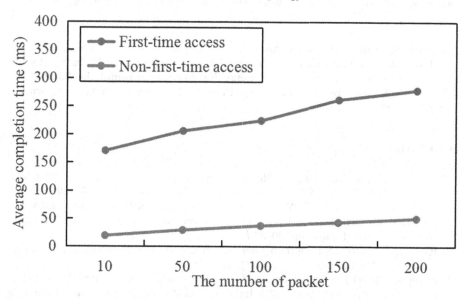

Fig. 4. Average completion time comparison for first-time access and non-first-time access

5.2   Time Overhead for Terminal First Access and Non-first Access

In our solution, there are two scenarios for secure access to the SDN network for terminals: first-time access and non-first-time access. As described in Sect. 4, we simulate the process of terminal first and non-first access to the SDN network, and we test the time overhead for both cases separately, which is shown in Fig. 4.

As can be seen from Fig. 4, in the case of first-time access, the average completion time of authentication for different numbers of packets is about 197 milliseconds. In the case of non-first-time access, considering the parsing of packets in the P4 control plane and performing Token authentication, the average completion time of authentication for each packet is about 35.6 milliseconds, which is less than the average completion time of first-time access. Therefore, the non-first access method in this scheme can make up for the time-consuming first-time access.

6   Conclusion

Due to the lack of an effective access control mechanism in the SDN network, we utilize the ABAC model for fine-grained control of terminal access to the network and implement the ABAC model using smart contract technology to make the access control policy and terminal-related attributes secure and reliable. In addition, we realize fast access to terminals based on P4 programmable technology. Through the above work, the security of the SDN network is further guaranteed.

Acknowledgments. This work was supported in part by the National Natural Science Foundation of China under Grant 62162018 and Grant 61861013, in part by the Innovation Research Team Project of Guangxi Natural Science Foundation 2019GXNS-FGA245004, in part by the Innovation Project of Guangxi Graduate Education YCSW2022296.

References

1. Sun, S., Kadoch, M., Gong, L., Rong, B.: Integrating network function virtualization with SDR and SDN for 4G/5G networks. IEEE Netw. **29**(3), 54–59 (2015)
2. Hu, Z., Wang, M., Yan, X., Yin, Y., Luo, Z.: A comprehensive security architecture for SDN. In: 18th International Conference on Intelligence in Next Generation Networks, Paris, France, pp. 30–37 (2015)
3. Kim, H., Feamster, N.: Improving network management with software defined networking. IEEE Commun. Mag. **51**(2), 114–119 (2013)
4. Jiang, B., He, Q., Li, X., Huang, H.: QoS control method based on SDN for mobile cloud service. In: 2020 IEEE 13th International Conference on Cloud Computing (CLOUD), Beijing, China, pp. 275–283 (2020)
5. Cox, J., et al.: Advancing software-defined networks: a survey. IEEE Access **5**, 25487–25526 (2017)
6. Chica, J., Imbachi, J., Vega, J.: Security in SDN: a comprehensive survey. J. Netw. Comput. Appl. **159**, 102595 (2020)
7. Porras, P.A., Cheung, S., Fong, M.W., Skinner, K., Yegneswaran, V.: Securing the software defined network control layer. In: Proceedings of the Network and Distributed System Security Symposium (NDSS) (2015)
8. Duy, P., Do, H., Nguyen, A., Pham, V.: B-DAC: a decentralized access control framework on northbound interface for securing SDN using blockchain. J. Inf. Secur. Appl. **64**, 103080 (2022)

9. Zou, D., Lu, Y., Yuan, B., Chen, H., Jin, H.: A fine-grained multi-tenant permission management framework for SDN and NFV. IEEE Access **6**, 25562–25572 (2018)

10. Kammoun, N., Abassi, R., Guemara El Fatmi, S., Mosbah, M.: A new SDN architecture based on trust management and access control for IoT. In: Barolli, L., Amato, F., Moscato, F., Enokido, T., Takizawa, M. (eds.) WAINA 2020. AISC, vol. 1150, pp. 245–254. Springer, Cham (2020). https://doi.org/10.1007/978-3-030-44038-1_23

11. Weng, J.-S., Weng, J., Zhang, Y., Luo, W., Lan, W.: BENBI: scalable and dynamic access control on the northbound interface of SDN-based VANET. IEEE Trans. Veh. Technol. **68**(1), 822–831 (2019)

12. Awasthi, C., Sehgal, I., Pal, P., Mishra, P.: Software-defined network (SDN) for cloud-based Internet of Things. In: Al-Turjman, F., Yadav, S.P., Kumar, M., Yadav, V., Stephan, T. (eds.) Transforming Management with AI, Big-Data, and IoT, pp. 185–213. Springer, Cham (2022). https://doi.org/10.1007/978-3-030-86749-2_11

13. Matias, J., Garay, J., Mendiola, A., Toledo, N., Jacob, E.: FlowNAC: flow-based network access control. In: Proceedings of the 3th European Workshop on Software Defined Networks, Budapest, Hungary, pp. 79–84 (2014)

14. del Rey, M.: Internet Protocol - DARPA Internet Program Protocol Specification. Information Sciences Institute University of Southern California (1981)

A Practical Detection and Defense Scheme Against Smart Contract Attacks Based on Transaction Features

Ruichi Yan[1], Guohua Tian[1], Shichong Tan[1(✉)], and Zhengtao Jiang[2]

[1] State Key Laboratory of Integrated Service Networks (ISN), Xidian University, Xi'an, Shaanxi 710071, China
yanruichi@stu.xidian.edu.cn, sctan@mail.xidian.edu.cn
[2] School of Computer Science and Cybersecurity, Communication University of China, Beijing 100024, China
ztjiang@cuc.edu.cn

Abstract. As a main component of blockchain technology, smart contracts support multiple functions and hold large amounts of assets, which makes them a target for attackers. Statistics show that attacks on smart contracts account for three-quarters of all attacks on the blockchain applications, causing huge economic losses to users of smart contracts. The existing research mainly focuses on vulnerability detection of contracts that cannot achieve real-time protection of deployed contracts. In this paper, we propose a practical detection and defense scheme against smart contract attacks. Specifically, We use an attack detection method based on transaction features to detect attacks using miner nodes and use the attack detection results as a consensus to block the executions of attacks and achieve real-time defense against attacks. Theoretical analysis and simulation results show that our scheme only requires a small increase in storage and computational overhead to achieve effective defense against smart contract attacks.

Keywords: Blockchain · Smart contract · Attack detection · Defense

1 Introduction

A smart contract is a computer protocol designed to disseminate, validate or enforce a contract in an informational manner. After a contract is deployed, it can be used by other users through transactions with the help of mobile wallets. At present, it has been widely applied in the fields of finance, medical care, logistics and so on. Smart contracts also exposed many vulnerabilities in the blockchain. Like ordinary computer programs, smart contracts have vulnerabilities, such as integer overflow, call injection, and reentrancy attacks. Since smart contracts cannot be modified once they are deployed and they hold a large number of assets, if vulnerabilities incidents in the contracts are exploited by attackers, they will cause incalculable financial losses. After The DAO attack, blockchain

I. You et al. (Eds.): MobiSec 2022, CCIS 1644, pp. 280–291, 2023.
https://doi.org/10.1007/978-981-99-4430-9_21

security became a hot topic, and various vulnerability detection methods have been proposed to improve the security of blockchain.

In previous research, the protection for smart contracts is mainly divided into two categories, offline analysis and online detection. For offline analysis, they mainly detect vulnerabilities in smart contracts through code analysis [1–5] and fuzzing [6–9], or find out the abnormality in the smart contract code through formal verification [10–13]. However, due to the lack of runtime information about the contract, offline analysis cannot guarantee that all attacks can be detected. Once the smart contract is deployed, it can no longer be protected. Online detection schemes usually detect attacks by instrumenting the Ethereum client [14] to monitor the operation of smart contracts [15–18] or inserting protection code into smart contracts [19–22]. However, since these methods need to insert extra code into a smart contract, they will increase the gas consumption of deploying and invoking the smart contract.

The essence of a blockchain attack is maliciously tampered with the state of the blockchain, and the state can only be changed through transactions. According to the analysis of attack events, the transactions that launched the attacks have unique features. Therefore, we choose to detect the smart contract attacks through the feature analysis of transactions. At the same time, to defend against attacks, we leverage miner nodes to detect attacks, and then use the detection results as a consensus to block the execution of malicious transactions, achieving an effective protection for smart contracts.

In this paper, we propose a detection and defense scheme against smart contract attacks. Specifically, our contributions are summarized as follows.

- We analyze multiple smart contract attacks to extract transaction features that cause the attacks and propose a real-time attack detection method based on transaction features.
- We propose an attack defense scheme based on hybrid consensus, miners are responsible for detecting attacks and preventing their execution, and stakeholders are responsible for defending against attacks.
- Theoretical analysis and simulation experiments show that our scheme can effectively defense against smart contract attacks with only a small increase in storage and computational overhead.

2 Related Work

Due to the openness and transparency of the blockchain system, smart contracts are subject to various attacks in recent years. Research on smart contract security is mainly divided into two categories: offline vulnerability analysis and online attack detection.

Offline Analysis. The offline analysis mainly uses static code auditing, usually used for security analysis before contract deployment. Oyente [3] is the first tool that use symbolic execution to automatically detect smart contract vulnerabilities. Maian [4] is a tool for specifying and inferring trace properties that uses interprocedural symbolic analysis and concrete validators to reveal real vulnerabilities. Securify [13] is a static analysis tool that detects vulnerabilities by analyzing Ethereum Virtual Machine (EVM) bytecode. ZEUS [10] leverages both abstract interpretation and symbolic model checking, along with the power of constrained horn clauses to quickly verify contracts. Mythril [23] uses EVM bytecode to detect vulnerabilities in smart contracts. It uses taint tracking and control flow graph detection to detect vulnerabilities in smart contracts. Vandal [1] is an Ethereum-based smart contract detection framework that uses an analysis pipeline to convert EVM bytecodes into logical semantic relationships to detect potential security vulnerabilities in smart contracts.

Online Detection. The online detection method is considered a supplement to the offline detection method. Cook designs DappGuard [24], which is a real-time monitoring and protection system. Sereum [18] is an online dynamic detection tool that uses dynamic taint tracking to detect reentrancy attacks in smart contracts. SODA [15] is a general smart contract online detection framework, which uses the method of instrumenting the Ethereum client to smart contract information, and provides an interface for vulnerability detection applications. Zhou et al. [25] proposes an attack detection and defense method based on transaction logs; in particular, they decoupled the attack into two parts, the action and the result, which analyzed the attack more clearer. ContractGuard [19] obtains contextually marked acyclic paths by embedding intrusion detection systems into smart contracts and then uses these paths to detect and defend against malicious transactions. EthScope [26] proposes a transaction-centric approach to detecting malicious smart contracts on Ethereum. It determines malicious behavior by replaying transactions and can detect six types of attacks.

3   Problem Formulation

3.1   System Model

The blockchain is a transaction-driven distributed ledger. Based on the general blockchain system model, our system model is shown in Fig. 1. The system mainly includes three entities: users, PoW miners, and PoS holders.

User: A user is a blockchain account entity with a balance. Users can transfer money and deploy or call smart contracts by initiating transactions.

PoW miner: PoW miners are entities that can verify transactions and pack blocks. PoW miners extract features of the transaction data flow during the trans- action execution and then detect whether the transaction is malicious according to the attack detection rules.

PoS holder: A PoS holder is an entity that validates a candidate block. A PoS holder obtains the right to validate a block and vote on it during a window period by staking a certain number of tokens.

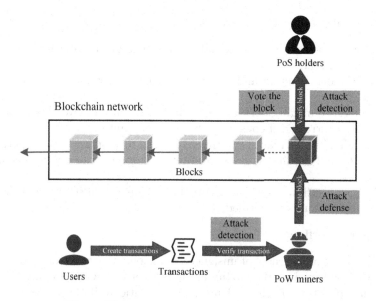

Fig. 1. The system model of proposed scheme

3.2 Threat Model

Blockchain users may use vulnerabilities in smart contracts to launch attacks and illegally steal access to contracts or assets. Miner nodes use their computing resources to verify transactions and create blocks, thus contributing to the proper functioning of the blockchain. However, miner nodes may collude with attackers or act as attackers to modify malicious transactions within blocks, leading to attacks. Therefore, the adversary model considered in the scenarios includes malicious users and miners.

Malicious users: As the party with the power to initiate transactions on the blockchain, a malicious user may attack the vulnerable contract to steal contract privileges or assets. Due to some internal or external factors, it may also interfere with the services of the smart contract and cause it to become unavailable.

Malicious miners: First, miners have the power to verify transactions and create blocks, so miners may intentionally tamper with transactions to their benefit. Second, miners may collude with attackers to encapsulate malicious transactions into the block as valid transactions, so that the malicious transactions in the block can be validated after the block is confirmed, resulting in an attack.

4 Feature-Based Attack Detection Method

For different smart contract attacks, we design a feature-based attack detection method. We analyze the features of attacks and design the detection rules for these attacks based on their features.

Reentrancy Attack

- Cyclic calls occur in an external transaction or in internal transactions between contracts;
- With the same function and parameters, same contract call occurs multiple times;
- The difference in call depth between the same contract calls is the same;
- The same contract call consumes the same amount of gas;
- As the call depth increases, continuous storage read operations are performed, and as the call depth decreases, continuous storage write operations are performed;
- An integer overflow occurs in the arithmetic operation in the contract when a write operation is performed.

Integer Overflow

- For the addition overflow of unsigned operations, the result of the arithmetic operation is less than the maximum number of the two operands;
- For multiplication overflow of unsigned operations, if the multiplicand and the multiplier are not zero, the result of the arithmetic operation is less than the maximum of the two operands;
- For the subtraction overflow of unsigned operations, the subtrahend of the arithmetic operation is greater than the minuend.

Short Address Attack

- Get the first 4 bytes of the transaction input data and determine whether the transaction calls the *transfer* or *transferFrom* function;
- Get the length of the input data of the transaction. For the transaction calling the *transfer* function, check whether the length of the input data is less than 68 bytes (function identifier of 4 bytes, destination address of 32 bytes, transfer amount of 32 bytes). For the transaction calling the *transferFrom* function, check whether the length of the input data is less than 100 bytes (function identifier of 4 bytes, token sender address of 32 bytes, destination address of 32 bytes, 32 characters The transfer amount of the section). Finally output the detection result.

Denial of Service

- For bidding smart contracts, check whether the bidder is a contract user;
- Detect whether the external call of the bidding smart contract is an insecure call method, such as *transfer* or *call* method;
- Detect whether the logic of the *fallback* function of the contract account is equivalent to the *revert* function. For example, the source code of the *fallback* function includes the *revert* function or an infinite loop judgment condition.

5   The Proposed Scheme

5.1   Scheme Overview

We design a feature-based attack detection method and propose a hybrid consensus-based attack defense scheme. Figure 2 shows the workflow of our scheme.

For attack defense, our scheme can be divided into two layers. In the first layer, when miners discover a malicious transaction during the transaction validation phase, they can block the execution of the transaction while sealing the block. In the second layer, if a miner node is malicious, it may intentionally pack malicious transactions into a block. Therefore, the PoS holders need to verify the transactions in the block again and then vote to reach a consensus based on the verification result, thus achieving a defense against the malicious miner.

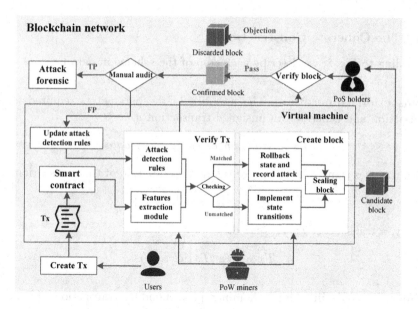

Fig. 2. The workflow of proposed scheme

5.2   Definition of the Scheme

Our scheme consists of the following six algorithms.

– **Setup**$(\lambda) \to pp$: Given a security parameter λ, and output the initialization parameter pp of the blockchain system.

- **KeyGen**(pp)→ $\{sk, pk\}$: Given the security parameter pp, a user can get the public and private key pair $\{pk_i, sk_i\}$, the private key sk_i is used for signature $\pi \leftarrow Sign_{sk_i}(Hash(M))$, where $Hash(M)$ is the signed message digest, and the public key pk_i is used for signature verification.
- **NewTx**(uTx, sk_i)→ Tx: The user inputs the unsigned transaction uTx and the private key sk_i, outputs the transaction Tx and broadcasts it.
- **VerifyTx**(Tx)→ $\{1/0\}$: PoW miner selects transactions set $\{Tx_0, Tx_1, ... Tx_{n-1}\}$ from the transaction pool and verifies them.
- **NewBlock**($Txs, root, nonce, t, ...$)→ B: The transactions are divided into two categories according to the verification result. Then the miner seal a candidate block B and broadcast to the blockchain network for verification.
- **VerifyBlock**(B)→ $\{1/0\}$: After the candidate block B is broadcast to the network, PoS holders first verify the proof-of-work of the candidate block and then similarly apply the same transaction verification method to verify each transaction in the block.

5.3   The Concrete Construction

According to Fig. 2, we describe each step of the scheme in detail.

Transaction Generation. The user fills in the parameters required for the transaction and generates an unsigned transaction uTx.

$$uTx \leftarrow (to, \ nonce, \ value, \ ..., \ data)$$

Then the user signs uTx to ensure the non-repudiation of the transaction.

$$\pi \leftarrow Sign_{sk_i}(Hash(uTx))$$

Finally, a transaction Tx is created.

$$Tx \leftarrow NewTx(uTx, \ \pi)$$

Transaction Verification. A miner picks pending transactions $\{Tx_0, Tx_1, ..., Tx_{N-1}\}$ from the transaction pool, for each transaction Tx_i while executing the transaction in the blockchain virtual machine, extract the data flow information of the transaction, and then match the features according to the attack detection rules, and finally output the detection result.

$$VerifyTx(Tx_i) \rightarrow \{1/0\}$$

Block Generation. After miners complete the transaction verification, the transaction will be decided as a benign or malicious transaction. When the block is confirmed, benign transactions will take effect and change the state of the blockchain and malicious transactions will be aborted by miners and rolled back. At the same time, the miner will record the failure in the transaction receipt and deduct the transaction fee, which prevents the attack from happening. For recording attacks and forensics, miners need to record the attack evidence e in the extraData field in the block header, including the location $index$ of the malicious transaction in the transaction tree and the attack $type$, that is $e \leftarrow \{index, type\}$.

Block Verification. PoS holders first need to verify whether the proof of work of the candidate block is correct, and then verify the transactions in the block. When all verification results are the same as that of the miner, the PoS holders will consider the block valid and vote to add the block to the blockchain ledger.

6 Security Analysis

In this section, we discuss the security of our scheme in the threat model described in Sect. 3.

For malicious users, they can conduct malicious transactions by constructing special parameters. When a transaction enters the transaction pool, miners first verify the legitimacy of the transaction, and detect whether the transaction is malicious according to the attack detection rules, realizing the first layer of defense against malicious users. In addition, after the miners seal the block, the PoS holders will verify the legality and security of the transactions in the block for the second time. If there is a malicious transaction, the block will be discarded directly, thus achieving a second layer of defense against malicious users. In this two-tier detection model, a malicious user must break through both the PoW and PoS, otherwise it is almost impossible to achieve an attack.

For malicious miners, they can encapsulate malicious transactions from malicious users into blocks or intentionally sequence transactions within blocks for illicit gain. When a candidate block is broadcasted, PoS holders have the right to second-validate the transactions within the block and vote to prevent blocks with malicious transactions or unreasonable ordering from being added to the main ledger. Thus, the ultimate defense against malicious miners and protection against smart contracts is achieved.

From the analysis, it can be seen that the hybrid consensus-based mechanism can improve the difficulty of attacks and can effectively defend against attacks and protect the security of smart contracts.

7 Theoretical Analysis

In this section, we compare storage overhead and computational overhead of our scheme with the original blockchain system. For clarity, we explain the meaning of symbols used in subsequent sections: N, Number of transaction in a block ; n, Number of malicious transaction; $|e|$, Length of the attack evidence; $|r|$, Length of the transaction receipt; $|tx|$, Length of the transactions; $|hd|$, Length of block header; H, Cost of Hash algorithm; ad, Cost of attack detection; $Sign$, Cost of sign algorithm; Ver, Cost of Signature verification algorithm.

7.1 Storage Overheads

Table 1 summarizes the storage overheads of our scheme and the original blockchain. It can be seen that the transactions executed in the blockchain are the same size.

Table 1. Comparisons of storage overhead

Scenarios	Transaction	Block
Original	$N \times (|tx| + |r|)$	$N \times |tx| + |hd|$
Ours	$N \times (|tx| + |r|)$	$N \times |tx| + |hd| + n \times |e|$

In our scheme, in addition to the data stored in the block header, additional space of $n \times e$ size needs to be opened in the block header to store malicious transaction information, where $0 \leq n \leq N$, e is stored in the block header. e's fixed size is 4 bytes, of which 2 bytes record the index of the malicious transaction in the transaction tree, and the other 2 bytes record the attack type. In terms of storage overhead, compared to the fixed size of 508 bytes for the block header, single attack evidence e only occupies 4 bytes, and the total occupied space is related to the number of malicious transactions n in the block. If there are no malicious transactions in the N transactions, that is, $n = 0$, the storage overhead of the proposed scheme is the same as the original blockchain system.

7.2 Computation Overheads

The computational overheads of each stage are compared in Table 2.

Table 2. Comparisons of computation overhead

Scenarios	Transaction Verification	Block Generation	Block verification
Original	$N \times Ver$	$(2N - 1)H$	$2N \times H + N \times Ver$
Ours	$N \times (Ver + ad)$	$(2N - 1)H$	$2N \times H + N \times (Ver + ad)$

In the transaction verification stage, compared to the original blockchain system, our scheme needs to perform feature extraction and attack detection on the data flow information of N transactions, so an additional $N \times ad$ calculation is required to verify the transactions, where ad is the attack detection calculation. The block verification phase is the same as the transaction validation phase, where the PoS holder first needs to verify the proof of work of the block by hashing and then perform a secondary validation of the transactions within the block, thus also adding $N \times ad$ computational overhead compared to the original blockchain system.

8 Experiments

To test the performance of our scheme, we built an original blockchain system and a blockchain system embedded in our scheme under the same conditions, and then performed the same test by creating some smart contract and transactions on both systems. Our experiments are run separately on Windows 10 with a 1.60 GHz Intel Core i5-8265U CPU and 8GB memory using Python 3.7.3.

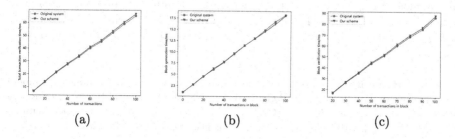

Fig. 3. Computational overhead between our scheme and the original system

As shown in Fig. 3(a), in the transaction verification stage. Compared with the original system, the growth trend of computational overhead is consistent, and the computational overhead of our scheme is negligible, only an increase of 2.2%. However, these calculations are all done by the miners' local computing resources and will not occupy the computing resources of the blockchain system.

In the block generation phase, our scheme uses the same block generation method as the original system, so the computational overhead is essentially the same for the same batch of transactions. As shown in Fig. 3(b), as the number of transactions within a block increases, the time to generate the block also increases, and the overhead of our scheme is consistent with the original system.

Figure 3(c) shows the computational overhead of block verification phase. It is easy to see a slight increase in the total computational overhead of the block verification phase compared to the transaction verification phase for the same number of transactions. Specifically, for the validation of a single transaction, the verification time is still in the order of milliseconds. Compared to the original blockchain system, the computational overhead of the block verification phase of our scheme increases by approximately 2.2%, and as PoS holders are a minority in the blockchain network, this increase in computational overhead hardly affects the overall efficiency of the blockchain system.

According to the analysis above, our scheme can protect smart contracts on the blockchain and realizes real-time defense against attacks with only a little increase in storage and computational overhead. The extra computational overhead of our scheme is all in the order of milliseconds, which is almost negligible compared to the 15 s out of the block.

9   Conclusion

In this paper, we design an attack detection method based on transaction features, then use the power of miner nodes to detect attacks, and abort the execution of attacks while sealing the block. Meanwhile, to defend against malicious miners, we propose a defense scheme based on hybrid consensus. When a candidate block is broadcasted by the miner, the PoS holders must verify the candidate block and vote to add the block to the blockchain ledger based on the block verification result, achieving a double defense against malicious miners and malicious transactions. Finally, we perform theoretical analysis and simulation experiments on our scheme and demonstrate that our scheme can effectively defend against attacks on the smart contract with low storage and computation overheads.

Acknowledgment. This work is supported by the Key Research and Development Program of Shaanxi (No. 2020ZDLGY08-03) and the Fundamental Research Funds for the Central Universities (No. ZDRC2204), Beijing Municipal Natural Science Foundation (M22002, 4212019), National Natural Science Foundation of China (621 72005).

References

1. Brent, L., et al.: Vandal: a scalable security analysis framework for smart contracts. arXiv preprint arXiv:1809.03981 (2018)
2. Chen, W., Zheng, Z., Cui, J., Ngai, E., Zheng, P., Zhou, Y.: Detecting ponzi schemes on ethereum: towards healthier blockchain technology. In: Proceedings of the 2018 World Wide Web Conference, pp. 1409–1418 (2018)
3. Luu, L., Chu, D.H., Olickel, H., Saxena, P., Hobor, A.: Making smart contracts smarter. In Proceedings of the 2016 ACM SIGSAC Conference on Computer and Communications Security, pp. 254–269 (2016)
4. Nikolić, I., Kolluri, A., Sergey, I., Saxena, P., Hobor, A.: Finding the greedy, prodigal, and suicidal contracts at scale. In: Proceedings of the 34th Annual Computer Security Applications Conference, pp. 653–663 (2018)
5. Torres, C.F., Schütte, J., State, R.: Osiris: Hunting for integer bugs in ethereum smart contracts. In: Proceedings of the 34th Annual Computer Security Applications Conference, pp. 664–676 (2018)
6. He, J., Balunović, M., Ambroladze, N., Tsankov, P., Vechev, M.: Learning to fuzz from symbolic execution with application to smart contracts. In: Proceedings of the 2019 ACM SIGSAC Conference on Computer and Communications Security, pp. 531–548 (2019)
7. Jiang, B., Liu, Y., Chan, W.K.: Contractfuzzer: fuzzing smart contracts for vulnerability detection. In: 2018 33rd IEEE/ACM International Conference on Automated Software Engineering (ASE), pp. 259–269. IEEE (2018)
8. Nguyen, T.D., Pham, L.H., Sun, J., Lin, Y., Tran Minh, Q: sfuzz: an efficient adaptive fuzzer for solidity smart contracts. In: Proceedings of the ACM/IEEE 42nd International Conference on Software Engineering, pp. 778–788 (2020)
9. Wüstholz, V., Christakis, M.: Harvey: A greybox fuzzer for smart contracts. In: Proceedings of the 28th ACM Joint Meeting on European Software Engineering Conference and Symposium on the Foundations of Software Engineering, pp. 1398–1409 (2020)

10. Kalra, S., Goel, S., Dhawan, M., Sharma, S.: Zeus: analyzing safety of smart contracts. In: NDSS, pp. 1–12 (2018)
11. Permenev, A., Dimitrov, D., Tsankov, P., Drachsler-Cohen, D., Vechev, M.: VerX: safety verification of smart contracts. In: 2020 IEEE Symposium on Security and Privacy (SP), pp. 1661–1677. IEEE (2020)
12. So, S., Lee, M., Park, J., Lee, H., Oh, H.: Verismart: a highly precise safety verifier for ethereum smart contracts. In: 2020 IEEE Symposium on Security and Privacy (SP), pp. 1678–1694. IEEE (2020)
13. Tsankov, P., Dan, A., Drachsler-Cohen, D., Gervais, A., Buenzli, F., Vechev. M.: Securify: practical security analysis of smart contracts. In: Proceedings of the 2018 ACM SIGSAC Conference on Computer and Communications Security, pp. 67–82 (2018)
14. Geth. https://geth.ethereum.org/
15. Chen, T., et al.: Soda: a generic online detection framework for smart contracts. In: NDSS (2020)
16. Torres, C.F., Baden, M., Norvill, R., Pontiveros, B.B.F., Jonker, H., Mauw. S.: Ægis: shielding vulnerable smart contracts against attacks. In: Proceedings of the 15th ACM Asia Conference on Computer and Communications Security, pp. 584–597 (2020)
17. Grossman, S., et al.: Online detection of effectively callback free objects with applications to smart contracts. In: Proceedings of the ACM on Programming Languages, (POPL), 21–28 (2017)
18. Rodler, M., Li, W., Karame, G.O., Davi, L., Sereum: Protecting existing smart contracts against re-entrancy attacks. arXiv preprint arXiv:1812.05934 (2018)
19. Wang, X., He, J., Xie, Z., Zhao, G., Cheung, S.-C.: Contractguard: defend ethereum smart contracts with embedded intrusion detection. IEEE Trans. Serv. Comput. **13**(2), 314–328 (2019)
20. Azzopardi, S., Ellul, J., Pace, G.J.: Monitoring smart contracts: Contractlarva and open challenges beyond. In: International Conference on Runtime Verification, pp. 113–137. Springer, Cham (2018). https://doi.org/10.1007/978-3-030-03769-7_8
21. Li, A., Choi, J.A., Long. F.: Securing smart contract with runtime validation. In: Proceedings of the 41st ACM SIGPLAN Conference on Programming Language Design and Implementation, pp. 438–453 (2020)
22. Ayoade, G., Bauman, E., Khan, L., Hamlen, K.: Smart contract defense through bytecode rewriting. In: 2019 IEEE International Conference on Blockchain (Blockchain), pp. 384–389. IEEE (2019)
23. Mythril. https://github.com/ConsenSys/mythril, 2018
24. Cook, T., Latham, A., Lee, J.H.: DappGuard: active monitoring and defense for solidity smart contracts: active monitoring and defense for solidity smart contracts (2017). Accessed 18 July 2018
25. Zhou, S., et al.: An ever-evolving game: Evaluation of real-world attacks and defenses in ethereum ecosystem. In: 29th USENIX Security Symposium (USENIX Security 2020), pp. 2793–2810 (2020)
26. Wu, L., et al.: Ethscope: a transaction-centric security analytics framework to detect malicious smart contracts on ethereum. arXiv preprint arXiv:2005.08278 (2020)

A Blockchain-Based Framework for Audio Copyright Deposition

Ridong Huang, Jianmao Xiao[✉], Jing Zhao, Jiangyu Wang, Yuhang Zhang, Siqi Chen, Jianyu Zou, Yuanlong Cao, and Youliang Ma

Jiangxi Normal University, Nanchang, Jiangxi 330027, China
jm_xiao@jxnu.edu.cn

Abstract. Based on the defects of existing audio copyright transaction processes such as complicated deposition models, long periods of rights maintenance, and ambiguous benefit distribution, this paper mainly proposes a model of depositing audio with unique identification on a real and transparent blockchain. Based on blockchain technology, which is famous for its decentralization, powerful tamper-proof function, and smart contract, the model transforms the audio data uploaded by music owners into uniquely identified audio fingerprints using the audio fingerprint recognition library (Dejavu) in python. Through the signature of the user's private key and the confirmation of each node in the blockchain, it is finally uploaded and broadcasted to complete a series of tamper-evident deposition processes. In this way, based on the decentralization, traceability, and anti-tampering features of blockchain, the audio owner can transact directly with the buyer, and the process of defending rights is greatly simplified and has strong legal proof.

Keywords: Blockchain · Audio Fingerprinting · Hash Algorithm · Copyright Depository

1 Introduction

In the current information age, traditional music recordings break through the physical medium of distribution to be presented to the public in multiple ways. People can access music works released by music authors quite easily on the internet, thanks to the internet making the distribution of digital content less costly. The Internet has always been a double-edged sword. Although the Internet has enabled a higher level of distribution and development of digital products, it can breed considerable problems, with more ways and channels of distribution and lower costs for piracy. It is understood that the cycle of copyright registration by the Copyright Protection Center is generally about 30 working days. Since copyright arises from the completion of creation, registration of works is based on the principle of voluntariness, and most of the approval takes the form of examination, these three points have caused the inherent defects and shortcomings of the current work registration system, and its negative effects are increasingly apparent [1].

Blockchain technology has attracted a lot of attention in recent years. The root cause of why blockchain technology has such magic is its weak centralization, which makes all its users enjoy the true and reliable "right to know" instead of only a few people holding the core information, truly making information sharing and transparency. Blockchain technology is an emerging technology that relies on cryptographic methods to establish trust relationships in a distributed environment, and is an innovative combination of hash algorithms, asymmetric cryptography, timestamps, consensus mechanisms, and other technologies with features such as decentralization, collective maintenance, immutability, anonymity, traceability, and programmability [2].

Since the traditional copyright registration system has high costs, confusing registration procedures, and no uniform standard, blockchain technology can be introduced to promote the change of the traditional copyright registration system [3]. Here we propose the "blockchain + depository" model. The audio created by a music author is used to generate a uniquely identified audio fingerprint through the Dejavu audio algorithm. The tracks are uniquely identified by the key features of a frequency band of the audio. In combination with Hyperledger-fabric, a blockchain-based audio copyright deposition system is architected using a federated chain framework. We build an audio deposition model that is fast to confirm copyright, simple to trace infringement, and tamper-evident after deposition. After analyzing the experimental audio recognition, the dissonance matching accuracy, dissonance matching accuracy, song matching accuracy, and matching time can basically meet the requirements of this system.

The contribution of this paper is:

1. In this paper, we study the problems of today's online music copyright deposition and transaction process and propose a solution based on the blockchain audio deposition framework.
2. We propose a Dejavu-based audio fingerprint retrieval technique and analyze the algorithm from the principle point of view.
3. We design experiments to compare the audio fingerprint extraction method in this paper with the traditional PRH method to analyze its practicality and efficiency.

2   Related Work

2.1   Blockchain

With the rapid development of digital currencies such as Bitcoin, ether, and digital collections, the underlying blockchain technology is coming into the public eye. A blockchain is a chain of several blocks generated by cryptographic algorithms that are linked together in a complete block-like structure. A block organization is like a page in a ledger, where each block is filled with information and data. A distributed database system is formed within the blockchain, which is jointly maintained and supervised by multiple blocks, thus blockchain technology is also a distributed shared ledger. As a new technology using a new data architecture and calculation method, blockchain technology can check and store database information through a block-chain structure, generate and edit information using smart contracts, calculate and adjust data using consensus algorithms, and guarantee the security of the whole process by combining with cryptography technology [4]. Therefore, compared with other technologies, blockchain technology has decentralization or no-centralization as its core logic, with the characteristics of openness and transparency, automatic portability and real anti-counterfeiting, which can fundamentally solve the problem of trust crisis and value transmission [5].

There are many types of blockchain, private chain, public chain, and alliance chain, each of which applies to its field and also has certain limitations. Usually, a complete blockchain system consists of a data layer, network layer, consensus layer, incentive layer, contract layer, and application layer. Among them, the data layer encapsulates the underlying data blocks and related basic data and algorithms such as data encryption and timestamps, and the other layers also have their corresponding roles. Timestamp-based chain block structure, consensus mechanism of distributed nodes, economic incentive based on consensus arithmetic, and flexible programmable smart contracts are the most representative innovation points of blockchain technology [6]. The core technologies of blockchain include distributed ledger, asymmetric encryption algorithm, consensus mechanism, and smart contract, as shown in Fig. 1. Distributed ledger technology differs from traditional distributed storage in that each node of the blockchain is stored according to the blockchain. On the blockchain's asymmetric encryption technology, the transaction information stored on the blockchain

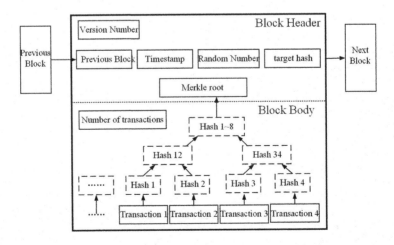

Fig. 1. Blockchain schematic diagram.

is public, but the account identification information is highly encrypted and can only be accessed with the authorization of the data owner, thus ensuring data security and personal privacy. Blockchain abolishes centralization because it has its unique consensus mechanism, which enables each node to reach consensus and has the characteristics of "majority rule" and "equality for all" [7].

2.2   Status of Digital Audio Deposition

Digital Music and Digital Music Rights. Digital music is a genre of music that is stored in a digital format and can be transmitted via digital media such as the Internet, wireless networks and cell phones. The quality of digital music does not change as a result of downloading, playing and copying. Compared with traditional music, digital music is a form of music production, creation and distribution based on digital technology, which is characterized by low production cost, high efficiency, easy storage and distribution, and personalization.

In the Internet field, digital music copyright, also known as "digital music copyright", is a micro-level category of digital copyright. Digital music copyright refers to a set of rights that a right holder enjoys for a certain period of time over a digital music work that he or she created or owns [8].

For digital music in the Internet era, the proof of copyright ownership is not so smooth, first of all, because orphan works are created in large numbers by the Internet. The so-called "orphan works" are those works for which the copyright holder cannot be found even after trying to locate them [9]. A typical "orphan work" is a musical work that is usually found with an anonymous author. The Internet has lowered the threshold of individual works creation and provided a convenient way and platform for individual works creation, but the lack of awareness of rights protection among some groups has led to a large number of "orphan works" flooding the Internet. They do not know the specific scope of the objects protected by copyright law and do not understand the legal significance of signing the works, so they upload their improvised individual works to Internet music service platforms for sharing, making it impossible to match the effective information of works and creators with a large number of anonymous digital music works, thus bringing certain difficulties to the determination of rights ownership of digital music works [10]. At the same time, under the existing copyright depository system, the copyright transaction process is too complicated, and the shortcomings of the long transaction cycle also bring difficulties to the digital music copyright transaction.

Analysis of Existing Copyright Depository Systems. Most traditional music rights depository systems such as Pandora, Spotify, etc. receive nearly 40,000 audio data uploads per day. Even with such a large system, there are still many problems with these centralized agencies hiding data such as song sales and download numbers, and charging authors a variety of fees in disguise. This is extremely unfair to audio creators, and it is quite common in today's music inventory systems. Therefore, there is an urgent need for a reliable, non-tamperable, transparent, and real decentralized copyright depository platform.

Sondrio player is a blockchain-based music platform whose main functions are music streaming, i.e., mining SoundArio DB, which will be mined and distributed according to the playing time. By sharing music, users can bring more play time to the author and will gain revenue themselves. Sondrio simplifies the music industry into 4 steps: upload, set the conditions, start streaming and get paid. It also has immutable visual data that is fair, transparent, and accurate, and users can view their DB balance and playlist earnings details in their digital wallets. They can also view song revenue and airtime, as well as their airtime and DB revenue percentages through the airtime log page. It is essentially a blockchain-based music community but lacks some legal proof. In contrast, the system studied in this paper has some credibility and legal proof due to the generation of an audio fingerprint with a unique identifier after the author has created the audio.

The literature [11] investigates the audio deposition model based on business chain and public chain, using business chain and public chain cross-chain anchoring heterogeneity to upload user data to the public chain (Ether) for deposition. The consensus mechanism is adopted based on the trust penetration model of 21given witnesses. This system uses a public chain. Although the public chain has high security, the public chain has a disadvantage relative to the fabric federated chain proposed in this paper, namely, the public chain is relatively slow in processing data. It cannot be adapted to the specific application scenarios of copyright registration and trading.

3   The Blockchain-Based Audio Copyright Deposition System

This paper designs a blockchain-based audio copyright deposition system using Hyperledger Fabric federated chain architecture. the transaction process of Hyperledger fabric refers to the consensus process of the ledger data by each node in the network. Different servers are configured as different nodes during actual operation, and each step of the transaction process is assigned to a different node, with each node taking on a different function, thus realizing the functions of each module in the system architecture. The system uses blockchain technology to achieve credible registration and authentication of audio copyrights and fast transactions of audio copyrights. The audio copyright is decentralized deposited and traded through the fabric smart contract written in the go language. The audio fingerprint is extracted using Dejavu-based audio fingerprint extraction and retrieval algorithm. The system operation flow is shown in Fig. 2.

Users can use this system for audio upload registration, audio copyright inquiry, audio copyright transaction, user asset inquiry, and other functions. The core of the system is the registration and deposition of audio copyright. The user uploads the original audio to this audio deposition system, the system calls Dejavu audio fingerprint extraction algorithm to store the original audio

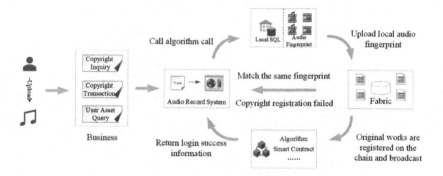

Fig. 2. System flow chart.

and the extracted audio fingerprint to the local Mysql database, and at the same time uploads the audio fingerprint to the fabric distributed database for fingerprint retrieval and comparison, if the same fingerprint is matched, the audio is copied and the registration fails, if there is no same fingerprint, the work is original and the registration is carried out. The user information and the audio fingerprint information will be registered and broadcast, and the successful copyright registration information will be returned to the user and counted as the user's assets.

3.1 System Architecture

The audio copyright deposition system is divided into four layers, data layer, security layer, business layer, application layer, and the basic architecture of the system is shown in Fig. 3 below. Users register their accounts in the application layer, and the security layer issues CA certificates to user accounts (digital certificates are the unique identifiers of user identity). The business layer is divided into three modules: user management module, audio algorithm module, and copyright deposit module. The user management module functions as user registration processing, user asset query, and audio copyright query. The audio algorithm module generates audio fingerprints and audio identification and retrieval. The copyright storage module carries out copyright registration broadcasts and copyright transactions on the blockchain. The registration and transaction records are automatically broadcasted on the chain by fabric smart contracts. The data storage structure and data organization of the system are based on the fabric federation chain architecture [12].

3.2 Business Layer

The business layer is divided into three main modules: user management module, audio processing module, and copyright storage module. The audio processing module and the copyright deposit module are the core of the system and carry out the main functions of the system. The advantages of blockchain technology

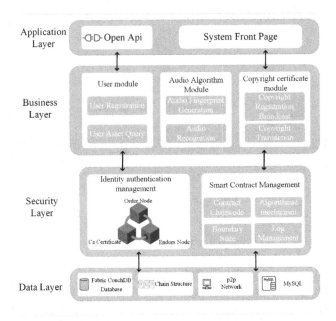

Fig. 3. System architecture.

can fully automate the registration and storage, transaction, and traceability of audio copyright, and decentralize the processing, which is safer and more convenient [13].

Audio Fingerprint Upload. The unique identification and retrieval of the original audio uploaded by the user is the key to the audio copyright deposition processing. After successful registration, user nodes can upload their original music works to the system for copyright registration. In this paper, we use Dejavu-based audio fingerprinting technology to extract and upload audio fingerprints, and the specific implementation process is as follows. The user needs to upload an uncompressed audio wave file. The system first samples the audio. In the uncompressed .wav file, the music is processed and encoded as a long string of numbers. Each channel is 44100 per second. This means that a 3-minute-long song has almost 16 million samples.

$$3\,min * 60sec * 44100\ samples\ per\ sec * 2channels = 15,876,000samples \quad (1)$$

In the case of recorded audio, the accepted rule is that we can miss frequencies above 22,050 Hz because humans cannot even hear frequencies above 20,000 Hz [14]. Therefore, according to the Nyquist-Shannon theorem (to recover the analog signal without distortion, the sampling frequency should be greater than or equal to two times the highest frequency in the analog signal spectrum), the number of samples is:

$$Samples\,per\,sec\,needed \;=\; Highest - Frequency \;*\; 2 = 44100\,samples \qquad (2)$$

Since the amplitude of the audio signal changes continuously with time, it is necessary to frame it, and by framing, the characteristics of the audio signal can be kept largely unchanged over time. For a long speech signal, the frames are divided, windows are added, and then the fast Fourier transform is done for each frame, after which the results of each frame are stacked along another dimension to obtain a graph (similar to a two-dimensional signal), which is the sound spectrum graph. Above, we can repeatedly use FFT (fast Fourier transform) in a small time window in a song sample to create a sound spectrum map of the song.

$$f(x) = a_0 + \sum_{n=1}^{\infty} \left(a_n \cos \frac{n\pi x}{L} + b_n \sin \frac{n\pi x}{L} \right) \qquad (3)$$

Its amplitude is a function of time and frequency. The FFT shows us the intensity (amplitude) of the signal at that particular frequency, If we do it enough times with the sliding window of FFT, we put them together to get a 2D array spectrogram with the horizontal axis indicating the time t(s), the vertical axis indicating the frequency f(Hz), and the value of the coordinate points is the magnitude of the audio signal. The maximum value, i.e., the peak point, is extracted to form the maximum value coordinate diagram. The frequency and time values are discrete, while the amplitude is real-valued. The colors show the actual values of the amplitude at the discrete (time, frequency) coordinates (yellow $\rightarrow$ higher, green $\rightarrow$ lower) as shown in Fig. 4.

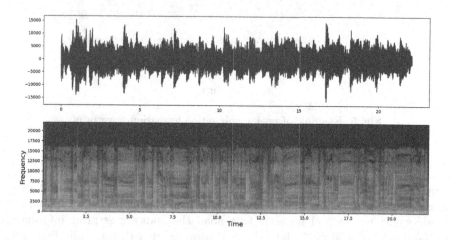

Fig. 4. Test audio sonogram and sound spectrum

After obtaining the sound spectrum of the audio signal, peak finding is performed. We define a peak as a (time, frequency) pair that corresponds to the largest amplitude value in its surrounding local "neighborhood". Other (time, frequency) pairs around it have lower amplitudes and are therefore less likely to survive in the noise. The spectrogram is treated as an image and an image processing toolkit and the technique is used to find the peaks, i.e. using a combination of filters (highlighting high amplitudes) and local maxima structures. Once these noise-resistant peaks are extracted, i.e., the peaks are found, the spectrogram is compressed and the processing of the data volume becomes more concise and intuitive [15].

The hash function is then used to make the combination of peaks form a fingerprint as shown in Fig. 5. A hash function takes an integer input and returns another integer as the output. The advantage is that a good hash function will not only return the same output integer each time the input is the same but also that a few different inputs will have the same output.

By looking at the spectrogram peaks and combining the peak frequencies and the time differences between them, we can create a hash that represents a unique fingerprint of the song.

$$hash(frequencies\ of\ peaks, time\ between\ peaks) = fingerprint\ hash\ value \tag{4}$$

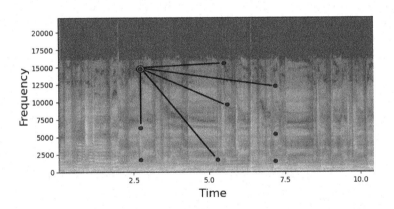

Fig. 5. Example of peak combination formation fingerprint

Copyright Deposit and Transaction. After getting the fingerprint of the user's original audio by Dejavu audio fingerprint technology, the system calls fabric smart contract chain code to upload the audio fingerprint information in the user's local MySQL database and compare it with the audio fingerprint information already stored in the fabric CouchDB database for retrieval. The copyright is stored in the blockchain ledger in the form of a transaction.

After the audio is judged as original, the audio metadata that needs to be uploaded by the user is (the song name, author, song file size, song duration, copyright owner ID), and the unique identification of the audio: the audio fingerprint information is corresponded to the song information data by the system in the form of key-value pairs. Also encapsulated is the block information such as transaction timestamp.

After the song information is successfully registered, it is automatically counted into the copyright owner's user assets (Owner. assets) After the copyright registration is successfully packaged on the chain, users can make copyright inquiries and personal assets inquiries. The core code of the copyright registration smart contract is shown in Fig. 6.

```
var audio = Audio{Song_Name: args[1], Author: args[2], Size: args[3], Time: args[4], Owner_ID: []string{}}
audioAsBytes, err := json.Marshal(audio)
    if err != nil {
        return shim.Error("Marshal error !!")
    }
    APIstub.PutState(args[0], audioAsBytes)

    return shim.Success(nil)
```

Fig. 6. Copyright registration smart contract code.

Users can transfer the audio copyright they own, i.e. the system can support audio copyright trading. The system uses the characteristics of blockchain, which is non-falsifiable and traceable and invokes smart contracts to realize copyright transactions between users. Compared with the traditional copyright trading process, the system is not only short, decentralized, and highly reliable, but also supports cross-border trading. Users can search for their favorite music IDs to purchase them, and the transaction is broadcasted through the fabric P2P network. For each completed transaction, the fabric blockchain will add a transaction record accordingly, and the record cannot be modified once the verification is completed and broadcast. The transaction record consists of the purchase user ID, author ID, transaction amount, copyright update timestamp, etc. The smart contract code for copyright trading as shown in Fig. 7.

```
func (a *AudioRecognitionChaincode) UpdateOwner(APIstub shim.ChaincodeStubInterface, args []string)
pb.Response {
    if len(args) != 5 {
        return shim.Error("Incorrect number of arguments. Expecting 5")
    }
    ownerAsByte, _ := APIstub.GetState(args[0])
    own := Owner{}
    json.Unmarshal(ownerAsByte, &own)
    own.Owner_Name = args[1]
    own.Upate_Time = args[2]
    own.Sex = args[3]
    own.Country = args[4]
    ownerAsByte, err := json.Marshal(own)
    if err != nil {
        return shim.Error("Marshal error !!!")
    }
    APIstub.PutState(args[0], ownerAsByte)
    return shim.Success(nil)
}
```

Fig. 7. Copyright trading smart contract code.

4   Performance Testing and Analysis

To verify the performance of the system, the test environment used in this paper is a Windows 11 operating system configured with a CPU Intel Core i7 2.50 GHz and 16 GB of RAM, and Ubuntu 20.01 installed on a VMware virtual machine.

The system has a total of three major functional modules, of which audio fingerprint retrieval is the core and most basic function, using the Dejavu-based audio fingerprint retrieval algorithm, which uses audio spectrograms for peak finding to generate audio fingerprints, using methods such as Fast Fourier Transform [16].

The Dejavu project has the advantages of high audio recognition accuracy, fast recognition rate, ease of use, etc. The audio fingerprint retrieval module of the system is tested next.

The experimental data set used in this paper is 60 songs downloaded randomly from the Internet, mainly popular pop songs, the song file type is MP3, the standard sound quality is selected when downloading, the sampling rate of the songs is 73.1 kHZ, the bit rate is 127 kbps, the average length of the songs is 3.5 min, and the file is converted to wav format in order to get the sound spectrum map of the audio. In this 60 music songs, each music extracted feature fingerprint data on the Mysql database consumes the storage space as shown in Fig. 1. The average space consumed for each of the 60 music tracks is about 19 MB as shown in Fig. 8.

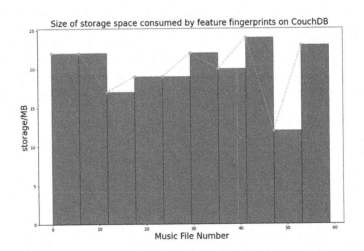

Fig. 8. Average space consumption per piece of music in the audio set

4.1   Audio Anti-interference Analysis

We examine the effect of signal amplitude change on the audio fingerprint. Let $y(t) = ax(t)$, $x(t)$ be the original audio, a be the amplification factor, and $y(t)$

be the audio after the change of amplitude. The experimental results show that the audio fingerprint extracted from the same audio is the same for any change in signal amplitude (a value is chosen randomly), i.e., the audio fingerprint is not affected by the change in amplitude. Next, we investigated the effect of noise on the audio fingerprint. 30s-long audio was randomly selected from the database and then superimposed with Gaussian white noise with different signal-to-noise ratios to generate noisy frequency data, and we counted different signal-to-noise ratios (the ratio of signal-to-noise in an electronic device or electronic system. The signal in this case refers to the electronic signal from outside the device that needs to be processed by this device, and the noise refers to the irregular additional signal (or information) that does not exist in the original signal after passing through this device, and this signal does not change with the change of the original signal) [17]. The BER of audio fingerprints at noisy frequencies was tested, and the experimental results are shown in Fig. 9.

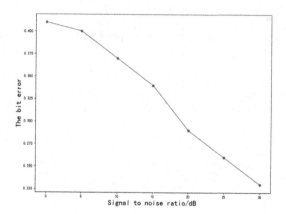

Fig. 9. BER of noise on audio fingerprint extraction.

4.2   Audio Fingerprint Extraction Time Test

The Dejavu audio fingerprint retrieval method used in this paper extracts typical energy feature points from the spectrogram and selects feature points within a certain region to form a feature point pair called music fingerprint (also called an audio fingerprint), and uses a hash query structure for retrieval, making the query overhead of constant order. The advantage of this method is that it does not need to retain the global information in the frequency spectrum, the feature point storage space occupation is less compared to PRH (Philips Robust Hash), and the noise immunity is strong, its disadvantage is that if the feature points are not selected to be representative, more hash collisions are generated [18]. From Fig. 10, it is clear that the fingerprint extraction method used in this paper consumes significantly less time compared to the PRH hash fingerprint method, which greatly reduces the user's waiting time and achieves the extraction of audio fingerprints with high efficiency.

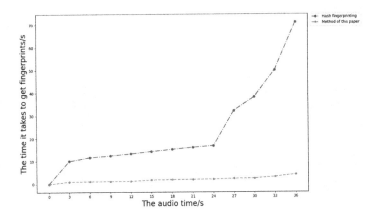

Fig. 10. Time comparison between audio fingerprint extraction method and traditional PRH method in this paper.

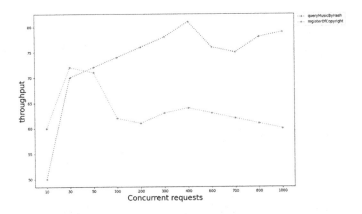

Fig. 11. Blockchain throughput versus transaction requests

Blockchain Transaction Processing Performance Testing. In order to verify the blockchain transaction processing speed and reliability, this paper uses the transaction volume per second as the judging criterion of the system throughput (TPS). The throughput of the relevant smart contract is calculated under different concurrent requests, and the number of concurrency is set to 10, 30, 50, 100, 200, 300, 400, 600, 700, 800, 1000, and the average of 11 experiments is shown in Fig. 11.

a) System throughput refers to the number of transactions that can be processed by the system per unit of time and is an important metric used to measure system performance. For online trading systems, system throughput refers to the number of transaction requests that are successfully processed and responded to per unit of time [19]. Calculation of the average number of concurrent users:

$$C = nL/T \qquad (5)$$

where C is the average number of concurrent users, n is the average number of users accessed per day, L is the average time from login to logout of users in a day (average time of operation), and T is the length of time examined When no performance bottleneck is encountered, there is a relationship between throughput and the number of virtual users, which can be calculated using the following formula:

$$F = VU * R/T \qquad (6)$$

where F is the throughput, VU denotes the number of virtual users, R denotes the number of requests made by each virtual user, and T denotes the time taken for the performance test.

b) The throughput of the system increases as the number of concurrent requests increases, and when the number of concurrent requests reaches a -certain value, the throughput of the system stabilizes because the number of connections in the blockchain network connection pool has reached the upper limit, but it does not affect the transactions of each node, and each transaction is completed in the form of a queue.

c) The throughput of the smart contract for copyright registration is kept around 65 and the throughput of the smart contract for copyright information query is kept around 70. Since the throughput of the audio copyright depository system can be stabilized at 66 tps with the draft algorithm, it is capable of carrying the practical application function of the audio copyright depository system.

In this paper, we build a music copyright protection and trading system including work verification, copyright registration, and copyright trading using fabric federated chain and Dejavu audio fingerprint retrieval technology, which has comprehensive functions and secure storage.

5   Conclusion

Music can bring people happiness and is a way for people to send their feelings. The rapid development of the Internet also brings opportunities and challenges to the digital music copyright industry. The blockchain-based audio deposition system designed in this paper can solve to a certain extent the problems of opaque information, long deposition period, cumbersome procedures, and excessive centralization in existing digital music copyright deposition and transaction. We propose a "blockchain + deposition" system, which adopts the Hyperledger

Fabric federated chain framework to extract the audio fingerprints of original music as the unique identification of audio and upload them to the chain, to construct an audio deposition system with no tampering, real and transparent information and high deposition efficiency. The feasibility of this method has been demonstrated. In the subsequent stage, we will continue to optimize the system and put it into practical application to promote the healthy development of the digital copyright trading market and the prosperity of the music culture industry.

Acknowledgements. This work is supported by Jiangxi Provincial Natural Science Foundation Under Grant No. 20224BAB212015, Jiangxi Province Science and Technology Project (03 Special 5G Project) Under Grant No.20224ABC03A13, the Foundation of Jiangxi Educational Committee Under Grant No. GJJ210338, the National Natural Science Foundation of China (NSFC) Under Grant No. 61962026, the National Natural Science Key Foundation of China Grant No. 61832014 and No. 62032016, the Natural Science Foundation of Jiangxi Province Under Grant No. 20192ACBL21031.

References

1. Ji, Y.: Problems of China's copyright registration system-also commenting on article 12 of the new copyright law. Publication Reference (3), 5 (2021)
2. Xinyi, Y., Yi, Z., He, Y.: Technical characteristics and model of blockchain. In: 2018 10th International Conference on Communication Software and Networks (ICCSN), pp. 562–566 (2018)
3. Tian, Z.K.: Innovative application of blockchain technology in copyright registration. Computer Applications Digest (038–010) (2022)
4. Yue, W., Junxiang, L.: Blockchain p2p network protocol evolution process. Comput. Appli. Res. **36**(10), 7 (2019)
5. Quluzada, J., Maharramli, S.: The development of blockchain technology (2019)
6. Yong, Y., Feiyue, W.: Blockchain technology development status and outlook. J. Automat. **42**(4), 14 (2016)
7. Yan, Z., Guohua, G., Di, D., Fei, J.F., Aiping, C.: Research on security in blockchain key technologies. Inf. Secur. Res. **2**(12), 8 (2016)
8. Mengyuan, F., Gongbo, Z., Tianchong, Y.: Exploring the copyright protection of digital music from a blockchain perspective. Indust. Technol. Forum **21**(10), 28–31 (2022)
9. Surhone, L.M., Tennoe, M.T., Henssonow, S.F., Plaintiff, Track, R., Park, V., Federation, A.R.: Victoria park racing and recreation grounds co. ltd v. taylor (2010)
10. Jianli, S., Xiunan, W.: Research on digital music copyright protection from the perspective of blockchain. J Shaoguan College (2021)
11. Liu, J., Liu, B., Peng, T., Jiang, D., Li, K., Chen, Z.: Blockchain-based audio copyright deposition model. Comput. Sci. **48**, 438–442 (2021)
12. Cai, X., et al.: Blockchain principle and its core technology. J. Comput. Sci. **44**(1), 48 (2021)
13. Tetarave, S.K., Tripathy, S.: PJ-sec: secure node joining in mobile p2p networks. CCF Trans. Perv. Comput. Interact. **3**, 13–24 (2021)
14. Holm, F., Hicken, W.T.: Audio fingerprint recognition system and method (2007)

15. Wang, H., Wei, J.: Research on fingerprint retrieval technology of music clips based on artificial intelligence recognition. Automat. Instrum (2019)
16. Wang, A.: An industrial-strength audio search algorithm.In: ISMIR 2003, 4th International Conference on Music Information Retrieval, Baltimore, Maryland, USA (2003)
17. Chang, S., et al.: Neural audio fingerprint for high-specific audio retrieval based on contrastive learning (2020)
18. Zhang, M., Ouyang, J., Li, Z., Liu, W.: A fast method for specific audio fingerprint extraction. Comput. Eng. (2), 3 (2010)
19. Exploitation, C.: Blockchain throughput optimization study based on improved dag and PBFt

A Trust-Based Blockchain System for Secured Migration of BLE Devices in IoT Networks

Erukala Suresh Babu$^{(\boxtimes)}$ ⓘ, Aguru Aswani Deviⓘ, and Bhukya Padmaⓘ

National Institute of Technology Warangal, Hanamkonda, India
esbabu@nitw.ac.in, {aa720086,padmajyo}@student.nitw.ac.in

Abstract. The Internet of Things (IoT) has gained popularity recently, leading in the rapid invention and enormous advancement of ubiquitous applications that are seamlessly interwoven into our daily life. Because privacy is becoming more important, questions about secure management and effective access control of IoT devices have gotten a lot of attention. Hacking BLE modules in devices that have previously validated a connection is nearly impossible. However, devices must first pair in order to connect, and this is where the fundamental risk of BLE-enabled systems lies. In this study, we focused on blockchain-based pairing of BLE devices in Bluetooth enabled IoT devices and proposed the architecture of a blockchain- connected gateway that adaptive and safely maintains user privacy preferences for IoT devices in the blockchain network. Individual privacy leaks can be prevented because the gateway successfully protects users' sensitive data from being accessed without their permission. In this paper, the seamless secured communication and migration of BLE enabled IoT devices is achieved by utilizing the full potential of blockchain technology.

Keywords: Internet of Things · Bluetooth Low Energy · Secure communication · Blockchain Technology

1 Introduction

The Internet of Things (IoT) is a term used to describe a device or thing that has embedded technology that can sense, communicate, and transport data from one network to another. The IoT ecosystem consists of many smart devices that can be connected amongst each other anywhere and anytime [1]. A multitude of architectures are available for defining the physical, functional and conceptual framework of IoT networks. [2]. There are multiple IoT communication protocols and standards for interconnecting IoT devices and the internet, including Wi-Fi, Bluetooth Low Energy, Zigbee, Satellite, NFC, and RFID standards. Bluetooth Low Energy (BLE), also known as "Bluetooth Smart," with the Bluetooth 4.0 core specification, is a lightweight subset of original Bluetooth. BLE-enabled IoT devices offer very low power consumption, encrypted data communication

I. You et al. (Eds.): MobiSec 2022, CCIS 1644, pp. 308–322, 2023.
https://doi.org/10.1007/978-981-99-4430-9_23

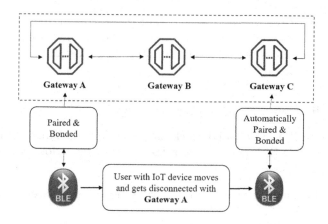

Fig. 1. Scenario of BLE-compliant Device Migration

with 128 bit AES, interference-free connections, reliability, robustness, faster connection establishment and data transfer.

The BLE-enabled smart devices are paired and bonded to its nearby gateway. When the device is in motion, it is disconnected with the current gateway and automatically paired and bonded with the gateway which is in its proximity. Figure 1 depicts this scenario of BLE-compliant device migration among multiple gateways. But, multiple challenges arise in BLE migration, as IoT devices are unmodified, the only option is to change the BLE implementation of gateways. Identifying the state variables, gateway selection while device migration, secure and fast connection transfer by withstanding the gateway impersonation. The BLE-compliant IoT devices can be hacked easily, so we have leveraged blockchain to enable security and privacy.

A blockchain is a series of interconnected blocks, where each block contains a collection of transactions. Each block's header includes the hash of the preceding/parent block, providing a link to the prior block. The genesis block is the first block, and it is the only one without a parent block. Many studies have provided the essence of blockchain technology for achieving IoT device security. The gateways for BLE-based IoT devices can be connected using blockchain technology for realizing security and privacy [14]. Motivated with the advantages of blockchain, We have employed the blockchain network for building the trust among multiple gateways by ensuring the security and privacy preservation of BLE-enabled IoT devices. While establishing the gateway pairing while device migration, the current gateway needs to establish a trust relationship with that untrusted/foreign gateway using the blockchain network.

Nowadays, privacy is a very big concern for every individual, we all want our data to be secure. Recently, IoT has gained so much popularity. But as we know privacy plays a huge role, questions about secure management and effective access control of IoT devices have gotten a lot of attention. Hacking these devices is quite impossible if they already have a previously validated connection.

However, the devices must pair first in order to connect, and that's where the fundamental risk of BLE-enabled systems lies. We got inspired from A BLE-based IoT gateway simulation with blockchain implementation and implemented our proposed scheme in NS3.

1.1 Contributions

We have designed a trust based blockchain system for secured communication among IoT enabled BLE devices. For achieving this, we performed the following contributions.

- Created blockchain network by registering the different gateway devices and BLE devices.
- Identified and authenticated the BLE devices before and after pairing.
- Performed a Secure communication among gateway and BLE devices using blockchain System.

2 Literature Survey

We have performed the literature survey on the existing works on secured communication and migration of BLE devices in IoT networks.

Table 1. Analysis of existing works on BLE Security

Ref.	Proposed Mechanism	Conclusion	Limitations	BL	GW	SE	ID	AU	RG
[3]	BLE Security Scan (BLESS) framework to discover BLE-Apps	At least 93 percent of these apps are found to be insecure	Application scope has some limitations	✓	✗	✗	✗	✗	✗
[4]	Smart contract enable gateway	Reduced risk of tampering with confidentiality	Higher computing complexity	✗	✓	✓	✗	✗	✗
[5]	Realistic blockchain based IoT architecture	Actors and interaction based framework	Not completely decentralized mechanism..	✗	✓	✓	✓	✗	✓
[6]	BLE capable mobile IoT gateways based forward secrecy	Improved connection migration security features.	No heterogeneous applicability	✓	✓	✗	✗	✗	✗
[7]	SCO mode based initiators & responders for mission critical BLE systems.	To combat security risks including man-in-the-middle (MITM) attacks.	Different suppliers may implement BLE protocols in a variety of methods	✓	✗	✗	✗	✓	✓
[8]	Secure authentication procedures based on master and slave impersonation attacks	Assaults are stealthy as the notification features of BLE-Are not enabled.	Role Switching and Mutual Authentication are both legacy features	✓	✓	✓	✓	✓	✓
[9]	Secured and decentralized communication scheme for wireless networks using BLE	The security and energy consumption issues of IoT can be solved with BLE-And blockchain	The security ensuring phases such as authentication and identification of IoT devices are not addressed	✓	✓	✓	✗	✗	✗

The seamless connectivity can be extended by enabling the communication among BLE devices and IPv6 hosts by tuning the lower layer of BLE stack using IPv6 over BLE. Table 1 presents the state of art mechanisms on BLE security and the notations used as **BL** for BLE, **GW** for gateway, **SE** for Security, **ID** for Identification, **AU** for Authentication and **RG** for Registration. We have considered these parameters, to indicate whether they are addressed in the literature or not. From the perspective of security performance, identification, registration and authentication are the mandatory phases through which each BLE device must undergo for ensuring the robust security and transparency.

3   Preliminaries of the Proposed Framework

3.1   Gateway Transfer Protocol

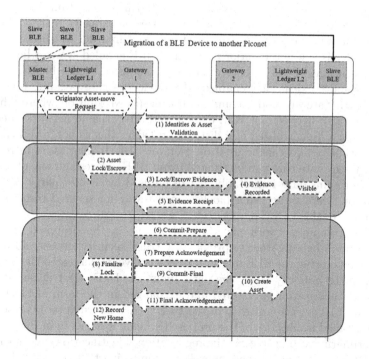

Fig. 2. Gateway Asset Movement Protocol

The pairing of BLE devices can be performed through Legacy connection Pairing and Secure Connection Pairing. We are using a gateway for secured communication among IoT enabled BLE devices. Figure 2 presents the gateway asset movement protocol among the BLE devices.

3.2 Assumptions for the Proposed Blockchain Framework

- There are three gateways: GW1, GW2, and GW3 (in real time, there could be more than three, but we're simply using three for demonstration purposes), each of which is already trusted and registered in the ledger's genesis block.
- Each gateway has a BLE device that requests registration to the gateway, such as 12 BLE1 requesting to GW1, BLE-A requesting to GW2, BLE-M requesting to GW3, and so on.
- The access to the blockchain network is controlled by each of the gateways, and BLE devices cannot access the global blockchain directly.
- The BLE device opens a secure communication channel with the nearest gateway and requests registration.

4 Proposed Framework

The proposed model work is described in detail in this section. In the present BLE module devices that are already validated hacking is nearly impossible. However, for validating the devices must pair first in order to connect and validate, and this is where the major problem of BLE-enabled systems lies. In all of the aforementioned cases, a better solution is required, and a blockchain-based solution would be ideal "IoT enabled BLE devices, a gateway, and a blockchain network with gateway nodes comprise the proposed solution where The gateway acts as a go-between for BLE devices and a blockchain network" because a blockchain is a decentralized and distributed ledger that is not governed by any central authority and can be used by everyone [10]. It may assist in retrieving previously sent data that can be trusted by all BLE devices and any other device because it retains data immutably, it can be used by a third-party program or organization. Here we're using blockchain gateway for secured communication between IoT enabled BLE devices.

The blockchain network plays a crucial role in the proposed framework. The blockchain-based gateways provide the trust, security, decentralization and transparency during the BLE migration. As we have implemented the blockchain network in the gateway layer, the data about the BLE registration, identification and authentication are stored and exchanged in the form of blocks of the blockchain [11]. So, the integrity of the BLE device information is preserved.

The detailed framework of the proposed scheme is depicted in Fig. 3, A gateway is primarily responsible for the registration, identification, and authentication of BLE devices in its zone, as well as monitoring their activity [12]. When a BLE device seeks registration from a gateway, it first checks to see if the BLE device is already registered by looking in the global ledger; if it is, it will contact the gateway that holds information about the BLE device in its local ledger. If it is not registered, one of the gateways with the privilege to create a new block will request the Static Variable data of BLE devices from all the other gateways, and the other gateways will send the required data to this gateway, which will combine its own data with the Static Variable data received from all the other gateways in a new block as transactions and send a copy of this block

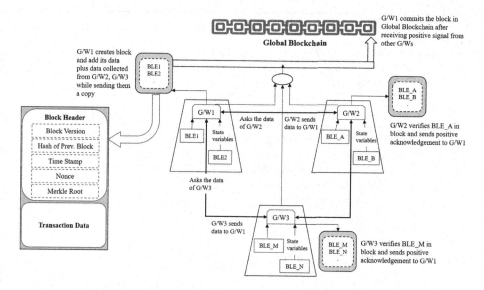

Fig. 3. Proposed blockchain System

to all the other gateways for verification before sending it to the main blockchain network to commit. When all gateways have properly verified the block, they recognise the gateway that created it with a positive signal, and the block is then permanently added to the blockchain network. All gateways will have their own merkle Tree containing hash values for various transactions, and as we all know, a hash value for the entire block is stored in the block header, which is known as the merkle Root Hash. Gateway generates this hash value by creating a merkle Tree of the Block, where all the leaf nodes of the tree are the hash values of the transactions in the block, and all the non-leaf nodes, including the root node, are the hash values of their children. If a gateway creates a new block and a new merkle Tree, the old and new trees are merged by creating a new root hash using the root hash values of the two separate trees. If a BLE device enters the range of gateway GW1 from another gateway with gateway GW2, GW1 will check in the global ledger if it is there or not, if it isn't there, it will register it, and if it is already registered, and GW1 requires more information about the device, it will request further information from GW2. It can't collect information about that BLE device by itself because it doesn't have access to the merkle tree of GW2, so it will ask GW2 to validate the BLE device.

4.1 Gateway Registration Process

Here we're considering gateway nodes, or gateways that are already trusted in the system, it's also critical to register gateways in the blockchain network (As presented in Algorithm 1). The process for registering the gateway is the same as for any other BLE device, with the exception that gateways will be

Algorithm 1. Registration of Gateways

1: **for** i in 0 to n **do**
2:     $key \leftarrow ECCGenerateHexKeyPair(3072 + i)$
3:     $ssk \leftarrow PrivateKey$
4:     $spk \leftarrow PublicKey$
5:     $signature \leftarrow (ECCSignString \leftarrow privateKey, a)$
6:     **if** $Verify\ String$ **then**
7:         $Print(Signing\ key\ pair\ Signatue\ is\ valid.)$
8:         $Transactionblank\ Block\ Data \leftarrow address,\ signature$
9:         $regismap \leftarrow blank\ Block\ Data$
10:         $usekeys \leftarrow ECC\ Generate\ Hex\ Key\ Pair$
11:         $usk \leftarrow use\ keys(private\ Key)$
12:         $upk \leftarrow use\ keys(public\ Key)$
13:         $a1 \leftarrow i + 1 + upk$
14:         $signature \leftarrow (ECC\ Sign\ String \leftarrow private\ Key, a1)$
15:         $Print(signature)$
16:         **if** $ECC\ Verify\ String$ **then**
17:             $Print(use\ key\ pair\ Signatue\ is\ valid)$
18:             $Transactionblank\ Block\ Data1 \leftarrow address,\ signature$
19:             $regismap \leftarrow blank\ Block\ Data$
20:             $Print(Registration\ Completed)$
21:         **end if**
22:     **end if**
23: **end for**

registered ahead of time and their credentials will be stored in the first block of the blockchain, known as the Genesis Block, while the credentials of BLE devices will be stored in subsequent blocks.

4.2   BLE Device Registration Process

A BLE device that has to be registered first creates a secure communication channel with the nearest gateway and then makes a registration request to that gateway. Similarly, BLE devices from various gateways send registration requests to their nearest gateway.

Now gateway will check to see if the BLE device has previously been registered, and if it has, it will request that the gateway from which this device has arrived verify the BLE static data. The reason gateway wants data from another gateway is that it does not have the data of this BLE device because it has not registered it in its local ledger. As a result, it requests data from another gateway. If it is not registered, one of the gateways will have the privilege to create the block on a Round-Robin basis, so it will request data from other gateways, then create a block by adding its own data plus data from other gateways as transactions in the block body part, and information like merkle root hash, previous block hash, and so on in the block header, and send a copy of that block to all gateways for verification purpose, the other gateways then validate

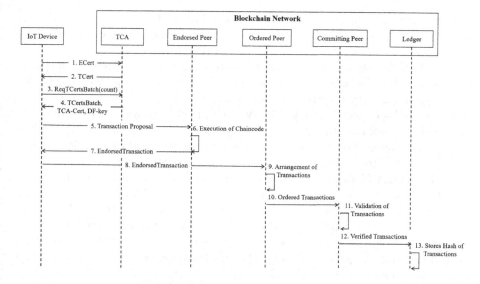

Fig. 4. Flow Chart of BLE Device Registration Process

their data in that block. And if their data is properly verified, they acknowledge the primary gateway with a positive signal, after which the block is eventually added or committed to the blockchain, and registration is completed. Figure 4 depicts the flow chart for BLE device registration.

5 Overall Registration Process

5.1 Assumptions

- Assume there are three gateways in them: GW1, GW2, and GW3.
- There is a BLE device in each gateway asking for registration to the gateway of that particular range, such as BLE1 requesting GW1, BLE2 requesting GW2, and BLE-A requesting GW3.
- All gateways will first check their Global ledger to see if this BLE device has previously been registered, and if it has, they will be able to request more data from one another. Assume that all of the BLE devices BLE1, BLE2, and BLE-A have not yet been registered.
- This time, assume gateway GW1 is a Home gateway and BLE1 comes in the range of gateway GW1.
- In the sequence diagram the GW1 is referred to as the Home gateway.
- In sequence diagram all the remaining gateways are referred as Foreign gateway.

5.2 Process of Registration

1. **BLE DEVICES ⟶ HOME gateway**: BLE DEVICE which enters in the region of GW1 asks for registration.

2. **HOME gateway** ⟶ **MAIN blockchain**: Home gateway sends the request to Main blockchain to assign the gateway of its choice of registration.

3. **MAIN blockchain** ⟶ **HOME gateway**: A message request response is send to all the gateways, but only the desired gateway will accept the response and all the other gateways deny it.

4. **HOME gateway** ⟶ **BLE DEVICES**: Home gateway asks for the static variables from the BLE DEVICEs and generates "blockchain Id, IPv6, Time Stamp" along with the public-private key pair and send to BLE device with Public key to verify and to pursue the pairing, bonding process.

5. **BLE DEVICES** ⟶ **HOME gateway**: BLE DEVICES has to accept the message and verify the "blockchain Id, IPv6, Time Stamp" using its public key. After the verification the BLE device stores the credentials in it's own storage, and also send the pairing-bonding static variables to other end so Home gateway can store the required pairing-bonding information along with the generated public-private keys and request HOME gateway to do further process.

6. **HOME gateway** ⟶ **FOREIGN gatewayS**: HOME gateway requests all the FOREIGN gatewayS to send their BLE DEVICE reg. requests.

7. **FOREIGN gateway** ⟶ **HOME gatewayS**: HOME gateway receives all the registration requests.

8. **HOME gateway** ⟶**BLOCK CREATION**: When HOME gateway receives data from other gateways, it generates a new block in which it stores its own static variable data from BLE devices as well as data received from FOREIGN gateways.

9. **HOME gateway** ⟶ **merkle TREE**: HOME gateway will generate the merkle Tree from the block's transactions, which will be kept in the HOME gateway's local ledger. The merkle Tree's root, as well as additional fields like as a nonce, block version, prior block hash, and so on, will be kept in the block header.

10. **HOME gateway** ⟶ **FOREIGN gateway**: For verification of their own data, HOME gateway sends a copy of the block to all the FOREIGN gateways.

11. **FOREIGN gateway (positive-acknowledgement)** → **HOME gateway**: FOREIGN gateways deliver a positive acknowledgement to HOME gateway after successfully checking the data in the block.

12. **HOME gateway (block-submission)** → **MAIN blockchain**: After obtaining a positive response from all gateways, HOME gateway will finally submit that block to the blockchain network, completing the registration process of the BLE devices.

6   BLE Device Identification and Authentication

6.1   Identification

Identification is a unique process of identifying each and every BLE device present in our blockchain network, so that we can perform further operations or perform secure communication.

- BLE device comes in the range of Home gateway.
- A Home gateway is a gateway which has the privilege to create a new block.
- Gateway checks the Main blockchain about its registration.
- Since every registered device has static variables stored in the main blockchain signed with the Private key of PUBLIC-PRIVATE pair Key, and every BLE device has public key of it so it is used to identify the data in the main blockchain.
- If verified successfully in the above step then it means the device is registered else we can say that the device isn't registered.
- If the BLE device is not registered then we register the device by BLE Registration (As explained above.)
- The whole process of registering the credentials of a BLE device in the blockchain network is called BLE device Identification.

6.2   Authentication

- BLE device comes in the range of Foreign gateway.
- An authentication request is send to the FOREIGN gateway which is signed by a private key.
- The gateway first checks the global ledger or main blockchain database to see if the BLE device is already registered.
- The device is already registered and the Foreign gateway requests other required credentials from the home gateways.
- Home gateway accesses their local ledger and retrieves the required details of the BLE device.
- Home gateway sends the required details to the current gateway.
- By verifying signed private key, if signatures are valid and the device is already registered it means the authentication is successful else it fails.
- This process of authenticating credentials of a BLE device in the blockchain network by the gateway when it enters a new gateway is known as BLE device Authentication.

7   Experimental Results

This section contains the results and that we used to determine the viability of our proposed work, we used the network simulator NS3 to construct the suggested Trust based blockchain system for secure communication among IoT devices. There are three types of nodes in the proposed IoT simulator, namely,

BLE nodes, blockchain nodes, and gateway nodes. In the proposed solution, we have simulated the IoT network for the BLE modules in NS3 using the libraries required for IoT architectures. Our proposed solution successfully completed all the objectives as mentioned below:

- To set up a blockchain network by registering the different gateway devices and BLE devices.
- To identify and authenticate the BLE devices before and after pairing.
- Secure communication among gateway and BLE devices using blockchain System.

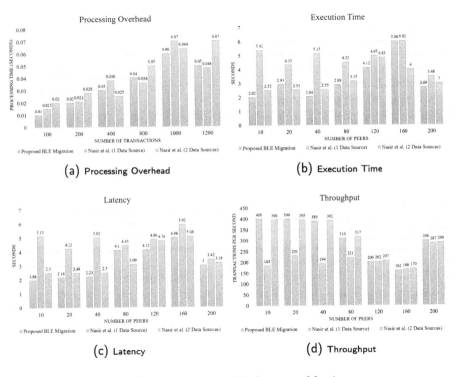

(a) Processing Overhead

(b) Execution Time

(c) Latency

(d) Throughput

Fig. 5. Comparison of Performance Metrics

We have created gateways (validator nodes) by using the application of BLE nodes. The stream of results are indicated in red font on the screenshots which are extracted from the results of NS3 implementation. The detailed implementation results are presented and described using (a), (b), (c) and (d) of Fig. 6 respectively.

(a), (b), (c) and (d) of Fig. 5 depicts the processing overhead, execution time, latency and throughput of the proposed scheme in comparison to the works in [13]. The analysis has shown that the proposed blockchain system is unique with BLE devices and gateways. In addition, we have achieved lower processing overhead, lower execution time, lower latency and higher throughput than the existing schemes.

Each application comprises blockchain code that conducts the output's operations when the code is executed. (a) of Fig. 6 depicts the process of creating genesis block where all the credentials of gateways can be kept. And How the gateways were assigned to BLE devices. It also depicts the address of BLE devices. The BLE generates a key pair and sends the public key to the gateway via the gateway during the registration procedure. The gateway and BLE-Agree on a format for the BLE registration request for signing keys to the gateway. The registration request from the BLE is received by the appropriate gateway. And the gateway confirms the request and sends a reply message to the BLE requesting confirmation. After confirming the transaction received from the gateway, the BLE device will confirm the gateway before registering the signing keys. If the gateway fails to add the block to the blockchain, the gateway will submit a registration request to the gateway (which is chosen at random in a round-robin fashion) to add the block to the blockchain. When the gateway receives fresh requests from other gateways, it will forward them to the other gateway in some agreed-upon format. In (b) of Fig. 6, the verification of signature is done using the generated shared key. As shown in (c) of Fig. 6, the registration of BLE devices is completed. The (d) of Fig. 6 shows the Secure communication among BLE to gateway to gateway to BLE.

- The master BLE device sends a data request to the gateway, which is signed by a private key, in order to obtain the shared key from another gateway.
- The gateway verifies the request with the BLE device's public key to authenticate it.
- If the authentication fails, the process will be terminated. Similarly, after authentication, the gateway checks its own local ledger to see if the device is registered or not, and if it isn't, the process is terminated.
- For secure communication between BLE devices, both gateways now generate a shared key. However, when it comes to shared key generation, there are usually two scenarios
  1. The Master BLE device and the Salve BLE device are both registered in the same gateway. In that case, the gateway signs the shared key and sends it to the slave BLE device directly.
  2. In this case, the gateway requests the information and sends it along with the shared key to all other gateways in the blockchain network. Whether the device is registered in their gateway or not, the other gateways validate and check-in their independent local ledger. The shared key is accepted by only the gateway in which the Slave BLE device is registered, while all other gateways reject it. The gateways then sign the shared key and send it to the slave BLE device.
- Both BLE devices use the public key to verify the shared key generated by gateways, and after that, both devices temporarily store the shared key.
- The Master BLE creates a message, signs it with a private key, and sends it to the Slave BLE.

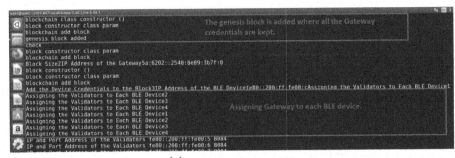

(a) Creation of Genesis Block

(b) Generation of Shared Key

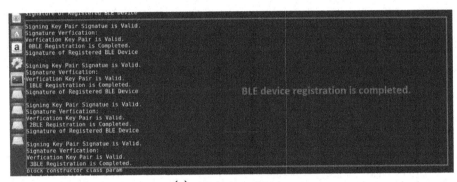

(c) BLE device registration

(d) Secure Gateway Communication

Fig. 6. The Sequence of Implementation Details

– The Slave BLE verifies the message with the shared key and responds by sending a positive acknowledgement to the Master BLE, allowing both devices to delete the temporarily stored shared key.

8   Conclusion and Future Work

Secure communication and migration of BLE devices in IoT networks is one of the major challenging issues which hinders the automatic bonding and pairing of BLE devices to nearest gateways. In this paper, we have addressed this issue using a trust-based blockchain system. The algorithms are presented for the registration of BLE devices and gateways, identification and Authentication of BLE devices. We have carried out the experimental result analysis and simulation of the proposed scheme using NS3. The main considerations of our proposed scheme is to experimentally prove the effectiveness of blockchain-enabled gateways in performing the secure migration of BLE devices. The results have shown that the proposed scheme is exhibiting the optimal results in terms of processing overhead, execution time and latency.

In the future, we will propose a trust-based blockchain network for secure communication of BLE devices using IPv6 over BLE technology. We will model this scheme to result in the optimal energy consumption and timely transmission among BLE devices.

References

1. Manogna Devi, M., Kirthana, K., Babu, E.S., Bhargav Raj. V.: A review on security issues and challenges of IoT. Int. J. Eng. Technol. **7**(32), 341–342 (2018)
2. Aguru, A.D., Babu, E.S., Nayak, S.R., Sethy, A., Verma. A.: Integrated industrial reference architecture for smart healthcare in internet of things: a systematic investigation. Algorithms **15**(9), 309 (2022)
3. Zhang, Y., Weng, J., Ling, Z., Pearson, B., Fu. X.: BLESS: a BLE application security scanning framework. In: IEEE INFOCOM 2020 - IEEE Conference on Computer Communications, pp. 636–645 (2020)
4. Lee, Y., Rathore, S., Park, J., Park, J.: A blockchain-based smart home gateway architecture for preventing data forgery. Hum-centric Comput. Inf. Sci. **10**, 9 (2020)
5. Fotiou, N., Pittaras, I., Siris, V.A., Voulgaris, S., Polyzos, G.C.: Secure IoT access at scale using blockchains and smart contracts. In: 2019 IEEE 20th International Symposium on A World of Wireless, Mobile and Multimedia Networks" (WoW-MoM), pp. 1–6 (2019)
6. Hussain, S.R., Mehnaz, S., Nirjon, S., Bertino. E.: Secure seamless bluetooth low energy connection migration for unmodified IoT devices. IEEE Trans. Mob. Comput. **17**(4), 927–944 (2018)
7. Zhang, Y., Weng, J., Dey, R., Jin, Y., Lin, Z., Fu, X.: Breaking secure pairing of bluetooth low energy using downgrade attacks. In: Proceedings of the 29th USENIX Conference on Security Symposium, SEC2020, USA, 2020. USENIX Association
8. Antonioli, D., Tippenhauer, N.O., Rasmussen, K: BIAS: bluetooth impersonation attacks. In: 2020 IEEE Symposium on Security and Privacy (SP), pp. 549–562 (2020)
9. Baucas, M.J., Spachos, P.: Permissioned blockchain-driven internet of things gateway using blue- tooth low energy. In: ICC 2020 - 2020 IEEE International Conference on Communications (ICC), pp. 1–6, June 2020

10. Suresh Babu, E., et al.: A distributed identity-based authentication scheme for internet of things devices using permissioned blockchain system. Expert Syst **39**, e12941 (2022)

11. Aguru, A.D., Erukala, S.B., Kavati, I.: Smart contract based next-generation public key infrastructure (PKI) using permissionless blockchain. In: Abraham, A., Siarry, P., Piuri, V., Gandhi, N., Casalino, G., Castillo, O., Hung, P. (eds.) HIS 2021. LNNS, vol. 420, pp. 625–635. Springer, Cham (2022). https://doi.org/10.1007/978-3-030-96305-7_58

12. Baert, M., Camerlynck, P., Crombez, P., Hoebeke. J.: A BLE-based multi-gateway network infrastructure with handover support for mobile BLE peripherals. In: 2019 IEEE 16th International Conference on Mobile Ad Hoc and Sensor Systems (MASS), pp. 91–99 (2019)

13. Nasir, Q., Qasse, I., Talib, M.A., Nassif, A.: Performance analysis of hyperledger fabric platforms. Secur. Commun. Netw. **2018**, 1–14 (2018)

14. Cha, S.-C., Chen, J.-F., Chunhua, S., Yeh, K.-H.: A blockchain connected gateway for BLE-based devices in the internet of things. IEEE Access **6**, 24639–24649 (2018)

Web API Verifier for IoTtalk and Its Applications

Wen-Yu Lin, Min-Zheng Shieh$^{(\boxtimes)}$ ⓘ, and Yi-Bing Lin ⓘ

National Yang Ming Chiao Tung University, 1001 University Road, 300 Hsinchu,
Taiwan
{rreexxllii0310.cs09,mzshieh,liny}@nycu.edu.tw

Abstract. With the vigorous development of Internet of Things (IoT) applications, many IoT applications based on IoTtalk, such as EduTalk, ScratchTalk, and other X-Talk systems, have been created in recent years. Most of these IoT applications are developed using Web application programming interface (API) and thus enable web browsers to transfer data to applications. But in the development stage, unknown errors or unexpected results may occur. It is hard to manually design test cases to detect such flaws efficiently, and automatic testing tools often require much domain knowledge. This work combines Fuzzing technology to develop a graphical user interface (GUI) test system, Web API Verifier (WAV), for IoTtalk and X-Talk developers to automatically test their applications easily.

WAV integrates Swagger Editor and RESTler-fuzzer. According to the uploaded source codes, it generates the corresponding drafts of OpenAPI documents. By filling the several fields in WAV GUI, developers can quickly describe the Web API specification of their applications and build the settings required for the RESTler-fuzzer test. After the test, WAV provides a GUI displaying the file location and row number for each buggy function. With WAV, users can write API documents and test their IoT applications conveniently.

Keywords: Internet of Things · IoTtalk · Fuzz Testing

1 Introduction

The concept of the Internet of Things (IoT) was first proposed by Kevin Ashton in 1999 [10]. After years of development, many IoT applications, such as smart homes, smart farming, smart campus, and smart health, are proficiently collaborating with IoT devices and have increased rapidly. However, the data collected by IoT applications is quite sensitive and private to users. Steinberg pointed out that many people in their own homes could be monitored by smart home

This work was financially supported by the Center for Open Intelligent Connectivity from The Featured Areas Research Center Program within the framework of the Higher Education Sprout Project by the Ministry of Education (MOE) in Taiwan.

I. You et al. (Eds.): MobiSec 2022, CCIS 1644, pp. 323–337, 2023.
https://doi.org/10.1007/978-981-99-4430-9_24

devices [26], such as web cameras, air conditioners, and air purifiers. The medical devices in smart health are very sensitive to patients as well. Hewlett-Packard also found that 70% of IoT devices connected to the Internet are vulnerable to various attacks [9,11].

More and more physical objects can connect to the Internet of Things as IoT devices [21], such as refrigerators, automatic doors, fans, and air conditioners. As a result, researchers have started noticing the issues of IoT security. Many studies address various security issues in IoT, such as Prediction Model [29], Penetration testing [13], and CyExec (Cyber Security Exercise System) [23]. Ensuring the security of applications and services is crucial for users to trust and use the Internet of Things [21].

Developers often implement IoT applications on top of several application-level protocols and frameworks [1]. REST (The representational state transfer) [8] is one of the most popular approaches to building Web APIs [12,20] in applications. However, vulnerabilities in Web APIs can have hazardous consequences, such as sensitive data exposure, injection attacks, parameter tampering, and Man-In-The-Middle-Attack (MITM). However, there is still no efficient way to test web APIs in IoTtalk [15,16,27,30] and its applications, such as EduTalk [17] and ScratchTalk [28]. Therefore, verifying that the Web APIs are secure becomes critical. In this section, we describe the related work and then give the idea behind our approach.

1.1   Related Work

Nowadays, most cloud services, such as AWS and Microsoft Azure, use REST APIs to access their services. Meanwhile, OpenAPI (formerly Swagger) [25] has become the most prevalent REST API interface description language [2]. The OpenAPI specification describes how to access a service through its REST API. The specification includes the API's Uniform Resource Locator (URL) Rules, the methods used by the service, the request parameters sent by the clients, the responses from the service, and the response format. In addition, the open-source project Swagger Editor [24] is an online editor for writing OpenAPI specifications. The validator in Swagger Editor will display an error message on the GUI to notify the user if the user types any of the OpenAPI definitions wrong on the editor. After users complete the document, they can save it on their local computer.

Tools for automated testing of web APIs are just beginning to emerge. For example, RESTler-fuzzer (RESTler) [18], an open-source tool, is the first stateful REST API fuzzer developed by Microsoft, and its core technology is Fuzzing [22]. Fuzzing is a software testing technique that exploits software vulnerabilities by repeatedly sending different input values to an application to attempt to interrupt or crash the process of the target program. RESTler analyzes the OpenAPI specification of a web-based service and generates a request sequence to test the service through its REST API automatically. In RESTler, all input values sent to the application are defined in a JSON-formatted [4] Dictionary Settings File. After fuzzing, the client receives a response with a HyperText

Transfer Protocol (HTTP) status code, such as 500 - Internal Server Error, which is a bug reported in RESTler. However, setting up RESTler requires some knowledge about fuzzing and HTTP [7]. Hence, we propose Web API Verifier, an online platform that can easily create the OpenAPI documentation and set configurations in RESTler, to solve this problem.

1.2   Web API Verifier

In this paper, we propose Web API Verifier, a web-based testing platform, to provide a fast OpenAPI specification writing and user-friendly fuzzing environment, where users can obtain the corresponding OpenAPI specification draft based on the uploaded source codes. Users no longer need to find all APIs manually since Web API Verifier automatically parses the uploaded source codes and fetches all APIs. Moreover, Web API Verifier generates template specifications that are easy to modify. Web API Verifier also extracts important information from the hard-reading report files produced by RESTler-fuzzer. Web API Verifier stores this information into a database and displays it on the web GUI. Consequently, users can easily read the bug report on the testing report page. They can also view the corresponding API source code snippets under bug reports.

2   Web API Verifier Architecture

The Web API Verifier (WAV) subsystem (Fig. 1 (f)) is associated with a web-based GUI (Fig. 1 (e)). We will elaborate on the WAV GUI in Sect. 3. When developers need to test their X-Talk system, they execute the Initialization program (Fig. 1 (b)) in X-Talk Subsystem (Fig. 1 (a)), then upload a copy of the X-Talk source code via WAV GUI. Through the GUI, users upload their X-Talk source codes (Fig. 1 (q)), which will be stored in the WAV Subsystem. The WAV then generates a template specification for further modification on WAV GUI (Fig. 1 (e)). The WAV also provides a GUI for the users to set the configurations of the RESTler (Fig. 1 (j)) and start testing. During testing, the Test Engine (Fig. 1 (n)) acts as the X-Talk GUI (Fig. 1 (d)) and interacts with the X-Talk Event Handler (Fig. 1 (c)) via HTTP.

WAV Subsystem stores the uploaded source code in WAV File System (Fig. 2 (q)). The Specification Management Procedures (Fig. 2 (r)) is responsible for managing OpenAPI specifications. The Configuration Management Procedures (Fig. 2 (s)) support the CRUD (create, read, update, and delete) operations. The Configuration Management Procedures are also responsible for setting up the Compiler Config (Fig. 2 (k)). The Testing Management Procedures (Fig. 2 (t)) take responsibility for starting the test of RESTler-fuzzer (Fig. 2 (j)), getting the bug report, and searching for the source code. The Testing Management Procedures (Fig. 2 (t)) feed the Compiler Config (Fig. 2 (k)) into RESTler Compiler (Fig. 2 (l)), and RESTler Compiler outputs the Testing Config (Fig. 2 (m)). Then, the Test Procedure feeds the Testing Config into RESTler Test Engine (Fig. 2 (n)). Finally, RESTler Test Engine interacts with X-Talk Event Handler

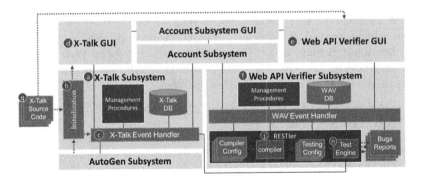

Fig. 1. The Web API Verifier architecture.

(Fig. 1 (c)) and generates the Bugs Reports (Fig. 2 (o)). The Account Management Procedures (Fig. 2 (u)) take responsibility for the management of authentication with the Account Subsystem (Fig. 2 (y)). When an unauthorized user accesses the WAV GUI, Account Management Procedures will redirect the user to the Account Subsystem GUI (Fig. 2 (x)) to log in.

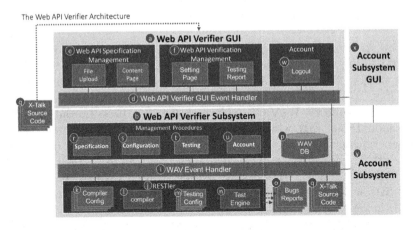

Fig. 2. The Web API Verifier GUI & Subsystem Architecture.

If the users need to test their X-Talk Subsystem as a specific role, they can provide the pair of usernames and passwords of the particular account. The Test Management Procedures (Fig. 2 (t)) will request the Account Subsystem (Fig. 2 (y)) to log in with the user-provided username and password stored in WAV DB (Fig. 2 (p)). WAV request the X-Talk GUI (Fig. 1 (d)) to get HTTP Cookies [14] that maintain the login state. Then, the Test Management Procedures use the obtained Cookies to set header information in the Compiler Config (Fig. 2 (k)) for later testing.

3   The Graphical User Interface

fWAV provides a user-friendly web-based Graphical User Interface (GUI), so users can easily check the API list in the uploaded source code and quickly perform fuzz testing.

In the IoTtalk ecosystem, users must log in to the Account Subsystem before they use subsystems under IoTtalk. Thus, when unauthorized users access WAV, they will be redirected to the login page of the Account Subsystem (Fig. 3). The new users need to register first by clicking the "Register now" link (Fig. 3 (d)). Otherwise, the users are required to fill in their username (Fig. 3 (a)) and password (Fig. 3 (b)) and then click the "Login" button (Fig. 3 (c)) to log in to the Account Subsystem. For the usage of other functions, please refer to the thesis about the Account Subsystem [5].

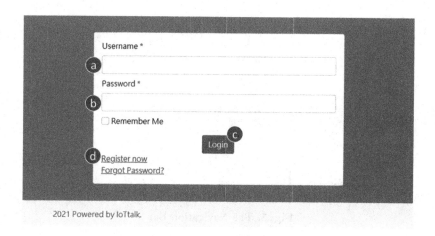

Fig. 3. The login page of the Account Subsystem.

3.1   The Navigation Bar

Users can see the WAV GUI home page (Fig. 4) after they log in to the Account Subsystem. The WAV homepage navigation bar has four components, the Logo (Fig. 5 (a)), the Specification (Fig. 5 (b)), the Verification (Fig. 5 (c)), and the Logout button (Fig. 5 (d)).

Fig. 4. The home page of the WAV.

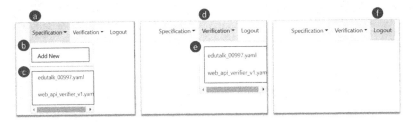

Fig. 5. The Navigation Bar.

- The Logo is a hyperlink that redirects users to the home page (Fig. 4) once the users click on it.
- The Specification (Fig. 5 (a)) is a pull-down list that, in addition to listing the names of existing specifications, also provides an option for users to upload their source codes to generate a new specification. Users can click "Add New" (Fig. 5 (b)) to upload their source code with the Files Upload Pop-up (Fig. 6 (d)). Then, users can click "Specification Name" (Fig. 5 (c)) to enter the content page of the specification. In the next section, we will elaborate on the content page.
- The Verification is a pull-down list that lists the names of existing specifications, and users can select these specification names (Fig. 5 (e)) to enter the setting page. We will give a detailed description of the setting page in Sect. 3.3.
- The Logout is a button to log out the current user. After the users click the Logout button, they are redirected to the login page of the Account Subsystem (Fig. 3).

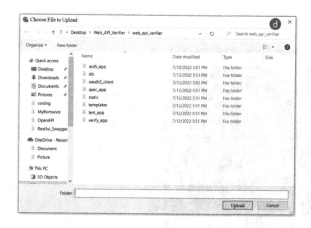

Fig. 6. The Files Upload Pop-up.

3.2 Specification Development and Management

In WAV GUI, Web API Specification Management (Fig. 2 (e)), called content page, provides functions including uploading source code, modifying an existing specification, and deleting a specification.

The content page consists of two buttons (Fig. 7 (b) and (c)) and the Swagger Editor iframe (Fig. 7 (d)).

In Fig. 7, the Specification Name (Fig. 7 (a)) specifies the file name of the specification in YAML [3] format. Users edit OpenAPI definitions in YAML format inside the Edit Area (Fig. 7 (g)) and preview documentation in Swagger-UI in real time. The "Save" button (Fig. 7 (b)) allows users to save the content once they complete their specifications in the Swagger Editor (Fig. 7 (d)). The Rename Pop-up (Fig. 8 (a)) will show up after the users click on the Save button. As soon as users fill in the valid string and click the "OK" button (Fig. 8 (c)), the new specification name and the content will be sent and stored in the database. Otherwise, users can click the "Cancel" button (Fig. 8 (d)) to cancel the save operation.

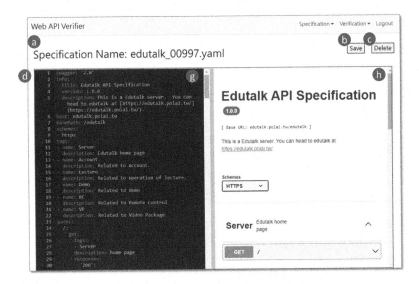

Fig. 7. The Content Page of the new Specification.

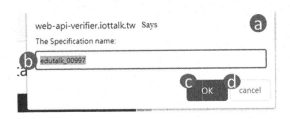

Fig. 8. The Rename pop-up.

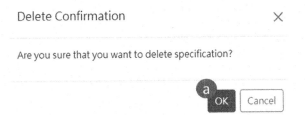

Fig. 9. The Delete Pop-up.

When the specification is no longer needed, users can delete it by clicking the "Delete" button (Fig. 7 (c)), and the Delete pop-up (Fig. 9) shows up. After clicking the "OK" button (Fig. 9 (a)), the users will be redirected to the home page.

3.3   The Verification Management

The setting page consists of the Configuration pull-down list (Fig. 10 (c)), the Test Settings Block (Fig. 10 (b)), and the buttons "save" (Fig. 10 (e)) and "test" (Fig. 10 (g)).

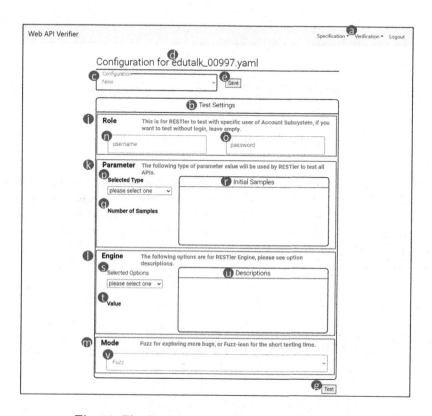

Fig. 10. The Setting page of the new Configuration.

A setting page maps to a specification with its name displayed at the top (Fig. 10 (d)). A specification can has multiple configurations. Hence, users can create a new configuration by clicking the dropdown list (Fig. 11 (b)) and selecting "New" (Fig. 11 (c)) or selecting an existing configuration (Fig. 11 (d)). The "delete" button only appears if an existing configuration is selected.

Here we take a new configuration as an example. Users will see the "Test Settings" block (Fig. 10 (b)) under the configuration dropdown list (Fig. 10 (c)). Test Settings has four blocks: Role (Fig. 10 (j)), Parameters (Fig. 10 (k)), Engine (Fig. 10 (l)), and Mode (Fig. 10 (m)). The "Role" block (Fig. 10 (j)) is for obtaining a Cookie of the system under test (such as EduTalk). Web API Verifier writes the Cookie into the Dictionary Settings File (Fig. 12 (d)) so that the system under test can authenticate the requests when RESTler is fuzzing. The username (Fig. 10 (n)) and password (Fig. 10 (o)) are the users that the system under test uses to log in to the Account Subsystem. For example, in EduTalk, different roles, including teachers and students, can log in with different usernames and passwords.

Fig. 11. The Configuration dropdown list.

The "Parameter" block (Fig. 10 (k)) is for setting up the Dictionary Settings File (Fig. 16). Currently, we support three types, String, Integer, and Number. The "Number of Samples" (Fig. 12 (c)) represents the initial number of samples expected by the users. The minimum number of samples is one, and the maximum number of samples is ten.

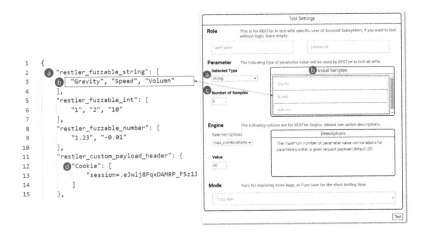

Fig. 12. The Dictionary Settings File and Test settings.

The "Engine" block (Fig. 10 (l)) is for the RESTler Engine Settings (Fig. 13 (d)). Many options can be set [19]. So far, we support the most common options (Fig. 13 (a)), such as max_combinations, no_ssl, and time_budget (Fig. 13 (c)).

- max_combinations is the maximum number of parameter value combinations for parameters within a given request payload.

- no_ssl indicates to disable SSL or not for requests.
- time_budget means that once this time is reached, the RESTler will stop. The units are hours.

The descriptions of the options will be displayed on the Descriptions block (Fig. 13 (b)) so that the users can understand the functions of the options. After selecting an option through the Selected Options (Fig. 14 (a)), the Input Box (Fig. 14 (b)) is displayed so that the users can set the value of the option.

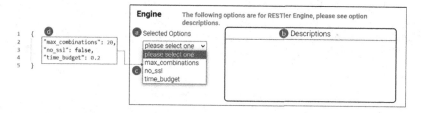

Fig. 13. The Engine Settings

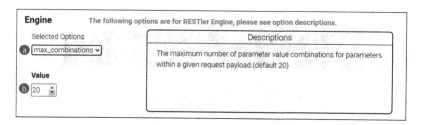

Fig. 14. The Engine Settings (An option is selected)

The "Mode" block (Fig. 10 (m)) indicates the RESTler testing mode. There are two test modes, Fuzz and Fuzz-lean.

- Fuzz mode (Fig. 15 (a)): RESTler will test the service for a longer period to try more combinations. In this mode, RESTler can find more bugs.
- Fuzz-lean mode (Fig. 15 (b)): RESTler will execute once with a default set of checkers for every endpoint and method. In this mode, RESTler can find bugs quickly.

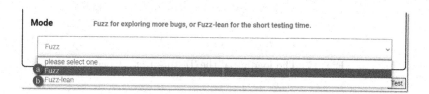

Fig. 15. The Mode Settings

Finally, once the users complete all settings, they can click the "Save" button (Fig. 10 (e)) to save the configuration or click the "Test" button (Fig. 10 (g)) to start testing the specification with the configuration.

3.4 The Testing Report

If the users click the "Test" button (Fig. 10 (g)) and the test starts successfully, the browser opens the Testing Report page (Fig. 16) in a new tab. Initially, loading (Fig. 17) is displayed.

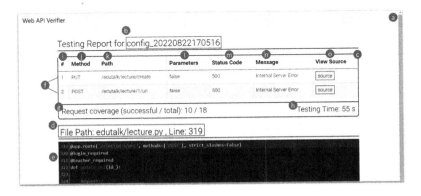

Fig. 16. The Testing Report Page

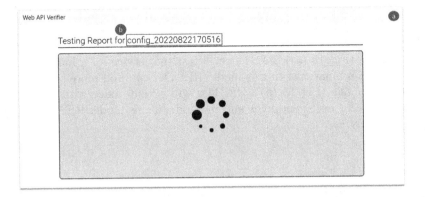

Fig. 17. The loading of the Testing Report page

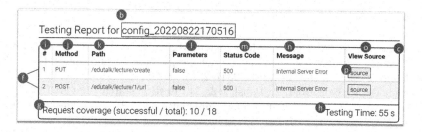

Fig. 18. The Configuration Name and Report Table.

The Testing Report page maps to a configuration with its name displayed at the top (Fig. 18 (b)) of the Report table. A configuration may have multiple testing reports. However, users can only see the latest testing report in our current implementation.

After the test is done, users can see the Report Table (Fig. 18 (c)). There are seven columns. The "#" column (Fig. 18 (i)) is the id of the bug. The "Method" column (Fig. 18 (j)) is the HTTP method of the Web API. The "Path" column (Fig. 18 (k)) is the URL pattern of the Web API. The "Parameters" column (Fig. 18 (l)) is the parameter that produces the bug. The "Status Code" column (Fig. 18 (m)) is the response with the HTTP status code from the system under test. The "Message" column (Fig. 18 (n)) is the received message from the system under test. The "View Source" column (Fig. 18 (o)) contains a button "Source" (Fig. 16 (o)) that displays the Web API's file information (Fig. 16 (d)) and code snippets on the Code Area (Fig. 16 (e)) under the Report Table. The source code snippets are displayed by CodeMirror5 [6], an open-source project which is a versatile text editor for the browser. We use selected APIs to search user-uploaded source code for file information such as file paths, line numbers, and source code snippets. Thus, users can find bugs by comparing the parameters of the request and the source code snippets. There are two fields at the bottom of the Report Table, Request coverage (Fig. 18 (g)) and Testing Time (Fig. 18 (h)). Request coverage is the ratio of responses received with HTTP status code 200 to HTTP status code other than 200. Testing Time shows the total test time for the test.

4   Conclusion

In this paper, we proposed Web API Verifier (WAV), a web-based Web API test system. With WAV, users can generate the OpenAPI specifications, configure the RESTler fuzzer, test their system with the specifications, and view bug reports with source code snippets. WAV reduces the effort of writing the OpenAPI specification and also lowers the knowledge required to perform fuzzing tests.

References

1. Al-Fuqaha, A., Guizani, M., Mohammadi, M., Aledhari, M., Ayyash, M.: Internet of things: a survey on enabling technologies, protocols, and applications. IEEE Commun. Surv. Tutorials **17**(4), 2347–2376 (2015)
2. Atlidakis, V., Godefroid, P., Polishchuk, M.: Restler: stateful rest API fuzzing. In: 2019 IEEE/ACM 41st International Conference on Software Engineering (ICSE), pp. 748–758. IEEE (2019)
3. Ben-Kiki, O., Evans, C., Ingerson, B.: Yaml ain't markup language (yaml^{TM} Working Draft 2008, vol. 5, p. 11 (2009)
4. Bourhis, P., Reutter, J. L., Suárez, F., Vrgoč, D.: JSON: data model, query languages and schema specification. In Proceedings of the 36th ACM SIGMOD-SIGACT-SIGAI Symposium on Principles of Database Systems, pp. 123–135 (2017)
5. Chang, Y.H.: Design and implementation of iottalk aa subsystem and account subsystem. https://etd.lib.nctu.edu.tw/cgi-bin/gs32/tugsweb.cgi?o=dnctucdr& s=id=%22GT070856505%22.&searchmode=basic. Accessed July 2022
6. CodeMirror. Codemirror5. https://github.com/codemirror/codemirror5. Accessed July 2022
7. Fielding, R., et al.: Hypertext transfer protocol-http/1.1. Technical report (1999)
8. Fielding, R.T.: Rest: architectural styles and the design of network-based software architectures. Doctoral dissertation, University of California (2000)
9. Fortify, H.P.: Internet of things security study: Smartwatches. Technical report, Technical Report (2015)
10. Gurunath, R., Agarwal, M., Nandi, A., Samanta, D.. An overview: security issue in IoT network. In 2018 2nd International Conference on I-SMAC (IoT in Social, Mobile, Analytics and Cloud)(I-SMAC) I-SMAC (IoT in Social, Mobile, Analytics and Cloud)(I-SMAC), 2018 2nd International Conference on, pp. 104–107. IEEE (2018)
11. Iqbal, W., Abbas, H., Daneshmand, M., Rauf, B., Bangash, Y.A.: An in-depth analysis of IoT security requirements, challenges, and their countermeasures via software-defined security. IEEE Internet Things J. **7**(10), 10250–10276 (2020)
12. Jacobson, D., Brail, G., Woods, D.: APIs: A Strategy Guide. O'Reilly Media Inc., Sebastopol (2011)
13. Johari, R., Kaur, I., Tripathi, R., Gupta, K.: Penetration testing in IoT network. In 2020 5th International Conference on Computing, Communication and Security (ICCCS), pp. 1–7. IEEE (2020)
14. Kristol, D.M.: Http cookies: standards, privacy, and politics. ACM Trans. Internet Technol. (TOIT) **1**(2), 151–198 (2001)
15. Lin, Y.B., et al.: Easyconnect: a management system for IoT devices and its applications for interactive design and art. IEEE Internet Things J. **2**(6), 551–561 (2015)
16. Lin, Y.-B., Lin, Y.-W., Huang, C.-M., Chih, C.-Y., Lin, P.: IoTtalk: a management platform for reconfigurable sensor devices. IEEE Internet Things J. **4**(5), 1552–1562 (2017)
17. Lin, Y.B., Shieh, M.Z., Shih, M.F., Cheng, C.C.: EduTalk: an IoT environment for learning computer programming and physics. IEEE Internet Things J. (2022)
18. Microsoft. Restler-fuzzer. https://github.com/microsoft/restler-fuzzer. Accessed July 2022
19. Microsoft. Restler settings files. https://github.com/microsoft/restler-fuzzer/blob/main/docs/user-guide/SettingsFile.md. Accessed July 2022

20. Brian, M.: Web API design (2013)
21. Rose, K., Eldridge, S., Chapin, L.: The internet of things: an overview. The Internet Soc. (ISOC) **80**, 1–50 (2015)
22. Sargsyan, S., Kurmangaleev, S., Mehrabyan, M., Mishechkin, M., Ghukasyan, T., Asryan, S.: Grammar-based fuzzing. In; 2018 Ivannikov Memorial Workshop (IVMEM), pp. 32–35. IEEE (2018)
23. Shin, S., Seto, Y.: Development of IoT security exercise contents for cyber security exercise system. In: 2020 13th International Conference on Human System Interaction (HSI), pp. 1–6. IEEE (2020)
24. SmartBear Software. Swagger editor. https://github.com/swagger-api/Swagger. Accessed July 2022
25. SmartBear Software. Swagger specification. https://swagger.io/specification/. Accessed July 2022
26. Steinberg, J.: These devices may be spying on you (even in your own home). Forbes. Accessed 27 2014
27. Wang, H.E.: Design and implementation of IoTtalk and its application. https://hdl.handle.net/11296/yw74yp. Accessed July 2022
28. Wen, Z.X.: ScratchTalk: an open-source programming education platform with IoT. https://etd.lib.nctu.edu.tw/cgi-bin/gs32/tugsweb.cgi?o=dnctucdr&s=id=%22GT070856514%22.&searchmode=basic. Accessed July 2022
29. Yang, H., Zhang, L., Zhang, X., Zhang, J.: An adaptive IoT network security situation prediction model. Mob. Netw. Appl. **27**(1), 371–381 (2022)
30. Yen, T.H.: Design and implementation iottalk based on message queuing telemetry transport protocol. https://hdl.handle.net/11296/9upc7x. Accessed July 2022

Author Index

Printed in the United States
by Baker & Taylor Publisher Services